Praise for *The Indispen...*

"Tommasini cheerfully acknowledges the ... mation, especially in a field like classical ... tory can become ossified. ... The book's subtitle is *A Personal Guide*, and both terms apply. He is warmly open about his preferences. ... Tommasini does a fine job of conveying the inner life of a piece, through his rhythmic sentences and sculpted paragraphs. ... One cannot help coming away from it with a more rounded understanding of classical music at its peak."
—Phillip Lopate, *The New York Times Book Review*

"The story of four centuries of music in essays on seventeen composers, from Monteverdi to Stravinsky ... all suffused with memoir and colored by a lifelong love of opera." —*The New Yorker*

"A pianist himself, Tommasini infuses his essays with insights from a lifetime of playing and listening." —*San Francisco Chronicle*

"These masters feel relatable—and their musical feats are made all the more impressive. Tommasini weaves an engrossing narrative, one that musicians and non-musicians alike will enjoy." —*The New Criterion*

"A must for musicians and music lovers alike." —*Pittsburgh Post-Gazette*

"Every case [Tommasini] makes is convincingly argued, and his style is accessible without being patronizing, enthusiastic but never gushily so. It's a superb read. Indispensable, even."
—Jeremy Pound, *BBC Music Magazine*

"A spirited musical compendium to the best of the best ... [Tommasini's] goal is to keep his assessments simple, insightful, and jargon-free, and he succeeds. ... Entertaining, highly enthusiastic, and very knowledgeable, he's the perfect guide [to the great composers] ... all exuberantly presented for your edification and enjoyment." —*Kirkus Reviews*

"Insightful ... Tommasini twines engaging biographical sketches of the maestros and their tragic ailments, love affairs, and endless scrambles for money with appreciations of masterpieces, the latter enriched by his memories of hearing and performing them. ... He excels at the difficult task of capturing music in words. . . . The result is an engrossing study that will appeal to both classical music aficionados and novice listeners who want a road map." —*Publishers Weekly*

"A treasure trove of biographical information and a primer on the language and notation of music itself . . . Tommasini makes a potentially dry and academic subject accessible." —*Library Journal*

"This wonderful and indispensable book is written by an indispensable and fabulous music critic, Anthony Tommasini. This marvelous publication is both a great addition to the body of tributes to these magnificent composers and a perfect educational vehicle about the grandiose field of opera. It is a pleasure to add my voice to the others singing its praises!"
—Leontyne Price

"Anthony Tommasini's book is itself indispensable—not only for those who already know how immortal are Monteverdi, Bach, and Haydn down to Schoenberg, Stravinsky, and Bartók, but for those who want to read Tommasini's take on what makes our great composers lifelong companions from whom we would ask nothing more than to hear a few last notes before leaving them forever." —André Aciman, author of *Call Me by Your Name*

"Anthony Tommasini is an engaging, authoritative guide to the careers and works of the great composers. Writing accessibly about even the more technical aspects of the music, he shares what these creations have meant to him in ways that should also make them essential listening for his readers."
—Walter Frisch, H. Harold Gumm/Harry and Albert von Tilzer Professor of Music at Columbia University; author of *Arlen and Harburg's "Over the Rainbow"*

"Few critics in history have been as rigorously trained or deeply versed in music as Tony Tommasini. Page after page of this exuberant book shows not only his comprehensive knowledge—he writes with the music under his fingers—but also his infectious love for the great classical repertory."
—Alex Ross, author of *The Rest Is Noise*

PENGUIN BOOKS

THE INDISPENSABLE COMPOSERS

Anthony Tommasini is the chief classical music critic of *The New York Times*. He graduated from Yale University and later earned a doctorate of musical arts at Boston University. He is the author of three books, including a biography of the composer and critic Virgil Thomson. As a pianist, he made two recordings of Thomson's music on the Northeastern label, which were supported by the National Endowment for the Arts.

THE

INDISPENSABLE

COMPOSERS

A PERSONAL GUIDE

ANTHONY TOMMASINI

PENGUIN BOOKS

PENGUIN BOOKS

An imprint of Penguin Random House LLC
penguinrandomhouse.com

First published in the United States of America by Penguin Press,
an imprint of Penguin Random House LLC, 2018
Published in Penguin Books 2019

Copyright © 2018 by Anthony Tommasini
Penguin supports copyright. Copyright fuels creativity, encourages diverse voices,
promotes free speech, and creates a vibrant culture. Thank you for buying an authorized edition
of this book and for complying with copyright laws by not reproducing, scanning, or distributing
any part of it in any form without permission. You are supporting writers and allowing
Penguin to continue to publish books for every reader.

Excerpt from page 27 from *Amadeus: A Play* by Peter Shaffer. Copyright © 1981, 2001
by Peter Shaffer. Reprinted by permission of HarperCollins Publishers.
Excerpts from *A Virgil Thomson Reader,* with an introduction by John Rockwell (Houghton Mifflin, 1981).
Reprinted by permission of the Virgil Thomson Foundation, Ltd., copyright owner.
Quotation of letters from *Beethoven's Letters* with explanatory notes by Dr. A. C. Kalischer,
translated by J. S. Shedlock, and *Beethoven: Impressions by His Contemporaries,* edited
by O. G. Sonneck. Reprinted by permission of Dover Publications.
Quotation from "Gretchen am Spinnrade" from *Franz Schubert: The Complete Songs,*
translated by Richard Wigmore. Copyright © 2014 by Yale University Press.
Reproduced by permission of Yale University Press through PLSclear.
Quotation of letters from *Selected Letters of Richard Wagner,* translated and edited by Stewart Spencer and
Barry Millington (W. W. Norton and Company, 1988). The author gratefully acknowledges
Barry Millington and Stewart Spencer for granting permission to reproduce.
Quotation of letters from *Debussy Letters,* translated by Roger Nichols (Harvard University Press, 1987).
The author gratefully acknowledges Roger Nichols for granting permission to reproduce.
Excerpt from "Spring Is Here," words by Lorenz Hart and music by Richard Rodgers.
Copyright © 1938 (renewed) EMI Robbins Catalog Inc. Exclusive print rights controlled
and administered by Alfred Music. All rights reserved. Used by permission of Alfred Music.

Illustration credits appear on pp. 465–66.

ISBN 9780143111085 (paperback)

THE LIBRARY OF CONGRESS HAS CATALOGED THE HARDCOVER EDITION AS FOLLOWS:
Names: Tommasini, Anthony, 1948– author.
Title: The indispensable composers : a personal guide / Anthony Tommasini.
Description: New York : Penguin Press, 2018. | Includes bibliographical
references and index.
Identifiers: LCCN 2018031755 (print) | LCCN 2018033228 (ebook) |
ISBN 9780698150133 (ebook) | ISBN 9781594205934 (hardcover)
Subjects: LCSH: Composers—Biography.
Classification: LCC ML390 (ebook) | LCC ML390 .T608 2018 (print) |
DDC 780.92/2—dc23
LC record available at https://lccn.loc.gov/2018031755

Printed in the United States of America

Designed by Gretchen Achilles

For Ben

CONTENTS

AUTHOR'S NOTE

I have been thinking and writing about these composers and their music for decades. While I have endeavored not to quote passages of my previous work in this book, I inevitably have drawn on thoughts, stories, and descriptions from earlier articles, reviews, and talks. In these chapters I have blended long-held ideas with fresh impressions. I hope the reader will benefit from what I have to say.

THE GREATNESS COMPLEX

I must have been about thirteen when I first listened to a recording of Bach's Mass in B Minor. As a child I was essentially alone in my passion for music. No one in my family (not even an uncle or aunt, from what I knew) had sung in a chorus, played the guitar, or anything. So the finished-basement den of our house on Long Island was my private musical refuge, where I practiced the piano, one of those boxy old uprights, and listened to classical records.

About a year earlier I had begun studying with a new piano teacher, Gladys Gehrig, an awesome woman in her late sixties. A Bach devotee, Mrs. Gehrig had me learning several of the composer's Two-Part Inventions, and my first Prelude and Fugue. One day she urged me to get to know Bach's mass, the greatest masterpiece of all time, she said. Her words made me eager to hear the piece, but also a little wary. It sounded intimidating. And the recording I found in a store—Herbert von Karajan's weighty, full-orchestra version from 1952, on three LPs—certainly looked daunting.

I may not remember the exact moment I put on Side One, but I remember vividly how those opening choral pleas of "Kyrie eleison" (Lord, have mercy) affected me. Today, after decades of experience with the piece—from hearing numerous performances and recordings, from studying the score in college classes and playing it through on the piano—I still find the music overwhelming, though for me it will always be imprinted by my first reaction long ago in the den.

The mass opens with a five-part chorus, buttressed by the instrumental forces, singing "Ky-ri-e" in three stern chords of increasing intensity. The melodic line, taken by the Soprano I section, rises up a step, and the harmonies seem to lift with it. This simple musical gesture—an imploring melodic phrase that ascends step-by-step with each urgent statement—is a timeless music trope. As that third chord on the final syllable of "Kyrie" cuts off, the members of the Soprano II section, only they, start to sing "eleison" on a pleading three-note ascending phrase, as if saying to their brethren, "Don't give up yet."

Before they finish, though, most of the other choristers, too impatient to wait, burst in with a second, even more wrenching cry of "Kyrie." The Sopranos I again carry the top melodic note, having slipped up a scale step to F-sharp. You expect this short phrase, just like the first "Kyrie," to rise with anguished fervor up higher still, to a G.

At least that's what I expected hearing it that first time. Something in the way the notes of the chords mingled made it seem like that was where the harmonies were headed.

Instead, as it sounded to my adolescent ears, Bach has the sopranos cling to that F-sharp for a piercing moment, digging in with more vehemence, clashing with other voices and instruments.

Now, at the time, though I dutifully practiced scales on the piano, I knew almost nothing about harmony, voice-leading, suspensions—all the musical elements Bach was utilizing to make this passage so powerful. But intuitively I must have grasped some of what was going on. I certainly knew what I felt about it. There is a touch of angry desperation in that second cry of "Kyrie." It's as if the chorus were saying, "Lord, are You hearing us down here? Hey, we're talking to You! How about some mercy?"

With the third and final "Kyrie" plea, the melodic line finally crests and touches that top note I had anticipated as a kid, before the whole imploring opening statement of "Kyrie eleison," having vented its anguish, settles down, ending on a solid, sonorous dominant chord. What next?

Beseeching the Lord for some attention through those choral declamations obviously did not do the job. So the chorus, standing in for all of us, tries an earnest entreaty. The main section of the Kyrie begins: a long, elaborate fugue, astonishing music that unfolds mostly with somber penitence, driven, but not overly so, by a calm, relentless gait of steady quarter notes and flowing eighth notes.

In crucial ways, that early experience of listening to my first recording of Bach's mass set the course for my life in music. Yes, I was emotionally overcome. And, yes, I sensed immediately that Mrs. Gehrig was right about this masterpiece. It felt like I was venturing into a realm of greatness that only certain lucky people knew about.

Yet at the same time, the budding musician in me wanted to know more, to know why this music, even this opening phrase of just four measures, moved me so much. How did the music work? My passion for music was not enough. I needed to understand it as well. I had to try to grapple with these giants, starting with Bach, always a good place to start. Who was he? How did he relate to his era? How does one account for, let alone explain, his music and its unshakeable hold on us to this day?

The Baroque period was in full swing when Bach was born in Eisenach, Germany, in 1685. By the time he died, in 1750, all manner of new styles and genres had taken root, including the early symphonic schools, and, of course, opera, which had been around for a century and a half. The era of Viennese Classicism was about to take off; Haydn was eighteen.

But Bach had no interest in being fashionable. Instead, he looked deeper into prevailing styles and techniques. His music is an uncanny synthesis of what had been and what was to come. No piece reflects this duality more than the Mass in B Minor. Though lasting about two hours and written in multiple, mood-shifting sections, the work comes across as an organic entity. This is all the more amazing when you consider that Bach composed the mass over decades in a piecemeal way, finishing the score only the year before he died. While it is possible that the first two main sections, the Kyrie and the Gloria, were tried out in performance in Dresden in 1733, historians are not sure. There is no evidence that the mass was performed complete in Bach's lifetime.

Whenever I hear Bach's Mass in B Minor, or other of Bach's incomparable works, I usually come away thinking that, for his matchless combination of technical mastery, ingenious musical engineering, profound expressivity, and, when so moved, unabashed boldness, Bach was the greatest composer in history.

But what is greatness in music? Does it matter? Does there need to be a greatest composer in history? Does the canon expand? And who gets to say what is canonical now?

The field of classical music has justifiably been criticized for its obsession with greatness, with certifying a repertory of canonical masterpieces. And the religious connotation of the word "canon" is not helpful, with its suggestion of accepted dogma. As my friend Alex Ross, the music critic of the *New Yorker,* argues in "Listen to This," the title essay of a collection of his pieces published in 2010, the very term "classical music" makes the whole field seem dead; it traps "a tenaciously living art in a theme park of the past." Classical music, of course, can be "great and serious," as Alex writes, but greatness and seriousness are "not its defining characteristics." It can also be "stupid, vulgar, and insane."

It makes sense that the nickname *Eroica* (Heroic) has stuck to Beethoven's Third Symphony, a colossal piece. Yet this music is also audacious and unpredictable. On the surface the symphony's four movements might seem, at first, to come from different spheres: a brisk, purposeful Allegro with a searching development section that climaxes midway in a gnashing burst of dissonant chords; a grimly imposing Funeral March; a breathless Scherzo, at once godly and giddy; a romping, mischievous Finale that is somehow the ultimate statement of the heroic in music. Yet the movements are linked, almost in a subliminal way, by a small group of short musical motifs that run through almost every moment of this fifty-minute score, lending the overall work inexorable sweep and structural cohesion. Talk about greatness.

And yet the idea that greatness does not matter implanted itself in me early. As a child my first favorite composer was Edvard Grieg, who would not make anyone's list of all-time greats. I had a recording I adored, *Rubinstein Plays Grieg.* The main work on the album, recorded in 1953, was Grieg's Ballade, Op. 24, a seventeen-minute score in the form of variations

on a bittersweet folk song. Some of the variations become quite tumultuous; the piece both hooked and baffled me.

I especially loved the short works Rubinstein played, selections from
Grieg's ten volumes of *Lyric Pieces:* sprightly dances, songs without words
that evoked wistful folk tunes, character pieces with evocative titles like
"March of the Dwarfs" and "Little Bird." My favorite was "Shepherd Boy,"
with its achingly sad melody, a series of descending lyrical phrases that actually seem to sigh. In the middle section the melodic line goes through
twists and generates agitation. The piece sounds not like the song of a
shepherd boy but a musical depiction of his inner thoughts. At my young
age, I couldn't articulate what I was feeling about this short piece. In retrospect I realize that I must have wondered what made this Norwegian shepherd boy so sad. I could be a sad kid too, especially when, alone, I listened
to recordings like this one and felt the music so deeply.

Decades later, in 2002, I went to Norway for the first time and had the
chance to trace Grieg's steps in Bergen, where he was born in 1843. I finally
learned why, for all his success in Europe as a composer and a pianist, who
often accompanied his wife, Nina Hagerup, a fine soprano, in song recitals
on tour, Grieg remained attached to the "great, melancholy, natural scenery" of his rugged, misty homeland, with its spectacular mountains and
fjords, as he wrote to a friend. I gained a sense of why Grieg was so touched
by the wistful, elegiac folk music of Norway, and what he meant when he
said self-effacingly that his music had a "taste of cod" about it.

While there, I visited the two-story wooden house that Grieg lived in
with his wife on the outskirts of Bergen, a home they designed. On the
piano in the main living room there remains in its special place a framed
photograph of the couple's only child, Alexandra, who died of meningitis
at thirteen months in 1869. The house is now part of the Grieg Museum.
On this visit, after introducing myself to a security guard, I was allowed to
try Grieg's piano. So I played another one of his *Lyric Pieces,* the tender
"Cradle Song," while looking at the photograph of Alexandra and glancing
though the window at the vista of a nearby lake.

The case for denying Grieg greatness is easy to make. At twenty, urged
to do so by a mentor, he wrote a symphony but soon withdrew the work

and never attempted another. He came under pressure to compose a stirring Norwegian national opera and tried to do it but got no further than
some choral scenes and sketches. He wrote the wonderful, if modest, *Lyric
Pieces;* some chamber works, including three engaging violin sonatas; and
a few volumes of elegant songs. There is his incidental music for Ibsen's
play *Peer Gynt,* from which Grieg fashioned two popular orchestra suites.
And, of course, his justly beloved piano concerto.

But a great? No. Should that matter? Absolutely not.

Before switching tacks, though, and arguing that lovers of music, like
lovers of any art form, cannot help being swept up in the search for greatness, let me fortify the case against the greatness obsession in classical music by briefly discussing a recent piece, John Adams's *The Gospel According
to the Other Mary,* an ambitious and powerful oratorio that the composer
completed in 2012.

One of the most rewarding things about music by living composers, as
with new work in any artistic field, is that questions of the greatness of
a piece, all predictions for its longevity, are rendered irrelevant. Creators,
performers, and audiences alike understand that we are simply too close to
a living artist's work to be able to make such judgments. If an exciting new
novel comes along, literary-minded people want to read it, talk about it,
maybe argue over it. But the question of whether the novelist is another
Dickens or Proust is absurd. The same goes for new plays, new films, new
pop groups, and new television dramas.

We know from reading music history that contemporary audiences
could be clueless judges of a composer's work. Beethoven was widely recognized as a towering figure in his time. Many of his pieces quickly found
favor with the public and professionals. But a lot of his music was considered confounding, even bizarre, and I'm not just talking about the late-
period works, which many people, including some in awe of Beethoven,
thought were the products of a deaf composer who had turned a little crazy
in his fifties. Many earlier scores baffled listeners as well. This attitude
lingered among those who should have known better, including critics.
Consider an assessment of Beethoven's exhilarating Seventh Symphony by
a London critic in 1825, twelve years after the work's Vienna premiere.

In this score Beethoven "indulged a great deal of disagreeable eccentricity," the critic wrote, adding that "we cannot yet discover any design in it, neither can we trace any connection in its parts." The critic could only conclude that the symphony was intended as "a kind of enigma—we had almost said a hoax."

If Beethoven's music routinely divided opinion in his day, the compositions of the Austrian composer and virtuoso pianist Johann Nepomuk Hummel were almost universally hailed, his place in the pantheon confidently predicted. Hummel was a solid composer. Still, the relative achievement of these two contentious rivals looks pretty lopsided today. For the record, they reconciled at Beethoven's deathbed. Hummel, a pallbearer at his competitor's funeral, performed at the grand Beethoven memorial concert in Vienna.

To return to John Adams's *The Gospel According to the Other Mary*, this is a perfect example of an arresting work that pushes aside questions of lasting greatness because we know we are too close to it, and to Adams, to make any such assessment. With new music, we become swept up in the immediacy of the experience of hearing it.

Adams's oratorio tells the story of Christ's Passion from the perspectives of Mary Magdalene, Martha, and Lazarus, presented both as biblical and modern-day characters. I first heard it live in 2013 when Gustavo Dudamel, who had conducted the premiere the previous year with the Los Angeles Philharmonic, brought that orchestra to Lincoln Center for a semi-staged performance. The oratorio contains some of Adams's most fraught and complex music. He has always had skill at writing multi-layered scores in which different swirling elements unfold simultaneously, something he does in this ambitious piece with exceptional brilliance. You hear passages inspired by everything from big band jazz to Bach passions, from Ives to Ravel to Steve Reich. Yet it all sounds personal and urgent. And for all the density of the music, its layers and textures are impressively audible.

There is a problem, though. The piece is too long. Act I is seventy minutes; Act II an hour. The version I heard in New York had already been trimmed by Adams after the premiere. Even so, stretches of the score that were riveting at first lost their punch and seemed overextended.

As I listened I kept thinking: Well, what can you do. Adams is an exciting composer, but he has never written a piece that doesn't seem too long. The run-on quality that affects his scores may be a remnant of his early days, when he was excited by Minimalism. But what was radical about pioneering Minimalist works like Philip Glass's haunting opera *Satyagraha* is that the music is, you might say, radically Minimalist. *Satyagraha* is truly "music with repetitive structures," the description Glass has always preferred to the term "Minimalism."

This is the take, I admit, of a listener who has been hearing Adams pieces over the years fresh from the studio. I could easily be wrong. Who knows what future commentators might say? The idea that an Adams work is too long may be considered as oversimplified a response as saying that Schubert's sonatas and chamber works are too long, which was once an accepted assessment but now seems a small-minded way to think of Schubert's sublime pieces. Then again, maybe historians will look back and wonder why any fuss was made over Adams in the first place.

The point is that in the moment, when you're listening to new music, these questions, if ever important, are out of mind.

Okay. That's my case against the greatness fixation.

Now here is an argument for it, which matters to me, since in these chapters I will try to account for what makes select composers indispensable by discussing elements of greatness in the music as I perceive it.

For one thing, it's human nature to want to affirm the greatness that impacts and inspires your life. Your first time hearing some exhilarating or mystifying work by a composer of the past—Mozart's justly nicknamed *Jupiter* Symphony, Beethoven's searching Fourth Piano Concerto, Wagner's trance-inducing *Tristan und Isolde,* Stravinsky's shattering *Rite of Spring*—can be as formative a moment as anything that happens to you personally. These works, and the composers who wrote them, become living presences; we need to know what places they hold in our consciousness. People everywhere date their lives, especially their youths, by the music they love. That was certainly true for a member of the Beatles generation like me. My college years at Yale were almost framed by the release of, first, *Sgt. Pepper's Lonely Hearts Club Band* and, in senior year, *Abbey Road.*

I experienced the most amazing confluence of two of the musical greats who have helped me through life one Saturday afternoon in June 1979 at a Broadway theater in New York. I was living in Boston at the time, having just finished my first year teaching music at Emerson College while also working on my doctoral degree at Boston University. I had come to New York to visit some friends.

Stephen Sondheim was already a giant to me, and *Sweeney Todd* had opened in March at what was then called the Uris Theatre. I was heading to Penn Station to see my family on Long Island, wearing jeans and a T-shirt, unshaven, backpack in tow, not having thought of going to see *Sweeney*. I assumed it would be sold out. Then I thought, Why not check? To my surprise there was a ticket available, fourth row center, no less. If I remember, it cost twenty-five dollars, which would have seemed a lot at the time. I grabbed it.

I found my seat, stuffed my backpack under it, and felt lucky to be there. Then who came walking down the aisle? John Lennon, in a cream-colored summer suit, and Yoko Ono, in a simple print dress. They wound up sitting right in front of me. Now, when I was in college, the idea that you might bump into John Lennon anywhere seemed unfathomable. The crowd control problem would have made it impossible for him to go to a Broadway theater. But at this stage in his life he had been trying to be like any New Yorker, taking in shows, shopping at Zabar's, grabbing coffee at an Italian cafe near the Dakota, where he lived. Still, there I was staring at the back of his head.

It's a tribute to Sondheim that from the first moments of the musical— the strange, wayward organ music that sets the ominous mood; the blast of the factory whistle; the undulant orchestral accompaniment that introduces "The Ballad of Sweeney Todd"—I was hooked, despite the out-of-body experience of sitting immediately behind John Lennon.

At the end of the performance, people went up to Lennon and tried to greet him, to say something, as he and Yoko quickly headed for an exit. I was able to catch his glance and say, "Your music is very important to me." He muttered, "Thank you, thank you," and slipped away.

A year and a half later he was dead, shot at the entry to the Dakota by a deranged fan, having made himself vulnerable by attempting to live normally and mingle among his fellow New Yorkers.

Maybe we are too obsessed with greatness in the arts. But, I'm sorry, Stephen Sondheim and John Lennon define it.

There are other reasons that many of us, after hearing an exciting performance, find ourselves thinking, "That is the greatest opera," the "greatest string quartet," the "greatest twentieth-century composer." To make these pronouncements in the flush of enthusiasm is a shorthand way of affirming the work's mastery, yes, but even more its hold over us. Also, deciding that some piece or composer is the greatest prods me to want to know more, to grapple with the qualities of the music that make it great.

Often a composer seems not at all to be striving for greatness in a work, as with those lovely Grieg piano pieces. A composer might simply think: I'm just practicing my craft, working out something that's been kicking around within me. Now, if it's considered great, well, wonderful.

Actually, it's hard to know if the giants in the arts consciously aimed for greatness. Did Shakespeare? From what we understand, he thought of himself as a professional, a man of the theater. Did he write those plays hoping they would endure? I doubt it, which may be why so many of the scripts were left in jumbled states, with missing pages and confusing rewrites.

In a way, even Beethoven, who really did strive for greatness, conducted his day-to-day life as a professional musician. I love the story about Beethoven's Quartet No. 13 in B-flat. This is one of the five late quartets that the deaf composer wrote in the mid-1820s, works that mystified even the finest musicians of that period. This six-movement quartet, which Beethoven finished in early 1826, the year before he died, originally ended with the Grosse Fuge, a gnarly, vehemently complex movement of nearly seventeen minutes: it sounds like some frenetic Promethean dance is swirling within a tangle of counterpoint. At the time, the skilled musicians who looked at the fugue considered it not just bewildering but almost unplayable.

Well, after a first performance, Beethoven's publishers, who had good reason to fear this hot-tempered, ornery man, gently suggested that he substitute something else for the sixth and final movement of the quartet. Did

Beethoven protest furiously that the Grosse Fuge was the only music to end this work? Did he denounce the publishers for their timidity and denseness?

No. He took their sensible advice and wrote instead a fairly agreeable, eight-minute finale that was vastly simpler than the fugue. With this finale the quartet was published as Op. 130; the Grosse Fuge was published separately as Op. 133.

Only in recent decades have many string quartets, even student ensembles, chosen to perform the Quartet in B-flat with the Grosse Fuge as the finale. Though it remains technically and musically daunting, musicians have learned how to tame it. Audiences seem thrilled to hear this great quartet (yes, great!) as Beethoven conceived it.

THE TOP TEN COMPOSERS PROJECT

My most unabashed venture into grappling with greatness came with a two-week series of articles I wrote in 2011 for the *New York Times,* what I called my Top Ten Composers project. And the seeds of this series were probably planted in high school, when my mother bought me Harold C. Schonberg's 1963 book *The Great Pianists.* I was a very serious piano student at the time and Schonberg, the respected chief music critic of the *New York Times,* was an informed admirer of great piano playing and great pianists. I loved the book, so full of colorful stories about historic figures I'd never heard of, along with whole chapters on legends like Liszt. I still have it.

Back then, I never remotely imagined that I would someday have the same job Schonberg held. Of course, even in my student days, as I developed my own take on things, I sometimes disagreed with Schonberg, especially his rough treatment of Leonard Bernstein as a conductor and composer. Bernstein was a hero to me. Also, by the time I went to Yale to major in music, Schonberg's lack of sympathy for challenging modern compositional styles bothered me. Still, I had to admit it was fun to read the august *Times* critic's dismissals of contemporary music. "I thought the serial-dominated music after the war was a hideously misbegotten creature sired by Caliban out of Hecate," Schonberg wrote in a valedictory essay on the occasion of his retirement in 1980.

Throughout his career Schonberg made clear that part of his responsibility as the *Times*'s chief music critic was to inform readers about music, a big motivation for his writing general-interest books like *The Great Pianists* and, in subsequent years, *The Great Conductors* and *The Lives of the Great Composers*.

Implicit in these titles was the assumption that music lovers cared deeply about "greatness" and that we all knew who the truly great composers and performers were. And if we were confused about who made the ranks, Schonberg, of course, would be a trustworthy guide.

I too take the educational component of being a music critic seriously. Of course I have strong opinions and a personal vision of the ways the art form I revere can thrive. Yet in our current musical culture, with the practice of amateur music making nothing like it used to be in earlier eras, even many people who consider music central to their lives admit to knowing little about its inner workings. So there is a hunger for insight, I've found. I've thought through these matters, immersed myself in music, and written extensively about it for decades.

And, here I am, to my surprise, doing something pretty close to a Harold Schonberg book on the "great" composers.

In truth, my Top Ten Composers project, an intellectual game that turned into a surprising, if hotly debated, success, was the initial motivator.

Over those two weeks I wrote a series of articles, supplemented by five videos and numerous blog posts, with the goal of determining a list of the top ten composers in history.

As I admitted from the start, the very idea of a top ten list was absurd. Yet the process of determining it was fascinating. On what basis would someone make the cut or not? Do you somehow measure compositional skills? Or seriousness of purpose? How much does influence matter? Arnold Schoenberg was arguably the most influential composer of the twentieth century. Every composer in his wake had to grapple with his development of twelve-tone music, even if only to reject it. Does that make Schoenberg a top ten composer? In asking such questions, you force yourself to pinpoint what exactly it is in a composer's music that makes it exceptional and timeless.

Yes, the whole thing was an intellectual game. But the only way to play any game is seriously. So I did. I analyzed pieces and composers, I agonized in public over the winnowing process, and I invited readers to weigh in. Did they ever. The *Times* posted more than fifteen hundred comments on our website.

There were wonderful comments and posts from musicians and music lovers who entered into the spirit. Many responders dismissed the whole exercise as pointless, even outrageous. On his blog the composer Nico Muhly called the project "a horror." Somehow I took it as a kind of compliment that the project provoked such condemnation from a gifted young composer. That this game and the questions it raised really stirred people up came through in the scores of comments on the website from readers who strongly criticized the venture while also offering their own top ten lists, often with warnings to me, like "Don't you dare leave off Mahler!"

The range of responders was inspiring. I think my favorite comment came from the cellist Gwen Krosnick, then twenty-four, whose father was Joel Krosnick, the renowned cellist of the Juilliard String Quartet. (He retired from the ensemble in 2016, after forty-two years.) Though Gwen rarely reads about music, she explained, she had enjoyed my articles and videos. "I found myself wishing I could have taken my Music History 101 class with you," she wrote, which was very flattering.

After a day spent immersed in the series, Gwen had a long phone chat with her father, who was on tour with the Juilliard Quartet; they spoke at length about my "wonderful and impossible project," she wrote. One issue that came up was whether a composer "who changes everything" is "necessarily great." The Juilliard Quartet had long championed Schoenberg's works. Gwen asked her dad if he would put Schoenberg in his top ten list.

"Dad said, quite slowly and sounding a bit surprised, 'You know, I don't think I would.' I was pretty surprised myself, hearing him say that," Gwen wrote.

The dilemma encountered by the two cello-playing Krosnicks over

Schoenberg was exactly what I had hoped for with the project. This intellectual game forced Joel Krosnick to think hard about how he valued and accounted for Schoenberg's indisputable achievements and many amazing works.

Of course, there is no need to bump Schoenberg from the list because there is no need for the list. But trying to compile one sure is fascinating.

Some of the most interesting responses, though, came from music lovers who found the game not innocent, but harmful. Take the reaction of the conductor Leon Botstein, the music director of the American Symphony Orchestra and longtime president of Bard College, who pronounced my Top Ten Composers project as "dangerous and despicable" when I interviewed him in 2014 as I began working on this book.

Botstein has essentially dedicated his career to rectifying what he sees as oversights in classical music, a field long dominated by performances of a certified canon of works while deserving scores that captured the imagination of the public in their day remain all but unknown. Botstein makes an impassioned and astute case against classical music's obsession with greatness.

To approach an art form like music with the idea that you are only interested in the very best, he said, is like shopping for a handbag and deciding in advance that you "only want Vuitton and forget everything else."

Of course there is bad music, Botstein said, lots of it, and Beethoven's *Eroica* is indisputably great. "It is astonishing, yes," Botstein said. But, he added, "I've never understood why I'm being asked the question is it better or worse than whatever. I don't get it."

The revitalization that results from exploring overlooked music of the past is crucial to the life of new music, Botstein believes. I completely agree. He is exhilarated by the lateral cross-fertilization that thrives today between classical, contemporary, pop, rock, folk, and film music. But, he asked, why not apply that approach vertically? Or chronologically? This has been his mission.

The classical music repertory needs revitalization. Still, there are ways to keep these beloved pieces alive for musicians and audiences without consigning these staples to storage shelves.

A masterpiece can be placed in programs that provide musical and historical context. Michael Tilson Thomas, among other adventurous conductors, is expert at this. He has said in interviews that performing a work like Tchaikovsky's Fifth Symphony is one of the hardest challenges he and the players of his dynamic orchestra, the San Francisco Symphony, deal with. This is because it's hard to perform such a staple in a way that conveys what a daring, wrenching, and modern piece it was when new, and, in a real way, remains. A conductor does not want to distort the piece by performing it in a manner that exaggerates its emotional and musical extremes or goes against the Russian Romantic style.

But if the Tchaikovsky Fifth is presented on, say, an all-Russian program that opens with a recent work by a living Russian composer, followed by a lesser-heard Stravinsky piece—or something comparable by Prokofiev or Shostakovich—and ends with the Tchaikovsky, then the audience is going to hear the Fifth afresh, as part of a heritage of Russian musical styles and experimentation.

Contextual programming has become increasingly common. Many performers push the idea even further by boldly juxtaposing the old and the new to tease out resonances between works written centuries apart.

The thoughtful Israeli pianist David Greilsammer is another practitioner of juxtapositions. For those concertgoers who judge artists by their expertise in older repertory, Greilsammer has plenty of credentials. A lively Mozart interpreter, he has given marathon concerts of the composer's complete piano sonatas, and during a single season played (and conducted from the keyboard) all twenty-seven of Mozart's piano concertos with a chamber orchestra in Geneva. He has also gained notice for his programs that alternate the old and the new, including music by figures seemingly as far removed from each other as the Baroque composer Domenico Scarlatti and the American maverick John Cage.

Scarlatti wrote some five hundred fifty wonderful, imaginative single-movement sonatas for keyboard. Yet when a pianist plays a group of these pieces in a recital, this segment of the program can seem just a nod to an earlier era, an offering of lighter Baroque fare before the artist tackles a mighty Beethoven sonata, the monumental Liszt sonata, or whatever.

In the spring of 2014, Greilsammer played a group of Scarlatti sonatas at the inviting Greenwich Village music club Le Poisson Rouge, interspersed with selected sonatas from Cage's pioneering work of the mid-1940s *Sonatas and Interludes,* a cycle of twenty pieces for prepared piano. (Greilsammer has taken this unlikely program on the road and recorded it as well.) Cage calls for the performer to "prepare" the piano by inserting screws, bolts, paper strips, rubber erasers, and other such items in between certain strings on the piano in specified places. Cage's idea was to turn the piano into a de facto percussion orchestra. And the strange, plunking, thwacking allure of the sound world Cage creates with his prepared piano pieces still seems fresh and startling today.

Hearing Greilsammer play a Scarlatti sonata on the standard piano and then, quickly swiveling on a rotating stool, play a Cage sonata on the prepared piano was transfixing and revelatory. The Cage works, for all their percussive energy, came across as delicate, textured, and fanciful. And hearing Scarlatti played in this context, and so vibrantly, I noticed more than even the willful, wild elements that churn beneath the surface sparkle and elegance. On this night, Scarlatti and Cage seemed kindred creators.

THE INDISPENSABLE COMPOSERS

During my Top Ten Composers project, quite a few readers wrote to me saying that, though engrossing, the series was frustrating, because they sensed I had much more to say about the composers I discussed.

So I thought I would put the game aside, open up my exploration, and look again at the issue of greatness. Hence, *The Indispensable Composers.* Of course, to say that certain composers are indispensable is to suggest that certain others are not. In these pages I'm embracing that concept as I discuss what makes some extraordinary composers indispensable to me.

This book is in no way a comprehensive historical survey. Whole periods and many significant figures are not discussed. This will be a series of essays on composers, seventeen in all, and their achievements, drawing upon elements of biography, historical background and influences, the composer's relationships with colleagues, shifting attitudes toward a composer's work over time—anything that strikes me as relevant. My goal is to keep it simple and try to explain what I find important and helpful to know. What's the big deal about Mozart? About Verdi? That's what I've attempted to explain.

For all the intellectual sport of my Top Ten Composers project, deciding which composers made the cut forced me to ask tough questions and reexamine their achievements. In dropping the game here, I had to grapple more seriously with these big, elusive questions in choosing the subjects of these chapters. I made what might seem some arbitrary calls, for example, including Debussy but taking a pass on the slightly younger Frenchman with whom he is so often linked, Ravel. Why? The more I learn about music, the more I've come to see Debussy as an epoch-altering figure. Yet though there are works of Ravel I revere, in recent years I've found his most famous pieces, like the sumptuous, sensual ballet score *Daphnis et Chloé*, too slick and extravagant for comfort. Maybe I'll change my mind in time. For now, I'm going with my gut.

Also, now and then I take a moment to explain (in the most nontechnical ways I know) some essential theoretical concepts, like major and minor keys, recitative, and such. Most of all, I've tried to make these essays personal pieces about indispensable composers. Though I break no biographical ground whatsoever in relating the stories of these composers, I focus on known aspects of their lives that strike me as meaningful. In assessing their work, I bring in impressions from significant performances I have heard, sometimes performances I have given, and even personal anecdotes that seem revealing.

I found that in coming to terms with these towering figures, I was freshly engaged by questions I've long pondered. For one, though I deal with my chosen composers in chronological order, I don't view music history as linear. Music doesn't necessarily advance as an art form. Not all giants are pathbreakers. Many composers achieved greatness by essentially working within the parameters of a tradition—Verdi, for example. Verdi's mission for most of his career was to invigorate the heritage of nineteenth-century Italian opera, not cast it aside.

Alas, this gallery of greats is an all-male club. Though most art forms have sorry legacies of misogyny, classical music during its formative centuries was especially uninviting to aspiring women composers.

The good news is that institutions and audiences have been increasingly eager to hear the music of women composers, to the point of pressuring stodgier institutions to open up. In one encouraging indicator of overdue change, as I write this four of the last nine winners of the Pulitzer Prize for Music have been women, the most recent being the Chinese-born Du Yun. But it will take time and dedicated effort to right this historic imbalance.

Also, after taking this guide into the early twentieth century by comparing three pioneering giants—Schoenberg, Stravinsky, and Bartók—I end with just an overview of what happened afterward, offering my own brief and personal take. To look in depth at the last one hundred years felt to me like another book with a different orientation.

Every day in my work at the *Times,* I face the challenge of trying to say something insightful about music while avoiding insider jargon as much as possible and not making assumptions about general knowledge among my readers. If I review, say, a new production of a Wagner work at the Metropolitan Opera, I am writing both for conductors, singers, and historians who are steeped in Wagner and for music lovers who may never have seen a Wagner opera. I must try to say something of interest to everyone.

This is even more the case when I'm reporting on the premiere of an ambitious piece at the New York Philharmonic. I have to describe music that no one has yet heard in language that makes it vivid, I hope, not only to other composers and music insiders, but especially to concertgoers with little background in music. What did the piece sound like? How did it come across as an entity? Who is this composer influenced by, or stealing from?

To me, these same questions apply when describing a piece by Bach, Mozart, or Brahms. That's what I'm up to in this book.

CHAPTER ONE

CREATOR OF MODERN MUSIC

CLAUDIO MONTEVERDI (1567–1643)

Monteverdi: Creator of Modern Music is the bold title the musicologist Leo Schrade gave to his important 1950 book on this towering Italian master. Schrade used "modern" in the same sense that traditional college surveys of Western civilization are divided into semester courses on ancient and modern history. The modern era of music, Schrade argues, dates roughly from 1600, with the coming of the Baroque period, following the age of the late Renaissance. And Monteverdi, who was born in Cremona in 1567 and died in Venice in 1643, was the seminal figure in this transition.

At the time of its publication, Schrade's book encountered pushback from musicologists who thought the author made Monteverdi seem almost single-handedly responsible for the coming of "modern" music. Still, by any measure Monteverdi was one of the most pioneering figures in music history, and his achievements shaped the art form for centuries to come. I essentially agree with Schrade's historical take.

The Renaissance, especially during its late decades, was the high age of polyphony, that is, counterpoint, music written in several distinct overlapping lines (or voices). During the late Renaissance composers pushed the techniques of counterpoint to new heights of complexity, especially in sacred and secular vocal works. A corrective of a kind was in order, and the Baroque period, which saw a growing fashion for simpler textures, including seventeenth-century equivalents of songs with supportive accompaniments, provided it.

In a way, music went public during the Baroque era, and Monteverdi rode that wave; you could even say he churned it up. He began his career working in the elite court of a duke, but wound up playing a defining role in developing the new genre of opera and opening it to general audiences. In his final period, directing music at the Basilica of St. Mark in Venice, while keeping his hand in opera, Monteverdi composed lush, extravagantly beautiful sacred works that seem Baroque prototypes for current-day surround-sound spectaculars.

Also, during the early decades of the seventeenth century the musical language of diatonic (major and minor) harmony was essentially codified. Monteverdi wrote exquisitely in the older language and mastered the new one. No composer was a more influential bridge during this period of change.

In truth, starting this survey with Monteverdi may be somewhat arbitrary. Still, he strikes me as the first towering figure with whom we, composers and audiences alike, can identify today. Consider the breadth of his works.

In his nine books of madrigals alone—vocal pieces he wrote throughout his long life that were collected and published over six decades, winning him fame while making him some money—you can trace Monteverdi's restless growth. He consolidated the achievements of the Renaissance masters who practiced that high art of polyphony while exploring the new styles and aesthetics of the Baroque.

When Monteverdi was born, the Italian madrigal was the most popular and important genre of secular vocal music: an unaccompanied piece written usually for three to six voices (five voices became the standard). Wrenching expression from the words of the text was the defining element of the genre. Many madrigals came close to being through-composed, that is, structured so that the music almost seemed to ebb and flow without internal repetitions. Monteverdi was a madrigal-writing prodigy; his first collection was published in 1587, before he turned twenty.

The subsequent books are almost a catalogue of musical developments that brought about the Baroque age. Monteverdi steadily experiments with innovative harmony, spiked with daring dissonance; he thins out the dense layers of counterpoint that had been standard practice, instead writing lucid madrigals that emphasize the top and bottom lines (the soprano and bass). Before long, pieces that are essentially Baroque songs with instrumental accompaniments were included among Monteverdi's madrigal books, culminating in the monumental Eighth Book, titled *Madrigals of War and Love*.

An exhilarating highlight of that volume is the amazing eighteen-minute dramatic scene *Il Combattimento di Tancredi e Clorinda*, which tells the ill-fated love story of the Christian hero Tancredi who falls for the Saracen Clorinda, whom he then meets on a battlefield, both of them unrecognizable in combat gear. They fight furiously. Clorinda is mortally wounded; Tancredi realizes his horrible mistake. This piece—for two solo singers in the title roles and a third as narrator, with an elaborate instrumental ensemble—is almost a mini-opera, quite a leap from the old idea of a madrigal. *Il Combattimento* a madrigal? It's like calling "Revolution 9" on *The White Album* a rock song.

Monteverdi was not among the initial group of composers, singers, poets, and princes in Florence around 1600 who, inspired by the example of ancient Greek tragedy (or what they understood it to be), came up with the idea of writing continuous music dramas, experiments soon seen as the beginning of opera. Still, Monteverdi, who was working for the Duke of Mantua at the time, knew all about what was going on in Florence. In 1607 he took a crack at the new genre, working with the poet Alessandro Striggio to compose *Orfeo*, a stunning masterpiece generally considered to be the first music drama that really worked as both music and drama, a piece rightly seen as the first great opera.

It is hard to see Monteverdi's hometown and family background as conducive to the musical revolutionary he became. Claudio Monteverdi was the eldest son of a surgeon and apothecary. The household must have been musical, though, because both Claudio and his brother Giulio Cesare became musicians. If Cremona was no major music center, it was easy traveling distance from places that were, like Parma and Mantua. The main locus of music making in Cremona was, naturally, the cathedral, which had a choir and maintained an instrumental ensemble under the direction of a maestro di cappella, the most important musician in town, at the time Marc'Antonio Ingegneri. There is no definitive record of Monteverdi becoming a choir member. But he definitely studied with Ingegneri, a skilled composer who instructed his star pupil in singing, text setting, and the art of writing contrapuntal textures for multiple voices. Monteverdi also learned string playing.

Monteverdi was a prodigiously talented, ambitious, and savvy careerist who managed, at just fifteen, to get a prominent house in Venice to publish his first collection of pieces—sacred motets for three voices suitable for domestic devotional singing. The first two books of madrigals already reveal Monteverdi as not only aware of the most innovative harmonic practices of the day, but exploring new realms of sophistication.

To comprehend the innovations of the new Baroque approaches, you have to grasp this matter of counterpoint in music and what it means. So, with apologies to those who need no help, let me briefly try to describe what counterpoint is.

The word derives from the Latin phrase "punctus contra punctum," which means "point against point," and that is a pretty good description of what's involved. Counterpoint refers to music written in two or more independent lines, or voices. The lines have to go together harmonically, of course. But linearly and rhythmically they must have independent natures for a passage to be considered contrapuntal.

Think of a solo melodic line. Then add, say, a lower line, not just a part that buttresses the upper one, but something that has independence, yet goes together. A canon, the fancy word for a round (like "Row, Row, Row Your Boat"), is actually a strict form of counterpoint because the second voice is the same music as the first, just delayed in time, which creates dynamic interplay between the two. A fugue is the most elaborate genre of counterpoint because, in the hands of a Bach, a fugue can be a complex spinning-out of three, four, and even more independent voices that mingle yet make sense together.

The challenge for audiences today, when we hear, say, a Renaissance motet or sacred work, is to orient our ears to try to hear complex contrapuntal music the way it was perceived at the time. Renaissance listeners found pleasure in trying to discern multiple lines unfolding simultaneously. The creative process was a little like what happens today in recording studios when extra tracks are laid atop (or below) already-recorded layers of a pop song.

The madrigal was an ideal genre for the contrapuntal entwining of voices. But—to oversimplify things a bit—during the Renaissance composers and their audiences became increasingly fascinated by what was happening vertically in the music—that is, harmonically—at any one moment. More and more, people were entranced by the power of harmony to drive music rhythmically through the use of dissonant intervals that craved resolution. To emphasize an earlier point, the emergence of Baroque styles, especially the growing popularity of music where a clear single melody was backed by a rhythmic and harmonic continuo group of instruments (the precursor of a 1960s folk singer accompanying herself on a guitar), was something of a simplifying corrective to complex Renaissance counterpoint.

By 1591, if not earlier (the record is unclear), Monteverdi had moved to Mantua to work for Vincenzo I, Duke of Mantua, of the illustrious Gonzaga family. The duke's father had been a cultivated champion of music and drama. Vincenzo maintained these passions, along with passions for women and gambling, when, at his father's death, he became duke in 1587. The duke maintained a large roster of court musicians and singers, headed at the time by a distinguished composer, Giaches de Wert, and had access to string and wind bands and virtuoso soloists. Monteverdi was first employed as a rather lowly viol player in the house ensemble. Over the next decade he steadily worked his way up, while still publishing books of madrigals and other works. In 1599 he married Claudia Cattaneo, a court singer, the daughter of a player in the string ensemble. This was probably an arranged match, which suggests how intent Monteverdi was on advancing his career, though he seems to have been happy with his wife. By 1601 he had attained the top post, maestro della musica.

The previous year, Monteverdi had been the subject of a critical attack from a conservative Bolognese theorist, Giovanni Maria Artusi, who wrote a book castigating the dissonant irregularities of modern music among a new generation of composers, focusing on some offending works by Monteverdi but refusing to name him. That Monteverdi was singled out indicates how influential he had become in Italy, though this young upstart might have been an easy target, as the musicologist Tim Carter suggests. One of the works Artusi seized on was a madrigal, "Cruda Amarilli," a work that had already circulated, though it was not published until 1605.

Listening today to this poignant madrigal, which sets a love lament, from Giovanni Battista Guarini's play *Il pastor fido,* a pastoral tragicomedy, you find it difficult to understand Artusi's indignation. Still, in previous approaches, the piercing harmonies were like fleeting bursts of musical intensity. Monteverdi's dissonant chords, Artusi argued, were unprepared for—that is, the harmonies seemed to appear out of nowhere.

Monteverdi, who had scant general education, responded with a manifesto: a composer's written note in his Fifth Book of Madrigals. He argued that there were now two practices in the composition of vocal works. The first approached music as the mistress of the oration, that is, the text; in the second, which Monteverdi championed, the oration was mistress of the music, hence, justifying harmonic boldness and "contrapuntal license in the service of text expression," as Carter puts it. The manifesto was a savvy tactical maneuver. Monteverdi basically said that there is the old way and there is the new way; let peace reign.

Monteverdi's most lasting contribution may have been the pivotal role he played in the development of opera. There had long been various kinds of music drama, including the liturgical dramas of the medieval period, spectacles and pastorals, interludes performed between the acts of spoken plays, even madrigal comedies that told a story in the equivalent of chapters. Still, those experiments to devise a new kind of music drama that began in Florence around 1600 proved momentous. It's too simple to say that the members of the Florentine Camerata, as historians would later dub this group of poets, composers, and aristocrats, invented opera. But they came pretty close. At the time, they were excited by the potential in a new technique called *stile rappresentativo* (or *stile recitativo*). This was simply a dramatically charged form of recitative with vocal lines written in ways that closely mimicked the natural rhythms and flow of the words being set to music. It is worth taking a moment, though, to explain more about the overall concept of recitative.

Every drama involving music, from Greek tragedy to rock opera, has to come up with a way of delivering dialogue. In many genres the dialogue is simply spoken. In most forms of opera, though, dialogue is primarily delivered in recitative. The clearest kind is so-called *secco* (or "dry") recitative, as in Mozart's operas, when the music seems to stop—at least the arias and ensembles backed by the orchestra—and the characters exchange chunks of dialogue in sputtering bursts of sung Italian accompanied by a harpsichord.

This is as close to sung speech as opera gets. On the other end of the spectrum is full-fledged melody: in Mozart, an aria; in a musical, a song. Conveying the words and the emotions of the text is still essential. But now music has the upper hand and the words emerge from the melodic lines.

There is also an in-between style, called arioso. Here the vocal lines are still composed in a way that mimics the rhythm and flow of the words but with more attention paid to melodic shapes and character. Arioso is quasi-melody.

To Stephen Sondheim, dialogue in a musical theater work should always be the province of the book writer and spoken by the cast. But, though he is no big opera fan, Sondheim embraces the concept of arioso. Whole stretches of his scores, *Passion* being a good example (the work that probably comes closest to being a Sondheim opera), unfold in what could be described as melodically charged vocal lines where words slightly rule. In other words, Sondheim-style arioso. I should say, though, that listeners often differ over whether a vocal line is recitative or arioso, or rises to the level of aria (or song) with a real melody.

The early days of Florentine opera is an instance in music history where a development that simplified things was seen as pathbreaking. The members of the Camerata believed that Greek dramas were more sung than spoken, probably in a style of music that relied essentially on monody, the musical term that describes just a single vocal line accompanied very minimally by instruments with maybe just hints of chords. The Camerata participants were making assumptions about Greek drama, since what they knew was sketchy. Still, they boldly set about to create a contemporary version of it, and their invention of *stile rappresentativo* was the means.

In the first operas the vocal writing of *stile rappresentativo* was closer to what would later be called arioso than to recitative, certainly nothing like the chatty sputtering of Mozart recitative. But after an age of complex Renaissance contrapuntal music, the birth of a new art form that relied extensively on long stretches of monody was momentous.

It's significant, and rather charming, that the story of choice those Florentines seized on to announce this new style of vocal writing and bold new genre of music drama was the myth of Orpheus and Euridice. The attraction was obvious: the character of Orpheus, the singer and poet whose music could tame beasts and soothe the very gods, embodied the power of music. A poet in the group, Ottavio Rinuccini, wrote a libretto, *L'Euridice,* a telling of the myth that plays much more like a pastoral drama with some solemn overtones than the Greek tragedies that supposedly were firing the imaginations of the Camerata.

For one thing, this version idealizes the tale: Orfeo and Euridice appear as a blissfully happy young couple when Euridice, as in the old myth, is bitten by a snake and dies. Orfeo's grief so moves the gods that Venus herself leads Orfeo to the gates of Hades to plead with Pluto to release Euridice from the realm of the dead. But not wanting to write a downer of a libretto, Rinuccini softens the story. Instead of being charged to lead Euridice home without looking back at her, no conditions are placed on Orfeo at all. The lovers simply return in triumph.

In 1600 two musical versions of *L'Euridice* emerged from Florence and were published by two composer/singers who by this point had their own followings and a brewing rivalry: Jacopo Peri and Giulio Caccini. These were not the first operas to be written, but they were the first ones for which we have adequate source materials. Also (and this is where the scholarly record is hard to fathom), each composer's *Euridice* contains music by the other! The commingling suggests that these works were like contributions to an ongoing experiment by, arguably, the most important private club in music history.

Peri's *Euridice* was first performed on October 6, 1600, at the Pitti Palace in Florence as part of the festivities surrounding the wedding of Henri IV, of France, and Marie de' Medici. It was soon published, though the ambitious, unpleasant Caccini, not wanting to miss out on such a high-visibility event, insisted that participating singers who had worked with him be allowed to perform excerpts of music he had composed. Peri, a more obliging sort, agreed. Peri's original score, containing additions by Caccini, was later published. Caccini's version was published around the same time, but not performed complete, it would appear, until 1602.

Peri's version is eloquent and refined. Emotional nuance, even tragic grandeur, inflect the vocal lines, which were accompanied, reports suggest, by lutes and a kind of early harpsichord. What these instruments actually played is hard to know, since the score just indicates bass notes with a few suggestions of chords or riffs. But today, with so many performers skilled in the art of improvising in historic styles, we can make pretty good guesses.

Caccini's *Euridice* is more varied and mellifluous. The vocal lines in *stile rappresentativo* are framed often with choral outbursts and instrumental ritornello, that is, refrains. Whole stretches of the vocal writing have a rhapsodic quality to me. In a good performance, it should seem as if the characters are almost improvising their parts.

Though this new venture in musical drama generated much buzz within aristocratic circles, the main shortcoming of Florentine opera was immediately clear: all that recitative got boring after a while. A theorist at the time urged composers to incorporate other kinds of music—choruses, instrumental episodes, arias with real melodies—to alleviate the tedium of recitative.

Other early opera composers acknowledged the problem. Monteverdi solved it.

At the time, opera was a plaything of princes. Duke Vincenzo, Monteverdi's boss, who had political and familial ties to Florence, kept abreast of artistic developments there. In 1607, anticipating the marriage of the duke's son and heir, there was an especially active festival season in Mantua. Monteverdi was asked to write a festival work. He too turned to the Orpheus tale, but with a libretto written by Alessandro Striggio that hewed closer to the myth, though not quite.

The triumph of Monteverdi's *Orfeo* was due not just to the composer's genius but to his astute analysis of the problems with the operas that had been written previously.

First, he understood that recitative had a built-in dullness factor. So his opera, which he called a *favola in musica* (legend in music), has a score of wondrous variety. There are instrumental numbers and episodes of fleeting dance; there are chorus segments sometimes evocative of madrigal, and other times in a fresh declamatory idiom; Monteverdi's arias, to call them that, are mostly structured in clear verses, usually with instrumental refrains.

Moreover, his way of writing recitative—that is, the *stile rappresentativo*—while closely depicting the contours of speech, has subtle melodic allure. In the great Act III climax, when Orfeo sings a long, pleading arioso to Pluto, "Possente spirto," begging for Euridice's release, the vocal writing in each successive verse becomes more elaborately lyrical and elegantly embellished. Even so, Monteverdi, an instinctive theater man, anticipated that this extended solo might try the patience of his audience, so each verse has a different orchestral accompaniment, with certain instruments being given an importance almost equal to Orfeo's vocal lines.

Because this work was produced for a festive occasion at the behest of a duke who wanted to show off his court composer, Monteverdi was allowed to write for a large ensemble of instruments, about three dozen, including a dozen *fundamenti*—that is, keyboards, harps, organs, and lutes, which provided harmonic support. The score that we have does not always specify which instrument plays what. Still, this Baroque ensemble could be considered a harbinger of big, lush opera orchestras to come.

Another crucial insight Monteverdi brought to this new genre involved the co-dependence, as he saw it, between form and drama. He intuitively realized that even though an opera presents a story in real time, it should also be a large-scaled piece with a musical structure. On a fundamental level, every great opera, even works like Verdi's *Otello* and Berg's *Wozzeck*, holds together like an elaborate composition. Monteverdi set that benchmark with *Orfeo*.

For example, Act I of *Orfeo* opens with a rousing instrumental toccata. A prologue follows in the form of an arioso in several verses sung by the personification of music, La Musica, who welcomes the guests, compliments the royal family, hails the soothing powers of her art, introduces the protagonist, and bids the audience to be silent.

Then the main body of the act begins. There is an introductory song for a shepherd, followed by a five-part chorus in praise of the gods; a transitional recitative for a nymph; a five-part balletic chorus of joy; an orchestral episode of dance; a repeat of the chorus and dance; and a short recitative for a shepherd that leads to the center of the musical structure, which is Orfeo's solo aria of contentment and love, "Rosa del ciel," followed by Euridice's tender reply. Then, in a savvy musico-dramatic stroke, Monteverdi reverses the order and goes backward through the forms of the sections we just heard, writing musical equivalents to them, and arriving at (that is, ending with) a final beguiling recitative for a shepherd. It's a butterflylike musical structure.

Now, as a member of the audience you might not consciously follow this structure; more likely you would just get swept up in the drama, as Monteverdi wanted. But you follow it subliminally. Act I comes across not just as an involving, tender, joyous opening to the story, but as a piece of music that has its own coherence and shape.

Monteverdi's rhythmic invention is another wonder of this work. During the celebratory choruses he demonstrates how to invest music written in a seemingly routine meter, like 4/4, with fetching rhythmic vitality. This is a good place to briefly explain what the term "meter" means. Any description is bound to make the concept seem complicated. Yet meter is probably the most perceptible element of music. The way composers handled it will keep coming up in this book.

Meter simply refers to regularly recurring patterns of beats that are grouped into measures, or bars. It's very similar to meter in poetry, in which words are grouped into symmetrical lines and verses with varying patterns of long and short, accented or unaccented syllables. Western music actually borrowed the term from poetry.

The meter of a piece, or a passage, is indicated in the score by a time signature with two stacked-up numbers. In 4/4, for example, the top number signifies that the music will have four beats per measure; the bottom number represents the unit of pulse, in this case a quarter note.

What matter to listeners are the musical results. Music written in the most basic duple meters, 2/4 and 4/4, seems to unfold in metrical patterns of two beats, or four, to the measure. The most basic triple meter has three beats to the measure. These meters are so pervasive in music, so familiar, that listeners take them for granted. The rhythmic patterns involve routine alterations of accented and unaccented beats. So in 4/4, the first beat, the so-called downbeat, is typically the strongest one: ONE, two, three, four, ONE, two, three, four. A triple-meter gait is the defining characteristic of the waltz: ONE, two, three, ONE, two, three (or, to use the charming colloquialism, OOM-pah-pah, OOM-pah-pah).

But all kinds of music throughout history—medieval dances, Eastern European folk songs, bebop jazz, rock—have played around with meter by throwing in unexpected accents that jostle the symmetrical patterns, like ONE, two, three, FOUR, one, two, THREE, four; or by employing lots of rhythmic syncopations (notes that fall between the regular beats). The possibilities are endless.

Compound meters, a complex-sounding term, are some of the most common, like 6/8, in which, within each measure, two larger units of pulse are continually divided into three, as in: ONE, two, three, FOUR, five, six. The tarantella, a popular Italian dance, is typically in 6/8 meter. Meters organized in seemingly asymmetrical groups of five or seven beats per measure are not uncommon. In Western music, the early twentieth century was a period of bold experimentation with rhythm, a time when composers like Stravinsky, during his radical Paris days, sometimes seemed to be waging war on regular meter.

From all reports, the first performances of *Orfeo* were triumphs. But Monteverdi was distracted by a personal crisis: the illness of his wife, who died that September in Cremona, where Monteverdi had taken her to be cared for by his father. He was left as the sole parent to three children.

Career responsibilities beckoned him back to Mantua.

The duke asked Monteverdi to write another opera, this one to be performed in 1608 as part of the festivities attending his son's wedding. Monteverdi complied with *Arianna,* based on the Ariadne myth. Alas, the score has been lost, every bit of it except for Arianna's lament, a piece that became the seventeenth-century equivalent of a hit tune, so popular that Monteverdi made other versions of it, including a five-part madrigal, "Lasciatemi morire," published in the Sixth Book of Madrigals in 1614. "Let me die," Arianna sings when she learns that the heroic Theseus has deserted her and she has been left alone on the island of Naxos. Earlier eras of music history are riddled with tales of lost works, and this was not just carelessness. The notion that pieces were conceived and written for posterity did not really take hold until the time of Beethoven, the era of the composer as colossus, writing works for the ages.

My favorite recording of the ravishing "Lasciatemi morire" comes from the first recording ever made of Monteverdi's music. In 1937 the French conductor and renowned teacher Nadia Boulanger, who in the early part of her career had been a composer, gathered a small ensemble of handpicked singers and instrumentalists and recorded nine vocal works, including madrigals, duets, and canzonettas, with small complements of instrumentals. Then fifty years old, Boulanger herself played the continuo keyboard parts on the piano; the strings were also modern instruments. However "wrong" the instrumental forces were, these performances radiate exquisite musicianship, tenderness, and palpable joy. This may have been the first Monteverdi I ever heard.

The album sparked renewed interest in the achievement of a neglected giant. Boulanger, who died in 1979 at ninety-two, must have been pleased when in 1964 the then-young British conductor John Eliot Gardiner founded the Monteverdi Choir at King's College Chapel in Cambridge specificaily to perform the composer's sumptuous "Vespers for the Blessed Virgin," commonly known as the Vespers of 1610, a monumental ninety-minute work for vocal soloists, large chorus, and orchestra with music that subtly mingles old and new styles.

Monteverdi was a slow, painstaking worker. And though he was a natural at writing dramatic music, he found the challenge exhausting, as he complained in a letter in 1608 to a wealthy counselor to the duke: "I assure you that unless I take a rest from toiling away at music for the theater, my life will indeed be a short one." His recent labors had caused him to have, he explained, a "frightful pain" in his head and "so terrible and violent an itching" around his waist that nothing—cauteries, purges, bloodletting—seemed to help.

There were certainly operatic elements of drama in Monteverdi's life as he gained fame and grew older. In 1612 Duke Vincenzo died and was succeeded by his son Francesco, which should have been propitious for Monteverdi, since the heir was a big opera enthusiast. But the new duke immediately reined in expenses at the lavish court, including scaling down the size of his house music ensemble. Monteverdi and his younger brother, also a court musician, were dismissed. As it turns out, by December of that year Francesco himself died suddenly. Monteverdi had already returned home to Cremona, exhausted and discouraged but determined. That he began composing an elaborate mass suggests he was angling for a church job. And the biggest one in Italy soon became available: maestro di cappella of the Basilica of St. Mark in Venice, the magnificent cathedral adjacent to the Doge's Palace, an embodiment of northern Italian wealth, power, and culture, and an institution with a renowned musical heritage.

The church overseers surely had their eye on Monteverdi already. But he went to Venice and presented his mass at what was, in effect, an audition. He won the post straightaway. As a pledge of good faith, the church officials gave Monteverdi fifty ducats. On his way to Venice to begin a thirty-year tenure that would become a milestone in music history, he was robbed by highwaymen with muskets who made Monteverdi and his couriers kneel on the ground, searched the caskets on the horses and carriage, and took all his money.

St. Mark's was built with musical acoustics in mind. Inside the cathedral, lofts and alcoves encircle the central space. This made possible wondrous musical effects: various choral, string, and brass ensembles could bounce musical passages antiphonally back and forth. Monteverdi's main responsibilities involved composing music for services and directing all the performances. He also proved adept at the administrative demands of his job: he reorganized the entire musical staff and even restocked the music library, which had become out of date.

This was Monteverdi's period of writing magnificent sacred music, though there are gaps in our knowledge of his life and work during the 1630s. But excitement was spreading about the emerging genre of opera, and in 1637 the first public opera house opened in Venice. Though select sections of the house were reserved for aristocratic patrons, anyone who could afford a ticket could sit in the upper galleries. This mingling of the moneyed set and the general public continues today in opera houses around the world. But the coming of the first public opera house was a turning point in the genre's history; within a few years, Venice alone had several of them.

Monteverdi was by now a grand old man of music. He had never really stopped writing dramatic works of various kinds, though the scores for quite a few have never turned up.

For me, it is fascinating to ponder the way he reconciled two seemingly different dimensions of his personal and creative life. On the one hand, he was the most prestigious composer of sacred music in Italy. Not only that, in 1632 he took holy orders and became a priest. Yet he was also drawn to dramatic music and in his last years wrote three major works in this genre. In 1640, following a revival of *Arianna* in Venice, there was the premiere of Monteverdi's complex, magisterial drama *Il ritorno di Ulisse in patria* (The Return of Ulysses to His Homeland), a story drawn from Homer's *Odyssey*. Despite the questionable quality of the sources for the score, *Ulisse* is produced frequently today and has been much recorded. In 1641 there was a Venice production of another new Monteverdi opera, *Le nozze d'Enea e Lavinia* (The Marriage of Aeneas to Livinia), but for that one no musical sources have turned up.

The work I want to focus on, and end this essay with, is Monteverdi's final opera, and probably his last work, *L'incoronazione di Poppea* (The Coronation of Poppea). This piece has a personal significance for me, as I'll explain in a bit.

The opera was first performed at a public theater in Venice during the carnival season of 1643, just months before Monteverdi died at seventy-six. The elegant, poetic, and very steamy libretto by Giovanni Francesco Busenello and the scandalous story, as set to Monteverdi's seductive, dramatically charged, dazzlingly varied music, still have the power to shock. The libretto, as the scholar Ellen Rosand has pointed out, emerged from a libertine intellectual movement in Venice whose adherents explored the relative domains of religion and sensuality. Judging by *Poppea*, they were not afraid to use historical subjects to shed light on the corrupting effects of power.

The story is loosely based on the episode when the Roman emperor Nero divorced his wife, Octavia, to marry his mistress, the lovely, ruthless Poppea. The opera departs from the most gruesome elements of the actual story: the real Octavia was banished, despite her popularity in Rome, then executed on Nero's orders and her severed head delivered to Poppea.

In Monteverdi's opera the key characters, if less bloodthirsty, are more psychologically intriguing. It opens with a prologue in the heavens, where Fortune, Virtue, and Cupid debate who has the most power over man. Fortune and Virtue concede victory to Cupid, who explains that a testimony to the power of love will be played out this very day.

There is nothing virtuous, though, about the kind of love that triumphs in *Poppea*. Working with his librettist, Monteverdi produced a complex, gripping, yet entertaining three-act opera. He provides music that fleshes out the individual natures of the disparate characters. The wronged Octavia sings mostly in agitated, wounded recitative. Ottone, Poppea's jilted lover, though a noble lord, is a vacillating, weak man, qualities conveyed in his fitful and at times self-pitying phrases. In this tale the bad guys, Nero and Poppea, triumph. Their romantic exchanges are rhapsodic and alluring. Yet the carnal excess that drives them comes through in the wily, twisting ways of their breathless recitative and seductive arioso phrases.

To make the best case for the continuing dramatic freshness of this music drama, I'd like to boast about a 1980 production for which I was co–music director, along with my colleague and friend the composer Scott Wheeler, when I was teaching with Scott at Emerson College in Boston. Emerson had a thriving musical theater program that drew many lively, gifted students. But there was no classical music program to speak of. Scott and I felt that the best voices among the students, including many singers in the college chorus, were often overlooked because the possessors of these voices were not necessarily strong actors or even theater majors. So we decided to stage at least one show a year overseen by music professors and cast with the best voices available, without regard to the acting strengths of the chosen students.

To kick off the workshop, we presented *Poppea* in a colloquial English translation of the libretto. Except for a bass whom we recruited from the Boston Conservatory to sing the role of the imposing Seneca, Nero's former tutor and preceptor, there were really no operatic voices in our production. But we had some very appealing musical-theater singers. It took our students time to adjust to the Baroque vocal style, though I enjoyed helping them figure out how to dispatch fleet strands of eighth notes and stuttering vocal embellishments. The cast members had to adjust to what was for them a very different kind of pit band: a harpsichord and a string quartet. We used an edition prepared by the conductor Raymond Leppard that early-music scholars today would consider far too tampered with. No matter. The Leppard version is theatrical and musically sound. And it was fascinating to see how these theater students immediately grasped the timeless dramatic elements of the opera.

In an early scene, Ottone, Poppea's lover, has just returned from a diplomatic mission that Nero had sent him on to get him out of the way. Ottone approaches Poppea's palace at daybreak and is horrified to see two soldiers, guards to the emperor, sleeping outside the entrance. This can mean only one thing: Nero is inside with Poppea. Ottone cries out, waking one soldier, who then rouses his comrade, since neither of them should have fallen asleep on duty. But they are exhausted because they have been spending night after night outside Poppea's palace while their emperor savors love.

One soldier gets up and, in a startlingly modern outburst, curses the god of love, who has wrought this spell on Nero. While he's at it, he also curses Nero, Poppea, Rome, and the whole stinking army! Eventually the soldiers break into a fleet yet suspenseful duo, where they sing florid runs in intricate overlapping lines, realizing that the safest course is to keep quiet and let their eyes see only what they are meant to see. Our Emerson *Poppea* had two young men singing these roles, neither of whom sounded remotely operatic. Yet the collegiate, virile energy they brought to their singing was exactly right for Monteverdi's characters.

Poppea is Monteverdi's final masterpiece. Unfortunately, the sources for this work are also contradictory and unreliable. Scholars have long believed that some of the music was likely written by other, younger composers in Venice, including Francesco Sacrati, it would appear, and Francesco Cavalli, who had already begun what would become a major career in opera. The practice of borrowing music from other works was common at the time and would remain so for a couple of centuries.

I was devastated to learn that "Pur ti miro," the astounding duet that ends *Poppea* so hauntingly, was probably not by Monteverdi. It's a mesmerizing ending to this psychologically complex opera. Poppea has been crowned empress and hailed by throngs of her new Roman subjects (who understand that they had better fall in with the new power structure). The crowd departs and the newlyweds begin the ravishing duet. Over a repeated descending four-note bass figure (often called a basso ostinato, or "obstinate" bass), Nero and Poppea exchange ardent, overlapping vocal phrases, though a flowing, lighter middle section shows a playful side to their attachment. This elegant duet creates emotional confusion for the audience. The music suggests that the tyrannical Nero and the scheming Poppea are blissfully, genuinely in love. Is this possible?

In any event, from what I understand, a body of recent research has suggested that Monteverdi, after all, may have composed this music. Or at least supervised its composition. The debate goes on. I've got my money on Claudio.

CHAPTER TWO

MUSIC FOR USE, DEVOTION, AND PERSONAL PROFIT

JOHANN SEBASTIAN BACH (1685–1750)

I n trying to account for Johann Sebastian Bach's staggering genius and superhuman achievement, even many great composers have resorted to deification.

"Music owes as much to Bach as a religion to its founder," said Schumann.

Schumann put his devotion into action, as he charmingly admitted to a friend, "I myself make a daily confession of my sins to that mighty one, and endeavor to purify and strengthen myself through him."

Debussy also affirmed Bach's divinity, while providing, as befits a Frenchman, more nuance. Bach was a "benevolent God," he wrote, "to whom musicians should offer a prayer before setting to work so that they may be preserved from mediocrity."

Leonard Bernstein, though prone to being emotional, tried to bring some rationality to the question. "Bach was a man, after all, not a god," Bernstein once said, "but he was a man *of* God, and his godliness informs his music from first to last."

But the humorist and music enthusiast H. L. Mencken accepted no such distinction. He summarized Bach simply as "Genesis 1,1."

Thankfully, if Bach is music's god (and the votes are in), this has not deterred intrepid performers from tackling his works. But how does one write about him?

John Eliot Gardiner has done both. This acclaimed Bach conductor has also written an insightful biography, *Bach: Music in the Castle of Heaven*, published in 2013. In the first sentence of the preface, Gardiner lays out the challenge of grappling with this master: "Bach the musician is an unfathomable genius; Bach the man is all too obviously flawed, disappointingly ordinary and in many ways still invisible to us."

I'll get to Bach, the "disappointingly ordinary" man. But why has his music over the centuries left even towering composers in such inarticulate awe?

That's the question. Before I too resort to deification, I'll make just a few points.

In his day Bach's reputation rested primarily on his acclaimed skills as a performer on organ and harpsichord. As a composer he absorbed every style, idiom, and technique he was able to explore, both old and new, a fixation that made him seem old-fashioned to many of his contemporaries.

Though Bach mastered the rooted, diatonic (that is, major and minor) musical language that had essentially been codified by the mid-seventeenth century, he went further, or, you could say, deeper, drawing out the inner workings, hidden potentials, and implications of this language in his distinctive approach to harmony.

Also, as I touched on in writing about the Mass in B Minor, Bach came to maturity during a time of enormous innovation. Notwithstanding new tastes and fashions, Bach retained a fascination with rigorous counterpoint, insisting upon the integrity of every voice in his scores.

The pianist Jeremy Denk, an engaging writer on music, gets at this central element in a smart essay on Bach for the *New Republic*. Bach is synonymous with the fugue, "the music of proposition, propagation, permutation," Denk writes. Yes, we want music to make us feel, to plumb our psyches. And a formidable multi-voiced, contrapuntal fugue might seem too stern an idiom for such an end. "But," as Denk puts it, "Bach is a multitasker: his logic is unassailable but is not tedious. His proofs soar. He captures the deepest feeling while remaining perfectly logical, thereby demonstrating that those imperatives are not at all opposed."

Bach had a less lofty take on his own achievement. When asked about how he mastered the art of music so impressively, as his first biographer later reported, Bach always replied: "I was obliged to be industrious; whoever is equally industrious will succeed equally well."

In part, Bach felt so obliged by the humble circumstances of his family background. Our knowledge of his private life is spotty and full of untrustworthy anecdotes. Few of his surviving letters deal with personal matters. He suffered devastating losses, including the deaths of his first wife and, over two marriages, half of his twenty children. But you find scant reference to these tragedies in his letters, which are dominated by obsequious dedications to potential patrons, detailed work reports to various employers, and in-depth analyses of church organs he was routinely commissioned to inspect and repair. (Bach, an exemplary organist, was equally prized for his expertise in organ mechanics.)

Bach spent his entire life living in and traveling among cities and towns in central and northern Germany. He never visited another country. We are not even that sure what he looked like. A painting from the late 1740s by Elias Gottlob Haussmann, the official portraitist in Leipzig, considered the most accurate likeness, shows Bach in his sixties, bewigged, jowly, and with a stern expression, though a corner of his mouth reveals a slight smile.

In his book, Gardiner adds dimension to the legend of Bach as a pious Lutheran humbly serving his God through dedication to his craft. Gardiner's Bach is "an artist driven to distraction by the narrow-mindedness and stupidity of his employers and forced to live, in his own words, 'amid almost continual vexation, envy and persecution.'"

That craft had been the Bach family business since the sixteenth century. For professional musicians in Germany of that era, there were not many career paths. You could win a post as a court musician to a noble patron or prince, or as a civic musician employed by a town council. You could be a church organist, or the music director (cantor) of a church, which involved directing choirs, preparing music for services, and teaching the boy choristers. Over many generations, the Bach family produced some significant composers and musicians; still, most of them were probably just solid professionals of no particular distinction.

Johann Sebastian Bach was born on March 21, 1685, in Eisenach, a town of about six thousand in the duchy of Saxe-Eisenach. He was the eighth and last child of Johann Ambrosius Bach, a town musician, and Maria Elisabeth, the daughter of a furrier and town councillor in Erfurt. Ambrosius held the desirable, if demanding, post of head town piper (*Stadtpfeifer*) in Eisenach, reporting to the council, which involved overseeing music for civic ceremonies, festivities, weddings, and such. Though not known to be a composer, Ambrosius was valued for his versatility as an instrumentalist and vocalist. We cannot be sure exactly how he trained the young Sebastian, though he probably instructed his son in the violin and in basic music theory.

Sebastian was fortunate, however, that an older relative, Johann Christoph Bach, his father's first cousin, worked in Eisenach as organist at the main church and court musician to the duke. Christoph grappled with lifelong financial troubles, owing in part to medical expenses for his wife and children, which left him prickly by nature. But within the Bach clan and beyond he was considered an accomplished composer and organist. Whether he systematically taught his young cousin is unclear. But he certainly guided Sebastian's development while conscripting him into helping maintain the church's great organ. In a family genealogy that Bach compiled late in life, he refers to Christoph as a "profound" composer.

Sebastian attended the Latin school in Eisenach. In 1694, when he was nine, Bach suffered a double tragedy. His mother died in early May at the age of fifty. In November his ailing father remarried, taking the thirty-five-year-old widow of a cousin as his wife. Three months later, Ambrosius died at forty-nine. In April, just turned ten and now an orphan, Sebastian moved with his thirteen-year-old brother, Johann Jacob, to Ohrdruf, a provincial town of twenty-five hundred residents some thirty miles southeast, to live with their eldest brother, Johann Christoph. As Gardiner points out,

Sebastian and Johann Christoph, who was fourteen years older, hardly knew each other. Culturally, the town was a step down from the musical hub of Eisenach. Still, Johann Christoph had a good job as organist at the town's main church. Married just a year, he and his wife were expecting their first child when his younger brothers arrived. Suddenly he found himself the guardian of two boys.

That summer Sebastian entered the Ohrdruf Lyceum. In Eisenach he had been an indifferent student prone to truancy. In Ohrdruf he applied himself and, reports suggest, excelled. Perhaps, as some biographers have speculated, Bach's involvement in his studies was the coping mechanism of an orphan still dealing with loss. There may have been more to it.

Eisenach was a bastion of orthodox Lutheran theology. In Ohrdruf, however, the tension between orthodox thinking and a more ascetic form of the religion known as Pietism played out every day in the town's civic and academic life. James R. Gaines, in his fascinating book *Evening in the Palace of Reason: Bach Meets Frederick the Great in the Age of Enlightenment*, offers an insightful take. Young Sebastian was "drawn to theology," Gaines proposes, "as he would be drawn to the cold logic of counterpoint, out of a wish for order in his life." Gaines adds, "From this time forward . . . Sebastian would pursue order, perfection, and spiritual meaning in his music, and never more movingly so than on the theme of triumph over death."

That young craving for knowledge of counterpoint and the salve of orderliness it provided may explain what strikes me as the most telling story of the young Bach's life: his clandestine copying of musical scores almost nightly over a period of months. This anecdote has been much told and embroidered. What actually happened, and why, is hard to know.

In his house Christoph kept a locked cabinet with a booklet of valuable musical scores: keyboard pieces by older masters, including Pachelbel (Christoph's teacher) and Froberger. For whatever reason, as Bach would later tell the story, which he often did, he was denied access to this booklet. But the young Sebastian could fit his small hand and wrist through the grille of the cabinet door, roll up the unbound booklet, and draw it out. So, with insatiable curiosity, he got up in the middle of moonlit nights and copied the precious scores, page by page, over six months, until he finished the job. Copying manuscripts had long been a traditional method of acquiring knowledge. Even late in life Beethoven continued to copy out scores by earlier masters.

When Christoph discovered his young charge's handwritten copy of the booklet, he reproached Sebastian and took it away. But why was the boy denied access in the first place? And why was he so bent on absorbing these pieces?

A possible explanation is that these unbound pages were fragile and Christoph wanted to protect them. He must have been annoyed as well that his defiant younger brother broke a household rule. Also, blank manuscript paper was expensive.

Perhaps, as some have interpreted the story, Christoph considered Sebastian too young to be given access to such precious musical knowledge, such a sacred text, almost as if a Jewish boy in preparation for becoming a bar mitzvah had not yet earned the right to study certain profound passages of the Torah.

For me, the story attests to the young Bach's determination to learn everything he could about music by exploring every learned piece he could get his hands on, whenever and however. Bach obviously had innate musical talents of astonishing depth. There are children, we know, whose brains seem almost prewired to comprehend numbers. Watching an episode of *Sesame Street,* these little tykes see Bert and Ernie work out two-plus-two on a blackboard and suddenly something clicks inside and all of mathematics opens up to them. Or so it can seem.

But this is just a first step. There is much more involved than neurological wiring. Something must have clicked in the musical mind of Sebastian Bach from his earliest exposure to music. He saw pathways stretching before him and realms to explore. But he had to set foot on those pathways, and scores by the masters provided musical maps.

Carl Philip Emanuel, one of Bach's sons, who in his day was more renowned as a composer than Sebastian, said that his father could hear a musical idea—a theme or a subject suitable for a fugue—and immediately know all the varied operations that could be carried out on it, that is, all the contrapuntal calculations—how to play it backward (in retrograde) or upside down (in inversion) or at half the speed (augmentation)—and then utilize these tweaked components to develop an elaborate piece. But this ingenious skill was hard-won, a self-teaching process that had begun for the young Bach even before those moonlit nights of clandestine copying.

Whatever the tensions between them, Sebastian made strides during his few years under his older brother's tutelage, gaining fluency at the keyboard and maturing as an organist, though from my reading, he must have developed his prodigious skill at improvisation on his own. And Christoph introduced the boy to works by important composers from other national traditions, including Italians like Frescobaldi and Frenchmen like Lully and Marais.

At fourteen, Bach, along with an older school chum, received a choral scholarship to attend the select St. Michael's School in Lüneburg. After graduating at seventeen, Bach applied for a job as organist at a church in Sangerhausen and received an offer, though the post wound up going to someone else. Instead, he found a fairly menial job as a musician in the court at Weimar.

And so began Bach's episodic professional career, which can be seen as a lifelong attempt by an ambitious musician to secure increasingly favorable appointments. Each new job had advantages and disadvantages, which I'll touch on only briefly since the details are less than engrossing, though the saga will resonate with professionals in many fields today who know what it's like to angle for a better situation in an increasingly fluid economy.

Six months after beginning his duties at Weimar, Bach was hired to assess an elaborate new organ in the Neukirche in Arnstadt, which led to his appointment as the church's organist, a nice improvement over his Weimar job. If his salary was modest, so were his responsibilities. Though his employers from the town council were initially pleased with Bach's work, they were dismayed by his prolonged absences, including several months during the winter of 1705–1706, when he went to the northern city of Lübeck to visit and observe the towering organist and composer Dietrich

Buxtehude. Legend holds that Bach made this long journey (some 280 miles each way) on foot, which seems improbable but could be true.

Just in time, in 1707, he won the post of organist at St. Blasius's Church in the Imperial City of Mühlhausen. With a good salary, and feeling more on his feet, he married a cousin, Maria Barbara. They would have seven children, of whom four survived to adulthood.

After just eleven months at Mühlhausen, Bach was amicably released from his post to take a coveted job as organist and chamber musician at the court of Weimar. In 1714 he was promoted to concertmaster of the court orchestra, which entailed composing a monthly church cantata. Things clearly soured for Bach at the court over time.

In 1717 he accepted a first kapellmeister post at the court of Prince Leopold in Cöthen, a step up and a promising post, though Bach first had to wrangle his freedom from the miffed councilmen in Mühlhausen, a dispute that led to detention of the stubborn Bach by a county judge.

Because Prince Leopold was Calvinist, Bach was not routinely expected to provide sacred works for church services. So during his years in Cöthen he focused on composing secular music: suites for orchestra, the suites for solo cello and solo violin, and the six *Brandenburg Concertos,* which remain among his most popular pieces. Bach seems to have been happy and productive at Cöthen. Then, in 1720, his wife died at thirty-five while Bach was traveling. The next year he married Anna Magdalena Wilcke, then twenty and a thoroughly trained musician. They would have thirteen children, of whom six survived.

Just at this juncture, the post of cantor at the St. Thomas School in Leipzig opened up. This was one of the most highly regarded positions in the Lutheran realm. Though the choir school was based at the St. Thomas Church, the cantor was charged with providing music for four churches in the city, as well as directing music for civic functions. Bach was not the first choice of the Leipzig council, whose members turned to him only after giving up on enticing Telemann or the now-obscure Christoph Graupner.

Bach was charged with overseeing not just the musical but also the general education of the young choristers, though he secured permission to hire a deputy to teach the boys Latin grammar. Overall, he tried to limit his responsibilities for classroom teaching so as to maximize his time for preparing performances and for composition. Despite endless haggling over his duties and chronic complaints to the authorities that they were inhibiting his efforts to improve the quality of music making at Leipzig, Bach wrote many of his greatest works while holding down this demanding post, including the St. John Passion, the St. Matthew Passion, and the Mass in B Minor.

Given the centrality of Bach today, it's hard to fathom that during his lifetime he was perceived as an old-fashioned composer. He enjoyed widespread respect in the German realm for his thorough mastery of his art, including unmatched skills at improvisation: given a theme (subject), Bach could improvise fugues in three or four parts that most musicians would have been hard-pressed to compose. His reputation as one of the finest organists of his era went beyond the borders of his native land.

Yet the new generation of composers, including Bach's sons, while deeply respectful, thought Bach out of the loop. Johann Christian, the youngest, affectionately dubbed his father "Old Wig."

It seems unfair of Bach's sons, not to mention a little dense, to think of him as dated. True, Bach was not trendy. New musical styles were springing up in France and Germany that favored lighter textures with elaborate filigree and a lot less counterpoint. Though Bach knew all about these developments, he was more interested in the roots of the various national styles and heritages. His lack of interest in opera was also suspect to his trendier contemporaries. By the time Bach got his first adult jobs, opera had been around for a century, evolving from the plaything of princes to an art form popular with the public (in cities where public theaters had been established). But Bach was never really tempted. He could certainly toss off a snappy dance movement for an instrumental suite when so inclined. Yet to the new generation he seemed sober and traditional, an Old Wig still cranking out complex chorale preludes for organ and industrious fugues.

One genre to which Bach brought indisputable freshness was the concerto, the genre in which a solo instrument plays with (or against, when things turn combative) a larger ensemble or orchestra. Bach greatly admired the Italian concerto tradition as practiced by Corelli and Vivaldi. In his own concertos, and in many other works, Bach appropriated the Italianate penchant for continuous rhythmic activity, with bustling streams of notes. And he adapted the concerto grosso setup favored by the Italians, where stretches of music were tossed back and forth between small groups of solo instruments and the larger orchestral ensemble.

Bach should probably be credited with developing the solo keyboard concerto. He likely composed his seven harpsichord concertos for entertainments at his home, or for the concerts of the Collegium Musicum, an informal organization founded by the young Telemann in Leipzig in 1704.

The Collegium was rather like a musical club that fostered the composition and performance of secular works. Its popular concerts sometimes spilled over into after-hours sessions at Leipzig coffeehouses. Bach took on the directorship of the Collegium in 1729 and held it for about a decade. Like Bach's cantatas and many other of his works, his inventive harpsichord concertos demonstrate his impressive recycling skills. In these scores Bach often refashioned and adapted existing pieces, including violin concertos and vocal works. The delightful Concerto in A was based on a concerto for oboe d'amore, for example. At times during episodes of the twisting, churning first movement, you can also sense Bach showing off, as the harpsichord's right-hand line goes on a melodic adventure, often breaking into swirling runs and elaborations that keep the listener on alert for surprises.

The best known of these pieces is the Concerto in D Minor, a dark, gripping work with long, obsessive, almost demonic passages of repetitive rhythms and oscillating chords played by the harpsichord. In 2012 Jeremy Denk played six of the seven harpsichord concertos at Alice Tully Hall in New York, performing on a piano and conducting from the keyboard, with an eager roster of eleven excellent string players from the Chamber Music Society of Lincoln Center, including a continuo group. I have seldom observed musicians having so much fun during a performance. Denk swayed along with the strings, his feet often dancing when not occupied with the sustaining pedal, which he used only lightly. And his colleagues positively beamed at the sheer ingenuity of Bach's music as they dispatched it. You could not listen to this program and perceive Bach as some Old Wig.

My mention of a continuo group calls for some explanation, since it's an essential element of most works by Bach and, indeed, all composers at the time.

Basso continuo is also known as thoroughbass or figured bass. An elaborate bass line, often of an undulant, quasi-melodic character, was crucial to the textures of Baroque music. So whether writing for a small chamber ensemble or an orchestra, a composer would provide a reinforcing bass line played by both a bass instrument (usually a cello or a viola da gamba) and a keyboard instrument (a harpsichord or a small organ). The keyboard part typically included chord symbols (figured bass), literally a system of numbers that indicated what the harmony above the bass should be. But the keyboard player had wide freedom to interpret those figures by playing chords and little runs in any way that more or less hewed to the symbols. Sometimes during extended stretches of recitative in a Bach oratorio, or even during an aria, the solo singer is accompanied by little else than the continuo group. Yet a continuo group will often play along during a big choral number as well, providing some grounding even when the instruments are barely audible.

In general, searching for evidence of Bach's trendiness misses the point. As I see it, and as I signaled at the start of this chapter, while many composers were exploring new fashions and developments, Bach kept looking deeper. He could sense the full implications of what had already been revealed. He explored the art of counterpoint and the larger practice through which contrapuntal lines are woven into chords and harmonic progressions as never before. He showed us all, not just the musicians of his time, but of all time, that we had not fully realized the ramifications of what we already knew. In all fields, true profundity comes from immersive examination. No composer has ever looked at music more deeply than Bach.

Take harmony, focusing on Bach's chorales. Almost all of Bach's sacred choral works, from shorter cantatas to spacious passions, contain chorales, in essence hymn tunes, many of which would have been well known to congregants at church. Bach set these to music in four-part harmony (four voices): soprano, alto, tenor, and bass. In the context of a cantata, a chorale provides a moment of reflection in which the choristers sing a consoling, or affirming, hymn. The challenge in harmonizing a chorale tune is twofold. The melodic notes must be supported by harmonies—that is, by progressions of chords that simultaneously cushion the melody and carry it forward. At the same time, each individual voice should have its own lyrical character and independence. Bach's chorales demonstrate the effortless and elegant blending of harmonic and contrapuntal elements, an ingenious matrix of vertical and horizontal lines.

Yet in harmonizing chorale tunes, Bach also explored every realm, every implication of major-minor harmony and modulations. The Bach chorales, taken from his various choral works, have been published as collections, the best known being a volume of 371 harmonized chorales edited by Albert Riemenschneider in the early 1940s. Often Bach harmonized a particular chorale tune several times: the Riemenschneider collection contains three chorale versions of *Ein feste Burg ist unser Gott* (A Mighty Fortress Is Our God), the well-known tune written by Martin Luther, and six of *Jesu, meine Freude* (Jesus, My Joy), a beloved melody by Johann Crüger. It's fascinating to explore the variety of ways Bach could harmonize the same tune. That collection of chorales, the definitive harmony textbook, is still used in music classrooms everywhere.

Bach's chorales explore and anticipate advanced approaches to harmony—so-called chromatic harmony. This important concept also requires a little explanation. While I'm at it, I should briefly explain the bare basics of scales (for the benefit of those readers who love music but understand little about music theory). Bach would want me to.

The basic pitch domain (to call it that) of Western music comes from the chromatic scale, the series of twelve pitches in which each is a half step (or semitone) above or below its neighbor. On the piano it's easy to see and play a chromatic scale: just play, for example, all the keys, black and white, between middle C and the C an octave higher.

Major scales (think do, re, mi, and so on) and their related minor versions use just seven of the twelve chromatic tones in various patterns of half steps and whole steps (the distance between two semitones). A scale is not just a series of pitches, but also a kind of hierarchy of pitches: certain notes are crucial to the harmonic grounding of a key, especially the first (tonic), the fifth (dominant), and the fourth (subdominant). Chords based on those tones are commonly referred to by Roman numerals: the I, V, and IV chords, and so on.

When a piece, or a passage, of music mostly hews to the tones and chords of a scale, it is said to be essentially diatonic in its harmonic functioning. But a passage written in a particular key is said to be chromatic when—to oversimplify—the music keeps using those in-between chromatic tones and chords based on those tones.

What matters to listeners is the resulting character of the music. When music veers into chromatic realms, the overall harmonic language, however rich and enticing, sounds more wayward, less centered on the main, stabilizing notes of a major or minor key. As music developed during the nineteenth century, composers grew bolder and bolder at exploring chromatic harmony to create a more ambiguous harmonic language. Wagner was a pioneer in this regard.

You could argue (I certainly would) that Bach was a visionary explorer not just of diatonic but of chromatic harmony. He anticipated most of what would happen as the nineteenth century segued into the twentieth and the tonal system became less grounded and more ambiguous, eventually opening pathways to atonal experiments by composers like Schoenberg.

Given my background as a pianist I might be biased, but as I see it, Bach the composer-searcher bent on plumbing music's depths comes through most clearly in his compositions for solo keyboard—in his day, the harpsichord. I'm thinking of the English Suites and the French Suites, and particularly the six Partitas. And, of course, the forty-eight Preludes and Fugues, written in two books, two installments, which together present a veritable treatise on the workings of counterpoint in the guise of intellectually awesome and musically exhilarating compositions.

Before discussing this, though, let me offer a quick primer on the technology of keyboard instruments in Bach's day.

On a harpsichord, a struck key engages a mechanism that uses a little hooklike device to pluck a corresponding string. The early fortepiano replaced that hook with a leather-covered hammer; this mechanism allowed for gradations of pressure and, hence, volume, reflected in the name of the new instrument, which translates to "loud-soft." The pianos of the early nineteenth century started using thicker and longer metal strings, and eventually steel frames over which those strings were stretched, which enhanced the volume and power even further.

The sustaining pedal was another new development. The piano has a system of dampers, which stop the strings from vibrating when the pianist's finger leaves the key. Without this mechanism, the sounds would linger and blur together. Engaging the sustaining pedal raises the dampers off the strings during passages when the pianist *wants* the sounds to linger and blend. Bach wrote his keyboard works for the harpsichord and was no fan of the early fortepianos that were gaining advocates during the later decades of his life. He was impressed, though, by a large Silbermann fortepiano he tried out at the court of Frederick the Great in 1747, three years before his death.

In the fall of 2012 the great pianist András Schiff, widely acclaimed as a masterful interpreter of Bach (who plays nearly all the composer's solo keyboard works), performed the complete Preludes and Fugues at the 92nd Street Y in New York on two programs: Book I the first night; Book II just five days later. Had Bach been in attendance he would have been stupefied by almost everything about Schiff's concerts. And hearing pieces conceived for harpsichord played on a modern piano would probably have been the least of it. Bach would have been baffled by the very idea of performing these works in concert for an audience of some nine hundred people. He intended the Preludes and Fugues as study pieces for musicians to practice and learn from, though "study piece" conveys the wrong notion since for all the stretches of rigorous counterpoint, the Preludes and Fugues abound in inventive, beguiling, and beautiful music.

The title page of Book I, completed in 1722, includes Bach's statement of purpose: "For the use and profit of the musical youth desirous of learning, as well as for the pastime of those already skilled in this study, drawn up and written by Johann Sebastian Bach."

Bach surely would have been flabbergasted that Schiff played all of these works—more than four hours of music over two nights—from memory. In Bach's time there was composed music, which was naturally performed from printed or handwritten scores, and there was improvised music, which of course entailed no scores. I bet Bach would have found it easier to improvise an entirely new Fugue in A-flat (from Book II) than to play that very complex piece from memory. Why, he would have thought, would a musician waste time memorizing a written-out piece?

Schiff has said in interviews that for him, playing the Preludes and Fugues from memory is not the hardest part of performing them complete. Clearly his brain, rather like Bach's, is wired to grapple with complex counterpoint.

Though the formal title of the collection, *The Well-Tempered Clavier*, is familiar to audiences, not many non-musicians know what it means. "Tempered" refers to a tuning system that was coming into vogue at the time Bach wrote these pieces. Tuning is a complicated subject, even for musicians. What is important to understand, though, is that pitch in music is not fixed. For example, string players can adjust a pitch—a little higher or lower, sharper or flatter—so as to make a particular chord sound almost elemental and in tune. But keyboard instruments, like the organs and harpsichords of Bach's day, had pre-fixed tunings that didn't allow for tweaks in the moment. Without getting into the complexities, the well-tempered approach to tuning provided somewhat equal spacing between the twelve pitches of the chromatic scale (from C to C an octave higher). The result was that a particular interval (that is, the space, or the distance, between two notes) played on a well-tempered harpsichord might have sounded slightly "off," that is, not as "pure" as it could be if rendered by string players, who could slightly adjust each interval or chord. But this compromise to "purity" made it possible for music on the harpsichord to explore all the ins and outs of the chromatic scale and chromatic keys.

Bach took advantage of this "defect," in a sense, by composing a series of twenty-four paired preludes and fugues, one pair for each of the twenty-four major and minor keys: Prelude and Fugue No. 1 in C Major, Prelude and Fugue No. 2 in C Minor, and so on. Then, twenty years later, he completed another twenty-four pairs of preludes and fugues, for a total of forty-eight.

And that's as much as I'll say about tuning. The point is that when you listen to these pieces, especially as Schiff played them in his brilliant and beautiful survey, you should forget all about tunings and temperaments and just follow Bach on his adventure.

And what an adventure. Bach begins invitingly with the gently lapping Prelude No. 1 in C Major, a piece every child taking piano lessons learns to play. It's just a series of chords, really, with no melody. The bass note of each one is struck and sustained in the left hand as the other fingers flesh out the chord in elegantly rippling ascending arpeggios (an evocative term that almost sounds like what it means: when the notes of a chord are played in succession, either upward or downward). Throughout this C Major Prelude, there is just one rippling chord per measure, played twice. It couldn't be simpler, or more charming. Except that in the most subtle way imaginable, Bach takes us through a sophisticated harmonic journey as the chords shift and wander, often with piercing bits of dissonance sustained in one measure, then resolved in the next. The paired Fugue in C Major that follows is not at all a piece for beginners. The subject, which begins with a steady ascent up the first four notes of the scale, seems straightforward at first, almost rudimentary. But this fugue involves intricate contrapuntal writing in four voices. Still, the overall character of the fugue is welcoming. You can practically hear Bach reassuring us not to fear anything, that he is leading us on a long exploit and everything is going to be just fine.

Then we're off. The next piece, Prelude in C Minor, takes us to the dark side. It's a fearsome, furious rush of sixteenth notes in insistent figures moving through a series of somber chords, again one per measure, until the wild final section, when the music bursts into a dramatic cadenza, like a penultimate passage of stormy improvisation. The paired Fugue in C Minor, written in just three voices, though still sober in mood, is dancelike and oddly perky.

Though this project of writing preludes and fugues in all the major and minor keys may seem intellectual, many of these pieces are captivating and fanciful, like the graceful Prelude No. 3 in C-sharp Major. The Prelude No. 21 in B-flat Major, a toccatalike whirlwind, is practically prankish, with bursts of runs that seem improvised; the Fugue in B-flat is so jocular and industrious that you don't notice how intricately complex the counterpoint becomes.

Yet there are grave, searching works in this collection. At my high school, St. Paul's in Garden City, on Long Island, I was the daily chapel organist for four years. Friday's service was always a mass, and when communion was distributed I usually played, very quietly, the Prelude No. 24 in B Minor, which unfolds as three slow, steady intermingling voices. Performed on the organ, this harpsichord piece seemed ideal for pensive self-reflection.

In keeping with my general perception of Bach as a composer who probed deeper into what was already known, I'd argue that with Book II of *The Well-Tempered Clavier*, Bach looked deeper still into his own Book I. To be sure, there are some delightful pieces in this collection. But overall, Bach explores more complex intellectual realms in these later Preludes and Fugues. Some of the fugue subjects (the common term for a fugue's theme) are strangely angular; for example, the subject in Fugue No. 22 in B-flat Minor, with its asymmetrical mini-phrases and jagged contours.

The composer Virgil Thomson had a pet theory about Bach's fugue subjects in Book II. Throughout his life Thomson wrote musical portraits of people, mostly miniatures (though not always), short pieces he "sketched from life," as he put it, in the presence of the "sitter," the subject of the portrait. When writing portraits, Thomson put himself in a mode of compositional spontaneity, giving free rein to his musical instincts. These portraits often came out quirky, which Thomson saw as evidence that the pieces truly were portraits of people. (In 1984 he composed a portrait of me, from life, while I read a magazine at the dining room table in his Chelsea Hotel apartment. He titled it "Tony Tommasini: A Study in Chords," a dramatic, imposing piece thick with chords in both hands.)

Thomson pointed out that Bach spent most of his adult life living in various bustling households full of children and came into continual contact with family members and colleagues. Perhaps, Thomson thought, Bach's fugue subjects were musical portraits of people in his life. It's an intriguing theory.

The simpler explanation, though, is that Bach challenged himself more this time around. Having achieved so much in Book I, he purposefully fashioned fugue subjects in Book II that seem utterly unwieldy, only to create astonishing fugues from these unlikely themes.

There has long been great debate over how to play Bach, especially the keyboard works. Bach somehow knew and conveyed that his scores were so thoroughly realized on the page, that the notes were so complete, so inevitable, so "right," in a sense, that choices of tempo, dynamics, phrasing, and articulation were not that important. Almost any approach would work. Now, composers in those days, it's true, tended not to clutter scores with too many phrasing indications, tempo markings and such. Still, Bach was especially stingy in this regard, and it was surely an intentional choice. It could be seen as Bach's way of emphasizing the "rightness" of his own music, that the notes on the page conveyed everything performers needed to know.

This seeming rightness in the music has led many performers over generations to adopt what's been called a "just the notes" approach to playing Bach. Somehow, simply playing the lines with clarity, energy, and integrity is thought to suffice: you don't want to muck up Bach with excessive expressivity or romanticize the music. Yet many "just the notes" Bach performances can sound anemic and intellectual.

This issue came up for me in talking with the superb Norwegian pianist Leif Ove Andsnes. An eloquent musician and a scrupulous technician, Andsnes believes that in any great piece every note matters, that no detail should be skirted. He recalled a conversation he had had about Bach with the formidable Polish pianist Piotr Anderszewski, a friend and colleague born in 1969, a year before Andsnes. Though Anderszewski plays a wide repertory he is especially renowned for his Bach, a composer Andsnes almost never performs.

"Piotr asked me why I don't play Bach," Andsnes told me that day. "He knew I loved the music. I told him I find Bach the hardest of all. Piotr answered, 'That's interesting, Leif Ove. I find Bach the easiest.'"

Now, Andsnes, who dispatches gnarly Prokofiev and Rachmaninoff concertos with command, has what it takes to play anything written for the piano. What did he mean by saying Bach was the hardest? I think I know. As a pianist who insists on giving every note its due, Andsnes is thrown by the way whole stretches of a Bach piece—a toccata, a dance movement from one of the partitas—often involve long lines of winding counterpoint, sometimes just two voices, one for each hand. The music is exposed, almost naked. What do you do with such spare lines? How can you bring interpretive sweep to the music?

Anderszewski is temperamentally bolder, more of a Romantic by nature. He too has exquisite technique and projects textures lucidly. But he unabashedly plays Bach with full-fledged impetuousness and passion. His artistic integrity never lets him go too far. If you want to know Bach the questing giant, Bach the composer who probes deep in the essence of music, listen to Anderszewski play the Partita No. 6 in E Minor.

Here is a visionary thirty-minute work comprising seven movements, starting with an elaborate Toccata that alternates somberly majestic episodes that sound like written-out improvisations with stretches of stern yet purposeful two-part counterpoint. The shocker, though, is the final movement, a hard-driving Gigue with a defiant theme that erupts in insistent two-note rhythmic spurts and keeps leaping high and low. The demonic fervor in the music comes in part by the unabiding complexity of the counterpoint. For whom did Bach write such a work? Where would it have been performed? It's too long, ornery, and amazing for a court entertainment. Again, I think Bach was exploring the far reaches of music in this piece and sharing his findings with keyboard artists willing to learn.

It's not surprising, given the indestructible integrity of Bach's music, that during the twentieth century his works, more than those of any other towering composer, were latched on to by musicians who boldly performed, arranged, and adapted them in all manner of ways, from the conductor Leopold Stokowski's juiced-up orchestral transcripts of organ works to

Wendy Carlos's electronic realizations for synthesizer in the 1968 hit album *Switched-On Bach*.

My favorite among the Bach experimenters was the Swingle Singers, the French vocal ensemble founded in Paris around 1962 almost as a lark by the Alabama-born vocalist and jazz musician Ward Swingle, whose surname just happened to denote the approach he took to Bach. With an ensemble of eight soft-spoken yet virtuosic singers, the group performed Bach pieces with a jolt of jazzy swing. The group mostly avoided Bach's vocal works, instead singing instrumental pieces using tried-and-true bebop syllables like *baba-daba-daba* and *doot-doo*. With just a rhythm section (drums and plucked double bass) providing a gentle backdrop, the Swingle Singers presented joyous, jazzy, and supremely musical takes on a whole range of Bach works. The pioneering Italian composer Luciano Berio was such a fan that he wrote his seminal, stylistically eclectic Sinfonia for Eight Voices and Orchestra for them in 1968 (commissioned by the New York Philharmonic).

Though the Swingle Singers enjoyed popular success, winning Grammy Awards for their recordings and a loyal following, they also drew some stinging dismissals from established classical music critics, including Harold Schonberg of the *New York Times*. Yet to me and to countless lovers of classical music, the Swingle Singers rendered Bach with impressive subtlety, lending just a touch of swing to the lines while executing every detail wondrously. I'd listen to them "swing" some Bach piano piece—a prelude, a fugue, a bourrée from one of the suites—with awe and envy, only wishing I could play it with such character and élan.

The pianist Glenn Gould was a Swingle Singers fanatic. Which brings up Gould. In a blunt comment, the eminent conductor George Szell may have summed up Gould best when he said, "That nut's a genius."

Born in Toronto in 1932, Gould emerged from classical music to become a cultural icon for a new generation. A maverick who grew to abhor performing for live audiences, an eccentric who used a makeshift piano chair custom-built by his father that was only fourteen inches high (as opposed to the typical twenty inches or so), a hypochondriac full of phobias, Gould was a protean pianist, a prodigious technician, and a visionary artist. Though he played a repertory of unusual breadth, he was first and foremost associated with Bach. Indeed, his artistic life was eerily framed by two recordings of Bach's formidable *Goldberg Variations.*

This work, an aria with thirty variations, can last some ninety minutes when all of the structural repeats in the score are observed. It had been performed by major Bach pianists like Rosalyn Tureck before Gould came along. Still, it was generally perceived by mainstream audiences as a theoretical, almost scholarly piece. In the preface to the score Bach described the variations as "composed for music-lovers, to refresh their spirits."

In 1955, aged twenty-two, Gould recorded the piece for Columbia Records. The album became a top-selling sensation. There had never been Bach playing, or, in a way, any piano playing, like this.

Gould's technique was extremely finger-oriented: his fingers appeared to be doing all the work, without much support from his arms and upper body. This approach was reinforced because he sat so low, which made his fingers almost curl over the keys. His touch was spindly, like the tinkling touch you associate with the harpsichord. Every note had uncanny clarity.

Gould's 1955 recording of the *Goldberg Variations* took listeners on a nonstop adventure. Some of the tempos are breathlessly fast, courting chaos. Yet, amazingly, Gould maintained command at every moment. The more pensive variations were not just ruminative but mystical, yet still somehow taut with forward-moving tension. The playful variations had a sly, stealthy quality, as if Gould had cut through the music's contrapuntal games to expose its dangerous subtext. Eschewing the repeats, he dispatched the entire piece in under thirty-nine minutes.

For Bach lovers who valued the "just the notes" approach, Gould delivered. Has anyone played those notes with such palpable transparency? Still, Gould was up to something. He pushed this piece, and all the Bach he played (and he recorded most of Bach's works), to interpretive extremes, with willful disregard of accepted norms. His command was so absolute, his identity with Bach so tight, that he could toy with the music in a way that was almost perverse. But have no fear; Bach could take it. At Yale, among my generation, coming of age with sixties rock, I had many classmates who had no particular interest in classical music. But Gould's recordings were the exception. At a time of switched-on Bach, Gould offered far-out Bach.

He retired from the concert stage in 1964, at thirty-two, and devoted himself to making studio recordings, producing eclectic radio programs (including fabricated conversations with interviewers for which he wrote both questions and answers), and writing some compulsively readable articles, however provocative his arguments.

But Gould grew to detest his landmark *Goldberg Variations* recording, calling it "the most overrated keyboard disc of all time." He returned to the studio in 1981 to record the piece again, offering an interpretation that was more sober and introspective, lasting just over fifty-one minutes, though still full of bracing vitality. Then, just days after its release, he died of a stroke, aged fifty, on October 4, 1982. You could argue that the popularity of this piece today, which almost every accomplished young pianist plays and which audiences everywhere revere, is due to Gould. Still, listening to him when in the throes of some agenda-driven performance of Bach (check out the bizarrely slow tempo he takes in the stormy Prelude in C Minor, *WTC*, Book I) can confound even his riveted fans, among whom I include myself.

Finally, the St. Matthew Passion.

For his post as cantor in Leipzig, Bach had to provide music for sacred services, including the most important one of the liturgical year, Good Friday. Bach composed the great St. John Passion in 1724. Alas, we have the text (libretto) but not the music for a St. Mark Passion from 1731.

Thankfully, there are quite adequate sources for the St. Matthew Passion, from 1727, the most ambitious of Bach's passions—indeed, a sacred work of previously unimaginable dimensions. Scored for a double chorus, a sizable orchestra, and vocal soloists, the Passion, if played right through, typically lasts more than two and a half hours. Utilizing a deftly integrated libretto by the German poet known as Picander, and mixing music of diverse genres (prayerful chorales, inspired arias, dramatically charged recitative) with an imaginative daring that exceeded what was then common in the opera house, the St. Matthew Passion must have overwhelmed the performers, let alone the parishioners, of Bach's day. Yet the piece was largely forgotten after Bach's death: historians believe that there were only occasional performances of parts of it, in Leipzig.

That changed in 1829, when the twenty-year-old Mendelssohn, having been given a copyist's complete score of the piece by his grandmother, performed the St. Matthew Passion in Berlin with a singing academy, to great acclaim, providing astonishing evidence that Bach was much more than the composer equivalent of a mathematician, as he had generally been regarded by the music-loving public.

Various directors have attempted to stage the St. Matthew Passion in order to make its narrative elements more viscerally dramatic. In 2010 the conductor Simon Rattle, working with the director Peter Sellars, did a semi-staged production with the Berlin Philharmonic and the Berlin Radio Choir that broke new ground. Four years later Rattle and his Berlin forces brought the production to New York, joined by a roster of superb vocal soloists and the Boy Choristers of St. Thomas Church. Within the expansive Drill Hall of the Park Avenue Armory, Sellars and his team essentially re-created the concert-hall-in-the-round setup of the Philharmonie, the orchestra's Berlin home. I left this astonishing performance shattered yet grateful, and with new insight into why Bach was never tempted by opera.

In this Passion, the choristers take many roles: the crowd witnessing the persecution and death of Jesus, high priests, disciples, Jews. A tenor sings the major solo role of the Evangelist, relating the Gospel of St. Matthew in wrenchingly expressive recitative. Jesus is a baritone soloist, whose utterings are accompanied by long-held string chords, which provides a wondrous halo effect. Other soloists (usually designated members of the chorus) sing the gripping solo parts for Judas, Peter, Pilate, and other smaller roles.

In a director's note Sellars wrote that, to him, Bach conceived this Passion not as a concert work or a theater piece, but as a "transformative ritual reaching across time and space." The sacred services of the church, after all, are participatory rituals: during Holy Eucharist we become disciples at the Last Supper partaking of Christ's body and blood; some religious sects even today practice ritualized self-flagellation in solidarity with the brutalized

Jesus. In the St. Matthew Passion, Bach wrenches you out of your safety zone as an audience member, pulling you into this story of faith and doubt, trust and betrayal, community and mob chaos. That's how Sellars and Rattle presented it at the Armory.

Even before it started, as the audience walked in, the tenor Mark Padmore, one of the most elegantly expressive artists of our time, who was singing the Evangelist, sat on a box, sunk in thought, looking already spent. This Evangelist was about to relate the most famous story ever told. He looked as if he had told it many times before and could almost not bear to do so again. But this was his obligation.

Both the chorus and the orchestra were separated into two groups on raked platforms, which allowed for musical and dramatic back-and-forth. In the opening chorus, "Kommt, ihr Töchter, helft mir klagen" (Come, daughters, help me lament), one group of choristers, sitting in rows behind the orchestra, began pleading, with cries of "kommt" and "helft." The other group, slumped atop small boxes, seemed rattled as they shouted back Bach's choral exclamations of "Sehet!" (See Him!) and "Wen?" (Who?).

Often the Evangelist is presented as a true narrator, almost separate from the action, delivering the words and telling the story. In this production, Padmore became the celebrant of a ritual of re-creation. It was he whom Judas kissed to betray Jesus; it was he who endured the whip when Jesus was scourged. Meanwhile, the superb baritone Christian Gerhaher, as Jesus, sang movingly but from a spatially and spiritually exalted place, looking on, not far from where the boy choristers contributed their parts, singing chorale melodies that float above the overlapping voices of complex choruses. Sometimes when a vocal soloist sang one of Bach's profound arias he or she would approach the suffering Evangelist tenderly and offer the music as a salve. And when you least expected it, a man sitting quietly near you would turn out to be the singer portraying Pontius Pilate during the trial of Jesus: he would just stand up, sing, and move to the performance area.

The musical performance was both searing and sublime. The staging convinced me that, far from being unsophisticated about opera, Bach thought that through his passions, especially St. Matthew, he could create his own kind of ritualized, participatory music drama. In comparison, opera presented in a theater may have struck Bach as too safe, too presentational, like a spectator sport. This staging of the St. Matthew Passion gave you no way out. Jesus took on our sins and gave his life. What was our role in this? What responsibility do we still carry? The performance left you awestruck, but wracked with guilt.

It says something reassuring about human nature that the composer who could conceive this St. Matthew Passion did so while going about the daily rituals of a busy musical career and family life with humility and devotion. In one of my favorite of his letters, written to a cousin in 1748, two years before he died, Bach thanks his relative for the gift of a cask of wine, while charmingly requesting that he not be given any more of this fine "liqueur." The cask, alas, was damaged en route and the wine lost. Also, its delivery entailed expenses on Bach's part, including payments to the deliveryman and the customs inspector, as well as inland duties. So Bach ends the letter by asking his "honored cousin" to judge for himself, that "each quart cost me almost 5 groschen, which for a present is really too expensive."

The year before writing this letter Bach suffered an illness that may have caused a mild stroke. He also developed eye trouble, probably cataracts, which impeded his vision. In the spring of 1750 he had two eye operations by a disreputable surgeon who made the problem worse. He was effectively rendered blind. During his last years he had been working on *The Art of the Fugue,* a collection of fourteen fugues and four canons, each one employing some variant of a single theme in D minor. Bach did not specify what instrument or instruments the collection was conceived for; only the content of the music mattered to Bach. As he grew weaker he dictated the music to one of his sons. A final attempted fugue (the fifteenth) breaks off halfway through. He died in late July 1750, aged sixty-five.

In *The Art of the Fugue* Bach intended to explore the entire range of possibilities contained in a single theme.

But hadn't he done this already, through his life and work? Here was Bach at the end, still looking deeper.

CHAPTER THREE

"VAST EFFECTS WITH SIMPLE MEANS"

GEORGE FRIDERIC HANDEL (1685–1759)

A s a foreign national, born in Germany, George Frideric Handel was prohibited from owning property in England. Still, he was quite content to rent a house in London when a suitable property in a comfortable neighborhood near St. James's Place came on the market in 1723. The location, on a sunny stretch of Brook Street, was convenient, but not uncomfortably close, to the hubbub of performing arts around Soho and Covent Garden, offering an easy walk to the King's Theatre in Haymarket, at the time the center of Handel's thriving career as a composer of Italian operas for English audiences.

Then thirty-eight, Handel was the first resident of this newly constructed Georgian-style house. He would live there until he died in his bed at seventy-four on April 14, 1759.

It wasn't until the 1990s that a group of Handel devotees, spearheaded by the musicologist Stanley Sadie, started efforts to reclaim the house at 25 Brook Street. A trust was formed; the building was restored; rooms were painted and furnished to approximate what they had looked like when the composer lived there, according to postmortem inventories of his possessions, which included some eighty paintings and drawings, many of them fine works by significant artists.

Handel House opened as a museum in 2001. Of all the houses of indispensable composers I have visited, this one may be the most revealing of its occupant's personal and creative life.

With a basement, a ground level, two upper floors, and a garret, the house served, in effect, as headquarters for Handel Enterprises, Inc. The basement contained the kitchen and pantry. Handel's cook and servants would have had quarters in the garret. The ground level, accessible from the street, was essentially a Handel shop where the composer's printed scores were sold and subscribers to the opera could collect their tickets. The commodious front room on the first floor would have been the main reception area, where Handel kept a two-manual harpsichord and a small portable organ. Dinner parties with musical entertainment took place there.

This room also provided Handel a rehearsal space in which to coach singers in his operas. It's amazing to think what occurred in it when you visit today. There Handel taught the tempestuous Italian diva Francesca Cuzzoni the title role of *Rodelinda* and the juicy part of Cleopatra in *Giulio Cesare.* There the superstar castrato Senesino reported to work on the title role of *Cesare,* among other assignments.

Handel likely used the adjoining room on the first floor for composing. In that cozy space he would have written *Messiah,* the beloved oratorio that defines him for most people today. In an unlikely historical twist, during the summer of 1968 the girlfriend of the rock guitarist Jimi Hendrix rented an upper-floor apartment in the building next door, 23 Brook Street. Hendrix moved in, decorated the place with piled rugs and ostrich feathers, and for nearly a year considered it his home base, when not off somewhere giving concerts. When he learned that Handel had lived on the other side of the wall, Hendrix thought the coincidence beyond cool. The Hendrix flat has also been restored; today a visitor can buy a single ticket to tour the Handel and Hendrix houses.

The second floor was the composer's private space: a smaller room for dressing and his modest yet airy bedroom, dominated today, as in Handel's time, by a full tester bed with a crimson harrateen cover, matching canopy, and puffy white pillows. That bed looks a little short to have accommodated Handel, a tall, stout man renowned for his hardy appetite, with a particular fondness for claret and chocolate. But, as visitors learn, it was customary for eighteenth-century gentlemen to sleep almost sitting up, leaning against pillows.

However comfy, that bed sure looks lonely placed against the wall in that Spartan room. And from the little we know, Handel probably spent most of his nights in that bed alone. Even though he meticulously preserved his musical manuscripts, he deliberately shielded his private life. Very few letters of a personal nature, and no diaries, survive. Secondhand reports by early biographers of Handel's possible relations with a couple of women seem unpersuasive. That an artist of Handel's fame, wealth, and high regard within aristocratic circles remained single all his life begs for an explanation. Speculation lingers that Handel may have been homosexual. But those fixed on adding Handel to the roster of great gay composers throughout history have nothing concrete to go on.

If he was attracted to men, it's entirely possible that, like many such people of his time, he found it less complicating to close off this dimension of his emotional life. Sexual mores in early eighteenth-century London, however restrictive officially, were fairly loose in practice. Men of all ranks did not blanch from visiting prostitutes. Still, if he lacked romance and domestic partnership, Handel maintained a small yet close circle of friends. Most of them, intriguingly, were not professional colleagues or fellow composers, but middle-class musical amateurs, tradesmen, lawyers, sociable widows, even the owner of a perfumery around the corner from his house, James Smyth, one of the last friends to be with Handel before his death.

In a rich, absorbing 2014 biography, *George Frideric Handel: A Life with Friends,* the music historian Ellen T. Harris brings fresh insights into the composer and his work by exploring his surprisingly diverse circle of intimates. Handel emerges as a cosmopolitan and fiercely independent man, already curious about other cultures during his boyhood in Halle, Germany. By instinct a self-directed musician, he gravitated early to the theater and spent nearly four formative years in Italy absorbing the latest styles, especially Italian *opera seria* (serious opera). In his youth Handel mastered

French. Eventually he spoke Italian freely, if imperfectly, and over time developed English well enough to thrive in his adopted home, though he never lost a thick German accent. Gruff, quick to offend, able to dispatch curses in several languages, Handel was also decent, generous, devoutly Christian, and, when in the mood, a gregarious fellow. It's touching to read of the composer late in life, after going blind, eagerly playing the harpsichord for company at the home of his long-widowed friend Anne Donnellan.

Most Londoners realized that the man residing at that Brook Street house was a looming figure in the cultural and public life of the entire nation. Just three years after he set foot in London for the first time in 1710, Queen Anne requested that Handel compose the Te Deum and Jubilate for the widespread celebrations of the Peace of Utrecht at St. Paul's Cathedral. His position as de facto composer to the realm was cemented in 1727 when George II, passing over the official Master of the King's Music, chose Handel to write a set of anthems to celebrate his coronation. And at least one of them, *Zadok the Priest,* has been performed at every coronation in Great Britain ever since.

During the last phase of his life and career, when Handel abandoned opera and turned to oratorios in English, these works began to represent, "even in some ways to create," as Harris puts it, the national Protestant identity of Great Britain. Something similar would happen in the mid-twentieth century when the Brooklyn-born, Jewish Aaron Copland, who lived a discreetly gay life, wrote pieces that came to define the "American" sound, music rich with wide-spaced harmonies and unsentimental affirmation, often ennobled with hymn tunes or enlivened with cowboy dances. Still, that Handel occupied such a place in his adopted homeland seems an even greater stretch.

At a time when the upper echelons of London society developed an insatiable, if somewhat inexplicable, taste for serious opera in the Italian style, works written mostly by imported Italian composers for virtuoso Italian singers, Handel not only rode this fad, but dominated the scene for some thirty years. His run had ups and downs. He essentially directed three opera company ventures during his career, each of which eventually went under. He both made and lost enormous sums. But his income was fortified by three royal pensions, the first bestowed by Queen Anne, the latter two by George I and George II, totaling six hundred pounds annually. (In today's currency, that would have amounted to roughly $135,000 dollars.) Yet Handel continually sank money into his opera companies, resulting sometimes in nice profits, other times in humbling losses. However, he made shrewd financial investments and died wealthy.

Handel has long been linked with his countryman Bach, since they were born the same year in cities not that far apart. Yet they never met. And they have fundamental differences, starting with their upbringings. Bach, born to a family that had practiced music as a profession for generations, had no choice but to continue in the family business. Handel's father, a barber-surgeon with scant feeling for music, tried mightily to push his musically gifted son into a pragmatic profession: civil law. Unlike Bach, who devoted himself to traditional career paths, Handel was full of ambition, fiercely independent, and cosmopolitan by nature, even as a young man.

Both brought awesome gifts and technique to their work. But succinct and strikingly similar assessments of Handel's music from two very different observers get at the core of what makes Handel Handel.

Charles Burney (1726–1814), an English composer and acclaimed music historian, who traveled throughout Germany, France, and Italy to collect materials for his books and reports on music history, left invaluable impressions of the composers of his time. Of all his comments on Handel, one leaps out for me. Handel was, Burney wrote, "perhaps the only great Fughist exempt from pedantry."

Fugues of that era, being complex contrapuntal compositions, had an almost built-in tendency to turn pedantic. Many of Bach's fugues, for all their musical awesomeness, are like contrapuntal obstacle courses. Part of the excitement of these pieces comes from hearing Bach surmount the obstacles he himself erects. The thrill is enhanced when a performer nails the challenges as well. But in his observation Burney suggests that for all their ingenuity, Handel's fugues never seem entangled with counterpoint or hobbled by gnarly passages. Handel never clobbers listeners with overt complexity or shows off profundity. The intricacies are folded elegantly into the contrapuntal textures.

Beethoven, a Handel devotee, had a similar take. Calling Handel the "unattained master of all masters," Beethoven urged composers to "go and learn from him how to achieve vast effects with simple means." Beethoven would not have known the Handel operas, of course, since they disappeared from the scene during the last decade of Handel's life, when he gave up on the genre and turned to oratorios. But Beethoven knew and admired some of Handel's oratorios, as well as orchestral music, organ concertos, keyboard works, and more. Shortly before he died, in Vienna, Beethoven was overwhelmed to receive a gift from a British admirer of a multi-volume set of Handel's works.

What did Beethoven mean in praising the "vast effects" Handel attained by "simple means," as he put it? As an example, I'd point to a work so familiar that audiences for generations have taken it for granted: the instrumental Sinfony that opens *Messiah*. In this introduction, lasting about three minutes, Handel nods to the style of a French Baroque overture, structured in two parts. It begins with a short section in E minor, marked "Grave," slow, a stern fanfare prodded along by relentlessly clipped dotted-note rhythms. It's repeated, and then settles on a dominant chord that segues into an Allegro moderato main section, essentially a stirring yet serious fugue for strings in which three lines of counterpoint mingle intricately over a basso continuo group. The Sinfony is rigorous and purposeful, yet generous and lucid, with clearheaded, accessible counterpoint. Even so, for a lesson in the sophisticated handling of contrapuntal lines, you could do no better than this short piece, long a staple of analysis classes in conservatories.

That Handel was so drawn to dramatic genres—first opera, then oratorio—suggests that reaching the public was crucial to his aesthetic, even while the genius in him drew upon the most sophisticated elements of musical composition without a trace of pedantry. That's what both Burney and Beethoven were getting at.

But to develop his talent, Handel had to grapple with the opposition of his father, who from all reports seems to have been a musical dunderhead.

———

George Handel, born in 1622, was a barber-surgeon who at twenty married the widow (twelve years his senior) of the barber to whom he had apprenticed. When she died in 1682, George, then sixty, married the thirty-two-year-old daughter of a clergyman. Their first child died at birth. Their second, George Frideric, was born on February 23, 1685, in the Saxon city of Halle.

In those days very few physicians performed minor surgical procedures. So barbers, with ready razors, dealt with everything from hangnails to hernias, from pulling teeth to stitching wounds. George had an honorific appointment as barber-surgeon in the service of the Duke of Saxe-Weissenfels, though his practice centered on the general populace of his provincial hometown.

Handel's mother and her sister, who lived with the family, may have had modest musical training, some scholars surmise. Not George, who upon seeing signs of his young son's talent ordered that no instrument be allowed in the house. For accounts of Handel's life we are mostly reliant on the Reverend John Mainwaring, whose memoirs of the composer were published in 1760, the year after Handel's death. Though the book, based primarily on secondhand reports, is unreliable, especially concerning dates, it's the best we have to go on.

Mainwaring tells of the young Handel contriving to sneak a clavichord into the house. The truth may be that the boy's father looked the other way as long as the instrument was kept in the attic. Still, the elder Handel decided early on that his young son would pursue a career in civil law.

The boy was sent to a local Lutheran grammar school where surely he had singing lessons and routine musical instruction. The turning point came when, in 1691 or 1692, George senior set out for Weissenfels, where a son from his previous marriage, who had followed his father's profession, was working for the duke. Passed-down lore holds that young George Frideric, who would have been six or seven, set on meeting his half brother (some thirty years older), followed on foot for the first leg of the trip and caught up with his father when he stopped for the night. His father, "greatly surprised" at his son's "courage" and "somewhat displeased with his obstinacy," as Mainwaring tells it, reluctantly took the boy along.

At court, with his father often busy, young George enjoyed "getting at harpsichords," and also played the organ, one time attracting the attention of the duke himself. While acknowledging a father's prerogative over the rearing of a son, the duke argued that it would be wrong to squander such a talent and urged George to provide his boy proper training in music.

His father relented to the extent that George Frideric started studying in Halle with Friedrich Zachow, the organist of the Marienkirche, an excellent musician and a prolific composer, who gave the boy lessons at the organ and harpsichord, taught him the basics of composition, and introduced him to the finest German and Italian works. By nine the young Handel was writing sacred cantatas for voices and instruments.

In 1697 Handel's father died, a shattering loss for the twelve-year-old boy, despite his parent's opposition to music. Young George's resolve to keep perfecting his art was reinforced when at sixteen he met and began a lifelong friendship with the composer Georg Philipp Telemann, four years his senior, who lived in Leipzig. Actually, Telemann was studying law in Leipzig. The next year, 1702, as if bowing to parental imperative, Handel enrolled at the University of Halle to study law. Just a month later, however, he also took a job as organist at the Calvinist Cathedral in his hometown. Music soon won out.

Within a year Handel dropped out of school, quit his organ job, and moved to Hamburg, which had a thriving public opera house. He found work as a violinist and harpsichordist in the house orchestra, directed by the composer Reinhard Keiser, and began a collegial, if competitive, association with the composer and performer Johann Mattheson, a proud, touchy artist, pivotal to the house not just as a composer of operas, but also as a singer, actor, and harpsichordist. Their relationship turned strained as Handel's skills became apparent. Before long, Handel assumed responsibility for leading performances from the harpsichord.

The joint absence of Keiser, who left Hamburg due to financial troubles, as Harris reports, and also Mattheson, bound for London to pursue opportunities there, caused a crisis at the opera house in 1704. A new opera by Keiser had been commissioned for the coming season. A libretto had been written; sets and costumes were in preparation. But there was now no composer. Handel was drafted into writing his first opera, *Almira*. And it's an oddity.

I am among what must be the minority of opera lovers who have seen a production. In 2012 Operamission, an enterprising company in New York, presented a semi-staged modern-dress performance in an unconventional space: the ornate lobby of the Gershwin Hotel, in the Flatiron district of Manhattan. Billed as the North American premiere production, this *Almira* presented pretty much the complete score, lasting four hours with just one intermission.

The fictional story, set in Spain in an unspecified time, is one of those trademark Baroque opera intrigues. Having reached her twentieth birthday, young Almira is crowned Queen of Castile, in accordance with her father's will, which also stipulates that she must marry someone from the family of her guardian, Consalvo, a prince of Segovia, which whittles the choice down to Osman, Consalvo's decent, if distressingly ambitious, son. But Almira loves her orphaned secretary, Fernando, who, in a classic plot twist, turns out to be a long-lost son of Consalvo. So all ends happily.

The text is a German translation of an Italian libretto. But in arias where Handel's music is clearly beholden to ornate Italian operatic styles, the composer sets the original Italian words, as if to advertise the music's nod to the Italian tradition.

The score abounds in arias of the traditional da capo structure, which merits some explanation.

Italian Baroque opera favored a standard aria format, a ternary (ABA) structure whereby an opening section (sounding like a complete musical entity) is followed by a contrasting middle one in a different key and mood, usually shorter and less ornate, often more reflective. At the end of the middle section the score is marked "da capo," meaning "repeat from the beginning." But for the recap the singer is invited, even expected, to embellish the vocal lines with more elaborate ornaments and runs. A common complaint about Baroque opera, including those by Handel, is that the drama unfolds as a seemingly endless series of da capo arias, as they came to be known, with short passages of recitative in between to convey the dialogue and advance the story. But from the beginning of his involvement in the genre, Handel embraced this convention, confident that he could write arias so musically rich and alluring—or gripping or spectacularly brilliant or poignant, depending upon the dramatic imperative—that boredom was impossible.

That gift for composing elegant, inventive arias came through even in the stylistically confused *Almira,* Handel's first crack at opera. The production in early 1705 was a considerable success. Mattheson, back in town, sang the leading male role. Moreover, this experience conditioned Handel to an opera scene where Italian composers, singers, and conventions, along with German imitators of Italian styles, were suppressing the development of native opera. This is the situation he would also encounter in London, where the popularity of Italian *opera seria* stunted the growth of English music drama.

Shortly thereafter he wrote another opera for Hamburg, *Nero* (for which the music is lost). Now, galvanized by the opera genre and flush with enthusiasm for Italian musical styles, Handel decided to get himself to Italy to absorb things firsthand. Whole swatches of the story of his sojourn there, which lasted more than three years, remain sketchy, including which prince of Tuscany (probably one of two Medici brothers) offered him an invitation to Florence with a promise of a position in the first place. Handel tactfully declined to join the prince's entourage but by the latter part of 1706 had settled in Florence. At first he devoted himself to listening, learning, demonstrating his virtuosic keyboard skills, and collecting librettos, already thinking about future operatic possibilities. Once an opera was written and performed, it was standard practice for other composers to take a crack at setting the same libretto, something hard to fathom today.

Scholars do agree, however, that Handel dazzled aristocratic audiences in Rome with his keyboard playing, and acquired patrons who put whole palazzos at his disposal. Since public operatic performances were banned by papal order, Handel instead composed several dozen chamber cantatas, works that were essentially embryonic opera scenes. Venice, where the first public opera house had opened in 1637, was still an opera hub, and Handel triumphed there in 1709 with his *Agrippina*. Mainwaring reports that the audience, enthralled with the grandeur and sublimity of Handel's style, resounded with shouts of "Viva il caro Sassone!" (Hooray for the dear Saxon!) after every aria.

Handel never intended to remain in Italy. It was probably during the production of *Agrippina* in Venice that he was invited to visit London by the English ambassador, the Duke of Westminster. There he also met the deputy Master of the Horse to George Ludwig, elector of Hanover (later George I of Great Britain). The elector, clearly comprehending that Handel could be a prized acquisition, appointed him kapellmeister to his court. He immediately granted the composer a year's leave from his duties; at least, that's the way Handel perceived the arrangement, as Harris relates it. There would later be acrimony between the elector and the composer over Handel's assumption. But with his appointment in hand, Handel arrived in London in the autumn of 1710. Except for some extended return visits to Germany, and following some diplomatic gestures to untangle himself officially from the Hanover court, Handel remained in what turned out to be his adopted homeland. In 1727 he became a naturalized British subject.

Dr. Johnson understood why the average Englishman might see *opera seria* as "an exotic and irrational entertainment." Here was a curious cultural import that "retained the aroma of its origins in the princely courts of Italy," as the musicologist Winton Dean wrote in his insightful book on Handel. Nevertheless, starting in the early 1700s, *opera seria* took hold of London. Many audience members and all of the patrons came from aristocratic circles, though most theaters were dependent upon the general public as subscribers. In crucial ways, the scene was not unlike the situation today in most American cities, where opera companies are funded by our financial royalty yet rely upon everyday fans.

Burney, reporting on the fancy for Italian opera in London, admitted that "concerts in costume" was not an unfair way to describe these presentations. "No one will dispute," he wrote, "but that understanding Italian would render our entertainment at an opera more rational and more complete." Yet for lovers of music, he explained, opera was the "completest concert" available, offering perfect singing, a disciplined band, and "often excellent acting," not to mention splendid scenes and decorations.

From all accounts, the art of singing had reached its glory in Italy at that time, and English audiences were utterly entranced by the dazzling prima donnas and castratos who performed in London's theaters. Before I go on, though, for those who might be vague about it, I should explain the castrato singer.

Castration as a way of punishing, humiliating, and subjugating males goes back to ancient times. Realization of its potential value to the art of singing came later. The procedure involved castrating vocally gifted boys before puberty to preserve the natural high boy-soprano range. The Catholic Church advanced the practice to maintain high voices for all-male choirs. But when opera burst forth in the seventeenth century, the best castrati became superstars in the field. Because of resulting hormonal imbalances, young males so altered sometimes grew to have oversized bodies and lungs. So the best castratos had an uncanny combination of high range and penetrating power.

There were many sorry tales of boys with vocal talent being forced by poorer families into undergoing the surgery in hopes of attaining wealth and fame. The best castrati could become fabulously successful, like the megastar Farinelli (a stage name), born in 1705 to a family of musicians that had come upon hard times. Farinelli had conquered his native Italy before turning twenty-one and Vienna and Paris by twenty-five. Composers fought over his services. He was admired by artists, royalty, and glamorous women. During just two years working in London's opera houses he amassed a lifetime's fortune.

Roles from Baroque operas written for castrati are sung today by either countertenors (men with high voices who primarily sing in falsetto) or mezzo-sopranos in male garb. But the famed castrati of that era probably sounded a little closer to the mezzo-soprano Marilyn Horne in her powerhouse prime than to most countertenors today, even those with bright, penetrating voices.

For Londoners, the dazzling singers from Italy were the main attraction of *opera seria*. That these convention-bound works came across essentially as a series of da capo arias, with a few duets and ensembles sometimes mixed in, actually appealed to the public. The operas usually had five or six important roles. So the evening became a rotating cavalcade of singers, one after the other. The audience could cheer their favorites and pass the time chatting and socializing when a less interesting vocalist took the stage. Naturally, audiences often divided into rowdy camps supporting rival singers.

The entire genre was beholden to artistic conventions. The plots—favoring stories from mythology, the travails of historical figures, wars between nations, and pastoral dramas—had to be twisted so that after an aria a character would exit the stage on some dramatic pretext, allowing another singer to come on for the next aria.

Many lesser composers for London's stages were flummoxed by these expectations. Not Handel, however, who was, as Dean argues, not just a great composer but a "dramatic genius of the first order born in an unfavorable age, a period whose operatic convention was as near as possible antidramatic." Handel's solution to the challenges of the stilted *opera seria* was to embrace the genre as a framework that he could modify to his own needs.

There's a rich history of comparable genres in which creative artists used the conventions of a form to showcase their individuality and inspirations. Think of the 32-bar song form that was a staple of American popular music in the middle decades of the twentieth century. Songs as seemingly different as "Over the Rainbow" and "Blue Skies" hewed to a basic four-part structure that audiences anticipated: an A1 section, a modified A2 section, then a contrasting B section (the so-called bridge), and a final A3 segment. The A sections would have the same basic melody, with slight variations, though different lyrics. The B (or bridge) section usually involved a significant melodic contrast. That a standard form could inspire such wondrously varied songs enchanted audiences.

Or think of bebop jazz. The basic structural device of this uniquely

American art is somewhat like the theme and variations form in classical music. A tune, either a standard popular song or some intricate melody by, say, Charlie Parker (often written with complex chord changes), would be played by an entire group of five or so instruments. Then, one by one, the players would take turns improvising variations on the theme (or variations on the chords, rhythms, or structure of the theme), backed by the bass and drums, with occasional interjections by the other members. Even the drummer would take a turn with a rhythmic variation on the melody. At the end, everyone would join together to repeat the tune as first presented. These great artists played to—in a sense, played with—the expectations of listeners who were immersed in this basic formal convention of bebop. The seeming restrictiveness of the form actually generated artistic creativity.

This was more or less Handel's approach to the *opera seria* conventions that had taken hold in London. If his audiences expected an opera to be a parade of showpiece arias, well then, Handel would make each aria a magnificent float. He brought matchless skills to the task. The sensual richness of his music, the inventiveness of his melodic writing, the sure sense of dramatic pacing, the uncanny insight into the emotions of the characters that comes through in scene after scene, all combined to make Handel, as Dean writes, the "greatest and most successful theater composer of his age."

Yet after Handel retired from the stage and turned to oratorios in English, his operas quickly fell into neglect. After his death these incomparable Handel works, wrongly dismissed as dated and hopelessly hobbled by the conventions of the genre, languished for some 160 years, until the first stirrings of a Handel opera revival in the 1920s.

Aaron Hill, a young entrepreneur intent on making it big, was running an opera company at a new venue in the Haymarket called the Queen's Theatre, named after Her Majesty. (It would become the King's Theatre in 1714 with the coronation of George I.) In early 1711, Hill asked Handel, already the talk of cultural circles in London, to compose music for a story loosely drawn from Tasso's *Gerusalemme liberata*, with an Italian libretto by Giacomo Rossi adapted from Hill's English sketches. This work would be the first Italian-language opera written to order for the London stage. It was a terrible rush job.

The libretto and music were created in tandem, and Rossi complained that Handel, who churned out the score in a fortnight, hardly left him time to write the verses. To compose at this pace, though, Handel resorted to borrowing and adapted extensively from earlier works he had written during his sojourn in Italy. The music for the sublime soprano aria "Lascia ch'io pianga" (Let me weep), a popular concert piece today, was lifted by Handel from one of the cantatas he had written in Rome. Though recycling music was common practice during the Baroque era, Handel sometimes took it to extremes.

Still, on February 24, 1711, less than three weeks after music by Handel was performed at court for the celebration of Queen Anne's birthday, this much-anticipated new opera, *Rinaldo,* had its premiere and immediately established Handel's reputation as a composer for the theater. Indeed, this work—a Crusader tale of love, conquest, and sorcery, a score rich with eloquent arias and stirring music, a fantastical entertainment full of the magic and spectacle Hill considered essential to this emerging theatrical endeavor—set a new standard for Italian opera in London.

The story tells of Christian forces during the First Crusade, led by a formidable general, Goffredo, and the renowned knight Rinaldo, as they lay siege to Jerusalem to vanquish its king, Argante. The formidable king is abetted by, and enamored of, Armida, the willful Queen of Damascus, Argante's mistress, and an expert in sorcery.

For audiences today, a traditional production of an opera like *Rinaldo* can actually call attention to the genre's conventions and make them seem creaky. For decades now, the field of opera has been energized (or undermined, depending upon one's point of view) by directors who boldly update the settings of repertory operas and draw upon contemporary stage imagery, like Michael Mayer's 2013 staging of Verdi's *Rigoletto* for the Metropolitan Opera. The "Rat Pack" *Rigoletto* takes Verdi's bleak tale of a hunchback jester in sixteenth-century Mantua and zaps it to the Las Vegas Strip in the early 1960s, turning the philandering Duke into a nightclub headliner. Conservative opera fans condemn what's become known as "regie" productions (short for "regisseur"), that is, director-driven productions.

To me, it all depends on the intrinsic merit and execution of the concept. I've seen profoundly insightful updated productions and glibly facile ones. I'd argue that no opera composer has benefited more from good contemporary productions than Handel. The operas almost beg for directors who can penetrate the formal conventions to reveal the emotional, psychological, and spiritual depths of these seemingly problematic works.

I had always been enchanted by the music of *Rinaldo* but never bought its dramaturgy until I saw Francisco Negrin's production for the Lyric Opera of Chicago in 2012, with a terrific cast headed by the countertenor David Daniels in the title role and the conductor Harry Bicket tending smartly to musical matters.

So *Rinaldo* was primarily meant to dazzle audiences? That's what this production did, through surreal contemporary imagery. To Negrin, *Rinaldo,* like Mozart's *Magic Flute,* is a parable about the difficult quest for enlightenment and the lure of the dark side. Here, the massive wall of the city of Jerusalem became a series of illuminated vertical panels under clear plastic, like something out of Robert Wilson. Entry was barred to intruders by huge granitic blocks spelling out the city's name in Italian. The Christian soldiers wore uniforms of leather and burlap; the Muslim forces wore long black suit jackets over skirts that seemed patched together fancifully from Persian carpets.

When King Argante, facing defeat, calls upon his beloved sorceress Armida to bolster him, she rises from the ground in a hellish red-leather dress, then swears to get Rinaldo out of the way by putting him under her spell. However, she winds up feeling romantic yearnings for Rinaldo and determines instead to vanquish her rival, the lovely Almirena. Those psychological ambiguities and conflicting emotional agendas course through Handel's music, with arias that seem courtly on the surface yet stir subtly with yearning. Or is it calculating manipulation? Somehow this production's imagery tapped deep into these undercurrents.

And talk about spectacle that serves the story rather than distracting from it! When Armida decides to ensnare Rinaldo, she summons a huge harpsichord that descends from the sky, literally her "instrument" of enchantment. The cover opens and party balloons on strings (keyboard strings!) pop out. This staging touch, though a little silly, somehow conveyed the power of music to cast a spell, a power that permeates Handel's astonishing music in this scene, yet often falls flat in traditional stagings. This contemporary production chillingly linked the story to the never-ending bloody turmoil in the Middle East yet also invited you to bask in a marvelous entertainment.

It's helpful to remember that Handel's operas were presented in London in what passed then for updated concepts, usually with elaborate modern-dress costumes that loosely suggested the characters of the story: crusaders, generals, mythological beings, haughty aristocrats, shepherds, and sorcerers. Handel might not have been all that flabbergasted by "regie" productions today. He would have been stunned, however, by the sheer size of the houses where his operas are now routinely performed. The intimate Queen's Theatre had about eight hundred fifty seats. The Metropolitan Opera House seats more than thirty-seven hundred.

Yet the Met has been on a surprisingly successful Handel streak in recent years. The breakthrough for contemporary Handel productions at that house came with the 2004 staging of *Rodelinda*, directed by Stephen Wadsworth. By the time of this opera's premiere in 1725, Handel was entrenched as an impresario at the resident company of the King's Theatre, the Royal Academy of Music. He wrote the title role for Francesca Cuzzoni, then his most popular Italian diva. The Met featured Renée Fleming in a career high. With a cast of charismatic singers, scenic grandeur, and subtle but sumptuous playing from the orchestra under Harry Bicket, the performance managed to fill the house yet draw you in, making the vast space feel more intimate.

The story is freely based on the history of the Lombards, a wealthy migrant European people who invaded northern Italy toward the end of the sixth century and ruled the region for two hundred years. Bertarido, the King of Lombardy, has been driven from the Milanese throne by Grimoaldo, a usurping duke, who keeps the king's wife, Rodelinda, and young son, Flavio (a silent role), under house arrest. He intends to make the queen, who believes her husband is dead, marry him. In fact, the exiled king, though shattered, has survived, and he returns in disguise hoping to reclaim his family and throne.

Handel's opera acutely conveys the internal twists of characters who form uneasy romantic and political alliances as they scheme for position in a dangerous society, and simply try to live. This production set the story in early eighteenth-century Milan, with stage-filling sets depicting airy courtyards, palace rooms, and, in one scene, an imposing, well-stocked library. The opera begins with Rodelinda, alone and weeping, singing an aching aria of grief over her poor husband. But in this concept, after a wistful minuet that follows the overture, as the orchestra plays the halting, melancholic introduction to Rodelinda's short aria, we saw Fleming's queen asleep on a solitary bed, her hand affixed to the railing by a long chain.

Her son, first seen sleeping next to her restlessly, sat up and tried to shake his mother awake. No luck. He stepped down and shook her harder. Fleming shifted uneasily, as if trying to ignore him, an overwhelmingly human reaction. Here was a woman who, if only for five more minutes, didn't want to be a prisoner, a queen, a widow, even a mother. She just wanted to sleep a little longer and forget everything.

But Rodelinda *is* a mother, and her boy needed her. So Fleming's queen groggily sat up, comforted her child, and started to sing. Yes, the aria was a defenseless expression of loss and loneliness. But the first step in coping is to vent such feelings. In Handel's day, formulaic *opera seria* librettos may have been cranked out to meet demand. Today it's easy to look back and dismiss these texts. But Handel took the words to heart. "Ho perduto il caro sposa" (I have lost my dear husband), "e qui sola alle sventure" (and alone here in misfortune) "vie più cresce il mio penar" (my suffering grows worse). In this performance, framed by this sensitive production, I realized that amid the intense sadness of this music, Handel embedded a remnant of Rodelinda's ardor, a fleeting memory of marital love.

Grimoaldo, one of the few leading roles in Handel operas written for a tenor, intrudes and again tries to persuade Rodelinda to marry him. This usurper is a classic tyrant, a vacillating, cagey man whose moments of self-doubt prod him to rash actions. Rodelinda, risking his anger, rebuffs him again and sings a stern, feisty aria.

One of the opera's glories comes at the end of Act II, when Bertarido actually arrives and embraces his stunned, ecstatic wife. Grimoaldo, seeing them together, turns furious. Bertarido defiantly reveals that he is the king. Rodelinda, trying to save him, swears that this stranger is lying. The usurper declares that whoever the intruder is, he will be put to death anyway.

Left alone, the couple sings a ravishingly sad duet. Finally a duet! In context, it almost seems the operatic equivalent of the invention of the wheel. Why didn't Handel introduce more formal variety into his operas? At the Met that night, hearing Fleming and the countertenor David Daniels perform this duet with subdued, melting magnificence, I realized how wise Handel was to keep these moments special, to make them really count.

For many American opera fans, certainly for me, the introduction to the idea of updated staging concepts came in 1982, when the American Repertory Theater in Cambridge presented the director Peter Sellars's production of Handel's *Orlando* in a forty-performance run. Sellars was just twenty-four, and though updating had caught on in Europe's more adventurous houses, the practice was uncommon in American opera companies. The Sellars *Orlando,* controversial at the time in many circles, was in retrospect a breakthrough.

Handel wrote the opera in 1733, three years after the Royal Academy, plagued by debt, had gone out of business and a new venture, known as the Second Royal Academy, jointly managed by Handel and John James Heidegger, was established at the King's Theatre. In his new company Handel had inconstant financial backers and, more problematically, stiff competition from a rival company, Opera of the Nobility, which opened in 1733, initially with strong support from Frederick, Prince of Wales. Some of Handel's star singers defected to the new theater, which managed to entice major composers like Johann Adolph Hasse. Despite the day-to-day hassles, Handel produced some astonishing works during the few years of this Second Academy, none more miraculous than *Orlando,* a work Dean places under the thematic category of "magic" operas in Handel's works.

The libretto, freely adapted from Ariosto, tells of Orlando, a valiant knight and crusading Christian hero. Weary of seeking glory through combat, Orlando turns his attention to love and falls for Angelica, Queen of Cathay, an imperious beauty. Having rejected princely suitors from all over Europe, Angelica is smitten with a young African soldier-prince, Medoro. The opera introduces two compelling characters who are not in Ariosto's tale: the winsome shepherdess Dorinda, who was loved by Medoro until he became entranced by Angelica, and the wise, wily magician Zoroastro who advises and cares for Orlando as he suffers with unrequited love for Angelica. Determined to prod Orlando back to deeds of valor, Zoroastro leads him to an enchanted wood where confusing romantic entanglements turn him mad. The sage conjurer cures the young knight by Act III of this long, multi-layered opera.

For the Sellars production, performed in Italian with no English supertitles, the audience was given a scene-by-scene English synopsis, just as Handel's London audiences were. In his review of the production, Andrew Porter, the influential *New Yorker* critic, made a point of contrasting the opening stage direction of the original with the Sellars's synopsis of the same scene.

The original:

Night. A country with a Mountain in Prospect; Atlas, on the Summit of the Mountain, sustaining the Heavens on his Shoulders; Several Genii at the Foot of the Mountain; Zoroaster leaning on a Stone, and contemplating the Motions of the Stars.

Sellars's synopsis:

The scene opens at Mission Control, Kennedy Space Center, Cape Canaveral. Zoroaster—scientist, magician, and Project Supervisor—is studying distant galaxies of the solar system.

Of course, at the space center Zoroastro studies the galaxies on a video screen with blinking lights. Orlando becomes an astronaut, a heroic yet endearingly comic figure in an orange space suit. Angelica looked like a

Katharine Hepburn high society type in smart riding clothes. I remember being delighted when the scene shifted to Dorinda's pastoral domicile, which the libretto indicates is a camp in the woods with cots of shepherds here and there. This adorable Dorinda, wearing cutoff jeans, lived in a gleaming Airstream camper parked in a clearing in the Florida Everglades. At one point, when Medoro is fleeing from Orlando, who is seething with jealousy, the libretto directs that Zoroastro cause a "large fountain" to rise from the earth, which Medoro hides behind. In this production, a steel drinking fountain—what you'd find next to the restroom at work—rose from the ground with a stream of gurgling water.

Along with seemingly everyone else in the theater, I laughed out loud at the stage image. But should we have been laughing? Was this at all irreverent? This was my first experience of an updated opera production.

I remember almost feeling relief when Porter's rave review came out. Here was the most respected critic of the day, an opera scholar who wrote brilliant English performing translations of Italian and German librettos, and he loved it. "Clumsily executed, or conceived in a spirit of prankishness, such a production would be intolerable," Porter wrote. "But this *Orlando* was brilliantly, gracefully, and precisely handled. (Entertainingly, too; the element of visual extravaganza is a necessary component of Handel's drama.)" He singled out the staging of the complex trio that ends Act I, in which Angelica and Medoro, now contentedly happy together, try to console the sweet, loveless Dorinda. Sellars had the three singers "move through intricate, mazy patterns that seem not a gloss on the music but a marvelous, living enactment of it," Porter wrote. "Mr. Sellars' control of the long phrase, of stillness, of sudden shifts of direction, of musical and emotional counterpoints struck me as near-miraculous."

Breaking with convention, Handel includes several intricate ensembles and poignant duets in *Orlando*. Act II may be a typically Handelian series of arias, but each one is in various ways breathtaking. This middle act culminates in Orlando's mad scene, which, as Porter wrote, when "violently and passionately enacted—as it was in Cambridge—is an incident to arouse pity and terror." Mad scenes for a suffering soprano heroine would become requisite elements of early nineteenth-century opera. But not one of them, including the touchstone mad scene of *Lucia di Lammermoor*, surpasses *Orlando's* wrenching descent into madness. For me, only the episode when Benjamin Britten's ostracized, tormented fisherman Peter Grimes lapses into violent, anguished outbursts matches the searing impact of *Orlando's* mad scene.

During the profound final scene, restored to reason, Orlando blesses the union of Angelica and Medoro. With a heavy heart he has come to understand, as Zoroastro explains, that all our thoughts travel through impenetrable darkness when spurred on by blind love. Only reason can divert us from chaos.

Four years after the premiere of *Orlando*, Handel suffered symptoms of "mental derangement," as contemporaries described it, and temporarily lost the use of his right arm due to a "stroke of the palsy." How greatly his "senses were distorted," his biographer Mainwaring wrote, "appeared from an hundred instances, which are better forgotten than recorded."

Handel traveled to Aix-la-Chapelle, on the border of France and Germany, for a health cure, including vapor baths. Mainwaring reports that the composer sat in the baths three times as long as usual, and "his sweats were profuse beyond what can well be imagined." It worked. The nuns there considered Handel's recuperation miraculous.

When Handel's five-year arrangement with Heidegger ended in 1734, the Opera of the Nobility took over the King's Theatre. Handel began one more—his final—venture as an impresario at a new location, Covent Garden Theatre (a precursor to the current Royal Opera House at Covent Garden). But the opera scene in London had changed.

In 1728 *The Beggar's Opera*, a grimly satirical ballad opera written by John Gay, with music arranged by Johann Christoph Pepusch, became a watershed of British theater. The piece played for sixty-two performances, the longest run in theatrical history at the time. With its antihero Macheath, the captain of a gang of robbers; Mr. Peachum, a ruthless profiteering middleman; and other charming miscreants, *The Beggar's Opera* skewered politicians and the powerful. It also lampooned the enthusiasm of the upper classes for Italian opera, which even its fans conceded, when pressed, was an "irrational entertainment."

The Beggar's Opera did not put the opera houses out of business right off. Handel kept on, working at Covent Garden until 1741. He wasn't ready to give up. You could argue that more than his audiences, more than his fellow composers, and more than even the highly paid star singers, Handel approached this genre with the most seriousness and the greatest artistic integrity.

Of course, Handel also had his show-biz side. For all his genius as a musical dramatist, he was perfectly willing to stoke the intensity of fans and cater to the whims of divas. In 1725, when the celebrated soprano Francesca Cuzzoni was at the height of her popularity in London, Handel's Royal Academy brought another Italian soprano into the company, the great Faustina Bordoni. The two divas appeared together in works written to highlight their respective talents, like Handel's *Alessandro* in 1726. Handel carefully supplied each singer with ample opportunities to enthrall the audience, including a duet. Naturally, camps of fans would cheer their favorite and hiss her rival. Things came to a madcap climax that year when both artists appeared in Giovanni Bononcini's *Astianatte*. At the final performance the audience grew particularly rowdy, not just cheering and jeering but breaking into fistfights. The brawls eventually consumed the dueling divas on stage, who cursed and clawed each other as fans urged them on.

During Handel's years at Covent Garden he had already begun his crucial shift to composing English oratorios, including ambitious works that won immediate acclaim like *Saul* and *Israel in Egypt*. Once he retired as an opera composer in 1741, he never looked back. His operas were no longer performed in London. Most of them would languish until the early twentieth century, awaiting the slow discovery of this extraordinary repertory.

I f Handel found ways to work within and subtly tweak the conventions of *opera seria*, he brought pioneering innovation to the development of the oratorio, defining the genre for generations to come. Taking this new direction must have felt not just relieving, but liberating. His dramatic genius found a natural outlet in the oratorio genre as he developed it. If a libretto contained a narrative gap, he didn't have to fill it with a stretch of stilted recitative, as he was forced to do in opera. His oratorio arias could be the Handelian equivalent of Shakespearean soliloquies. He could delve into the most profound resonances of a story through elaborate ensembles and fugal choruses without having to worry that a number was too musically complex to hold the stage. New opportunities certainly came at a propitious time.

In 1741, dejected over the failing fortunes of his Covent Garden opera company, Handel received an invitation to present a series of concerts in Dublin. The prospect of getting out of London for a while, far from the crumbling opera scene, appealed to him greatly. He arrived in November and stayed nine months, returning in the summer of 1742. By far his most momentous accomplishment in Dublin was the formal premiere of *Messiah* in April 1742, in the city's Great Music Hall.

Handel had composed the score while still in London, taking just over three weeks, working from a libretto assembled by his friend Charles Jennens, an English landowner and arts patron who was something of a dilettante. Yet the text Jennens adapted from the Bible and from psalms in the Book of Common Prayer balanced narrative elements and reflective passages in a fashion that inspired Handel. The work is divided into three large sections, dealing with first the prophecy and birth of Christ, then the vicissitudes of his time on earth, and finally the Resurrection, with its promise of eternal redemption.

I am hardly the only music critic to have questioned the institutionalization of *Messiah,* which is brought out during Christmas season in cities and towns everywhere and performed too often for its own good. Why not take a break now and then and substitute, say, Berlioz's exalted oratorio *L'Enfance du Christ,* among many possibilities?

Yet in a good performance, *Messiah* never disappoints. Like Tchaikovsky's *Nutcracker,* a work that keeps many ballet companies financially solvent during extended runs for family audiences at holiday time, Handel's *Messiah* may be the rare masterpiece that can withstand its own popularity.

Messiah was scored for relatively modest orchestral forces, and Handel's writing exhibits marvelous restraint and clarity. The dramatic thrust of the piece comes through at the start, after the Sinfony, with the tenor's poignantly expressive "Comfort ye" recitative. This beguiling music shifts in a flash to agitated recitative exhortations, "Prepare ye the way of the Lord." Then the tenor lets loose in the exuberant, captivating aria "Ev'ry valley shall be exalted." Virgil Thomson pointed to this aria as a prime example of how to write music that expresses, almost illustrates, the text, which continues: "and ev'ry mountain and hill made low, the crooked straight and the rough places plain." The tenor's vocal lines stride, twist, and climb when the words describe every valley being "exalted." But when every hill is "made low" and the rough places "plain," the vocal line settles down, narrows to a midrange two-note ripple, then ebbs into calming sustained tones.

Chorus numbers like the "For unto us a child is born" are justly beloved for the uncanny way passages of sprightly, childlike joy segue into stirring proclamations that "His name shall be called Wonderful, Counsellor, the mighty God, the Everlasting Father, the Prince of Peace." There is a tinge of incredulous intensity in these choral affirmations, as if the singers, on behalf of us all, cannot quite believe that this world-altering, long-prophesied birth has actually happened. And now? What will it mean? What do we do?

Messiah was presented in Dublin as a benefit for various charities, including the relief of prisoners and a hospital serving the poor. After this success, the premiere in London at Covent Garden provoked critical complaints that a sacred work of this sort should not be performed in a theater. The tradition of annual charity performances for the benefit of London's Foundling Hospital began in 1750 and continued beyond Handel's death.

Still, of his seventeen English oratorios, Handel's favorite was not *Messiah* but his penultimate one, *Theodora,* a piece that flopped at its 1750 premiere and never caught on during his lifetime, to the composer's chagrin. This elaborate, intensely complex score, with a libretto by Thomas Morell, is deemed a staggering achievement today. Every performance is an event.

Unlike most Handel oratorios, *Theodora* is a tale of ordinary people caught in extraordinary circumstances, and it ends tragically. Theodora is an aristocratic Christian in fourth-century Antioch, a region under Roman occupation ruled by Valens, a governor. Didymus, a Roman soldier, has secretly fallen in love with Theodora and converted to Christianity, in mortal defiance of military law. At the start, Valens decrees that to celebrate the Roman emperor's birthday there will be sacrificial rites and festivities. A Chorus of Heathens sings in vehement affirmation. Immediately, you sense the reason the work might have baffled Handel's audience: the music here, and throughout the score, explores the ambiguous emotions and calculations of the characters.

Handel tucks a sliver of forced enthusiasm into this boisterous first chorus. Valens's edict leaves Didymus in a quandary. Sounding more like a liberal philosopher than a Christian convert, he sings a wrenching aria exploring his confusion. "Ought we not to leave the free-born mind of man still ever free?" he wonders. Handel also gives us poignantly flawed and endearing characters, like Irene, Theodora's closest friend, who during an aria warns her fellow Christians to beware of prosperity, the "soother of vile inclinations." On the surface the music is purposeful and convincing. Yet Handel embeds suggestions—some primness in the rhythmic flow, moments of ornate smugness in the melodic twists—that Irene could be trying to convince herself of something.

Theodora may be Handel's most sympathetic heroine, a Christian wracked by confusion over her relationship to the world. Is it right to withdraw from civic society because it goes against one's beliefs? The composer gives her magnificent arias. In the end, she and Didymus are condemned to death. The oratorio concludes with a Chorus of Christians, at once shattering and consoling, with moments of anguish and pensive self-reflection.

Like Bach, Handel lost his sight by his sixties. He survived Bach by nine years, dying at seventy-four in 1759, and was mostly blind during this long period of decline. Yet, as Burney recounts, Handel kept active in his field. During performances of his oratorios, a friend would sometimes lead him to the organ, where Handel would play concertos between the acts, at first from memory, then increasingly working from his own powers of invention. It was a sight, Burney wrote, "so truly afflicting and deplorable to persons of sensibility, as greatly diminished their pleasure, in hearing him perform."

Maybe so. But imagine being there.

CHAPTER FOUR

THE "VIENNA FOUR"

AN INTRODUCTION

How did it happen that during a period of only seventy-five years, roughly from 1750 to 1825, in a single European city, Vienna, the cultural climate, the state of music, the historical context, the coincidence of genius, or whatever it was, fostered the work of four of the most titanic composers in music history? They were, of course, Haydn, Mozart, Beethoven, and Schubert.

Looking at the music that emerged from Vienna and its environs during that period, it's easy to assume that the city must have been a bastion of cultural enlightenment with an informed and curious public. Not exactly. For one thing, the last half of the eighteenth century brought a pivotal shift in how composers made their livelihoods and practiced their craft. Vienna was practically a laboratory for this development.

The era of patronage, in which composers were dependent upon aristocratic supporters of varying musical sophistication, still dominated the scene when Haydn came of age in the early 1750s. But this custom steadily gave way to a setup much closer to freelancing. After struggling as a musician for hire during his twenties in Vienna, Haydn worked for nearly thirty years in the court of Prince Esterházy, who had castles on the outskirts of the city and in the countryside. Yet during that last decade, in the 1780s, even while still directing music at the court, Haydn was in the vanguard of Austrian musicians who promoted performances of their own works outside aristocratic realms and were taken up by publishing houses. In his golden years, back in Vienna, Haydn was an internationally acclaimed master who could hardly keep pace with demand for his compositions.

Mozart, guided and pushed by his indomitable father, sought royal patronage from the time he was touring as a child prodigy. But as a young adult with a rebellious nature, he actually disdained the system. In any event, he never found a patron comparable to Haydn's prince. Mozart was essentially forced to be, for the most part, a free agent, with very mixed success, including periods of real hardship.

By the time Beethoven moved to Vienna from Bonn in 1792 to study with Haydn and make his way, the patronage system was shaky. Still, Beethoven enjoyed the support of some discerning aristocratic patrons, especially at the start, before he found commercial success. But his attitude was that these princes should be grateful for being allowed to bestow their patronage upon him.

And Schubert? That's another story, a sad one. He spent most of his short life (he died at thirty-one) in the vanguard of a different kind of artistic scene: the urban bohemians. He could have been a character in a Viennese version of *La Bohème*. He had important, established supporters on and off and secured some publishers for many of his works, especially piano duets and part-songs for the amateur music market. But mostly he struggled. Schubert was embraced by a group of good friends who thought they had a genius in their midst and called themselves the Schubertians. They stayed at each other's homes and spent each other's money. But Schubert only became "Schubert" posthumously.

Beyond the challenges of making a living as a composer in Vienna, the truth is that by the early nineteenth century, the place was no oasis for contemporary art. There was a new music scene with a network of intellectually formidable composers and performers who found an adventure-seeking audience. But as the writer Harvey Sachs makes clear in *The Ninth: Beethoven and the World in 1824*, "terms such as 'crossover,' 'kitsch,' and 'dumbing down' could as easily have been applied to the cultural life of Vienna in Beethoven and Schubert's day as to that of major cities throughout the Western world in our own."

Still, certain conditions must have made the Vienna Four possible. I have never quite bought into the concept of music as an art form that advanced over time to increasingly higher levels of modernity and sophistication. Of course, bold, radical innovations kept coming, but these shifts did not necessarily make music any greater, just different. That said, certain important trends and developments that coalesced in the mid-eighteenth century played out in Vienna.

The musical language of Haydn's youth was characterized by a strong, clear affinity for diatonic harmony (music written essentially in major and minor keys, as I discussed in connection with Bach). By the mid-1700s, this language had gained in strength, clarity, and a kind of built-in harmonic imperative. The emerging style of Viennese Classicism incorporated that language whole.

What I will try to make clear when I take up Haydn next is that, among the composers of his day, he truly figured out how to use this system of harmony to simultaneously fortify and activate the structure of a long piece. Listeners steeped in the musical language of the time grew to expect these built-in harmonic shifts. In other words, a composer could make it seem as if something very significant were happening when a symphony movement written in, say, C major, after announcing itself with a theme in that key, bustled along energetically, took a turn or two, maybe teased us by flirting with a remote key area, but eventually landed on a second theme in the anticipated dominant area of the key, in this case G major. Haydn did this ingeniously.

Another crucial characteristic of Viennese Classicism concerned what can be called the grammar of music, which came to resemble the grammar of language. The more complex forms of music in the Baroque period utilized almost continuously flowing contrapuntal writing, with lines spinning out and chugging along. By the mid-eighteenth century, the periodic phrase, as it was called, became a favored way to speak in music: long phrases were structured out of shorter ones, much the way sentences are structured out of clauses. As many historians have argued, this emerging musical characteristic reflected the Age of Enlightenment, or at least the idealized notion of the Enlightenment that was touted at the time: a movement that championed reason, logic, and discourse.

Of course, it took an incomparable talent to fashion these currents into the astounding works of the early Viennese Classical era. That composer was Haydn, whose career spanned the years when Bach wrote his final works through the start of the nineteenth century, when Beethoven's middle-period symphonies were shaking up Vienna.

Before getting to Haydn, though, I want to discuss briefly a twentieth-century development that profoundly altered our understanding of the Viennese masters and their Baroque predecessors: the early-music movement.

Starting as early as the 1930s, but especially beginning in the 1960s, intrepid groups of musicians and scholars closely studied the performance practices of the Baroque and Classical eras and the types of instruments that were played then. They argued that orchestras of Haydn's time sounded little like the New York Philharmonic of Bernstein's day. Violins from earlier centuries, for example, used gut strings that were mellower and richer in sound than the steel and synthetic strings of modern violins, which have brighter sound and more carrying power.

Ensembles and artists started performing early music on refurbished early instruments, "period" instruments, as they were called, or newly made ones modeled after the originals. Early-music aficionados combed through historical records to understand earlier approaches to matters of tempo, articulation, dynamics, and ornamentation. For decades now, lovers of classical music have been able to hear lithe accounts of Baroque and Classical works performed by musicians steeped in the practices of those eras and played on period instruments. Such performances can be revelatory.

As the movement developed, though, some of its proponents argued for the musical superiority of so-called historically informed performances on "authentic" instruments. To be sure, hearing Haydn symphonies played on period instruments by a lively chamber orchestra with an inspired conductor can be a bracing experience. But Leonard Bernstein was also a superb

Haydn conductor. He just "got" Haydn. His performances with the slightly reduced but still ample forces of the New York Philharmonic were both robust and insightful, humorous and heroic.

In a way I'm venting a bit about a problem that no longer exists. Yes, for a while many people in the early-music movement had a holier-than-thou attitude about their work. More recently, peace and mutual understanding have reigned between performers from the early-music movement and those who play old music on modern instruments, including adventurous artists who bring contemporary musical thinking to performances of the standard repertory.

Great Bach interpreters, like the pianist András Schiff, who perform the master's keyboard works on a modern concert grand piano, are respected by the general public and early-music advocates alike, even as other artists play this repertory on Bach's instrument, the harpsichord.

In all the arts our perceptions about earlier works inevitably change, as they should. It's interesting to explore how Shakespeare's plays might have been performed in his day. But most Shakespeare lovers today find it more interesting to present those plays in bold new productions that connect with our own times. In music, we will never be able to experience, say, a Beethoven symphony as it was experienced when it was new. Our ears can't block out the two hundred years of music written since.

The story of Mozart's *Messiah,* and I do mean Mozart's, is a cautionary tale both for period-instrument artists and for concertgoers who love hearing excellent early-music ensembles today. In 1789 Mozart was asked by his friend and sometime patron Baron von Swieten to prepare arrangements of a few Handel works, including *Messiah,* for performances in Vienna sponsored by the musical association Swieten had founded. As usual, Mozart needed money. Still, he was genuinely interested in the project. He had heard *Messiah* and loved the piece, which, in Vienna of the late 1780s, was not widely known. So Mozart readily accepted the commission.

Of course, as he and Swieten immediately agreed, Handel's score would have to be updated and the spare original orchestration redone. Naturally, the English libretto was translated into German. Mozart eliminated the continuo part—a vestige of Baroque practice—and rescored the work for a more modern orchestra, to which he added flutes, clarinets, trombones, and horns. He not only rearranged the piece, but recomposed parts of it.

In the now-beloved opening "Comfort ye" recitative and "Ev'ry valley" aria, Mozart's version adds lines for woodwinds that mingle with the solo tenor. During the alto aria "But who may abide," when the strings tremble ominously as the soloist warns us "For He is like a refiner's fire," you almost expect Mozart's scary Queen of the Night to descend from on high and demand vengeance. Some of Handel's choruses are given over to a solo quartet of singers; several arias are trimmed down, others eliminated outright.

It simply did not occur to Mozart when he took on this project to ask himself how *Messiah* would have been performed at its 1742 premiere. Even Handel, in presiding over later revivals, altered the scoring to suit the circumstances. Rather, Mozart honored Handel by bringing the master's piece up to date, which involved streamlining the score in certain ways and beefing it up in others.

Could the composer who approached *Messiah* in this way have minded when German opera houses in the early twentieth century beefed up the scoring of *Don Giovanni* to suit modern tastes? Or when some contemporary productions of the opera blare the offstage voice of the ghostly Commendatore through loudspeakers? Mozart would have expected such things to happen. I think he would have been thrilled.

CHAPTER FIVE

"I HAD TO BE ORIGINAL"

FRANZ JOSEPH HAYDN (1732-1809)

As a prepubescent choirboy in Vienna, Haydn was almost turned into a castrato. At least this is the story that, in old age, Haydn recounted to Georg August Griesinger, a lawyer in Vienna who became the composer's first biographer. Though some scholars today doubt it, contemporaries of Haydn affirmed the vivid account Haydn gave to Griesinger. I believe it. In any event, this tale of a young boy's close call is at once endearing, horrible, and revealing of the good and the bad of Haydn's childhood.

Born in Rohrau, Lower Austria, near the Hungarian border, on March 31, 1732, Joseph Haydn came from a family of artisans and tradespeople. Matthias Haydn, his father, was a master wheelwright and a town magistrate; his mother, Anna Maria, was a God-fearing woman who had been a cook in the local castle of the ruling count and, like her husband, nurtured hopes of Joseph becoming a priest. The house was filled with music. His mother sang songs accompanied by his father, who could not read a note but played the harp by ear. Another son, Michael, five years Joseph's junior, became a prominent composer in his own right. In old age Haydn could still remember the tunes he sang during these convivial family evenings.

It was soon clear, though, that Joseph was uncommonly talented. A man named Franck, a school principal in the nearby town of Hainburg who also ran the church choir, was so impressed by the six-year-old Haydn's gifts that he suggested the boy come live with him in order to study music thoroughly. Haydn's parents agreed. Joseph learned reading, writing, and religion from Franck, as well as singing, string playing, and some timpani. Haydn later told Griesinger that he would be indebted to Franck "even in my grave," though he also said, "I received in the process more thrashings than food"—which you can only hope represented the exaggerated memory of the elderly Haydn.

Around the time Haydn was eight, a kapellmeister Reutter passed through Hainburg in search of potential boys to join the choir school at St. Stephen's Cathedral in Vienna. He heard Haydn and recruited him on the spot for this prestigious institution. Young Joseph became a city boy.

Being away from his family was surely a terrible deprivation. Matthias Haydn must have felt guilty, if not horrified, when he received a letter from the choir director proposing that Joseph's soprano voice be surgically preserved.

This old-fashioned father, worried that the operation may already have taken place, rushed to Vienna, as Haydn later recalled. Matthias came into Joseph's room and asked, "Does anything hurt you? Can you still walk?" Matthias was extremely relieved to discover that Joseph was still intact.

At the choir school, Haydn received basic instruction in Latin, arithmetic, writing, and catechism, and was taught singing, harpsichord, and violin. In performing with the choir, both at the cathedral and in court, he was introduced to important works of Western sacred music. Though he seems not to have studied much music theory or composition, he began composing on his own. At this school he obtained an education that would have been otherwise impossible. And if discipline was tough, he emerged relatively unscarred, it would seem, and developed a reputation for impish humor and practical jokes. Still, he must have felt cut off from the love and security of his family.

At seventeen, if not earlier (the records are unclear), Haydn's voice broke. So he was dismissed from St. Stephen's and found himself on the streets. Another biographer, Albert Christoph Dies, who conducted an extensive series of interviews with Haydn in the composer's last years, gives a vivid description of the situation. Young Haydn, the "cashiered choirboy, helpless, without money, outfitted with three miserable shirts and a worn-out coat, stepped into the great and unknown world." His upset parents again urged him to consider the priesthood. But Joseph was determined to pursue music in Vienna.

He eventually rented an attic room in an apartment building, a flat with a leaky roof and no stove. For almost a decade Haydn eked out a living as a freelance musician.

Today's generation of composers and performers, who in the face of a shrinking job market have embraced entrepreneurial ventures with inspiring determination, should see a soul mate in the Haydn who had to make his own way in Vienna.

Haydn gave the equivalent, in his day, of piano lessons; he played string instruments, mostly viola, in ensembles and orchestras. And he was a natural at networking. Living downstairs in his building was the eminent poet and librettist Metastasio, who was then guiding the education of the daughter of friends. His student, Marianne Martinez, was an aspiring composer of Spanish descent. Metastasio hired Haydn to teach Martinez singing and piano, for which Haydn received three years of free rent. Through Metastasio, he met the distinguished elderly Italian composer and singing teacher Nicola Porpora, who hired Haydn to accompany his vocal students during lessons. From Porpora he gleaned invaluable insights into the heritage of Italian vocal music, opera, and singing styles, and became fluent in Italian.

Haydn moved to better quarters, composed pieces with diligence, apparently collaborated on an opera with the comic actor who went by the stage name Bernardon (the work is lost), and commanded higher fees for giving private lessons. He even mingled with aristocrats, including a baron who hired him as a music instructor to his children. Still, there were times, especially in the earlier years, when Haydn basically played music on the streets to collect donations. He learned what it meant to hover near poverty and never forgot it.

So in 1759 he leapt at the chance to become music director to Count Morzin in Vienna, with a good salary as well as free room and board at the staff table—a "carefree existence" that "suited him thoroughly," as Griesinger reports. While working for the count, Haydn composed industriously, including some fifteen symphonies, chamber works, concertos, and keyboard sonatas. He also got married—not a fortuitous turn in his life.

Haydn, who wore powdered wigs from his late teenage years until his death, gave music lessons to the eldest daughter of his wigmaker, named Keller, who may have helped Haydn financially during the lean times. Haydn had fallen for Keller's younger daughter, who had been bound, alas, for a convent. Sometime later, he taught music to Keller's eldest daughter, Maria Anna, three years Haydn's senior. Herr Keller kept urging Haydn to marry Maria Anna. Feeling financially settled and ready for marriage, and perhaps believing himself not much of a catch (he was short, solidly built, with a broad forehead, a darkish, pockmarked complexion, and a big nose), the easygoing Haydn eventually agreed. He married Maria Anna in November 1760. That the match was a bad one became clear early on.

Maria Anna was domineering and unpleasant, at least according to Haydn. What she thought, we don't know. Though a devout Catholic, Haydn made adjustments to his life. "My wife was unable to bear children," the composer told Griesinger, "and I was therefore less indifferent to the charms of other ladies." She spent money too freely, Haydn would later complain, constantly inviting clergy to dinner and making charitable donations. She seems not even to have appreciated Haydn's music. "It is all the same to her if her husband is a shoemaker or an artist." From all reports, both Haydn and Maria Anna, especially Haydn, sought extramarital comfort.

Count Morzin, a spendthrift, found himself in financial trouble and disbanded the musical coterie in his house. Around the same time, Haydn got a better offer, the post that would define his career and that still elicits debate among historians and music lovers over whether, on balance, it represented a great opportunity for Haydn or wound up restricting his creativity.

Prince Paul Anton Esterházy, the heir to the wealthiest, most influential family of Hungarian nobility, had long been an avid supporter of culture, especially literature and music. Haydn seems to have been brought into the prince's service around 1761, when Paul Anton was mostly living in his Vienna palace. Haydn's initial appointment was as vice-kapellmeister, a delicate assignment, since his superior, the long-serving Gregor Joseph Werner, was old and ailing. The prince, who wanted to expand and modernize his musical establishment, put his trust in Haydn, who, though officially the assistant to Werner, was the de facto music director.

When the childless Prince Paul Anton died in March 1762, he was succeeded by his brother, Nicholas, an even more enthusiastic music booster and an amateur performer.

Detailed accounts of Haydn's decades in the Esterházy court report some hitches along the way, including a tense period just prior to Werner's death in 1766, when the old kapellmeister accused Haydn of neglecting the maintenance of the court's instruments and musical archives and badmouthed Haydn the composer as a mere "song writer" and "fashion follower." But for the most part Haydn seems to have been an efficient musical administrator, and as a composer he was astonishingly prolific during his Esterházy period, which lasted almost thirty years.

The new prince preferred living at his estate in Eisenstadt, about twenty-five miles outside Vienna. At the time he was building a fine new palace at Esterháza, just over the border of what is today Hungary. As the years went on, his summertime stays grew to several months each year.

Recent scholars have dismantled the notion that Haydn was essentially a servant in the prince's household. He was a well-paid professional who lived in a well-appointed apartment in a building for the court musicians up a hill from the palace. Prince Nicholas maintained his own small opera company, with two theaters (one of them seating four hundred), a comedy

troupe, a marionette theater, and an orchestra, which under Haydn's stew-
ardship grew to an ensemble of about two dozen. There was also church
music to be written and performed.

Haydn had almost unlimited opportunities to compose chamber pieces,
symphonies, and serenades, and to present performances of works by others. Of course, as with any gig, there were tiresome routine duties. Nicholas
was an avid player of the baryton, a string instrument that, like the earlier
bass viol, was a cross between a viola and a cello. Haydn was conscripted by
his prince into composing pieces for baryton, which grew to a body of two
hundred works, including a hundred and twenty-three trios for baryton,
viola, and cello, which Haydn, on viola, would play with Nicholas. That he
played chamber music with the prince suggests how intimate they were.
Still, he grew bored with churning out pieces for the instrument, which is
only of historical curiosity today.

As I mentioned earlier, Haydn lived at a time when the patronage system was slackening and composers were finding independent ways to support their work. In this regard, the most striking concession Haydn had to
make in joining the prince's staff regarded the rights to his compositions,
which were controlled by His Highness. The contract stated that Haydn
was not allowed to compose a work for any other person without the prior
approval and consent of the prince.

Today composers tenaciously attempt to protect their works, and self-
publishing is common. That Haydn agreed to such conditions is hard to
imagine now. But at the time, this was the norm in the Hapsburg realm,
where there was no real publishing industry, as there was in London and
Paris. Haydn's works slipped out of the Esterházy court in manuscript versions and were published without authorization elsewhere. But things
changed in 1778, when Artaria & Co., Viennese dealers in the visual arts,
began a music-publishing business. Within a year Haydn had a contract
with the company. Over the next two decades he developed into a savvy
self-promoter and a powerhouse in the music-publishing world. There was
a growing market for printed music during this period, and Haydn, often
working through a middleman, would sell his works in different countries,
collecting a separate fee for each.

Compositionally, Haydn's tenure with the Esterházys had begun auspiciously. Among the first works he composed were a trio of symphonies (Nos. 6, 7, and 8) based on the times of day and nicknamed *Le Matin* (Morning), *Le Midi* (Noon), and *Le Soir* (Evening), a theme that may have been suggested by the prince. This first assignment involved a balancing act that Haydn executed deftly. You can imagine that he wanted to impress the prince and the players of the chamber orchestra and announce himself as someone to be taken seriously. Yet he also had to be careful to show deference to tradition.

All three of these beguiling, fresh scores pay homage to Baroque concerto grosso practice, where passages highlighting small groups of solo instruments were contrasted with full-bodied episodes for the whole orchestra. *Le Matin,* the first of this symphonic trilogy, begins with soft, glowing music that evokes the sunrise. This leads, almost sneaking up on us, to a hearty, fast main section, the Allegro. The slow movement has a wafting gait and a serenely alluring theme.

The ensemble included some outstanding players, none more notable, I hasten to point out, than the esteemed first violinist, Luigi Tomasini. (My ancestor? I can't say. But it also can't be disproved. So I claim him.) The symphonies contain extended virtuosic passages for what today we would call the orchestra's concertmaster, Tomasini, who became one of Haydn's closest colleagues.

Still, it's hard not to look back at Haydn's time in the Esterházy court as artistically limiting in certain ways. After all, he missed out on the challenge that comes from directly presenting one's works to a wide public and gauging the reactions firsthand. But Haydn made the best of things. Trying to explain his attitude toward his job to Griesinger, he came up with what may be the most self-perceptive observation any composer has ever made about his own music: "My prince was content with all my works, I received approval, I could, as head of an orchestra, make experiments, observe what enhanced an effect, and what weakened it, thus improving, adding to, cutting away, and running risks. I was set apart from the world, there was nobody in my vicinity to confuse and annoy me in my course, and so I had to be original."

He "had to be" original, Haydn said. In other words, with a supportive prince, the prince's guests at court as an audience, and top-notch players at his disposal, Haydn had nothing to lose by giving free rein to his inventiveness. Over time, Haydn's music got around and earned him an international reputation, the extent of which even Haydn didn't realize until later in life. But at the Esterházy court, Haydn was indeed "set apart from the world." This limitation particularly affected him as an opera composer.

Nicholas's enthusiasm for opera had been growing. By the 1770s he had turned his court, especially the new castle at Esterháza, into an operatic hotbed, though a private one. On a state visit to Esterháza in 1773, Empress Maria Theresa attended a performance of Haydn's light comic opera *L'infedeltà delusa* (Deceit Outwitted); she was later said to remark that to see a really good opera, she had to go to the country. If she actually made this interesting comment (and it seems plausible), it was a slap at the quality of opera in Vienna.

The Haydn operas are rich in stately, intricate, and engaging music. Stylistically, the works range from *Orlando Paladino,* described as a "dramma eroicomico" (mock-heroic drama), full of theatrical exploits and inventive musical flights, to the charming, fanciful *I'isola disabitata* (The Desert Island), utilizing a libretto by Metastasio. Still, Haydn's operas lack surefooted dramatic know-how, the kind of experience a composer can pick up only by putting pieces on a public stage and seeing what clicks.

By contrast, Mozart was a theater man through and through. Of course, functioning more as a freelancer, Mozart struggled to get support for operatic projects. But one way or another he got shows up and running and gained invaluable insight into the byways of music drama.

Compare what Mozart was up to operatically in 1786 with Haydn's lot in Nicholas's court. That year Haydn was almost a full-time opera impresario. As the scholar James Webster reports, there were eight new productions and five revivals, for an estimated total of one hundred twenty-five evenings of opera at the court, mostly pieces brought in from Vienna. Haydn was in effect the general manager, music director, and composer in residence of an opera company. And he still had his other duties to attend to, including composing all manner of instrumental works.

That same year Mozart, on his own initiative, enticed the noted librettist Lorenzo Da Ponte into working on *Le nozze di Figaro*, adapted from the notorious recent French play by Beaumarchais. Da Ponte had to remove the more incendiary political elements of the play, which depicted aristocrats being surreptitiously manipulated by their servants, at a time when resentment against entitled classes was seething in France. The project eventually won the backing of Emperor Joseph II, who approved the libretto. *Figaro* had its well-received premiere at the Burgtheater in Vienna in May 1786 and went on to have a sensationally successful, though limited, run at a theater in Prague. But despite Mozart's frustrations, from start to finish in working on this opera he was striving to connect with the theater-going public, trying to lure in listeners while also challenging them, and boldly shaping the operatic genre to his own pathbreaking ends.

If Haydn "had to be original," as he put it, this was much easier to do through instrumental genres. During his decades with the prince he excelled in two of them: the string quartet and the symphony.

In a 2002 review for the *New York Times,* the critic Bernard Holland, who yields to no one in his appreciation of Haydn, wrote: "Haydn invented the string quartet, said by many to be music's purest form of expression. No composer wrote better ones, not Mozart or Beethoven or anyone to follow."

The Beethoven quartets do not surpass Haydn's? For me the Beethoven quartets are not just great, but, by the late period, cosmic. Thinking about it, though, Holland had a point in arguing that Haydn's achievement in the genre is perhaps something rarer: the music is admirably self-effacing, with an expressive orientation nothing like the confessional soul-baring that become routine with the Romantics.

As developed by Haydn, the string quartet became musical composition as four-way conversation. Pressed into service by Haydn, the string instruments engage in much animated chat and intricate interplay. The music effortlessly balances grandeur and whimsy, good manners and impishness. Yet no matter the overall mood, whether somber or silly, Haydn's quartets are ingeniously structured and integrated works, though the coherence and logic are easy to miss, since moods can change in a moment and events get disrupted almost continuously.

If you leave out some early works and arrangements, Haydn wrote nearly seventy quartets. Prior to Haydn, composers had written pieces for the combination of two violins, viola, and cello, which became the standard string quartet. But these precursors were mostly divertimentos or lighter serenades. Those who want the quickest route into Haydn's greatness can do no better than pick up a boxed set of recordings of the quartets, which Haydn wrote, and eventually published, in groups, by opus numbers. Try the six amazing quartets of Op. 33, or the six late quartets of Op. 76 (one movement of which I will describe in detail).

It's a shakier case to claim Haydn as the father of the symphony, since whole schools of symphony writing had been happening in cities from Mannheim to Bologna when Haydn arrived on the scene. Still, as with the string quartet, Haydn showed the scope and potential inherent in the genre and wrote works—104 of them, to use the numbering of the most accepted catalogue—that defined the symphony for the Classical era and made the achievements of Mozart and Beethoven possible.

But before saying more about Haydn's quartets and symphonies, I want to delve into what's become known as sonata form (often called sonata-allegro form). Descriptions of it have long been rampant in program notes and music appreciation guides. To be sure, whole movements in symphonies, piano sonatas, and string quartets can be analyzed as roughly hewing to sonata form, as it's commonly explained. Yet the reality of how such movements unfold is in almost every instance more complicated.

I've found that music lovers, even those with a little training in music, are hungry to comprehend form. And writers about music, especially critics, myself included, cannot help talking about it, because form is the easiest thing to write about. Describing in everyday words how music actually sounds is far more challenging. By contrast, describing form is easy: First this happens, then this other thing happens, and then, oh wow, this new thing happens. And so on. Yet, such descriptions don't really aid audiences that much, because we cannot help listening to music moment to moment. The long arc of a form, the grand plan, happens over an extended period of time and is often hard to follow, at least consciously, though I'd argue that listeners intuitively discern the form of a great piece.

Sonata form, as it is typically explained, refers to a structure in three named parts, and it's rather complicated, especially regarding key relationships. There is an exposition that begins with a main theme presented in the tonic key area. As the music unfolds, it leads before long to a contrasting secondary theme in the dominant area of the key. (Now, this applies to pieces in a major key; if the piece is in a minor key, the secondary theme appears in that key's so-called relative major key: for C minor, that would be E-flat major. But let me focus on form here.)

After a while the exposition section ends. (During the Viennese Classical period the exposition was meant to be repeated in full.) Then comes the middle, or development section, in which the composer plays around with the thematic materials in all manner of ways. This section is often the most inventive and boldest episode of the whole movement. Eventually the main theme returns in the tonic key, signaling the arrival of the recapitulation section, which starts off by echoing the exposition. But this time there must be some tweaks to the music so that, following the protocols of the form, the secondary theme reappears in the tonic key area (rather than shifting as before to the dominant, or, as I just noted, shifting to the relative major if the piece is in a minor key). This leads inevitably to an extended coda, that is, a conclusion; and a coda can be prolonged dramatically if a composer so chooses.

Okay, that's the scheme as you can read about it today in music appreciation books. The problem is that this elaborate concept of sonata form (including the terms "exposition," "development," and "recapitulation") wasn't codified until around 1840. So Haydn and Mozart simply did not think of the opening movements of their symphonies and quartets as lining up with what we think of today as sonata form.

Still, it's tempting to keep using these terms and this concept. When the stirring main theme of the first movement of Beethoven's mighty *Eroica* Symphony returns after what has seemed a wildly inventive musical excursion in the middle of the movement, it certainly sounds like a recapitulation.

But neither Beethoven nor his audience thought quite this way about structure. Yes, these symphonic movements often had contrasting themes;

yes, there was an expectation that a movement beginning in a tonic key area would modulate to the dominant. And so on.

That said, the idea that composers were following a recipe or that the symphonic structure was a roadmap is just not the way things worked during the Classical era. Actually, many of Haydn's sonata-form movements have only one theme, which first appears in the tonic and then also in the dominant, though often with a few twists.

It's the getting from one area to the next that matters. If listeners today become fixated on trying to follow sonata form, they may miss the real inventiveness of the music. And Haydn's boldness occurs not just in intense pieces, but in seemingly affable ones.

Take, for example, the opening Allegro con spirito movement of Haydn's String Quartet in G, Op. 76, No. 1, a later work composed probably in 1796. This piece begins unassumingly with three emphatic chords: I-V-I, the tonic, dominant, and tonic. No big deal. Then the cello, alone, plays a bouncy tune, which seems a touch coy. The viola takes it up but turns the melody into a different strand of conversation. The second violin picks up the theme, but with a tweak, supported by the cello, which seems unwilling to let go of its stake in the argument. So the restless first violin intrudes with another, slightly altered version, this time with the viola undergirding the violin's remarks. Ah, well, why don't we all just try to get along? the instruments seem to be saying. So, the four prolong the discourse together, with no real disagreements. Soon, the violin dominates things, as the other three strings supply seemingly obliging accompaniment of staccato (meaning, played in a detached fashion) chords. Things turn agitated, however, as the first violin tries to be even more forceful, until its cohorts join in, not so much in assent as in a strategic maneuver to stay alert and wait for a moment to pounce on that pushy first fiddle.

This is my personal reading of the music. Whatever your take, who cares if the movement is written in sonata form? Have we yet heard a secondary theme? Got me. What does it matter?

Countless works by Haydn evolve in similar ways. But Haydn's compositional breakthrough—what made him a pioneer in demonstrating how to write a large-scale work in which all the movements and components seem part of an overall entity—was his sophisticated use of motifs, the practice known as motivic development.

A motif is not the same as a theme or a melody. A motif is a mini-gesture, a component of a theme: a few notes, or a little turn in a phrase, sometimes aligned to a rhythmic gesture. Haydn's themes are built from motifs. And in most pieces, a distinctive motif will appear, either clearly or in some guise, throughout the movement, even throughout the entire sonata or symphony. When listening, you may not consciously discern this little motif. But it works upon you in a subliminal way.

Basically, through motivic development a composer can generate an entire piece from a cell of pitches. For example, running through Haydn's Piano Sonata No. 38 in F Major, composed in 1773, is a recurring two-note gesture, in which the upper note, prolonged a bit, slips stepwise down and then get cuts off. That idea is introduced in the first measures of the first movement. What you pay attention to, though, is the entire theme—a jaunty tune, really a little fanfare riff—in a clipped, dotted-note rhythm that outlines the simple tonic and dominant chords of the key. But no matter what happens as the music goes on (and a whole lot happens, including sudden flourishes, showy passage-work, harmonic explorations of other key areas, a middle section that sounds almost like a free improvisation with hyperfast, scintillating, rippling runs), that sinking two-note motif keeps making itself present.

In the wistful slow movement that follows, the theme opens with a three-note gesture that this time *rises* from a lower to an upper note, then sinks back down: the inverse of the motif from the opening movement. And the presto Finale—one of those characteristic, joke-filled, breathless Haydn finales full of moments in which everything suddenly stops and then starts again—also keeps hammering us with that sighing two-note motif, even amid all the giddiness.

So even though these three movements are very different in content and character, that embedded motif makes the entire sonata seem organic and complete. Substitute a different Haydn slow movement for the one that appears in this score and the sonata as a whole would make much less sense. I am convinced that all listeners, whatever their background in music, would perceive the problem, at least on an unconscious level.

Of all the Haydn sonatas I've performed, this one, No. 38, is my favorite. I've paired it several times on a program with Beethoven's astonishing Sonata in A Major, Op. 101, the first of the five late sonatas. And in its playful way, the Haydn always struck me as just as awesome as the complex, elusive late Beethoven sonata.

I chose this Haydn sonata's first movement to play in the summer of 2013 when I took part in Sing for Hope, a project that placed old upright pianos, fancifully painted by various artists, outdoors in New York City, on corners, in squares, by ponds in parks, for anyone to play. I went around Manhattan playing the movement while a video crew from the *New York Times* filmed me. At various locations, little children not only listened but started to dance. How could they not? It's such joyous, beguiling music.

I will take up the technique of motivic development further when I discuss its greatest practitioner, Beethoven, who was Haydn's student.

A ll during his years in Esterházy's court, Haydn spent time in Vienna whenever he could, usually during a couple of months in the winter. He remarked that he was always ready to escape the "wasteland" of Esterháza and mingle with musicians in the city, a group that included Mozart for the last decade of that composer's life. Though these two giants did not spend all that much time together, and Mozart was twenty-four years younger, they were devoted friends, in their way, and mutual admirers.

In the fall of 1790, Prince Nicholas died and was succeeded by his son, Anton, who was less interested in culture and more frugal. Anton phased out the musical and theatrical establishment at the court. Haydn, at fifty-nine, was given a reduced but decent salary with no real responsibilities, essentially an honorarium for decades of loyal service. He moved to Vienna and began the last, triumphant period of his life. (He died at seventy-seven in 1809, some two weeks after the besieged city surrendered to the invading French army.)

The German violinist and concert producer Johann Peter Salomon, then living in London, came to Vienna to persuade Haydn to visit England for a professional engagement. Haydn didn't need much persuading.

Between 1791 and 1795, Haydn had two extended stays in London. Upon arriving in January 1791, he was astonished to realize that he was revered as a master by the English public. London was agog over Haydn. For three days he did newspaper interviews. He could have, as he wrote at the time, dined out every day, there were so many people, including nobles, who wanted to meet him. He reflected wistfully on his new independence in a 1791 letter to Griesinger's wife. "This little bit of freedom, how sweet it tastes!" he wrote. "I had a good prince," he explained, "but at times I was forced to be dependent on base souls. I often sighed for release."

Among the works Haydn composed for these sojourns were the *London* Symphonies, the final twelve (Nos. 93–104), astounding works that include many of the well-known nicknamed ones: the *Surprise,* the *Miracle,* the *Drum Roll,* and the *Military.*

That Haydn was not just basking in glory but still being ambitious during his London visits comes through in an exchange recounted by Griesinger. The biographer asked the elderly Haydn about the surprise moment in his *Surprise* Symphony (No. 94 in G). This may be the most famous surprise in all of music. It occurs when, without warning, the gentle, subdued, almost quaint theme of the slow movement is interrupted by a single, full-bodied fortissimo chord, complete with a thwack on the drum, at the end of a phrase. For the rest of the movement—written in a theme and variations form—the surprise does not reoccur, something that keeps you even more on edge: you are sure that Haydn is going to try to "get you" again and don't want to be caught unawares.

A story had long trailed this piece that Haydn put the surprise chord into the slow movement in order to awaken audience members who fell asleep during his beguiling slow movements. Griesinger asked Haydn if it was true. Haydn replied, "No, but I was interested in surprising the public with something new, and in making a brilliant debut, so that my student Pleyel, who was at that time engaged by an orchestra in London and whose concerts had opened a week before mine, should not outdo me." "Papa"

Haydn, as the master was dubbed in later life, was not about to suffer competition passively from the new generation.

During his visits to London, Haydn was inspired by some performances he heard of Handel oratorios. Even so, he had to be persuaded by Salomon to write a comparably ambitious oratorio of his own. After returning to Vienna in 1795 he received a gift from Salomon: an English libretto telling the Creation story with texts from Genesis, the Psalms, and Milton's *Paradise Lost*. Haydn had the text translated into German and, finally inspired, wrote "Die Schöpfung," the German title of the piece known as *The Creation* when it is performed in its English version. In either language, this ninety-minute score is among the most astounding works of all time.

It opens with an orchestral prelude, "The Representation of Chaos," an episode that evokes the earth without form and void. Haydn's music is hauntingly elusive and harmonically wayward, with melodic fragments and eerie instrumental effects. During the first halting, tentative choral episode, when the choir relates God's words, "Let there be light," at that climactic moment—the word "light"—the music bursts into a shimmering C-major chord, music so glorious and so bright you almost feel the need to squint. The entire score is comparably remarkable. Joyous choruses alternate with dramatic exchanges for the vocal soloists, culminating in a rousing final chorus on the words "The Lord is great," in the form of an intrepid and exuberant fugue.

On December 21, 2012, the conductor Harold Rosenbaum led the New York Virtuoso Singers and the Orchestra of St. Luke's in a performance of *The Creation* at Carnegie Hall. This was the very night that the ancient Mayan calendar had predicted the world would end (though Mayan experts had long tried to explain that this was a misreading of the sources). Haydn's *Creation* was presented as a kind of counterforce, a gesture of renewal.

As I wrote at the time, any apocalyptic forces kicking around that night did not have a chance against Haydn. *The Creation* triumphed. The world did not end.

⤛○ CHAPTER SIX ○⤜

"RIGHT HERE IN MY NOODLE"

WOLFGANG AMADEUS MOZART (1756–1791)

Nothing made the human dimension of the child prodigy Mozart more poignantly real for me than seeing a small music manuscript book that Leopold Mozart, Wolfgang's father, had used to teach his boy counterpoint. From the stories of young Mozart's astounding gifts it's easy to think of him as some sort of uncanny child-man. Portraits of the boy dressed in courtly attire, complete with powdered wig, reinforce that impression.

But the pages of exercises in this book, which I first saw long ago in an exhibition at the Mozart birth house in Salzburg, remind you that the prodigious Wolfgang was a little kid. In learning to write music in multiple voices according to the rules of counterpoint, Wolfgang was engaged in a sophisticated discipline. Here and there you see Leopold's corrections. What's touching is that, like all children, Wolfgang had difficulty controlling his pen, so when he wrote notes he often couldn't keep his circles and dots on the lines and within the spaces of the staff. For him this was the hard part of the task, not understanding the byways of counterpoint.

Wolfgang Amadeus Mozart, born on January 27, 1756, was the seventh and last child of Leopold Mozart, a violinist in the court of the prince-bishop of Salzburg, and Anna Maria, formerly Pertl. Only Wolfgang and his sister Maria Anna, known as Nannerl, who was four and a half years older, survived infancy. There is no reason to doubt Leopold's reports about his young son's miraculous musical gifts. Nannerl was also an extraordinarily talented child who played the piano beautifully and composed many works, almost all of which seem to be lost. By age four Wolfgang, mostly by observing his sister, could stand at the keyboard and play the pieces she was studying. At five he composed his first work, a little Andante and Allegro for piano. By six he was writing minuets and slightly more substantial pieces. He was a natural at the keyboard and the violin, playing a miniature violin designed for children. Most scholars suspect that Leopold had a hand in the composing of Mozart's juvenilia, at least until he was about ten. Still, we are dealing here with arguably the most gifted prodigy in music history.

Leopold, a respected composer and an influential pedagogue of the violin, rose through a series of musical posts in the employ of Salzburg's prince-archbishops, who lived amid the trappings of royalty and were essentially both the religious and secular head of a church-state. If Wolfgang in young adulthood developed a reckless drive for independence, he inherited some of his rebellious streak from his father. Leopold was born to a well-to-do bookbinder in Augsburg, Germany, and educated at a fine Jesuit school there. In time, though, he rejected the family business, went to law school in Salzburg, was thrown out after a year, and finally, to the dismay of his family, decided to pursue his passion: music.

Though he appreciated landing a good job at the prince-archbishop's court (and would be promoted to deputy kapellmeister in 1763), Leopold felt taken for granted and yearned for more. He nursed increasing bitterness about the submissive nature of his professional life. His talented daughter and uncannily gifted son offered a potential way out.

The children did not attend school; Leopold seems to have been their sole teacher, instructing them not just in music but in mathematics, reading, languages, literature, even dancing. In 1762, according to a recollection by Nannerl, Leopold took the two children to Munich, where they played for the elector of Bavaria. At the end of that year the entire Mozart family made a well-documented visit to Vienna lasting about four months,

during which Nannerl and Wolfgang played twice for Empress Maria Theresa and at the homes of noblemen. They received honoraria and gifts.
Midway through the stay, Leopold sent to his depositor in Salzburg a sum
equal to two years of his salary at court. And then there came an enticing
invitation from the French ambassador to visit the court of Versailles.

This led Leopold to devise the extensive European tour that would define the young Mozart's youth. The tour wound up lasting three and a half
years. (Leopold had not planned an itinerary in advance.) In undertaking
this arduous journey, Leopold had two long-term goals. One was the hope
that a monarch or culturally minded aristocrat would realize Wolfgang's
extraordinary promise and set the boy up for a future position, maybe with
a post for Leopold as well. The other was to expose his children, Wolfgang
especially, to the styles and customs of music throughout Europe. The latter goal was definitely accomplished. Not the former.

The family left Salzburg on June 9, 1763, traveling in a privately hired
coach with a servant across winding rural roads. Wolfgang was seven; Nannerl, almost twelve.

It's hard to generalize about this multi-year venture. Historical reports
are contradictory. For all the success and acclaim, there were hardships and
deprivation. They started in Munich, then went on to Augsburg, Frank-
furt, Brussels, and, eventually, Paris; they played for electors and kings before enchanted audiences at the great courts of Europe. But often they were
kept idling for days, even weeks, as they waited for a promised command
performance. They received gifts and at times made considerable money
from concerts, some of them benefits mounted with entrepreneurial daring
by Leopold. But many of the concerts attracted gawkers just curious to see
Wolfgang and Nannerl on display.

Also, both children were continually exposed to disease and suffered
long bouts of illness, the worst coming in the fall of 1765 in The Hague,
where first Nannerl and then Wolfgang came down with what was probably typhoid fever. Nannerl was actually administered the last rites. Wolfgang was grievously sick for two months. During the worst period he was
bedbound and speechless for eight days.

Still, Wolfgang was given unparalleled exposure to the music and musicians of his time. In London he came under the influence of the youngest son of J. S. Bach, Johann Christian Bach, the "London" Bach, as he was known internationally. If Christian Bach was not strictly Mozart's teacher, he became a pivotal mentor. In 1764 and 1765, as he turned nine, Wolfgang, inspired by Christian Bach, wrote three little symphonies in the three-movement, stately, texturally clear style of his mentor. In May 1764, from London, Leopold wrote to his good friend Hagenauer, a merchant in Salzburg from whom he rented the family apartment, to brag about the way Wolfgang dazzled George III and the queen: sight-reading scores the king put before him, playing the king's organ beautifully, accompanying the queen's singing and a solo flutist at the keyboard, improvising a melody upon a given bass line. "In a word," Leopold wrote, "what he knew when we set out from Salzburg was a mere shadow compared with what he knows now. It is beyond all conception."

Upon returning home in late November 1766, the Mozart family must have seemed celebrities to the citizens of Salzburg. Leopold emphasized to friends and colleagues how much money had been made, and talked of intimacies with royalty and evenings at palaces. Still, nothing that would promise a future for either of the children had come of it. Father Hubner, the librarian at the abbey in Salzburg, reported on his visit to the Mozart apartment, where Leopold had set up a display case for the trophies and gifts from monarchs they had collected during this costly journey, which included a trove of gold pocket watches, snuffboxes, rings, and necklaces. Naturally one could not sell a gold snuffbox that was a present from a king. So these items held only social cachet for the Mozart family.

Leopold, unhappy and frustrated, settled back into the routine of life at the prince-archbishop's court. Eventually he had the idea of traveling with Wolfgang to Italy to further his son's expertise, especially in Italian vocal styles and opera. Starting in December 1769, Leopold and Wolfgang would make three extended visits to Italy over a four-year-period. For these journeys the women of the family were left behind.

Obviously Leopold, a man of his time, had decided that a career for Nannerl, even as a performer, let alone a composer, would be impossible, given the barriers to women with professional aspirations. The conductor Jane Glover, in her perceptive 2005 book *Mozart's Women: His Family, His Friends, His Music,* looks at the composer through the perspectives of the women in his life. She is especially astute about Nannerl, who naturally bowed to her father's will. Glover points out, though, that Wolfgang did not share such attitudes about women. When in 1781 he made his break and moved to Vienna, he sometimes wrote to his sister encouraging her, along with their father, of course, to come join him in the city, where, he thought, she might acquire private students in fine homes and even give some concerts. Alas, her glory days behind her, Nannerl remained with her short-tempered father in Salzburg, fairly miserable, until, in what comes across as a desperate act, at thirty-three she married a government bureaucrat who moved her to a remote rural region of Austria. Nannerl became the stepmother to five truculent children and eventually had three of her own (one of whom died in infancy).

Professionally, the father-son trips to Italy were formative and promising experiences for the young Wolfgang. He received commissions for several operas, including *"Mitridate, re di Ponto"* (Mithridates, King of Pontus), an amazing work for a fourteen-year-old, written for the 1771 Carnival in Milan and performed at the Royal Ducal Theater an impressive twenty-one times.

Mitridate was, incredibly, Mozart's third opera, though the first full-scale one. When the news came that the boy would be composing an opera for this prestigious Milan house, the regular singers, players, and directors were miffed. They were not about to be told what to do by some pimply-faced Austrian who had never written for an Italian theater. Leopold wrote to Padre Martini, the eminent teacher with whom Wolfgang had had crucial lessons in Milan, complaining that his son's "enemies and detractors" were talking down what they assumed would be a "barbarous German composition" before hearing a note.

On the theory that you have to learn a tradition before you can put your personal spin on it, Mozart's score is beholden to the existing style of Italian *opera seria,* which had still not moved much beyond the Baroque idea of a numbered series of showcase arias for virtuosic singers. And yet there are flashes of beguiling lyricism, subtle writing for woodwinds, and bracing music that unfolds at times in boldly asymmetrical phrases.

The next year, 1772, the prince-archbishop died and was replaced by Hieronymus von Colloredo, who eventually offered the boy a modest post as a court musician. In time, though, he drove Wolfgang to break not just with the court and Salzburg, but with his father as well.

In the mid-1770s Mozart composed steadily, including a series of spirited violin concertos that he performed with some success, concerts that reminded the public of his skills as a string player. But he was exasperated in Salzburg, getting nowhere, and ready to bolt.

The period from early 1777 through the summer of the next year was life-altering for Mozart. As I see it, having seen the world and now feeling stifled in Salzburg, Mozart tried to break out vicariously through his ambitious compositions.

First, he wrote his Piano Concerto No. 9 in E-flat, an exhilarating work that comes across like a declaration of independence. The pianist and scholar Charles Rosen described it as "perhaps the first unequivocal masterpiece in a classical style purified of all mannerist traces." There are no remnants of late Baroque complexities or rococo graces. Here is Mozart showing off what he can do, indulging himself in a piece at once audaciously inventive and ingeniously integrated.

The first movement, a spirited Allegro, exemplifies the so-called periodic phrase, the style I described in the chapter on the Vienna Four. If flowing, continuous, and mingling contrapuntal lines were a hallmark of high Baroque style, the use of shorter, periodic phrases—the musical equivalent of grammatical writing—was a hallmark of Viennese Classicism. Haydn's pieces typically unfold in clear symmetrical phrases, like clauses that combine to form sentences in a paragraph, though Haydn was just as likely to play around with asymmetries and toss in disruptive bits.

From the opening of this Mozart concerto, you hear the composer staking a claim to the style in his own sly way. The first movement begins with the orchestra—just strings, two oboes, and two horns—playing a lively, simple statement in unison: a strong E-flat (the tonic note), which drops down an octave to the lower E-flat, and then skips up the basic tones of the chord in bustling eighth notes.

The tradition at this time called for concertos to begin with an extended orchestral exposition until the solo instrument finally enters. But in this work, ignoring expectations, Mozart has the piano boldly jump right in after that first short orchestral phrase. The piano plays a sprightly, almost cute reply, picking up the theme and completing the first statement, harmonizing it properly. But the charm masks the daring involved.

What happens next? This first four-measure phrase is repeated exactly. No tweaks, no little decorous alteration. It's as if Mozart were saying: Yes, you heard right. The piano jumps in and slyly asserts itself. And, yes, I am thrusting this symmetrical mini-phrase at you by repeating it.

The impertinent piano has shaken things up enough for now. So the orchestra continues on its own and calms things down, laying out the musical materials with elegance tinged with impishness, including, before long, a lyrical second theme.

When the piano is ready to jump in again, it sneaks back by playing a high sustained trill that segues into a fresh lyrical twist. Then the opening assertive theme in unison comes back, and the first movement unfolds, by turns brilliant and beguiling. Seemingly straightforward themes and riffs are put through wondrously inventive turns, especially harmonically.

The second movement, an Andantino, slow but not too slow, comes almost as a shock. The key is C minor and the first utterances of the orchestra are bereft. Nothing in the first movement has prepared you for this radical mood shift. At first it almost seems heavy-handed, as if Mozart were exploring some pat duality of existence. But the music is so profoundly beautiful that you are overwhelmed. For me, this is Mozart exploring a Buddhist-like realization: life is both joyous and tragic, which does not mean that we carry on in some middle ground of wistful daily pleasantries; no, we are at once happy and sad. This concerto conveys that insight better than any other work I can think of.

And then, wouldn't you know it, the last movement, a Rondo, is a perpetual-motion romp, with nonstop streams of running eighth notes in the right hand of the piano part, rhythmic displacements in the accompanying chords, and harmonic twists. The piano keeps breaking into outbursts of dizzying passage-work. There are playful exchanges between the soloist and the orchestra.

Then, in the most mischievous gesture of the movement, about halfway through, the rondo stops and, out of nowhere, segues into an endearing Old World minuet. Still, there are passing hints of intensity during this slight detour, and one long passage of stunning harmonic exploration. The perpetual-motion music returns, and the Rondo drives to its heady conclusion. From my reading of the historical records, the concerto may have only been performed at a private concert. It obviously did little to alter Mozart's circumstances at the time.

Mozart was increasingly exasperated to be stuck in Salzburg. Leopold wanted, yet again, to take his son on a professional tour. He wrote to the prince-archbishop requesting a leave, but His Eminence, thoroughly fed up with the Mozarts' frequent traveling and uppity airs, responded by dismissing both father and son. Leopold patched things up with his employer and, though frustrated and resentful, arranged for Mozart to undergo another tour, this time just with his mother.

Jane Glover sensitively explores what this trip must have meant to Anna Maria Mozart. Was she delighted to get away from her bossy, imperious husband? Was the prospect of being on the road with her ingenious but rambunctious son a delight? Or a mother's burden? It's hard to know. Probably all of the above.

The trip took them first to Munich, then to Augsburg, where Mozart bonded with his spirited younger cousin Maria Anna Thekla Mozart, known within the family as the "Bäsle" (little cousin), a coquettish young woman whom Wolfgang enjoyed immensely. During this period they exchanged scatological letters filled with toilet humor, nonsense rhymes, and sexual repartee. The astute musicologist Maynard Solomon, in his 1995 biography of Mozart, sees these letters as inhabiting "a self-enclosed world, remote from real events," where the correspondents could be "guiltlessly dedicated to the pursuit of pleasure."

Professionally, the trip was the same mix of sporadic advances, with commissions and performances, and frustrating setbacks. After giving concerts in Augsburg and fostering some professional connections, Mozart and his mother went to Mannheim, where they stayed for an extended time. Here Mozart became acquainted with the musical Weber family. The father, a successful copyist and double bass player, had four daughters, all of whom became singers. The twenty-one-year-old Mozart fell in love with Aloysia Weber, who was about eighteen (the record is unclear), the most talented and, under her later married name as the soprano Aloysia Lange, the most professionally successful. At the time, Mozart overlooked fifteen-year-old Constanze Weber, whom he would eventually marry. He was clearly smitten with Aloysia as a woman and an artist, so much so that he proposed in a letter to his father that he should take the young woman, with family escorts, to Italy and groom her as a prima donna in Italian houses.

Thus began a series of heated letters between Wolfgang and Leopold, the son trying to defend his attachment and its professional and personal possibilities. His father sent withering, bitter replies.

Though Solomon is tough on Leopold, the portrait he presents is persuasive. Left behind in Salzburg, Leopold despaired at what he considered his son's irresponsibility. Wolfgang had become "the object of a melancholiac's fantastic grievances against the world," Solomon writes. Leopold repeatedly accused his brilliant son of heartlessness and cruelty, and tried to make Wolfgang feel like an endangered child who could not care for himself, or even survive, without his father, Solomon argues.

As Wolfgang made his intimacy with Aloysia Weber clear and suggested the idea of the professional trip to Italy, Leopold replied with a diatribe. "I have read your letter of the 4th with amazement and horror!" The Italy plan? "It has almost deprived me of my senses!" Leopold continues. "How can you have allowed yourself to have been bewitched by such a monstrous idea even for an hour!"

Eventually Mozart, wounded and confused, headed to Paris. There he suffered a loss that dwarfed his professional frustrations: the illness and death of his mother in July 1778. In a letter written the day after she had died, Mozart told his father the distressing news that his mother was suffering simultaneously from chills and fever, accompanied by diarrhea and headaches. To break the news slowly, Mozart also described the enthusiastic reaction to a performance of the work that became known as his *Paris* Symphony (No. 31 in D), an ebullient, inventive three-movement piece presented at the renowned Concert Spirituel, one of the first public concert series, which had begun in 1725. That same day he wrote a family friend, asking him to prepare Leopold for the grave news, which Mozart delivered later that month in a poignant letter. For the first time in his life, Mozart was alone. But it did not feel like independence.

Heading home he passed through Munich, where Aloysia Weber had obtained a position as a singer and taken up residency, accompanied by her proud family. But when Mozart visited, she rejected him with an inexplicable suddenness and certainty. Though stunned, he moved on.

Back in Salzburg, Mozart received a modest appointment as court and church organist for the prince-archbishop, and it seems clear he accepted it because he had no other choice. The most significant composition of this stifling period for Mozart was the great opera *Idomeneo, re di Creta* (Idomeneus, King of Crete), commissioned for performance at the prestigious court theater in Munich.

The tradition of *opera seria*—that is, serious, lofty, and noble music dramas—had been reinvented during the early 1760s by the German-born, Prague-trained composer Christoph Willibald Gluck, who eventually became an international figure, hailed in Vienna and more or less adopted by Paris. Gluck took a reformist approach to *opera seria,* ridding the genre of showy excesses and pointless virtuosic displays, working with like-minded librettists to bring dramatic integrity and literary grace to the art form, and writing scores that combined sublime beauty and emotional intensity. His breakthrough work in this effort was *Orfeo ed Euridice,* first performed in Vienna in 1762 and a staple of today's repertory.

In composing *Idomeneo,* which tells of the king's fateful return to Crete after the Trojan wars, having nearly drowned at sea in a storm, Mozart was clearly influenced by Gluck, especially the majestic *Alceste.* But working with the librettist he was assigned, Giovanni Battista Varesco, Mozart brought in elements of elaborate Italian lyricism and vocal virtuosity. He began writing the piece in Salzburg and completed it in Munich as rehearsals were under way. The letters he wrote his father during these weeks offer almost a handbook of his thinking about opera at the time, as he wrestled with often conflicting demands of music, text, story, and pacing. He was continually accommodating his music to his desire to keep the drama vivid and urgent. Even after the dress rehearsal he jettisoned some passages he was proud of in order to make the opera move with more theatrical sweep and conviction toward its conclusion.

Mozart would probably be amazed that *Idomeneo* has found a solid place in the repertory today, let alone that superstar tenors like Plácido Domingo and Luciano Pavarotti embraced the title role as a sure dramatic vehicle. Though he learned a great deal by writing it, Mozart realized that this was not the style in which to create the kind of opera he knew he had in him. He was never going to find his way forward, he felt, in a town like Salzburg.

In 1781 the prince-archbishop of Salzburg traveled to Vienna, mostly to tend to his ailing father. He brought with him a typically extensive entourage and summoned Mozart as well, who on this trip found the city magnificent. "It seems as if good fortune is waiting to embrace me here. It is as if I *must* stay," he wrote to Leopold. Mozart felt increasingly certain that in this cosmopolitan center he could start anew: give concerts, get commissions, and make real money.

But the archbishop demanded that Mozart attend to his responsibilities. That was it for Mozart. He openly protested and was officially dismissed. His father thought his son rash and ungrateful, though secretly Leopold must have yearned to do something similar. In letters to his father venting antiaristocratic sentiments that were just then roiling in France, Mozart ridiculed his boss and stood firm.

"It is the heart that ennobles man; and though I am not a count, I have probably more Honor in me than many a count," he wrote in June of 1781. Whether dealing with a count or a lackey, "if he insults me, he is a scoundrel," Mozart added, stating: "When someone insults me, I have to avenge myself." Mozart's declaration is precisely the theme that would be at the core of *The Marriage of Figaro*, a barbed comedy in which servants outwit and teach lessons to their master, a count.

The political overtones of Mozart's stinging words are fascinating

because, overall, he was uncurious about history and unabashedly apoliti-
cal. He generally espoused the liberal ideals of his era and belonged to a
local chapter of the Masons, a secret society where these humanitarian
principles were discussed endlessly. Still, Mozart was so consumed by music that he had little space in his head for much else. He had no particular
feeling for nature and scant interest in the visual arts. In his letters home
during wide-ranging trips he took, he describes in detail everything he
heard and nothing that he saw.

During this period Mozart fomented a revolution in his own household. While in Vienna, he boarded with the Weber family, which had
moved there from Munich in 1779 in another career shift for Aloysia, who
married the court actor and painter Joseph Lange the following year. Mozart started courting young Constanze, and, in the interest of propriety,
was asked to live elsewhere by Frau Weber. The courtship had its ups and
downs. Naturally, Leopold was against it. But Mozart wrote that a bachelor
is only half alive, that the time had come for him to marry, and that Constanze was a "respectable, good girl of good parentage." They loved each
other, he insisted. In an intriguing remark, Mozart finally added that Leopold's fatherly advice, "however fine and good," was "no longer applicable
to a man whose feelings for a girl have gone so far as have mine." It makes
you wonder how "far" the couple had gone. Mozart's pent-up sexual drive
is barely disguised in these agitated letters to his dismayed father.

The twenty-six-year-old Mozart married the twenty-year-old Constanze on August 4, 1782. They would have six children, four of whom
would not survive infancy, which means that during their nine years of
marriage Constanze was pregnant about half the time.

In short order, Mozart had quit his post, broken away from his family,
gone off to Vienna, and gotten married.

His years in Vienna are the time frame of Peter Shaffer's play *Amadeus*,
which I saw—twice—in the Broadway production that opened in December 1980, directed by Peter Hall. The director Miloš Forman's 1984 award-
winning film adaptation would end up shaping the perception of Mozart
for much of the moviegoing public. While I have reservations about the
film, I love the play, though to appreciate it you have to go along with the

enormous artistic license Shaffer took in presenting the figures and their stories.

The play centers on the relationship between Mozart and Antonio Salieri, who was born in Italy in 1750, making him six years Mozart's senior. Salieri was mostly a resident of Vienna during the greatest decades of his career, though he achieved European renown and wrote operas for many cities, especially Paris. In Vienna he had a powerful supporter in the musically gifted emperor Joseph II and in 1788 became kapellmeister at Joseph's court. Mozart arrived in Vienna in 1781. There is solid evidence that during these years Salieri, a smooth operator, felt threatened by Mozart and manipulated things at court to keep this upstart in his place. Still, they seem to have had a respectful relationship. After Mozart's death, Salieri supervised the musical instruction of Mozart's younger son, Franz Xaver.

Salieri died in 1825 at seventy-four. He had become weak and doddering, and was hounded by rumors that he had poisoned Mozart, who had died at thirty-five in 1791. Though there was no truth to the rumors, in his play Shaffer presents Salieri as haunted by guilt over his dealings with Mozart.

What drives the drama is Salieri's bitterness, even wrath, toward God, to whom he had prayed so devoutly asking to become a great composer, and had served so well. But in what seems to Salieri a perverse trick of the heavens, God instead bestowed a talent so great as to seem divine on the uppity, uncouth, sex-obsessed, foul-mouthed Mozart, whose middle name, Amadeus, meaning beloved of God, says it all.

In his play, Shaffer certainly presents Mozart as infantile. We first see Mozart playing a cat-and-mouse game of pursuit with Constanze in a library at court, demanding that she marry him. He says: "I'm going to pounce-bounce! I'm going to scrunch-munch! I'm going to chew-poo my little mouse-wouse! I'm going to tear her to bits with my paws-claws!" A moment later, Mozart makes a farting sound and says, "Oh, what a melancholy note! Something's dropping from your boat!"

This is the immortal Mozart? Well, many of his letters are full of puerile nonsense and scatological shockers.

But, in the play, more clearly than in the film, the story is framed as the recollection of the old, dotty Salieri. During crucial stretches we see Salieri sitting in a chair in his apartment hearing ghostly voices more than thirty years after Mozart's death. So his memories of Mozart's crudeness, as he shares them with us, are exaggerated in the elderly man's mind.

For the original production of the play, during the scenes when old Salieri recalls performances of Mozart's music from long ago, rather than simply playing modern recordings of the pieces, Shaffer and Hall had the brilliant British modernist composer Harrison Birtwistle create electronic versions that slightly distorted the music—with chords blurring, voices fading in and out, notes lasting too long. It's as if we in the audience are hearing Salieri's faded memories of specific Mozart works along with him. But in recalling a piece, Salieri describes it in vivid, poetic, and penetrating language. Here is Salieri (that is, Shaffer) on the opening of the Adagio movement from Mozart's Serenade No. 10 for Wind Instruments (K. 361), which Salieri first heard, he explains, through a door to a music room for a concert he did not attend.

> It started simply enough: just a pulse in the lowest registers—bassoons and basset horns—like a rusty squeezebox. It would have been comic except for the slowness, which gave it instead a sort of serenity. And then suddenly, high above it, sounded a single note on the oboe. It hung there unwavering, piercing me through, till breath could hold it no longer, and a clarinet withdrew it out of me, and sweetened it into a phrase of such delight it had me trembling.

I wish I had written that. The play abounds in comparably rich descriptions of Mozart pieces, which we experience through Schaffer's words for Salieri and Birtwistle's hazy, slightly askew reworkings of the music.

The Forman film, in contrast, overflows with Mozart's actual music, which for me makes everything too literal. The story is told much more in the moment: we are there in the 1780s. And many, if not most, of those wonderful descriptions of Mozart's music are cut.

In the play and the film, Salieri becomes obsessed with the idea that the crude young Mozart, whose genius comes directly from God, did not have to work hard at composing the way Salieri did. In fact, Mozart berated himself constantly for being terribly lazy.

And yet he may have been the hardest-working composer who ever lived, if you think of the sheer number of works, especially the operas, he wrote during his short life. If Mozart felt lazy, that may have been because many pieces seemed to have come to him almost fully formed. In his preliminary sketches for, say, an aria from *The Marriage of Figaro,* you get a glimpse into his creative process. All Mozart needed to jot down was the vocal setting of the Italian words and a rudimentary bass line, with here and there a chord or two or a rhythmic figure. Clearly, everything else—inner voices, harmonies, orchestration, musical subtleties—was already in his mind, or, as the Mozart of Shaffer's play puts it: "Right here in my noodle. The rest's just scribbling."

Still, the process of "scribbling," of writing down what was left out of the sketches, must have been utter drudgery. You can imagine that he procrastinated all the time, which may explain why he felt lazy. A touching moment in the film version captures what this process may have been like for Mozart, played by the appealing Tom Hulce. Mozart is at home, in the wee hours, leaning on his billiards table. (Mozart was a passionate billiards player.) Music manuscript pages cover most of it. As Mozart, looking exhausted, jots down notes, with his free hand he distractedly keeps pushing a billiard ball, which slowly bounces back, and then mindlessly pushes it away again.

After leaving the archbishop's service and settling in Vienna, Mozart must have felt that the heavens were endorsing his boldness. No sooner had he arrived than a prestigious commission came to him, from the emperor himself, to write a comic German opera for the Burgtheater based on a libretto by Christoph Friedrich Bretzner titled *Belmont und Constanze.* Mozart embraced the project, a chance to write a fresh, funny opera in his native tongue for a popular theater. Naturally he wanted changes to the libretto, and these were made by the director of the theater. The result, *Die*

Entführung aus dem Serail (The Abduction from the Seraglio) was a break-through for Mozart, the piece with which he introduced himself as an artist-citizen of Vienna.

At the time, one criticism of this opera was that Mozart had lavished too much musical intricacy on a stock, slender comedy. The story tells of an earnest Spanish nobleman, Belmonte, who travels to an exotic pasha's palace in Turkey to rescue his fiancée, Konstanze, who is being held captive, along with Blonde, her feisty English maid.

But Mozart knew what he was doing. He understood that for comedy to be affecting as well as funny it had to be played straight and touch real emotions. A hint of ambiguity comes through even in the overture, which opens with restless martial music in the style of Turkish marches, complete with cymbals and drums, then shifts in the middle section to a forlorn minor-mode melody before returning to the march for a rousing conclusion, leaving you a little confused as to the intended mood of the opera to come.

Then we meet Belmonte, who, seeing the house where he believes his beloved is being held, sings a tender aria of relief and gratitude: a major-mode version of the poignant middle section of the overture.

Even in the opera's most excessive-seeming aria, Konstanze's "Martern aller Arten," Mozart reveals uncanny dramatic instincts. Here, the captive but defiant young woman declares that she would welcome pain and torture rather than betray her Belmonte. This nine-minute aria, which begins with an extended orchestral introduction, is at once a soprano showpiece replete with extreme vocal gymnastics and a mini–concerto grosso with elaborate solo parts for flute, oboe, violin, and cello. But in its very extremeness, the aria shows Konstanze seized with determination and roiling with emotion, a woman possessed. The stunning vocal difficulties the soprano must dispatch suggest that Konstanze is not someone to be doubted. The aria is at once mesmerizing and hilarious.

Some members of the emperor's inner circle and important figures in the Viennese theatrical establishment did not know what to make of *Abduction* at its 1782 premiere. Overall, though, Mozart scored a success. A production followed in Prague and eventually in other cities in Austria and Germany—more than forty during Mozart's lifetime.

Yet while upending German comic opera he was also engaged in more modest projects—for example, the Piano Concertos No. 11 in F (K. 413), No. 12 in A (K. 414), and No. 13 in C (K. 415), imaginative yet elegantly soft-spoken works scored for intimate orchestral forces. Writing to his father about these pieces he reveals striking self-awareness about his work: "These concertos are a happy medium between what's too difficult and too easy— they are Brilliant—pleasing to the ear—Natural without becoming vacuous;—there are passages here and there that only connoisseurs can fully appreciate—yet the common listener will find them satisfying as well, although without knowing why."

For the rest of his life, Mozart would compose works of all kinds: ambitious masses and symphonies, chamber music, songs, divertimentos, and dances. But opera and the piano concerto were the two genres that especially claimed him. And in 1784, a remarkable year for Mozart's instrumental output, he seemed at the height of his popularity among the Viennese, thanks in part to his success for a while at putting on subscription concerts.

This practice—in which a composer would contract a hall, sell tickets, and perform works—was taking hold in a field that had not much earlier been mostly the province of the nobility. That year alone on such programs Mozart wrote and performed six new piano concertos, numbers 14 through 19. These could only have been the works of a composer immersed in opera, a natural-born theater man. Slow movements become like arias for a "vocal" line in the piano and a supple orchestral accompaniment. The first movements overall, though loosely modeled on the sonata-allegro symphonic form with which Haydn had shown the way, are episodic and full of surprise turns.

Take the finale of the Concerto No. 17 in G, in which a jaunty theme is put through a series of variations that keep you guessing what will happen next. Toward the end, finally, impishly, the piano trails into a descending sequence of spiraling, elusive figures, chased by the perplexed orchestra.

There is a pause. And suddenly, a bustling theme over playfully dramatic string tremolos (rapid reiterations) in the orchestra signals what certainly sounds like one of those everyone-on-stage final ensembles in a Mozart opera. All the music lacks is a handful of singers and some Italian words.

For a season or so, the Vienna public could not get enough of Mozart's concertos. And for all the ingeniousness of the music, these are very public pieces. But Mozart also worked hard, uncommonly hard, on a series of works that were almost the opposite of public pieces: string quartets, inspired by a good friend, Haydn.

Haydn and Mozart, separated by twenty-four years, had become acquainted probably in 1783. With Haydn so often bound to the Esterházy household, he could only make periodic visits to Vienna. Still, he and Mozart become mutually admiring friends.

Haydn was the acknowledged master of the string quartet. Mozart studied Haydn's scores closely as they were published, even before the two had met. Sometimes he and Haydn joined colleagues for amiable readings of quartets at someone's home, usually with Haydn on one of the violin parts and Mozart playing viola. In late 1782, Mozart began composing a series of six quartets, numbers 14 through 19, that he would eventually dedicate to Haydn, commonly known as the *Haydn* Quartets.

Haydn first learned of them in February 1785, shortly after the last in the series was completed. Leopold Mozart had come to Vienna to visit Wolfgang, who with Constanze and their son Karl Thomas had moved to an apartment on the Grossen Schulerstrasse. Bad weather caused Leopold to arrive behind schedule, though just in time to attend a subscription concert at which Wolfgang conducted symphonies and arias and was the soloist in the dark, intensely dramatic Piano Concerto No. 20 in D Minor (a work Beethoven would later admire so greatly that he wrote cadenzas for the first and final movements). The concert was a triumph; Leopold was duly impressed.

The next night, Haydn was the guest of honor for an evening of chamber music at Mozart's home. This time he just listened, though Leopold played the violin and Wolfgang the viola, along with two aristocratic friends. On this momentous night for music history, Haydn heard three of the quartets

Mozart had been working on. Afterward, he told Leopold: "Before God and as an honest man, I tell you that your son is the greatest composer known to me either in person or by name. He has taste and, what is more, he has the most profound knowledge of composition." We know this only because Leopold later recounted Haydn's words in a letter to Nannerl.

Some months later, Mozart sent Haydn the six quartets with a dedication page that was published with the set. Perhaps Mozart was being overly effusive. To me, these words are the greatest tribute from one composer to another I know of (excerpted here from an elegant translation by Robert Spaethling): "A father, having decided to send his children out into the wide world, felt that he should entrust them to the protection and guidance of a famous Man who by good fortune also was his best Friend.—Here they are, distinguished Man and dearest Friend, my six children." Mozart adds that, "to be truthful," the quartets are "the fruit of long and laborious efforts." He begs Haydn "to consider with indulgence their flaws, which a Father's uncritical eye may have overlooked," and ends with a final expression of sincere friendship.

It's striking that Mozart emphasized how hard he worked on these pieces, how laborious the composition process was. Why were they so difficult to write? After all, here was a composer who could finish an elaborate piano concerto the night before he had to perform it.

I think it was this matter of motivic development, which I described in the chapter on Haydn, the technique of using small motifs and phrases as building blocks for an entire sonata, symphony, or string quartet—elements that run through and provide subliminal cohesion to a long score. Haydn practiced this technique with consumate skill; he practically invented it. Mozart could do it, but it did not come naturally to him, the way arias, operas, and concertos flowed from his imagination onto the page. He had an uncanny ear for adventurous harmony and a hard-won mastery of counterpoint that enabled him to tuck intricate, multi-voiced passages into his pieces, even into bustling ensembles in comic operas. But at his core he was a dramatist who found music to match the word, the moment, the emotion.

As I see it, in honor of Haydn, but also to challenge himself, Mozart decided to study Haydn's string quartets in order to learn more about motivic development and apply the technique to his own works. He succeeded stupendously. But it took enormous effort.

Mozart's determination to explore motivic development also may explain why a few years later, during the summer of 1788, he composed almost simultaneously what turned out to be his last three symphonies: No. 39 in E-flat, No. 40 in G Minor, and No. 41 in C (*Jupiter*). Though the scholarly record is unclear, these works seem to have been written neither on commission nor with the promise of a performance. Why did he compose them? I think he was again exploring the technique of motivic development and how it could be applied to ambitious symphonic structures. He certainly figured it out. Look at the Symphony in G Minor. Almost every bit of it can be heard as emanating from a pool of motifs that make up the first phrase, the opening theme. Having proven to himself that he could master this technique and write architectonic symphonies, Mozart put the genre aside and turned to other forms, especially opera. Had he lived longer he surely would have taken up the symphonic challenge.

Before returning to Mozart the stage composer, I'd like to discuss another issue relevant to the Piano Concerto No. 20 in D Minor: the concept of style. This also involves a personal recollection.

Performances of Mozart have long been hailed for their sensitivity to Mozartian style or criticized for their lack thereof. But what is this style? Refinement and crisp clarity are thought to be essential to performing Mozart. Lightness of texture, lithe tempos in faster pieces, elegance, and grace are considered almost requisite attributes of Mozart playing. But what about brashness and fervor, passion and intensity, heroic resolve and plaintive tenderness? These emotions run through his music as well. And think of the demonic hell-and-damnation finale of *Don Giovanni* or the overt anguish in the development section of the slow movement of the *Jupiter* Symphony. How do you convey such qualities while adhering to "Mozartian style," whatever that is?

As a teenage piano student with scant understanding of what made Mozart "Classical"—or Bach "Baroque," or Schumann "Romantic," for that matter—there was one thing I knew from direct experience: whatever its style, however it "should" be played, Mozart's Piano Concerto in D Minor was an overwhelmingly emotional piece.

I n the fall of 1963, when I was a sophomore in high school, and shocked, like Americans of all ages, by President Kennedy's assassination, I was immersed in learning the D Minor Concerto. My piano teacher had entered me in a concerto contest sponsored by an association of music educators in the greater New York City area, and my competition piece was that concerto. Though I studied the whole work, I played only the first movement for the competition. My teacher accompanied me at a second piano for the finals. I won.

The winners' concert in June 1964, shortly after I turned sixteen, took place at Town Hall, in New York City. During the first half, young pianists who had won various solo categories performed. After intermission, the Brooklyn Borough Park Orchestra, a hardworking amateur ensemble, conducted by Myron Levite, played for three student victors: a violinist in a movement of a Mozart concerto; a clarinetist in a movement of a Weber concerto; and, to end the evening, me, performing the Allegro first movement of the Concerto in D Minor. I can hardly remember the single rehearsal I had with the orchestra in a hall at a Y in Brooklyn, where the ensemble was based. But I remember being surprisingly un-nervous for the concert.

I have a recording of my performance on an old ten-inch vinyl LP. When I listen to it today, I realize why I felt no fear at the time. This is the playing of a young person swept up in the emotions of the music and the moment.

The performance is charmingly spontaneous and boldly emotional. I can hear myself feeling and expressing every yearning phrase, dramatic burst, and bout of anger in the music. Yet the piece challenged me technically. I had worked hard and knew it cold. Still, my passage-work, though pretty clean, even sparkling, sounds a little dutiful and well-practiced. I knew nothing of Mozartian style at the time. But the combination of deeply expressive feeling and carefully rendered execution sort of balanced out. Somehow I stumbled into a youthful approximation.

I played the somber, eruptive cadenza (a solo episode before the conclusion) that Beethoven wrote for this piece. For me at the time there was simply no difference between Mozart's writing and Beethoven's. The composer of the *Pathétique* Sonata, my first big Beethoven piece, could have written Mozart's concerto judging from the way I interpreted it.

How I wish I could still play that way. Now I know too much.

Mozart, an astute judge of librettos, was dissatisfied with most of the scripts he looked at. But in Lorenzo Da Ponte he found his ideal collaborator. The sought-after Da Ponte had studied for the priesthood in Italy and had been ordained but was expelled for luring women into adultery. He settled in Vienna in 1783 and quickly won appointment as poet to the Imperial Theater. Though he worked with every significant composer in Vienna at the time, he would probably be unknown today but for the three works he wrote with Mozart: *Le nozze di Figaro* (The Marriage of Figaro), *Don Giovanni*, and *Così fan tutte* (a phrase that resists easy translation, usually rendered as "Thus Do They All," meaning "They're all alike," referring specifically to women, who are by nature, the opera proposes, incapable of constancy).

Accumulated debts would force Da Ponte to flee to the United States in 1805, where he wound up teaching Italian literature at Columbia University and writing a risqué memoir in which he fashioned himself another Casanova.

Mozart, who had tried to entice Da Ponte into collaborating, finally hooked him with the idea for *The Marriage of Figaro*, which they began planning even before a commission appeared.

Anyone taking in *The Marriage of Figaro* today must remember that for audiences in Vienna in 1786, the work was viewed as a sequel, an operatic adaptation of the second in a trilogy of plays by the French ancien régime writer (and sometime watchmaker, diplomat, and polymath) Pierre-Augustin Caron de Beaumarchais. In Paris, Beaumarchais's plays had tapped into seething class grievances against the aristocracy that helped fuel the French Revolution.

The composer Giovanni Paisiello had enjoyed a triumph with his

Italian operatic version of the first play in the trilogy, *The Barber of Seville,* which played in Vienna in 1783. The story introduces Figaro, currently a barber by trade, but also a go-between and intrepid service provider. In Seville, Figaro bumps into his old boss, Count Almaviva, for whom he had worked as a servant. The Count is pretending to be a poor student in the hope of winning the affection of a pretty young girl, Rosina, the ward of the pompous older Dr. Bartolo, who plans to marry her, to the young girl's horror. There are complications galore. But by the end, Figaro has helped the Count to outwit Bartolo and win Rosina's love.

In the second play, *The Marriage of Figaro,* some years have passed. The Count, with his wandering eye, has grown tired of his wife, now the Countess Almaviva. Figaro, who has become the Count's valet, is engaged to sweet, feisty Susanna, the Countess's maid. But the Count, attempting to claim baronial privilege to the sexual favors of a servant before she marries, has been pursuing Susanna shamelessly. Meanwhile, Bartolo remains upset over having been duped and is seeking revenge.

Most of the audience members who attended the Mozart–Da Ponte *Figaro* would have known Paisiello's *Barber of Seville* and therefore been acquainted with these characters and their predicaments. Mozart was hoping to build upon that earlier success.

The Beaumarchais play had been banned from performance in Vienna by authorities concerned about the impact of a story in which clever servants manipulate their masters and dare to espouse ideals of equality. As the Count tries to compel Susanna to yield to him, the outraged Figaro delivers a bitter soliloquy denouncing the inherited rank and fortune that endow his master with such power. In the parallel moment of the opera, Figaro sings the slyly charming, subtly rebellious Act I aria "Se vuol ballare." To paraphrase, he says: Okay, Mr. Count. You want to dance with my bride-to-be? Fine, but you will dance to my tune.

Another composer might have had Figaro vent his frustration through vehement music. Mozart's Figaro lays out his intentions in a courtly yet muscular minuet, complete with pizzicato (plucked) violins and violas to suggest the strumming of Figaro's guitar, and softly insistent horn calls to lend the aria the air of a hunt. The musical subtext is powerful: Figaro is turning a dance genre with an aristocratic heritage into a vehicle for a servant's revenge.

The aria's effectiveness stems mostly from its rhythmic character. The harmonic inventiveness and melodic variety of Mozart's music have been much written about. For me, the best exploration of his approach to rhythm is in the 1983 book *Rhythmic Gesture in Mozart,* by Wye Jamison Allanbrook, an American musicologist. In this work, she analyzes *Figaro* and *Don Giovanni* to reveal that almost every aria and ensemble evokes, to some degree, a dance type, particularly social dances. Mozart, she argued, often chose the rhythmic character of an aria before settling on its melody and key. He had, in effect, a vocabulary of topical references, specific rhythmic gestures, and dance meters that would have activated specific associations among his listeners. Some of these dance types were obsolete when Mozart evoked them. Still, the character of the dance lingered in the public consciousness, much as a film score composer today might use swing, blues, or a foxtrot to subliminally convey something about a character or a dramatic turn in the story to an audience, including young listeners with no firsthand experience of those styles.

Having to soften the political barbs of the Beaumarchais play didn't really bother Mozart, who was drawn to the story for its exploration of relationships, sexual mores, gender roles, trust, and desire. During all the intrigues of Act I, the Count exudes courtly airs and, if the role is properly cast, dashing allure. Still, he comes across as menacing, sexually obsessed, and ultimately foolish.

Though we hear all about the Countess in Act I, we don't meet her until the opening of Act II, when, alone in her chambers, she sings the aching, ennobled aria "Porgi, amor," genuinely mourning the loss of her husband's affections. She and Susanna have an almost sisterly relationship. Yet when she agrees to contrive with Susanna and Figaro to entrap and expose her husband as a philanderer, the Countess feels humiliated that she must resort to such measures. After all, though not born to her position, she is a countess. All of this comes through in her other astonishing aria, "Dove sono," in Act III, when, bewildered, the Countess wonders how her marriage could have come to this point; then, in a rigorous, defiant, and vocally brilliant final section, she determines to make things right.

The other breakthrough achievement of Mozart as an opera composer, exemplified in *Figaro,* is the way he reinvents the operatic ensemble. Previously, in most comic operas, ensembles were vehicles for characters to sum up and state their feelings. Mozart turned the ensemble into a complex, dramatically charged device. Some of the most intricate elements of the story—complete with absurd turns and surprises—are advanced during these ensembles. Characters intrude upon one another, leap through windows, hide in closets, get into scrapes, overhear secrets, and escape close calls as an ensemble piece unfolds. The supreme example comes during the last twenty minutes of Act II in *Figaro,* during which a trio segues seamlessly into a quartet, then a quintet, then a sextet, until the dizzying final outburst with everyone on stage.

Figaro proved a success, but a short-lived one. During this period Mozart's chronic financial troubles began. The opera was presented in Prague, where it was a big hit. The citizens of that city loved Mozart and seemed to grasp his music. Admiring musicians there suggested he relocate. If only he had! Who knows, he might have lived decades longer and thrived there, away from Vienna, where the arts were overrun by royal power brokers, factions, and a fickle public.

Mozart did come away from that triumph in Prague with a commission to write an opera for the city's National Theater. The result was *Don Giovanni,* which had an acclaimed premiere there in October 1787.

When I first came to know this opera in college, productions tended to present Giovanni as a dashing libertine. More recently, many directors have emphasized the opera's bleakness and amorality, to make sure that audiences see through the surface charms of the title character and confront his depravity. For a production at the Salzburg Festival in 2002, the Austrian director Martin Kušej introduced a silent chorus of haggard, vacant-eyed, brutalized women who hover in the background almost continually, like the ghostly victims of Giovanni's lust. As I write this, American society has been galvanized by a wrenching and long-overdue scrutiny into the sexual harassment of women by powerful men. Yet Mozart and

Da Ponte described *Don Giovanni* as a "dramma giocoso," a phrase suggesting that the work has serious but also jocular elements. Is it still possible to enjoy the opera without recoiling at its content?

For me, and for countless lovers of this audacious work, Mozart and Da Ponte knew what they were doing—something theatrically risky, even radical. Yes, Giovanni is an aristocrat who uses his power, courtly grace, and manly allure to seduce women, and, when meeting resistance, rape them, by the thousands, if you believe the tally kept by his servant Leporello, who shares his findings in the so-called Catalogue Aria. But Mozart and Da Ponte also want us to be charmed by Giovanni, to envy his amorality and entitlement. And though we side with the honorable characters who make it a mission to bring Giovanni to account, as Mozart and Da Ponte wanted us to, at the same time we're invited to laugh at them, with their stiff moral rectitude.

The first scene opens with the appearance of Leporello, who immediately seems a stock comic character. He is waiting alone outside the home of the noble Commendatore and his virtuous daughter Donna Anna. Giovanni is in the midst of another attempted seduction, and Leporello mutters complaints about his lot in music that matches his mood—funny but a little forced, with a steady riff that ticks off the idle seconds going by. Donna Anna suddenly appears, chased by a masked man (Giovanni) who is determined to have her. The attempted rape is thwarted when the Commendatore arrives and draws his sword. In short order he is fatally stabbed by Giovanni, which leads to a short, stunning ensemble, a trio for three bass voices, each character absorbed with his own complex thoughts: the Commendatore, crushed that he is dying before being able to avenge his daughter; Giovanni, who convinces himself that, alas, he was forced to act once the foolish father challenged him, but seems a little shaken; and Leporello, distressed yet again by his violent master's recklessness, though he has long ago accepted his own servitude. But, he wonders, should he finally make a break?

In just minutes, Mozart's music conveys the moral quandary at the core of this opera. Giovanni is a proto-Nietzschean figure, a man who uses the privileges to which he was born to get what he wants. We are at once shocked by and envious of his amorality. That he is rich, powerful, and threatening enhances his allure.

Donna Anna, contentedly engaged to the upright Don Ottavio, is a tragic figure bent on finding and calling to punishment the mysterious man who assaulted her. Yet Mozart, risking it all, invites us to laugh a little at her high-minded airs. Later, Donna Anna, realizing that the attacker must have been Giovanni, describes to Ottavio what happened the night of her father's murder. Something in her high-charged dramatic recitative suggests, just a bit, that Giovanni's seductive powers almost rattled her. Ottavio, though an earnest young nobleman, comes across as full of stuffy honorableness and not up to the task of taking down Giovanni.

Donna Elvira is one of the most complex characters in all of opera. She has had relations with Giovanni and seems to think herself his wife. Fulminating over his abandonment and betrayal in jagged, leaping flights of coloratura, she often seems unnerved with lingering desire and desperation to get him back. Her innate decency and nobility come through. Yet, as Mozart presents her, Elvira also seems preposterous.

Virgil Thomson gets at this uncomfortable dichotomy in a penetrating analysis:

> The play implies a complete fatalism about love and about revenge. Don Giovanni gets away with everything, Donna Elvira with nothing. Donna Anna never succeeds in avenging her father's unjust murder. Punishment of this is left to supernatural agencies. Love is not punished at all. . . . Mozart is kind to these people and pokes fun at every one of them. The balance between sympathy and observation is so neat as to be almost miraculous. Don Giovanni is one of the funniest shows in the world and one of the most terrifying. It is all about love, and it kids love to a fare-ye-well. It is the world's greatest opera and the world's greatest parody of opera. It is a moral entertainment so movingly human that the morality gets lost before the play is scarcely started.

Even the supernatural scenes are ambiguous, at once amusing and chilling, including the turning point in Act II when, fresh from another attempted seduction, Giovanni encounters a life-size statue of the Commendatore. The statue, seemingly alive, speaks to Giovanni, calling this rapacious, unrepentant seducer and murderer to account. Rather than cowering, Giovanni invites the statue to dinner. Later, the statue shows up, pounding on the door to Giovanni's dining room, and then entering, as the ominous opening chords of the overture are reprised, along with those hypnotic rising and falling minor scales. Before long, the floor opens and Giovanni is sucked into an inferno amid fire, smoke, and a wailing offstage chorus.

The opera could have ended here. But Mozart and Da Ponte knew better. All the other characters assemble, peer down the cavern in Giovanni's floor, and basically say, Ah, well, right has been done. They then share plans for how each intends to move on in an ensemble that grows increasingly animated, with a touch of forced energy. The oddly cheerful end makes you uncomfortable. As it should.

We know little about how *Così fan tutte* came about. But after a successful revival of *Figaro* in Vienna in 1787, Mozart and Da Ponte were commissioned to write another work for the Burgtheater. For generations after its premiere in late January 1790, the opera was considered trivial because of its seemingly silly story. It was not until the mid-twentieth century that artists and audiences began to appreciate the opera's greatness and psychological complexity.

On the surface the tale, set in Naples, may be absurd. Don Alfonso, a cynical older bachelor, has grown tired of hearing Ferrando and Guglielmo, his young officer friends, bragging about the virtuousness of their fiancées, Dorabella and Fiordiligi, who are sisters. Declaring that women are incapable of fidelity, Alfonso challenges the naïve young men to a wager to prove his point. He concocts a plan that Ferrando and Guglielmo agree to.

The men explain to their fiancées that they have been called into action and must leave immediately. Later that day they return in disguise (usually looking like exotic Albanians). Each then proceeds to woo the other's beloved. After a convoluted series of ploys and plot twists, the men succeed. Not only do the women succumb, but they sign marriage contracts in a makeshift dual ceremony. When the outraged officers return and reveal all, they reject their former fiancées bitterly. But Alfonso urges them to accept that "all women are thus" and marry their sweethearts anyway. Yet at the end, who winds up with whom is left strangely unclear.

To me the opera is not really about the presumed faithlessness of women or the inflated pride of young men willing to put their fiancées through a cruel test. It's about the arbitrary element of romantic attachments and emotional fulfillment. *Così* suggests that romantic pairings are more capricious, more elusive, than we might like to admit. How much hold should raw sexual desire have over our life choices? Other needs and drives figure in: companionship, agreeability, even availability. This sister or that one, this officer or the other. How much does it really matter? Mozart, who was clearly consumed with music day and night, understood this firsthand. Having fallen in love with one Weber sister, when that didn't work out he just switched to another and got back to his music.

Still, the strands of unflinching duplicity for the sake of a mean romantic test that run through *Così* may make it even harder to produce convincingly today than *Don Giovanni*. And Mozart's music uncannily exposes all these strands at once. For example, there is the short yet astonishing quintet in Act I, when the two officers tell their fiancées that they must go to war, and teary farewells are exchanged. The orchestra plays a subdued yet restless chordal accompaniment while the distressed sisters haltingly ask their fiancées to write them daily. The men, faking it, of course, voice their good-byes in similarly broken phrases, as if struggling to speak. Then Fiordiligi begins a soaring melodic line, picked up by Dorabella, that becomes genuinely poignant. The four lovers eventually unite in overlapping phrases that crest into melting, pungent harmonies, buttressed by the orchestra. Meanwhile, Alfonso, in the background, mutters to himself that if this farce goes on another minute he'll break out laughing. Listening to this quintet, you don't know what to feel. It's hilarious and cruel; the young people have inflated sentiments yet come across as vulnerable, even the guys, who have moments when, the music suggests, they must wonder just how they got into this.

Mozart would write two more operas in 1791, the last year of his life, both rather makeshift projects. He hadn't planned to return to *opera seria* but did so when a commission came that he could not afford to turn down, to celebrate the coronation of Leopold II as King of Bavaria in Prague. Working with a collaborator, he adapted a 1734 libretto by Metastasio, *La clemenza di Tito* (The Clemency of Titus), that had already been set some forty times. This opera was a rush job, so much so that Mozart subcontracted the composing of most of the recitatives to another composer, probably his junior colleague Franz Xaver Süssmayr. There are grand elements and distinguished music in *Clemenza,* even though it is not the kind of integrated work that Mozart could have composed in better circumstances.

The other project, *Die Zauberflöte* (The Magic Flute), was a joy for Mozart from start to finish, though hectic in its creation. The fairy-tale story and text came from Emanuel Schikaneder, a theater impresario and actor who had taken charge of a kind of people's theater in what was then suburban Vienna. He wanted something light, a German singspiel, with spoken dialogue, a piece that would allow for stage tricks, magic, and special effects. Naturally he wrote a big, hammy part for himself to play: the bird catcher Papageno, who seems a little birdlike and pines for a wife. And, with some risk, he and Mozart, fellow Masons, dared to plant thinly disguised evocations of secret Masonic rituals in the opera. The character of Sarastro, the high priest of the brothers in the Temple of Wisdom, could be confused with a leader of a Masonic lodge in Mozart's Vienna.

Schikaneder kept altering the libretto, telling Mozart what tweaks he wanted and insisting that comic scenes be added. Mozart basically agreed to everything. Why was he so compliant? Because by this point, I'm sure, he was so confident of his skills as a composer for the theater that he could tap emotional resonances no matter how silly the plot.

Actually, I find *The Magic Flute* an uncannily spiritual work, the story of a confused young prince's quest for enlightenment. I prefer performances that draw out the mystical allure and depth of the music while basking in the comedic bits. My favorite recording remains Otto Klemperer's 1964 version with the Philharmonia Orchestra of London, the refined tenor Nicolai Gedda as Prince Tamino, the robust bass-baritone Walter Berry as a wonderfully hearty Papageno, and the soprano Lucia Popp as a demonically dazzling and ominous Queen of the Night. (The recording omits the spoken dialogue.) Then there is Ingmar Bergman's 1975 film version, performed in a Swedish translation, quite simply the best opera film ever made. There are hilarious scenes. Still, Bergman treats the story as a wrenching spiritual journey. This *Magic Flute* inhabits a realm not far from that of his film *The Seventh Seal.*

With *The Magic Flute* Mozart finally had a commercial success, though the run was not long enough. He made some money but still had accumulated debts to pay off. It was the prospect of future works like this one that lifted his hopes. I have often wondered what Schikaneder's people's theater was actually like. Who attended the show? Did those coming for the magic and pratfalls also respond to Mozart's sublime arias and austere choral anthems?

More or less in between composing *Clemenza* and finishing up *The Magic Flute,* Mozart received another commission when a rather mysterious messenger arrived asking for a requiem mass. It turned out that the messenger had been sent by his employer, one Count Walsegg, an amateur composer who was in the habit of paying others to write pieces that he passed off as his own at court. He wanted a memorial work for his wife, who had died recently.

As Mozart worked on the requiem, he grew deathly ill. Even if you include the sections of the score that Mozart was only able to sketch out, he composed no more than half the piece as it is known today. Constanze, desperate to collect the full commission after Mozart died, asked others to finish it. Süssmayr took on the job. The truth soon came out.

A myth emerged, fueled by Constanze, that in a horrific hoax, Mozart was poisoned by an enemy and had been set up to compose his own requiem. And the culprit pointed to in some circles was poor Salieri, who decades later, in his dotage, denied the accusation to visitors. Peter Shaffer could not resist drawing upon this juicy tale for his *Amadeus.* And in a way, Salieri may have poisoned the climate for Mozart at court by trying to keep him out of favor.

Mozart's death was probably caused by multiple illnesses, including renal failure, a condition that would have made him feel as if he had been poisoned, though his own body was causing the harm.

He died on December 5, 1791, survived by two sons and the despairing Constanze, frantic over how she would support the family.

In 2006, the two-hundred-fiftieth anniversary of Mozart's birth, I wrote an article speculating about what might have happened to him had he been in better health and lived as long as his sister, who died in 1829 at seventy-eight, an impressive age for that era.

Mozart would have made it to 1834. This means he would have survived Beethoven by seven years and Schubert by six. How would the symphonic output of Beethoven and Mozart have evolved had they overlapped in Vienna during those years? In 1829 the nineteen-year-old Chopin briefly visited Vienna and performed his first work for piano and orchestra, Variations on "Là ci darem la mano," the well-known duet from *Don Giovanni*. An old, flattered Mozart could have been in the audience.

Consider this. Over a span of about twenty-three years Mozart wrote twenty-two works for the stage, not all of them completed. That's nearly one per year. Imagine how many more operas he might have composed had he kept up that pace. Add forty-three years to his life and do the math.

ᥳᥱᥲ CHAPTER SEVEN ᥱᥲᥳ

THE GIFT OF INEVITABILITY

LUDWIG VAN BEETHOVEN (1770–1827)

During his many years on the Harvard University faculty, the formidable composer Leon Kirchner regularly conducted the Harvard Chamber Orchestra, a freelance ensemble hired by the college to give Kirchner an outlet for performing. Though awkward on the podium and not an adroit technician, Kirchner was a probing musician who conducted like a composer and excelled at revealing how pieces "work." His programs were always fascinating, including one I attended in the summer of 1984 at Sanders Theatre in Cambridge, during which I had an epiphany about Beethoven's Piano Concerto No. 4 in G Major, a work I had long revered for its strange combination of heroic and mystical elements, of feisty virtuosity and ethereal grace.

The Harvard program began with Walter Piston's Symphony No. 4, composed in 1950, a spirited Neoclassical score, a piece in which Piston deftly balances beguiling expressivity with clear formal design. I remember wondering at the time why the Piston symphonies were not played more often.

Then Kirchner conducted Debussy's *La Mer*. Now, as a composer, Kirchner, who studied under Schoenberg, was a complex modernist with a Germanic sensibility. Early in his life Debussy had been powerfully influenced by Wagner's music, and Kirchner instinctively drew out the weighty Wagnerian elements of this pioneering piece, completed in 1905. This was not the Debussy as atmospheric Impressionist. In this performance, *La Mer* came across as far more daring and contemporary than the Piston symphony.

Then, after intermission, the pianist Peter Serkin joined Kirchner and the orchestra for a performance of the Beethoven concerto. I should not have been surprised, I suppose, but on this night, in this performance, Beethoven's Fourth, completed in 1806, a century before the Debussy, seemed the most radical, risk-taking piece on the program.

A son of Rudolf Serkin, Peter Serkin, who had just turned thirty-seven, was born to an imposing musical family steeped in the great Classical heritage. In his youth Peter played Bach, Mozart, and Beethoven with insight, taste, and a sense of adventure. But he was also drawn early to contemporary music. Starting in his mid-twenties, for a decade or so, as he later told me, Peter Serkin played almost nothing but challenging contemporary works and did not even look at the Beethoven sonatas. When he started performing the classics again, he approached the repertory with renewed awareness for the startling, wild elements in the scores, for the intimations of music to come.

I had grown up with the recording of Beethoven's Fourth with Eugene Ormandy conducting the Philadelphia Orchestra and Rudolf Serkin, my early pianist hero, as soloist. At thirteen, I was thrilled to hear the elder Serkin play the concerto at Carnegie Hall with Ormandy and the Philadelphians, though I was too in awe to take away precise lasting impressions.

Still, many years before I heard Peter Serkin play the piece in Cambridge, I had formed a strong sense of its nature and shape, which seemed like a philosophical and often resolute dialogue between two characters, the piano and the orchestra.

The concerto begins with the piano alone, playing what seems less a thematic statement than a reflective proposition. The first sound we hear is a full, rich, calm G major chord, as if the piano were laying down not just the overall key of the piece but a starting point for discussion. That first phrase, initially all chords, is at once pensive, almost like a hymn, and restless, activated with a rhythmic riff of four eighth notes, a little reminiscent of the forceful dot-dot-dot-dash motif that opens Beethoven's Fifth Symphony, but here turned inquisitive. After a delicate rising flourish in the right hand, the phrase settles on the dominant chord, D major, which is what you might have anticipated, and awaits a reply.

The orchestra, just the strings at first, responds, starting from a completely unexpected B major chord, a bit outside the everyday realm of G major. The orchestra picks up the thought of the piano and puts it through some brief melodic and harmonic turns before settling on the tonic, G major. It's as if the orchestra has said to the piano: Hmm, that's interesting. I hadn't thought of it that way, but let's see.

At this point the entire orchestra goes through a full exposition of the piano's proposition, searching out every implication of the music, positing a contrasting, quizzical secondary theme that goes through minor modes, and building that initial reflective music into a teeming exploration of every inherent possibility.

For the rest of the movement the music maintains this dialectical quality. What's most astonishing is the way playful episodes—like when the piano tosses off rippling right-hand figures prodded by insistent left-hand chords—suddenly transform into mystical ruminations with probing melodic lines and lacy accompaniments. The development section, at its most intense, becomes fraught, dark, and eruptive. The piano's episodic solo cadenza, toward the end of the movement, becomes stormy, almost terrifying, but settles into a wistful, lovely trill that invites the orchestra to bask contemplatively on the theme. Yet the movement ends with a heroic, seemingly triumphant joint flourish.

Not so fast, though. The bleakly tragic slow second movement in E minor comes out of nowhere. I always feel as if some time has passed in the tale when this music starts. It's not a continuation of the first movement but another life episode.

The orchestra speaks up in stern unison octaves, sounding almost like some intimidating prophet, or an admonishing operatic basso profundo singing judgmental pronouncements in rhythmically clipped recitative. "What the hell is wrong with you?" the orchestra demands to know. The piano answers in meek chords, like a sad chorale. But this is less an explanation than a request: Please leave me alone. I'm crushed and I just have to feel this way for a while.

But the orchestra won't let up. It tries lowering its voice, being more sensitive. This approach works. Feeling less pushed around, the piano opens up and expresses sadness and confusion in despondent lyrical lines that could be wondering, What's the point of it all? A short, needling piano cadenza gets stuck on a prolonged trill that unravels into a defeated melodic fragment as the orchestra seems to relent, acknowledging that, yes, life sucks.

But then, as the piano traces the notes of a rising E minor chord, the orchestra, without break, tries out, quietly at first, a beguiling, dancelike theme that emerges in teasing bits, like mini-phrases, as if to say: C'mon, piano. When things look bad, get up and do something.

The piano immediately replies, and instantly seems to understand that the dancing theme is curiously ornate, for a dance, anyway. So in taking it up, the piano mischievously adds fancy trills and quick-spinning turns. The movement, a rondo (a form in which a main theme alternates with contrasting sections but keeps coming back), is off and running, an exhilarating yet somehow ambiguous dance, a dance that, using the same musical materials, can shift in an instant from heady to cosmic to crazed. I love that the last time the piano plays the theme, it has become so cocky it embellishes the melodic line with sort of mocking, *nyah-nyah* turns. The music settles down, seemingly content. Then a final, hypercharged coda breaks out. Yet there is still just a touch of the mystical in the triumph of the piano runs and spunky orchestra chords that conclude the concerto.

So what was my epiphany when I heard Peter Serkin play this piece with Kirchner at Harvard? Well, besides having intense feelings for contemporary music, Peter Serkin has a deeply spiritual side. He spent some youthful years exploring Eastern religions and mysticism. So he seemed especially alert to the cosmic elements of the concerto during this inspired performance.

And yet there was a kind of coolness, in the best sense, to his approach that made the Fourth Concerto seem more astonishing than ever. Nothing threw Peter that evening. Every strange, bold, beautiful, and mystical shift in the piece was presented as extraordinary, yes, but almost inevitable. This is Beethoven! This is life! What do you expect?

If you were to make a case for Beethoven as the greatest composer of all time, you would base the argument, I'd say, on the way his works—from a cheerful little piano bagatelle to the pathbreaking Ninth Symphony—sound inexorable and seem inevitable. For all their teeming restlessness, the strokes of wildness, the sudden shifts that come out of nowhere, and especially the mystical flights, the pieces sound like they have to be the way they are. Leonard Bernstein, in an inventive dialogue titled "Why Beethoven?" from his 1959 book *The Joy of Music,* describes Beethoven's gift of "inevitability." The composer "broke all the rules," Bernstein writes, "and turned out pieces of breath-taking rightness. Rightness—that's the word! When you get the feeling that whatever note succeeds the last is the only possible note that can rightly happen at that instant, in that context, then chances are you're listening to Beethoven."

It's not that Beethoven's pieces are monumental models of order and structure. Not at all. But they come across like audacious entities, even, I have found, in inadequate performances. Mozart depends upon good performances by artists with feeling for the style and a penchant for clear textures and crisp articulation. In a dull or careless rendering a Mozart piece can sound all tinkle-tinkle and superficial. But even in a shaky account of a Beethoven symphony or piano sonata, somehow the rightness of the piece manages to come through.

That Beethoven would become the master of inevitability is curious, given the chaotic household he was born into and the initial spottiness of his training.

His grandfather and namesake, born in present-day Belgium, was an exceptional musician who at twenty moved to Bonn, in the Electorate of Cologne, to accept a post as a bass singer at the court of the elector. He wound up as kapellmeister in that court. His son Johann worked as a tenor in the same musical establishment, supplementing his income by giving piano and violin lessons. Johann married a daughter of the head chef at the castle of Ehrenbrietsen. The couple had three children who survived into adulthood: Ludwig, the eldest, and his two younger brothers, Caspar Anton Carl and Nikolaus Johann, both of whom would figure prominently in Ludwig's later life.

Beethoven's life story has been subject to such mythologizing that it's hard to know the truth about him. What's indisputable, though, was his father's alcoholism. Johann recognized Ludwig's talents early on, and gave him keyboard lessons and some training in violin and viola. Johann was sociable and enjoyed partying at his home with colleagues from the court— gatherings at which there was lots of music making and plenty to eat. But while often gregarious, Johann could turn mean and, if you believe Beethoven's later accounts, abusive. Johann saw the potential to promote Ludwig as a child prodigy on the model of Mozart. Initially he discouraged Ludwig from writing his own tunes and pieces, and did not oversee a coherent program of training for the boy. At one point Ludwig's keyboard lessons were entrusted to an eccentric newcomer to his father's circle, Tobias Friedrich Pfeifer, an actor and musician at a theatrical company, who enjoyed carousing with Johann and boarded at the home of the Beethovens' neighbors. The lessons were sporadic and, if one believes the stories, sometimes torturous. Tobias and Johann would drag Beethoven crying out of bed and force him to stand at the piano and play, sometimes as entertainment for guests.

A great turn in Ludwig's young life came when, at around nine, he began lessons with his most important early teacher, Christian Gottlieb Neefe, who was appointed court organist at Bonn in 1781 and soon needed an assistant. At what point Neefe entered the picture is not clear. Still, he began grooming the young Ludwig for the organist job and taught him composition. He was also a Mason who imparted some Enlightenment ideals to his charge, including a belief in civic reform and liberal education.

Perhaps the chaotic nature of Beethoven's childhood drove him to seek order through music, especially composition. Yet from the start he showed an uncommon gift for improvisation.

During that era, most performing musicians were also composers, and every composer practiced the art of improvisation. By the time Beethoven moved to Vienna, at twenty-two, a young man determined to make it in the city of Haydn and Mozart, his skills at improvisation were from all reports extraordinary. The composer Johann Schenk recalled Beethoven improvising on the pianoforte at the home of Schenk's acquaintance the Abbé Gelinek in 1792. This was his first encounter with the young Beethoven, who invited Schenk to sit beside him at the keyboard as he improvised.

Beethoven "struck a few chords and tossed off a few figures as if they were of no significance," Schenk later recalled. Then, "the creative genius gradually unveiled his profound psychological pictures. My ear was continually charmed by the beauty of the many and varied motives which he wove with wonderful clarity and loveliness into each other, and I surrendered my heart to the impressions made upon it while he gave himself wholly up to his creative imagination, and anon, leaving the field of more tonal charm, boldly stormed the most distant keys in order to give expression to violent passions."

Throughout Beethoven's triumphant early years in Vienna, he consistently astounded audiences with his improvisations at the piano. Even those listeners who were baffled by his compositions acknowledged that Beethoven was a protean improviser.

What were his improvisations like? We can only guess from the hints he left in composed pieces, like the Fantasia for Piano, Op. 77, thought by many to be essentially a written-down improvisation. I find the piece a little cumbersome, with overwrought, flashy passage-work, curious non sequiturs, and a jaunty central section driven by a dumpy little tune.

Beethoven's improvisations might be better represented by passages in his works that were written so as to seem like sudden episodes of improvisation. There are, of course, the solo cadenzas he composed for his piano concertos. When he performed his concertos he likely would have improvised the cadenzas, though he probably had in mind a general idea of what he wanted to do. But he composed quite a few cadenzas, including the elaborate, promethean one for the first movement of his early Second Piano

Concerto. In some ways that astonishing cadenza is so long it throws off the structural balance of this entire Haydnesque movement. But this surely is the impression Beethoven wanted to create.

Beethoven's *Choral Fantasy,* for piano, four vocal soloists, chorus, and orchestra, begins with a long, fantastical introduction for solo piano that comes across like a majestic and ingenious improvisation. It's revealing to listen to the way Beethoven fixates on some little motif—an oscillating interval of a major third, or a series of rising chords—and transforms it into an extended improvisatory riff.

Somehow, thinking like an improviser enhanced Beethoven's feeling for dramatic narrative and structure, a quality that can reinforce the sense of inevitability in his pieces.

Family life with an alcoholic father may have been chaotic for Beethoven as he entered adolescence. But he adjusted, while thriving under Neefe's teaching. Beethoven composed three piano sonatas, which are among many early works not included in his official catalogue, though the pieces were published in 1783. In a classic strategic move, the young Beethoven dedicated the sonatas to Maximilian Friedrich, the archbishop-elector of Cologne, seated in Bonn. "May I now venture, most illustrious Prince," Beethoven wrote in a letter, "to place at the foot of your throne the first fruits of my youthful works?" The elector recognized Beethoven's promise and subsidized his studies. When he died in 1784, his successor, Maximilian Franz, the youngest child of the Empress Maria Theresa, continued to support the teenage Beethoven. The elector fostered reforms inspired by the Enlightenment thinking of the day, while also instituting budgetary restraints. Though he approved Neefe's request to appoint the young Beethoven his assistant as court organist, he transferred part of Neefe's salary to the boy. Maximilian became the first in a line of patrons who took an interest in Beethoven, including Count Ferdinand von Waldstein, who arrived at the Bonn court in 1788 and became not just an enduring supporter but a genuine friend.

Beethoven had conflicting attitudes toward the aristocracy throughout his life. He disdained the entitled airs of royalty and thought of himself as an artistic aristocrat, equal to any count or prince. History sides with Beethoven's self-regard. Waldstein might be forgotten today but for Beethoven's magnificent *Waldstein* Piano Sonata, dedicated to the count. When called for, the composer could flatter potential patrons with the best of them. Still, he never overcame his feelings of envy and exclusion over his common birth. And he kept falling for unattainable aristocratic women, which inevitably doomed these romantic attachments.

With support from Maximilian, the sixteen-year-old Beethoven traveled to Vienna in the spring of 1787, an arduous journey of some eighteen days, with ambitious but vague goals in mind. He hoped to give some performances, make contacts, mingle in musical circles, and perhaps have lessons from, or even find a mentor in, Mozart. At the time Mozart was working fiendishly on *Don Giovanni* and was, as always, haggard and overextended. That he made time to meet the young visitor from Bonn has long been central to Beethoven lore.

Apparently, the story goes, Beethoven played some of his flashier pieces for Mozart and showed him scores to some chamber works. Mozart was not especially impressed, until Beethoven asked the master to suggest a theme for an improvisation. This finally won Mozart's admiration. He told some guests, "Keep your eyes on him," or something to that effect. A great story. But from my reading of Beethoven biographies, there is no conclusive evidence that the meeting went like this, or even that it took place.

In any event, within a couple of months Beethoven learned that his mother was gravely ill. He returned home in time to see her before she died, of consumption, as Beethoven explained in a letter to Joseph von Schaden, a supportive town councillor he had met in Augsburg during his journey to Vienna. "She was to me such a good, lovable mother, my best friend."

At sixteen, Beethoven became the de facto head of his family, responsible for his two younger brothers, since his father barely maintained his position at court and wasted money on carousing. By the time he was eighteen, Beethoven obtained a legal order that directly paid him half his father's salary. Besides Beethoven's work for the elector, he earned income by playing viola in the orchestras of the court chapel and the theater.

Beethoven may have first met Haydn when the master composer was traveling through Bonn in 1790, en route to London, for the first of two triumphant extended stays in that city. It's more certain that they met in 1792, when Haydn was returning to Vienna. The young Beethoven showed the master a work of his. During this encounter the plan for Beethoven to go to Vienna to study with Haydn was probably devised.

Mozart had died in 1791, so Waldstein, who supported the Vienna proposal, wrote his famous farewell note to Beethoven, assuring him that with diligence, he would surely receive Mozart's spirit through Haydn's hands.

With the count's stipend to rely on, Beethoven arrived in Vienna at twenty-two, full of ambition, yet with a smart strategic plan. Rather than attempting to make an immediate impression, he put effort into setting himself up and fostering connections. Initially, he was more intent on honing his skills than introducing himself to the public, though he performed in salon settings before nobility and word spread of his skills as a pianist and an improviser.

Lessons with Haydn, though, became the focus of Beethoven's first two years in Vienna. He clearly revered Haydn as a master composer. In letters he describes Haydn's works with deep respect and insight. Yet Haydn, now retired from the Esterházy court and emboldened by the hero's reception he had received in London, was busy with his own work. As Haydn's younger colleague Johann Schenk put it in a recollection, Haydn was "intent on utilizing his muse in the composition of large masterworks, and thus laudably occupied could not well devote himself to the rules of grammar."

By "the rules of grammar" Schenk meant the traditional principles of counterpoint. Beethoven had been advised that his skills in this area were inadequate. Schenk claims that he actually took on this component of Beethoven's teaching for Haydn, at first surreptitiously but eventually with Haydn's sanction.

Maybe so. But Beethoven's close association with Haydn during this brief period was formative. Beethoven studied the master's scores in detail. Before composing his first string quartet, he copied out the score of a Haydn quartet in full, a tried-and-true method to uncover the inner workings of a piece. Even in his last years, Beethoven still kept at this practice in preparation for composing.

To me, the most important lesson Beethoven learned from Haydn, the technique that decisively helped him achieve that "rightness" and "inevitability," as Bernstein put it, in his works, involved the use of motivic development. As I discussed in the chapter on Haydn, this practice involves using little motifs from the main themes of a piece—a few notes, a fragment of melody, a rhythmic figure—as building blocks for an entire movement, even an entire symphony. Haydn was a master of this technique, almost its inventor. Beethoven absorbed his teacher's practice and took it to new levels of sophistication.

To be clear, this technique does not involve forcing a movement, even a whole piece, into a cohesive shape by running it through with little cell-like motifs. Rather, the cohesion comes across almost subliminally through motifs subtly embedded in the music.

Bernstein gave a vividly clear explanation of motivic development at Harvard in 1973 as part of his Norton Lectures. The talks were later published as a book, *The Unanswered Question,* and released on video. Motivic development comes up during the talk titled "Musical Semantics," in which Bernstein explores the grammar, in a sense, of music, the elements that lend music its purely musical meaning.

To explain, he takes apart Beethoven's Sixth Symphony, the *Pastoral.* Bernstein wonders whether it is possible to hear this piece, which listeners over centuries have cherished for its seeming evocations of sunny meadows, country dances, thunder storms, and cuckoo calls, as "pure music, divorced from all its extrinsic, nonmusical metaphors." It should be, he asserts, since Beethoven himself cautioned that his subtitles for the movements and such were to be taken only as suggestions, not as tone painting.

Bernstein then embarks on an exercise, asking his audience to approach the Sixth Symphony forgetting all about "birds and brooks and rustic pleasures" and concentrating only on the music "in all its *own* metaphorical pleasures."

He then proceeds to break down the first movement, focusing minutely on little motifs in the first four bars that seem on the surface to comprise a "blithe little tune in F major," beginning on the tonic chord of the key and ending on the dominant with a pause, or a fermata, as it is called in music. Nothing could be simpler.

But, Bernstein argues, "these first four bars are the material out of which the whole first movement is going to grow, and it's not just the main material but the *only* material." Then he reveals how every phrase to come in this entire movement derives essentially from motifs within those four opening measures: the contour of the melodic notes; the rudimentary use of the tonic-dominant sustained tones in the bass; the rhythmic figure in the second measure. He goes on to offer a perceptive and completely convincing analysis.

This business of motivic development is sophisticated and hard to explain in words. But, as I have suggested, subliminally all listeners hear these embedded motifs in Beethoven's pieces, and nothing is more essential to understanding the composer's greatness. For this he had Haydn to thank.

In 1794 Haydn went to London for the second of his two extended residencies in that city, and the lessons with Beethoven ended. In 1795 Beethoven gave his first public performance in Vienna, playing one of his first two piano concertos. (Historians are not sure which.) Around that time his first published work with an opus number was issued, the Three Piano Trios, Op. 1.

And maybe an explanation of opus numbers would be helpful.

The Latin term "opus," meaning work, had by this time become the standard way to designate published pieces. So these three trios were published under one opus number, broken down as Op. 1, No. 1; Op. 1, No. 2; Op. 1, No. 3. Now, in his youth Beethoven had written a few other piano trios, which are included in scholarly catalogues today without opus numbers. That same year, 1795, Beethoven wrote his first three piano sonatas, published as Op. 2. He had already written three piano sonatas during his early years. But the Op. 2 sonatas were, in a way, the first pieces Beethoven wanted acknowledged as such.

This cataloguing system can seem confusing, because, for example,

Beethoven's Piano Sonata No. 4 has its own opus number, Op. 7. Most music lovers find the numbering of pieces within a genre more helpful to know than the opus listing. Still, it's often revealing to see which pieces a composer like Beethoven grouped together for publication and in which order.

With composers who had very spotty success with publication, like Schubert, the opus numbers assigned to his work just muddle everything. In the mid-twentieth century, the scholar Otto Erich Deutsche prepared a chronological catalogue of Schubert's works with "D" numbers (for Deutsche), a contribution that cleaned up the clutter. But with Beethoven, these opus numbers stuck. Pianists refer to Beethoven's mystical final Piano Sonata in C Minor far more often by its opus listing, 111, than by its number in the canon, 32.

In any event, the Three Trios, Op. 1, dedicated to Prince Lichnowsky, who would become one of Beethoven's most important and reliable patrons, sold well, fortified Beethoven's income, and boosted his reputation. He dedicated the Three Piano Sonatas, Op. 2, to Haydn. And for me, these works are especially revealing of Beethoven's early style and achievements.

I love that in these and his other early pieces, Beethoven comes across as a confident composer intent not just on equaling but on one-upping his master. In many fields, emerging creative artists struggle over how to respond to passed-down traditions. Some of them, especially young composers, I've found, try to announce themselves as brash new voices, not beholden to any heritage, however great. Others seem hopelessly bound to tradition, writing works that emulate their masters, especially their teachers.

For me, the choreographer Mark Morris early in his career offered a model to creative artists in all fields of how to cope with an imposing inherited tradition. His dances exuded a healthy balance between genuinely honoring while also having fun with, even poking fun at, tradition. Clearly, Morris loved many styles and practices of dance: courtly Baroque, classical ballet, ballroom, jazz, even the tried-and-true waltz. His pieces were filled with loving, insightful allusions to all kinds of dance. Yet he also played around with the tradition, spiking an elegant work with a same-sex pas de deux, or with kicks right out of a Broadway chorus line. Suddenly the fluid motions of some Morris dancers would be jazzed up with angular twists. An exhilarating aesthetic attitude would come through. I love the tradition, Morris seemed to be saying; I've been steeped in it and worked hard to learn it. But that tradition is *mine* too! I own it. So I can do with it what I want.

The young Picasso had the balance right as well. Clearly, Cézanne was an enormous influence on Picasso's early paintings. Yet with every brushstroke, you see, and almost hear, Picasso saying: Take that, Cézanne!

A similar attitude comes through in early Beethoven. In those first three piano sonatas, he doesn't just carry on the Haydn heritage. Rather, he picks it up and runs with it. His young, confident voice comes through on every page of those pieces: I'll show you how to write an up-to-date Haydn piano sonata! And soon, just wait, I'll show everyone what a Viennese Classical symphony can really be!

I especially love the jocular Piano Sonata No. 2 in A Major. That it's written in four movements—an impish Allegro, a deceptively elegant Largo (a slow movement), a delightfully playful Scherzo, and an elaborate Rondo with humorously overwrought runs and filigree—announces that Beethoven is taking the model of the Haydn piano sonata and giving it symphonic dimension. If you want to know why Artur Schnabel was regarded as the most respected and influential interpreter of Beethoven in the twentieth century, listen to his recordings from the 1930s of the early Beethoven sonatas. He captures uncannily that mix of homage and audacity. He brings perfect comic timing to the scherzo of the Second Sonata, especially in the strategic pauses he takes between certain surprising phrases in his delivery (to borrow a term from stand-up comedy) of the music.

During those first years in Vienna, Beethoven attracted more attention for his piano playing than for his compositions. It's hard to know what his pianism was like. Clearly, from many reports, he had elemental force and power galore. Harold C. Schonberg, in *The Great Pianists,* put it dramatically when he wrote that Beethoven's performances had "an ocean-like surge and depth that made all other playing sound like the trickle of a rivulet." Beethoven's performances must have had an organic conception, much like his compositions. No doubt a pianist like Muzio Clementi, who had a huge following in Vienna, played with more refinement and fine-spun fingerwork.

Yet Carl Czerny, who would later study with Beethoven, recalled that no one equaled Beethoven in the rapidity of his scales, double trills, skips across the keyboard, and other matters of technical elegance. This must have been true.

As I suggested earlier, Beethoven's pieces, from the beginning, at once astonished and baffled audiences of his day. They exuded greatness and gargantuan ambition but also excess and crudeness. It's fascinating to read the reviews from critics back then. The outright denunciations of the music as shrill and incoherent, if amusing, are instructive. But the reviews that reveal more about how Beethoven's pieces came across to the public are the equivocal ones. In flowering prose, a Paris critic in 1810 expressed bewilderment over Beethoven's Second Symphony. Beethoven, who is often "bizarre and baroque," the critic wrote, "takes at times the majestic flight of an eagle, and then creeps in rocky pathways. He first fills the soul with sweet melancholy, and then shatters it by a mass of barbarous chords." Well, in a way he does. Sounds pretty compelling, actually.

By 1800, before turning thirty, Beethoven had become a leading figure in Vienna's musical life, with obliging patrons and enthusiastic fans. Contradictory reports also exist about Beethoven's eccentric manner and personal appearance. That he hobnobbed successfully with royalty suggests that he could dress up and behave when it was called for, though he defiantly refused to play a subservient role and was known to stop in the middle of a performance at a salon if he sensed talking and stirring from his listeners, however aristocratic their pedigree. Yet acquaintances from those first years in Vienna recall Beethoven as short and insignificant looking on first impression, with a homely, pockmarked face and dark, tousled, unkempt hair.

Ferdinand Ries, a composer and a pianist who studied with Beethoven in the early 1800s, left a famous description of him:

In his manner Beethoven was very awkward and helpless; and his clumsy movements lacked all grace. He seldom picked up anything with his hand without dropping or breaking it. Thus, on several occasions, he upset his ink-well into the piano which stood beside his writing-desk. No furniture was safe from him; least of all a valuable piece; all was over-turned, dirtied and destroyed. How he ever managed to shave himself is hard to understand, even making all allowance for the many cuts on his cheeks. And he never learned to dance in time to the music.

Beethoven could be violent at times, Ries says, especially with servants. Yet he could also be a softie. H. L. Mencken, in a 1927 review of a Beethoven biography, wrote that the hapless, erratic composer "managed servants by alternately overpaying them and heaving crockery at them."

Still, Beethoven's unkempt, burly, peremptory persona only enhanced his mystique as a pianist and a composer. And his published works sold strongly from the start. Between a yearly subsidy from Prince Lichnowsky, among other grants, and profits from publishers, Beethoven lived quite comfortably, as he wrote in 1800 to Franz Wegeler, a friend from his Bonn days. "My compositions are bringing in a goodly sum, and I may add, it is scarcely possible for me to execute the orders given. Also, for every work I have six, seven publishers, and if I choose, even more. They do not bargain with me; I demand and they pay."

Yet, in that same letter, Beethoven makes a stunning confession: his hearing was becoming impaired. "The humming in my ears continues day and night without ceasing," he wrote. "I may truly say my life is a wretched one. For the last two years I have avoided all society for it is impossible for me to say 'I am deaf.' Were my profession any other, it would not so much matter, but in my profession it is a terrible thing; and my enemies, of whom there are not a few, what would they say to this?"

Another letter from those weeks in June 1800, to his childhood friend Carl Amenda, is even more poignant: "Only think that the noblest part of me, my sense of hearing, has become very weak. Already when you were with me I noted traces of it, and I said nothing. Now it has become worse, and it remains to be seen whether it can ever be healed."

At what point Beethoven's hearing impairment started is unclear, though by his late twenties, it would seem, he had the condition known today as tinnitus, the persistent "humming" he describes in his letters. It's tempting to consider, as some biographers have, that Beethoven channeled premonitions of hearing loss into some anguished movements of various early works, especially the piano sonatas. For me, this seemed evident in the Sonata No. 8 in C Minor (Op. 13), the *Pathétique*, written in 1798.

I still have my old Columbia vinyl recording of Rudolf Serkin playing the three most famous of Beethoven's titled piano sonatas: the *Pathétique*, the *Moonlight*, and the *Appassionata*. During middle school I spent hours listening to recordings, especially this one. These three pieces thrilled me, the *Pathétique* most of all.

I loved that the grave, slow introduction to the first movement opened with a crashing, thick minor chord. Then, as the pummeled tones trailed off, the phrase continued with a sighing, harmonized melodic turn. That steely opening chord was like a burst of fury, followed by a poignant gesture of feeble comfort. At that age, trying to fit in but feeling a little isolated in my solitary passion for music, I identified completely with the stern, roiling emotions of Beethoven's *Pathétique*.

Imagine how awesome it was for me to hear Serkin play the piece at Carnegie Hall around that same time. I had to, I *needed* to play this music. But though I could navigate most of the grave introduction, the tempestuous Allegro main section was technically beyond me.

Until my sophomore year in high school. I learned that first movement and played it during the entertainment interlude of a school function with invited guests. My performance, if marred by tangled passage-work and clinkers, conveyed plenty of tragic intensity, as I remember it. I got a standing ovation from my indulgent audience, full of parents.

The next year, having grown a lot as a pianist, I played the whole piece, including the melancholic slow movement, on a recital program that included shorter works by Scarlatti, the late-Romantic American composer

Edward MacDowell, Bartók, and Schumann, ending with a sloppy but impassioned account of Chopin's Second Scherzo.

That was the last time I played the *Pathétique*, curiously. During graduate school, the *Appassionata* became one of my big pieces. My struggles to play the *Pathétique* must have become associated in my mind with enduring adolescence. I think I had been too emotionally entangled with that sonata to keep playing it.

From Beethoven's poignant, confiding letters to his friends about his encroaching deafness, it seems he felt confident that some way or other he would be able to continuing composing. What he feared was being laughed at, dismissed. Who could take a deaf composer seriously? I've often been asked how exactly Beethoven was able to compose when his hearing grew weaker and finally failed him.

In some ways, it's not as unfathomable as it might at first seem. Most composers write pieces at an instrument, usually the piano, but many do not. Some prefer to sketch out music on manuscript paper (and these days, electronic gadgets), away from any sound source.

Eventually, however, composers who work without a piano to help them can try out what they wrote and hear how it sounds. Also, the ability to hear music in your head, which every musician has, to some extent, would surely lessen if you were deaf and not able to reinforce your aural memory. That Beethoven continued to reach new realms as a composer as he lost his hearing constitutes one of the great stories of adaptation to a disability.

In 1802, on the advice of doctors, Beethoven spent some months in the rural outskirts of Vienna in the town of Heiligenstadt, where he wrote what has come to be called the Heiligenstadt Testament. The document, addressed to his two brothers, reads like a will, though it is also a confessional, an explanation for his withdrawal. He never sent it. Yet the way the document begins suggests that Beethoven was leaving history an account of his anguish and his fears, including thoughts of suicide: "O ye men who regard or declare me to be malignant, stubborn or cynical, how unjust are ye towards me," it begins. "You do not know the secret cause of my seeming so."

Beethoven was driven to retire from the world, he writes, to be solitary and miserable. He wanted to redouble back to society. "Yet," he explains, "it was not possible for me to say to men: Speak louder, shout, for I am deaf."

Eventually the public learned of Beethoven's condition. He composed with renewed purpose and even kept trying to perform. Attempting to play his *Emperor* Piano Concerto in 1811, he came to grief. His student Czerny gave the premiere of the piece. Beethoven never performed as a pianist again.

This crisis, though, inspired him to be even more intrepid as a composer, writing works of startling originality and depth, increasingly unmoored from the models of Haydn and Mozart. Take the Piano Concerto No. 3 in C Minor, first performed in 1803. For all the moody shifts and intensity of the suspenseful first movement, Apollonian coolness and control run through the music. The sublime, soft-spoken melody that opens the slow movement, played by piano alone, soon takes a surprising turn: an inspired episode of lyrical grace, with a theme played by the piano in double thirds over a simple chord accompaniment. To me this passage anticipates the opera-infused melodic writing of Chopin. And the impetuous final Rondo has bursts of Promethean humor, though the laughs are kept at bay by the piano's almost manic busyness, right through the seemingly celebratory yet wildly spiraling coda.

This piece is emblematic of Beethoven's middle period, often dubbed, not helpfully, his "Heroic" period. For whole segments of the public, Beethoven became not just a composer but a colossus. He assumed the "problematic status of a secular god, his shadow falling on those who came after him, and even on those who came before him," as Alex Ross, the music critic of the *New Yorker,* wrote in an astute 2014 article. Problematic? Yes, because "after Beethoven, the concert hall came to be seen not as a venue for diverse, meandering entertainments but as an austere memorial to artistic majesty. . . . The musicians' platform became the stage of an invisible drama, the temple of a sonic revelation."

Politically and culturally, this was a fractious era, a period of seething dissent, with revolutions against entrenched aristocracy fired by philosophical principles of enlightenment and common good, however imperfect and unbridled. The time was ripe for an artist-hero to emerge, even more than a military hero. The rough-hewn, impolitic Beethoven, with his supernatural ability to transcend deafness and compose colossal works, fit the image perfectly.

Piece after piece was heralded by many as a revelation from on high. Ross quotes the extravagant review of Beethoven's Fifth Symphony by the author and composer E. T. A. Hoffmann, from 1810. "Beethoven's instrumental music unveils before us the realm of the mighty and the immeasurable," Hoffmann wrote. "Beethoven's music sets in motion the machinery of awe, of fear, of terror, of pain."

Whew. How were mere mortal composers of Beethoven's day to reach this bar? Why bother? The mind-set of the composer as oracle writing pieces that intervene in our lives and transform the world lingers even today.

This hit me especially during the conductor Kurt Masur's eleven-year tenure as music director of the New York Philharmonic, which ended in 2002. Masur, a noted Beethoven interpreter, was an eminent maestro and a principled artist, who was rightly admired for courageously standing up to the East German government during his long association with the Leipzig Gewandhaus Orchestra in the years before the Berlin Wall came down. At the Philharmonic, when events demanded that a concert make an important statement, Masur was in his element.

But Masur's Philharmonic had a poor record of presenting contemporary music and too often seemed a fusty institution stifled by its own legacy. In interviews, Masur would always insist that the great New York Philharmonic, of all orchestras, had a special responsibility to perform the timeless works of the repertory at the highest standards and to keep these towering pieces before today's audiences. But shouldn't the New York Philharmonic, of all orchestras, have a New York identity? Shouldn't it champion American music and living composers?

And what would Beethoven have said about Masur's belief that unending devotion to the masters comes first? During his whole life Beethoven fought cultural power brokers who maintained such attitudes. He was a pathbreaker, an insurrectionist. Yes, he had boundless confidence about his own greatness and wrote pieces intended to last. Still, he wanted music to thrive, grow, and change.

It's important to remember how confounding Beethoven's music sounded to whole segments of his audience. Even in 1836, nine years after Beethoven's death, a London critic still found passages of the *Eroica* Symphony "confused and unintelligible."

To be sure, Beethoven invited listeners to experience his pieces as bold, restless, and heroic, no work more so than the *Eroica*. Beethoven initially conceived the symphony as a paean to Napoleon. As Ross writes, "At a time when Napoleon was overturning the old order, Beethoven seemed to launch a comparable coup, and he nurtured an ambivalent fascination for the French Revolutionary milieu, to the point of contemplating a move to Paris." And yes, after that era-defining leader crowned himself emperor, Beethoven crossed out the words "titled Bonaparte" on the title page.

Still, the phrase "written on Bonaparte," written in pencil in Beethoven's hand, remained at the bottom of the page, as the composer and author Jan Swafford points out in his comprehensive 2014 biography. The piece as we know it, complete with a slow, noble funeral march, can be heard as one of the defining statements of "the power of the heroic leader, the benevolent despot, to change himself and the world," as Swafford suggests. Sounds like Beethoven himself.

Still, I prefer to think of the *Eroica* as a work of revolutionary music. Easily lasting fifty-five minutes if all the structural repeats are observed, it was the longest piece ever written in which all the sections—four massive movements—were derived from the same pool of linking motifs. What I mean is that while Bach's Mass in B Minor is a much longer score, it is structured as a series of shorter pieces; the *Eroica* Symphony is an organic entity, a triumph of Beethoven's mastery of motivic development.

And for all its heroic stirrings, the music abounds in audacious humor, especially the finale, a theme and variations form that plays around with two main themes: an almost laughably elemental one built on the main notes of the scale and a sort of singsong, this-way-and-that-way melody that sounds like a beery folk tune. The master pianist Leonard Shure, one of my most influential teachers, used to describe this tune as the "most Jewish melody" Beethoven ever wrote. Shure, who was Jewish and could get away with such humor, used to sing the tune, which sways this way and that way, in his crackling basso voice, fitting it with made-up Yiddish. And though Shure's singing was hilarious, his point about the character of the melody was actually revealing.

I'll never forget hearing Leonard Bernstein conduct the New York Philharmonic in the *Eroica* in 1966, not at Lincoln Center, but for a summer performance in a concert tent at C. W. Post College on Long Island. The program was the *Eroica* in the first half, Stravinsky's *Rite of Spring* after intermission. Bernstein emphasized the wildness, daring, rawness, and discomfiting humor in the symphony. Hearing it performed this way, juxtaposed with Stravinsky's 1913 shocker, I was hard put to say which piece was the more radical.

Heroics by definition would seem to entail struggle. And Beethoven's scores often sound like titanic struggles between opposing forces. There is, to be sure, something effortful, almost by intention, in Beethoven's music. As Leo Carey, an editor at the *New Yorker,* suggested in a review of the Swafford biography for the *New York Review of Books,* Beethoven "wants us to hear effort, and above all struggle." Swafford points out in his book that the composer wrote to one of his publishers that "what is difficult is also beautiful, good, great and so forth."

And yet, struggle in Beethoven does not quite come across as combat. Struggle, in a militaristic sense, has never explained what takes place in these pieces. For me, Virgil Thomson, in a charming and penetrating review of George Szell conducting the New York Philharmonic in Beethoven's Fifth Symphony in 1945, gets closer to explaining the true nature of struggle in Beethoven.

Now, the Fifth Symphony might at first seem the ultimate expression of combat between good and evil. Thomson, in his review for the *New York Herald Tribune,* written during the last year of World War II, starts out by stating that the Fifth Symphony has long been seized upon as a symbol of political liberalism, or "fate knocking at the door," or, more recently, of "military victory." Szell, he said, conducted a "thoroughly demagogic and militarized version of it." Still, Thomson, somewhat impishly, put this in context:

> There is no intrinsic reason, in this work or in any other, for considering contrast to mean conflict. The expression of strength, even of rudeness, in one chief theme of a piece and of pathos or tenderness in another does not mean that there is a war going on between the two sentiments. . . . And I cannot find in the last movement of it, for all its triumphal trumpets, any representation, thematic or otherwise, of the victory of either sentiment. I find, rather, an apotheosis, in which the two are transformed into a third expression, which is one of optimism and confidence, a glorious but still dynamic serenity. Neither assertiveness nor lyricism wins; they simply decide to cooperate.

"This is no picture," Thomson continues, "of military victory. It is the purest Hegelian dialectic, by which thesis and antithesis unite to form a third element, or synthesis."

What an insightful reading of Beethoven's Fifth, as a Hegelian dialectic, not a battle to the death where the forces for good win out in the end. And Thomson's comment on contrast being not at all synonymous with conflict applies to all music, especially Beethoven's, this symphony in particular. The inherent struggle is never-ending and dynamic on its own terms, as Thomson points out, and as Beethoven demonstrates in his music. Even Beethoven's commanding *Emperor* Piano Concerto is a kind of struggle, but a cool, all-knowing one—a struggle without sweating. The music will shift in mid-phrase from a dreamy rumination to a burst of thumped-out, burly notes and chords. The finale is a multi-layered dance, playful and sly, yet insistent and obsessive.

The premiere of the Fifth Symphony took place on December 22, 1808, at the Theater an der Wien on a four-hour Beethoven program that also offered the premieres of the Sixth Symphony (*Pastoral*); portions of the Mass in C; the concert aria "Ah! Perfido"; and the first public performance of the Fourth Piano Concerto, with the composer as soloist. For good measure, Beethoven included one of his solo piano improvisations. From press reports, the audience and critics seem to have been impressed, of course, but also stupefied. The recollections of Czerny, Beethoven's student, about his master's performance in the concerto—he described it as "mutwillig" (mischievous)—strike me as trustworthy: the composer may have incorporated impetuous variants into the piano part. This turned out to be Beethoven's last performance as a concerto soloist. Surely his hearing problems made continued concert work almost impossible.

According to Ries, if the story is accurate, during May 1809, as Napoleon's forces bombarded Vienna, Beethoven, terrified that the remnants of his hearing would be further damaged by the noise, took refuge in the basement of his brother's house and covered his ears with pillows.

I t has long intrigued Beethoven devotees that someone who composed music of such dramatic intensity had trouble writing a music drama, an opera. It took him ten years, through three quite different versions, before he finished his only opera. Ultimately called *Fidelio*, it is a glorious work, though still not quite right.

In his music Beethoven can seem supremely sensitive to the emotions, confusions, and subtleties of human feeling. But in his personal life he was prone to irrational mood swings—irritability one moment and downright sentimentality the next. And for all his intellectual fascination with free will and liberation, he was often rigid and moralistic in dealing with family and friends.

It's not entirely surprising that, when approached in 1803 by the Theater an der Wien in Vienna to write an opera, Beethoven picked a two-dimensional subject with a too-obvious moral dilemma at its core, a story of heroic determination to overcome unjust tyranny.

Based on a French drama, two plot strands interact awkwardly in *Fidelio*. There is a lighter domestic drama involving Rocco, a jailor at a prison in Seville, whose pretty young daughter Marzelline has grown infatuated with Rocco's hardworking, serious young assistant, Fidelio, even though the boyish Jaquino, who also works at the prison, has long pined for her. The other strand concerns Fidelio, who is actually Leonore, the wife of an honorable nobleman, Florestan, who has been imprisoned by the repressive governor of the institution, Pizzaro, for espousing dangerous liberal views. Leonore, thinking her husband could be the mysterious inmate kept in a secret cell, has taken a job at the prison hoping to rescue him.

One problem with *Fidelio* is Beethoven's awkward approach to the lighter scenes. When Rocco sings a jaunty aria preaching the importance of money to a young couple about to wed, the music is heavy-handedly amusing and clumsily intricate. Some of the ensembles seem unmotivated stock setups.

Dramatically, this is true even of the great quartet in Act I: Marzelline, Leonore (Fidelio), Rocco, and Jaquino each voice their inner thoughts, reflecting on their different situations. As in a contrapuntal canon, the voices enter one at a time, each initially singing the same melody. For raptly beautiful and humane music, Beethoven never surpassed this quartet. At the start, the orchestra plays a choir of melting, sustained, hushed harmonies in lower strings, with just a bare pizzicato bass line, an effect Mahler would mimic in several slow movements of his symphonies.

For the opening of Act II, when we finally meet the isolated prisoner, who is indeed Florestan, Beethoven pulls off a tour de force of shattering power. The orchestra slowly heaves and shifts, in passages that anticipate weighty, halting episodes in Wagner's operas. Finally Florestan cries out, "Gott! Welch Dunkel hier!" (God! What darkness here!). The monologue evolves into an outpouring of despair that builds to a wrenching conclusion in which Florestan, delirious, is seized with an angelic vision of Leonore.

The great Florestan of my experience was the tenor Jon Vickers. I heard him in the role only once, in 1976, with the Opera Company of Boston, a production directed and conducted by Sarah Caldwell. In this staging, the dungeon was so dimly lit that at first you could hardly see Florestan on stage. You just heard clanking chains now and then as he moved. Then, cutting through the darkness, Vickers, with his powerhouse voice, sang an anguished, sustained G on the word "Gott!" that just grew louder and scarier, until he, and the vocal line, collapsed into the phrase "Welch Dunkel hier!" Beethoven must have imagined the scene just this way.

A couple of years before the premiere of the final version of *Fidelio* in 1814, Beethoven's productivity started to decline, a stagnant period that would last for several years, owing in part to serious health problems, but also to family crises instigated by his own emotional needs and obstinacy.

Beethoven, who had a prudish streak, disliked the wives of both of his brothers. Johann was living with a woman to whom he was not married, his nominal housekeeper, who had an illegitimate child from a previous relationship. Beethoven took his distress to civic and religious authorities in Vienna, and in late 1812 Johann married his companion.

Beethoven disdained even more his brother Carl's wife, Johanna, who also had an illegitimate child from an earlier relationship and had once been convicted of theft. Carl loved her, it would seem, and was proud of their son, named Karl.

Ill with tuberculosis, Carl died in November 1815. Beethoven, having spent enormous sums on his brother's care, became embroiled in a custody fight with Johanna, whom the composer considered too morally unfit and financially irresponsible to be a mother. In letters he called her the "Queen of the Night." Just before Carl died, Beethoven had bullied him, it would appear, into adding a codicil to his will granting Johanna and Ludwig joint custody of Karl. But Beethoven wanted to raise Karl, then about nine, as, in effect, his son.

The story of Beethoven's legal wrangling with Johanna is a convoluted and, finally, pathetic tale. From the boy's comments about his mother in letters, he seems to have had warm feelings for her. How could the courts have deemed the eccentric, disheveled, moralistic Beethoven a superior parent? He kept claiming in documents that Johanna was bribing his servants to lie about the disorder of his household and his ill treatment of Karl. Still, by 1816 Beethoven had wrenched Karl from his mother's house and by 1820 had won sole guardianship. The boy spent long periods in private schools and seems to have had, at best, complicated feelings toward his possessive uncle, who demanded that the young man live according to rigid moral standards.

In 1826 Karl attempted suicide by shooting himself in the temple, twice, with two pistols, but the bullets only grazed him. He survived, nursed back to health at his mother's home. Against Beethoven's wish, but finally with his help, Karl joined the army. He and his uncle last saw each other in early 1827, just months before the composer's death.

Beethoven's various houses must have been forbidding places for the young Karl to live. Beethoven's friend Anton Schindler, who would write the first substantial (if not entirely trustworthy) biography of the composer, amusingly recollected Beethoven's obsessive washing and bathing practices. Beethoven would stand before the washbasin "often in extremest negligée," and "pour great pitchersfull of water over his hands." His servant would laugh, sending Beethoven into a rage. His morning ablutions also resulted in constant battles with his landlords when the water inevitably leaked through the floorboards, which helps explain why Beethoven changed apartments frequently.

Yet while wrangling with judges and terrorizing servants, Beethoven composed the seminal works that would constitute his stunning late period, notably the last five piano sonatas; his Ninth Symphony (*Choral*); the Missa Solemnis, his longest sacred choral work; and especially the String Quartets Nos. 12–16, the last five, written in overlapping periods of work between 1823 and 1826, almost as a valedictory.

Though debate lingers about the extent of Beethoven's hearing impairment during his life, biographers concur that during this late period he was completely deaf, long reliant on his "conversation books," in which visitors wrote out what they needed to tell him. What Beethoven spoke in return is often not hard to figure out.

Beethoven took his music into a mystical realm during these last years, producing pieces beyond stylistic periods, fettered to no era, timeless, sometimes entrancingly inscrutable. Yet in basic ways he turned inward as a composer during this period, which can also be seen as a purposeful retrenchment. He closely studied the scores of older works, not just Mozart and Haydn but Bach and Handel and even Palestrina. He kept turning to the theme and variations form; he became fixated on counterpoint, writing whole sonata and quartet movements in the form of complex fugues.

To some degree, the Ninth Symphony, the most famous work of this period, is the outlier among his late works, being almost melodramatic in its narrative sweep. Beethoven altered the concept of what a symphony could be in this work, writing a teeming, seventy-minute, four-movement score that culminated in a choral setting, with four daunting solo roles, of Friedrich Schiller's "Ode to Joy," music that shifts from episodes of frenzied exuberance to cosmic stretches. Yet during these years, in his personal conduct Beethoven was boorish, bullheaded, and impossible.

"All men are brothers," the composer proclaims in his exhilarating setting of Schiller's words. Consider the exchange he had around the same time with one of the many beleaguered copyists who were hired by Beethoven's publishers to transcribe the composer's illegible manuscripts—notoriously full of scratched-out bits, ink blots, and indecipherable notation—into a clean, readable score that could be handed to the printers. When the copyist who had been hired to work on Beethoven's Missa Solemnis returned the finished pages to the composer there were inevitably errors, which Beethoven naturally blamed on the copyist's incompetence, not the messiness of his manuscripts. Rather than endure Beethoven's abuse, this valiant copyist quit, writing directly to Beethoven: "I therefore request you not to rank me among those common copying fellows who, even when treated like slaves, think themselves lucky to be able to earn a living."

Beethoven, not used to being challenged, scratched out the copyist's words and returned the letter, adding: "To such a rascal, who really robs one of one's money, am I to pay compliments instead of pulling his ass's ears?" And on the other side he wrote: "Scribbler! Stupid fool! Correct your own faults, caused through ignorance, arrogance, self-conceit and stupidity. This is far better than to try to instruct me; for this would be just like the sow trying to teach *Minerva*."

To whatever degree the mystique of Beethoven the composer as colossus is losing its sway on audiences today, especially young audiences, that's probably for the best, both for the vitality of classical music overall, and even for Beethoven. It's easier to come to terms with his staggering works if you can listen to them like the ingenious musical compositions they are rather than as messages from an oracle beamed down to concert halls.

And yet, my musical life—my entire life, really—was shaped by formative encounters with Beethoven at his most colossal, especially a Beethoven recital Rudolf Serkin presented at Carnegie Hall on December 16, 1970, the two-hundredth anniversary, to the day, of Beethoven's birth. It was the fourth and final in a series of Beethoven sonata programs. I attended with my piano professor from Yale, Donald Currier, an elegant pianist and, like me, a lifelong Serkin admirer.

The program opened with a vibrant account of the Sonata No. 11 in B-flat, a bold, joyous work, a personal favorite of Beethoven's. Then Serkin played the *Moonlight* Sonata, a performance of refinement and, in the finale, fire mixed with exacting rhythmic clarity.

After intermission, Serkin played the Sonata No. 29 in B-flat (Op. 106), the mighty *Hammerklavier,* by far the longest, hardest, most forbidding of Beethoven's sonatas. In Beethoven's day it was considered confounding, excessive, and eccentric, though Liszt would become a champion of the piece. In 1970 the *Hammerklavier* was still regarded a work for select, fearless pianists who had the artistic insight and boundless technique required to play it, especially the wild, crazed, supercomplicated yet—if dispatched in the right spirit—exhilarating final fugue. Even Serkin, a distinguished Beethoven interpreter, had resisted the piece.

Hearing it that night, I felt as if I were among a privileged group invited into Carnegie Hall to experience a towering artist sharing a lifetime of work. (He had recorded it for Columbia the night before.) My teacher had played most of the Beethoven sonatas, but not that one. The ovation for Serkin was ecstatic, of course. Afterward, Mr. Currier and I started walking, almost in a daze, hardly talking, to Grand Central Station to catch the late train back to New Haven. It was raining that night. We hardly noticed and got soaked.

But in the years following that performance, a new generation of pianists cracked the code, in a sense, of the *Hammerklavier.* Peter Serkin performed and recorded it excitingly, taking much brisker tempos overall, playing with less weightiness and exacting rigor, more lightness and spontaneity, de-emphasizing the piece's monumental heft to bring out its adventurousness.

As a critic I've heard splendid, confident, very personal performances from pianists like András Schiff and Jeremy Denk. Young virtuosos of new generations, more inspired than intimidated by the piece, have brought the *Hammerklavier* to new audiences. This is all to the good.

And yet I can't help hoping that we don't lose completely that sense of Beethoven as a colossus, drawing upon unfathomable genius to create the *Hammerklavier*.

A month or so after his concert at Carnegie Hall, Rudolf Serkin played a recital at Yale, a different program, ending with Schubert's late Sonata in B-flat. I was able to go backstage and greet Serkin afterward, along with other students. I mentioned that I had been at the concert on Beethoven's birthday and thought his *Hammerklavier* stupendous.

Serkin thanked me. Then, looking right at me, as if confiding something, he added, "It took me fifty years."

He meant it.

CHAPTER EIGHT

"WHEN I WISHED TO SING OF LOVE IT TURNED TO SORROW"

FRANZ SCHUBERT (1797–1828)

In the fall of 1814, the seventeen-year-old Franz Schubert felt stymied by his circumstances and thoroughly miserable. He had recently completed a ten-month course to gain certification as a schoolteacher, at the insistence of his father, who ran a grade school located on the lower floor of the family house in Vienna. Schubert reluctantly joined the faculty that fall as instructor to the youngest students. He hated teaching. Reports suggest he was irritable with the boys and would slap them to attention when he grew impatient. It's hard to imagine that Schubert—bespectacled, a little over five feet tall, and rather dumpy—commanded their obeisance. His friends nicknamed him "Schwammerl," Austrian dialect for "little mushroom," or "tubby." The youngsters must have given Schubert a hard time.

By this point Schubert had hoped to be immersed in a musical career. Though his father's profession brought little monetary gain or social status, Schubert enjoyed a childhood full of music, including family string quartet sessions with two of his brothers, Ignaz and Ferdinand, on violins, his father on cello, and Schubert playing viola. He had spent five tuition-free years as a choirboy in the Imperial and Royal City College, where he received room and board and a quality education. He took part in performances of important choral works of the day by Haydn, Mozart, and Beethoven. He wrote pieces for the student orchestra founded and led by Joseph von Spaun, who was eight years Schubert's senior and would become a lifelong friend. Spaun ran the ensemble as a kind of symphonic workshop, providing Schubert invaluable early experience in composing for orchestra. As a student Schubert impressed the esteemed kapellmeister Antonio Salieri, who began giving him private lessons in composition.

Still, when his time at court ended, Schubert had to find steady work. His father's burgeoning school was the family business. What other option did he have?

The frustrated Schubert could not have imagined that he would die tragically in just fourteen years, that he would be buried in a Vienna cemetery near Beethoven, and that future music lovers would deem his proximity to the formidable master very warranted. Yet during those bad days of 1814, feeling terribly restless and stuck in that school, Schubert must have sensed what he was capable of.

As if to prove this to himself, and to the world, for that matter, on a single day that fall, October 19, he composed a harrowing and ingenious song, "Gretchen am Spinnrade" (Gretchen at the Spinning Wheel), his first time setting a Goethe poem to music. (Over his life he would set seventy-four more.) Schubert had already written a few dozen songs, but nothing like this one. Here was young Schubert, in near obscurity, seizing on the genre of the German *Lied* (art song), to create a stunningly compact, proto-Freudian monodrama.

In his three-volume encyclopedia of Schubert's complete songs, the definitive guide to this body of more than six hundred lieder, the pianist and author Graham Johnson suggests that the young composer identified with the character of Gretchen, a proper young lower-middle-class German girl, the tragic heroine of Part One of Goethe's *Faust*. Here is a young woman "on the brink of being engulfed by her own turbulent emotions and the strictures of a cruel world," Johnson writes. He adds that in Gretchen,

Schubert "recognized the new frank reality of the romantic age, his own reality perhaps, and the full implications of his song-writing destiny."

In this lyric from the play, Gretchen is at home, trying to busy herself at her spinning wheel. The dashing Faust, having been diabolically transformed into a young man, has romanced Gretchen, flattered her and made advances, but not yet taken her to bed. The encounter has thrown Gretchen into a crisis, awakening her romantic longing and physical desires.

Johnson's volumes include English translations of the song texts by Richard Wigmore. The original lyric begins:

Meine Ruh' ist hin,
Mein Herz ist schwer,
Ich finde sie nimmer
Und nimmermehr.

In Wigmore's English rendering:

My peace is gone,
My heart is heavy,
I shall never, never again
Find peace.

"Wherever he is not with me," Gretchen says, "is my grave." Her poor head is "crazed," her poor mind "shattered."

Schubert situates the song in Gretchen's modest, confining room. The piece, in D minor, begins with stretches that seem almost "drained of expression," as Johnson comments, written in a steady, swaying 6/8 meter, not too fast. An incessant rippling figure in the right hand of the piano evokes the continuously spinning wheel. The left hand provides both grounding bass notes and a click-clack repeated riff that represents the sounds of the foot treadle.

Like Gretchen, we listeners become fixated on the operation of that nonstop spinning wheel. Here is a distraught young woman whose sexual yearnings have been unleashed trying to lose herself in a confining domestic chore. Even her melodic line is at first constricted to a narrow range of notes, except in passing moments when feelings overcome her and the line lurches higher, as in the first phrase on the word "Herz" (heart).

When she speaks of her poor, crazed head, the music shifts harmonically and the melodic line rises, until Gretchen—and the music—settle back into dark D minor and the opening words are repeated. She glances out the window only in hope of seeing the young man, she says; she leaves the house solely to look for him.

In an inspired stroke, when Gretchen reflects on Faust's fine gait, his noble form, the smile on his lips, the music transitions to melodic strands that begin in F major (the relative major key of D minor). For a moment, Gretchen's pleasure in Faust's handsomeness seems to ameliorate her guilt, and she seems almost proud. Still, the music remains unsettled as it pivots through jumpy harmonic sequences.

Raw desire suddenly overwhelms Gretchen. Recalling his kiss ("Und ach, sein Kuss"), she leaps to a high F, then lingers on an intense, anguished G, the highest note in the vocal part so far. We suddenly realize that the spinning wheel—that is, the piano accompaniment—has stopped. This outburst is buttressed only by fortissimo chords. Then, haltingly at first, the spiraling right-hand figure in the piano starts up again. Soon Gretchen is back at work, repeating the opening lines.

The last part of the song builds to a climactic declaration. If only she could grasp him, Gretchen swears, hold him and kiss him as she yearns to, she would die from his kisses ("An seinen Küssen/Vergehen sollt!"). Here, Schubert's Gretchen anticipates Wagner's Isolde, who actually seeks death, longing for it as the inevitable, transfiguring fulfillment of love. In a song lasting three and a half minutes, Schubert covers much the same emotional and sexual territory as Wagner does in *Tristan und Isolde,* an opera lasting more than four hours.

In a 2014 interview for *Deceptive Cadence,* National Public Radio's classical music online magazine, Johnson remarked on how amazing it was that a seventeen-year-old boy "can somehow enter into the female psyche with such an incredible amount of understanding as if he himself had experienced such feelings."

Well, what if Schubert *had* experienced such feelings? Perhaps he understood all too well what it felt like to have his secret yearnings toyed with, to be overcome with desire for a handsome, confident young man.

I'm referring to the speculation, long debated by scholars and biographers, that Schubert, who died in 1828 at thirty-one, might have been predominantly gay; or, since in the early nineteenth century there was no such thing as a gay identity the way it's thought of today, that Schubert at least had erotic feelings for and sexual experiences with men, whatever the full range of his intimate life, which may well have also included relations with women.

Fewer than a hundred of Schubert's letters exist, along with scattered diary entries, writings suffused with the composer's mood swings—from childish joy, to melancholic resignation, to fatalistic despair. Not one Schubert letter to a woman (or letter from a woman to Schubert) survives. Most of those we have overflow with affectionate longing for male friends. Writing in 1819 to Anselm Hüttenbrenner, a musician and lawyer who was away in Graz at the time, Schubert, almost twenty-two, asked: "What has become of all those supremely happy hours that we once spent together? Perhaps you do not think of them any more. But how often do I!" Still, the letters we have contain no explicit references to sexual intimacy with another man, or, for that matter, a woman, though now and then he dropped intimations of interest in women. Writing to his brother Ferdinand in 1819, Schubert related that "in the house where I am lodging there are eight girls, nearly all pretty. So you see one is kept busy!"—though this sounds like a younger brother trying to prove himself.

The question of Schubert's sexuality burst into fractious scholarly debate in 1989, when an article by the respected musicologist Maynard Solomon, intriguingly titled "Franz Schubert and the Peacocks of Benvenuto Cellini," appeared in the journal *19th-Century Music*. As if conducting a psychological investigation, Solomon presented a case that Schubert's primary orientation—and perhaps that of a few friends in his circle—was homosexual.

When Solomon's article made news, as a gay man I found the revelation fascinating and the incensed musicological pushback within staid circles of the field all too predictable. Still, I thought that this component of Schubert's character, if true, had to be seen for what it was. That Schubert might have been gay was biographically illuminating. It lent depth and nuance to our understanding of him as a man. But did it have relevance to Schubert as a composer? I wasn't convinced.

That was then. Over the years I've come to feel that Schubert's experience with his sexuality—his strong drives and chronic torment, his coping mechanisms—profoundly impacted his music. That he might have been homosexual may in fact open up some mysteries about his music. In many Schubert works—from a spirited little waltz for piano to a complex, moody string quartet lasting forty-five minutes—you often have the feeling that what you are hearing on the surface is not what it seems; or, to put it another way, that Schubert composed in a kind of covert language, like someone speaking in code.

Explaining how this works is difficult. But first, what can we say for sure?

In rebutting Solomon's article, some musicologists pointed to specific instances where the author's readings of source materials were questionable. I wouldn't know. Solomon presents his article as an exploration of Schubert's sexuality, a possible interpretation of inconclusive biographical materials. I find his overall analysis to be very persuasive.

As a young adult Schubert enjoyed the companionship and solid support of a group of friends who playfully treated the short, unbecoming composer like a mascot, while revering him deeply. These comrades thought they had an unappreciated genius in their midst. When they started having informal musical evenings together at the homes of various well-heeled supporters, the sessions were dubbed "Schubertiades." Schubert's music was the featured attraction at these gatherings, which always included the composer singing and playing his latest songs at the piano.

That most of the men in Schubert's intimate circle resisted marriage has to be seen in the context of the rather oppressive times. A stringent marriage consent law in 1815 required prospective husbands to certify that they had the means to support a family. Only a couple of Schubert's friends came from families with solid finances.

It's striking, as Solomon points out, that several of Schubert's friends suggested either in contemporaneous letters or in recollections after his death that the composer's unbridled sensuality had a disturbing side.

One was Anton Ottenwalt, a writer and early member of the circle. In an 1825 letter to Joseph von Spaun, Schubert's older musician colleague from the choir school, Ottenwalt observed that their mutual friend was subject to "the passions of an eagerly burning sensuality." Then there were pointed comments from a memoir by Johann Mayrhofer, a poet who had a major influence on Schubert's development as a song composer, who studied law and became an Austrian censor. For two years, starting in 1818, Schubert and Mayrhofer shared a shabby room with a worn-out piano on a gloomy street in Vienna. Mayrhofer wrote that Schubert's character was a "mixture of tenderness and coarseness, sensuality and candor, sociability and melancholy." Josef Kenner, who had been a schoolmate of Schubert's at the seminary and became a civil servant, also wrote of the composer's "two natures, foreign to each other." All his friends, Kenner asserted, observed how powerfully Schubert's "craving for pleasure dragged his soul down to the cesspool of slime."

Cesspool of slime? As least during their youths, the men in Schubert's circle embraced liberal causes, forsook established religion, flouted social strictures, and shared artistic passions. If Schubert did have involvements with men, why would it be so disturbing to his chums?

Several often-quoted passages from a revealing entry in Schubert's 1816 diary convey the pervasive melancholy he experienced and his conflicted feelings about attachment and marriage:

> *Happy moments relieve the sadness of life. Up in heaven these radiant moments will turn into joy perpetual, and ever more blessed will be the vision of worlds more blest, etc.*
>
> *Happy is he who finds a trusty friend. Happier still he who finds a true friend in his wife.*
>
> *Nowadays the idea of marriage is full of terrors to a single man! He sees in it only dreariness or wanton sensuality.*

But another passage from this poignant diary entry speaks to me most:

> *A man's natural disposition and education determine his intelligence*
> *and his heart. The head should be, but the heart is, the ruler. Take*
> *people as they are, not as they ought to be.*

Take people as they are. Couldn't Schubert's friends, who adored him, take him as he was?

Solomon's article offers one possible explanation. He writes that Cellini, the great Renaissance sculptor, who, daringly for his day, was an unabashed homosexual, had involvements with adolescent boys referred to in coded language as "peacocks." In the most contentious strand of Solomon's argument, he speculates that Schubert may also have engaged with underage boys, in Vienna.

To be fair, Solomon goes into other possible coded meanings of that phrase. Still, for me, this speculation is the least convincing element of his article and the least relevant to understanding Schubert's genius. It's enough to know that Schubert, like Goethe's Gretchen, may have nursed longings for men that filled him at once with sensual excitement and shameful anguish.

The effort to detect elements of a gay sensibility in music has long been dogged by a simple question: What exactly is a gay sensibility? For that matter, what's a straight sensibility?

The composer Ned Rorem, a gay pioneer who in his early diaries, published in the late 1960s, wrote with blasé frankness about his love life in Paris and New York, has long debunked the notion of a generalized gay sensibility. "Tell me what a gay sensibility is," Rorem has often said, "and I'll tell you whether it exists in music." Susan McClary, an influential American scholar who has combined musicology with feminist music criticism, building upon Solomon's article, took it further in lectures and books. She attempted to pin down specific elements of Schubert's music that emanated from a homosexual psychological makeup—for example, passages that intentionally avoid clear tonal harmonic identity, wandering from key to key, from one ambiguous chord to another. It would be hard, and unfair, to summarize briefly her intriguing and controversial analyses.

At the time, I must admit, I poked fun at McClary's notions of "regressive" chords being a telltale sign of Schubert's homosexuality. In recent years I've come around some.

Gay people may not share a common sensibility. But over centuries, countless gay people have adopted similar behavioral patterns, that is, ways of getting through life, particularly about being closeted. It's that quality of speaking (or composing) in code that so often comes through for me in Schubert's music.

It's long been said that, in a passage of Schubert, when a somber minor-key melody modulates momentarily to a major key the music somehow seems sadder than before. On the surface the theme and the major-key harmonies supporting it may sound cheerful, but an undertow conveys a different message: that this seeming relief is fleeting at best, that such happiness is ultimately impossible.

One of the most telling examples of this comes in the solemn slow movement of Schubert's Piano Sonata in B-flat (D. 960), his last sonata, written in the final months of his life and published posthumously. Marked "Andante sostenuto" (slow, though at a walking pace, and sustained, that is, steady), the movement is in C-sharp minor and written in 3/4 meter. The solemnly stately, deeply sad theme is played at first in thirds and unfolds almost like a duet. The melody unfolds as if it were sighing. Almost every measure starts with a long melodic note that sinks into a restless group of shorter notes packed into the third beat: it's as if the melody keeps needing to take a quick breath before sighing again.

The movement is defined, however, by a persistent figure that clings to the melody: at the beginning of every measure, a bass note is struck, then repeated an octave higher (a broken octave played in a dotted-note rhythm), then topped off, literally, by yet another repetition of that pitch an octave up. So every initial bass tone is re-sounded, in a sense, four times, spanning three octaves. This insistent rhythmic riff is like a tolling chime of doom that never stops. The overall effect—with the aching theme, poignant harmonies, and numbing repeated figure—is bleak and tragic. The beauty of the music just makes it more so.

Yet eventually the movement shifts into an episode in which the theme is heard in the relative major key, an effect that may seem like a brief break from misery, providing a glimmer of comfort. Not so. Somehow the mood shift comes across as implausibly hopeful, almost deluded. Why? For one thing, that numbing repeated riff simply will not stop! Here is the covert element of Schubert's language. What he means to convey is that bitter sadness is inevitable in life. At least in his life.

Though melancholia and fatalism permeate his letters and his music, Schubert also wrote an enormous number of cheerful pieces. Some of these are lighter fare, like four-hand piano music, or songs for vocal quartets that were aimed at amateurs. But there are also whole long movements of major scores that come across as joyous and animated—for example, the buoyant, bouncy scherzo of the great Trio for Violin, Cello, and Piano No. 2 in E-flat. It's hard to detect subliminal sadness beneath the beguiling surface of that jaunty movement. (Of course, the preceding movement is a profoundly tragic Andante.)

And yet, even many of Schubert's seemingly happy pieces contain disquieting subliminal elements. This realization hit me decades ago on a sunny afternoon in Cummington, Massachusetts, in the Berkshire hills. I was a member of a summer community of the arts where residents—musicians, writers, and visual artists, ranging from college students to established professionals—lived and worked together on bucolic grounds amid scattered cabins, converted barns, and two old houses. The residents also kept up the place, including tending to a community garden.

One day, just before lunch in the main house, a hearty pianist named Miriam showed up holding an impressively large zucchini—the first of the summer. Miriam wanted this community milestone to be celebrated, so a pianist friend, Janet, and I sat at the old Steinway in the dining hall and started sight-reading Schubert's well-known Military March in D Major (the first of his three *Marches militaires* for piano four-hands). This march may be Schubert's best-known melody. Arrangements exist for chamber ensemble, military band, and full orchestra. Liszt wrote a piano paraphrase of it; Stravinsky incorporated it into his *Circus Polka*.

It struck me and Janet as the perfect piece—full of summer cheer and pride—to celebrate our garden's first bounty. So we started playing it. Miriam, holding the zucchini aloft, marched and danced around the dining room, soon joined by other residents, including several giggling kids.

But as we played the piece, I noticed as I had not before that after the initial flourishes (evocative of military bands) and the stirring, joyous theme, the march turns a harmonic corner and modulates briefly into a related minor key, then keeps toying with distant key areas. This second episode of the piece, while retaining the overall mood of steadfast cheer, becomes a little mysterious, even questioning. During a contrasting middle section, the music slows down and turns softer, more tender, with a lilting tune and wistful passages. With this change of mood, Miriam and the revelers stopped marching and seemed a little puzzled. What had happened to Schubert's chipper music? What kind of military march was this? A little girl had come near me and Janet to watch; she suddenly looked pensive. Then the spirited main section of the march returned and the dancing resumed. When it was over there must have been thirty people applauding me and Janet, and, of course, the glorious zucchini.

Schubert had an instinctive feeling for the folk tunes and rustic dances of his homeland. So did Mahler, but his affection for folk music carries a different emotional message. In the midst of a tumultuous Mahler symphony a little dance tune (say, an Austrian ländler) or a nostalgic folk melody will break through fleetingly; or a whole movement will be based on a folkloric form. When this happens, I usually hear the composer saying, in essence: Let's face it. Life is tough, the sorry world is a cataclysmic mess, and the only hope is to achieve spiritual transcendence. But these simple songs, even if the contentment they promise is illusory, at least give us moments of comfort. Mahler's message is inclusive. The implication seems to be that we're all in this together.

But Schubert seems to exclude himself from the collective "we." He is more like the lyricist Lorenz Hart, the first song-writing partner of Richard Rodgers, and a deeply secretive gay man. In one classic song Hart wrote, and wondered: "Spring is here! Why doesn't my heart go dancing? Spring is here! Why isn't the waltz entrancing?" Hart soon answers his own question: "Maybe it's because nobody needs me." And later: "Maybe it's because nobody loves me."

In Schubert's music, the pleasures of comradeship, jollity, and simple song are like gifts to us, portraits of good feelings that are not impossible, just impossible for him. In a revealing first-person allegorical story, written down in 1822 and titled "My Dream" (though that title was given to it later by one of Schubert's brothers), Schubert tells of a son, of several siblings who are all devoted to their kindly parents. The father takes the family to a feast. The man's brothers are merry, but the son, he is sad. "My father then came up to me and bade me taste the delicious foods," the story continues. "But I could not, and at that my father in his anger banished me from his sight." With his heart burdened, the young man becomes a wanderer.

Years later, his mother's death draws the son home, where, tears welling in his eyes, he mourns his mother and is comforted by the family. One day the father takes the son to a favorite garden. The son finds the place inexplicably distressing. Furious, the father strikes the young man and turns him away, even though the scorned son's heart remains full of love. Again, he wanders to distant lands. "Through long, long years I sang my songs," he writes. "But when I wished to sing of love it turned to sorrow, and when I wanted to sing of sorrow it was transformed for me into love."

Actually, this dream touches on several circumstances of Schubert's youth. His parents—his schoolteacher father and his humbly born mother, the daughter of a locksmith, seven years older than her husband—had fourteen children, nine of whom died in infancy. His parents supported Schubert's matriculation at the choir school and were enthusiastic about his music. Still, when they discovered that Schubert was neglecting his academic studies to focus on music, his father became distressed and banned him from the family home for a time as punishment. In 1812, when Schubert was fifteen, his mother died suddenly, a crisis that drew the family together and healed all enmity. A year later, Schubert's father remarried. (The couple would have five more children.) There would be other ruptures between father and son, the most severe when Schubert quit his father's school for good.

Schubert's first act of liberation came in the fall of 1816, right before he was to begin his third year of teaching. Instead, he left home and moved into a spacious apartment where a good friend, Franz von Schober, lived with his widowed mother and sister. Schober is a major figure in Schubert's life.

Born in Sweden to Austrian parents, sophisticated and well-spoken, Schober briefly studied law but wound up dabbling in the arts as a poet, sometime librettist, and actor, all the while burning through an inheritance from his father. Charismatic and handsome, Schober was long pointed to by Schubert biographers as a corrupting influence on the tongue-tied, impressionable composer. Schubert's friend Josef Kenner, in an often-quoted memoir from 1858, wrote that Schubert's "genius" attracted "the heart of a seductively amiable and brilliant young man," a person "endowed with the noblest talents," but who squandered his potential by shunning "a stricter schooling" and considered discipline as beneath him. Without naming him, Kenner clearly meant Schober, who, all told, "won a lasting and pernicious influence over Schubert's honest susceptibility."

Schober's "pernicious influence" does not seem to have involved emboldening Schubert in any homosexual crushes he may have had. From the evidence of letters and diaries, Schober comes across as an unscrupulous ladies' man, though, for what it's worth, he had two years of middling success as an actor in Breslau playing a comic character in female drag. Schubert clearly adored him. When he was ill, broke, and scared about his future, Schubert wrote to Schober, away in Breslau, that "no one else can ever be to me, alas, what you once were."

Gay men today trying to get a reading on Schober from the sources we have might recognize a familiar type: the attractive straight guy who enjoys, and even encourages, the admiring attentions of gay friends, but stops things at that.

Schubert moved into the Schober family apartment in the inner ring of

Vienna in the autumn of 1816, quarters decorated with Persian carpets and other touches in keeping with Schober's artsy tastes. Between 1816 and his death, in 1828, Schubert spent several extended periods living in various lodgings with Schober.

Even while bogged down with teaching, the young Schubert composed as if frantic to write down as much as possible. For some fifteen months, starting in the fall of 1814, he had a burst of creativity that the scholar Robert Winter describes as "virtually unrivaled in the history of Western music." There were sacred works, including two masses; the second and third symphonies; chamber pieces, including string quartets; several singspiels (lighter operatic pieces); and, of course, songs galore. On a single day—October 15, 1815—Schubert wrote eight songs. Since manuscript paper was expensive, when Schubert went on a song-writing tear, after finishing one he would sometimes simply draw a line under it and begin the next on the same page.

Schubert was a natural at song writing. For one thing, he was a consummately gifted melodist. But this skill was just a starting point for his achievement. A relatively short Schubert song can feel like a momentous work, touchingly personal yet containing the scope and depth of a symphony.

Schubert's musical imagination was fired by poetry. He had a perceptive appreciation for great poems. In an 1816 letter to Schober describing a musical gathering at which he had sung some of his own songs, accompanying himself on the piano, Schubert reports that his setting of Goethe's "Restless Love" was unanimously applauded, whereas his song on Schiller's "Amalia" was less well received. He had performed the first one better, Schubert explains. Still, he adds, "it cannot be denied that the essential musicality of Goethe's poetic genius was largely responsible for the applause."

Yet literary sensitivity alone does not explain Schubert's achievement in lieder. As the tenor Ian Bostridge explains vividly in a review of the Johnson volumes, "There will always be so much more at stake in song than the mere setting of words by music. Faithful, responsible setting can issue in limp, drab music," Bostridge rightly argues. "The best Schubert songs involve bodysnatching, ripping the heart out of a poem and giving it back to us again, transformed." That, he suggests, is why great songs can be made of poor poems.

An example for me is one of Schubert's most beloved songs, "An die Musik" (To Music). The text, an ode to the consoling power of music, is by Schober, and it's pretty trite. The words are addressed directly to "du holde Kunst" ("beloved art"), an homage from a grateful music lover. In how many bleak hours, the poet confides, when enmeshed in life's tumults, have you kindled my heart to love and borne me to a better world (to paraphrase Richard Wigmore's translation); for revealing a heaven of happier times, beloved art, I thank you.

The song Schubert makes of the poem, for all its musical distinction, is fairly straightforward. It's basically a simple strophic setting, that is, a song structured in repeated sections that follow the verses of the poem. You might not notice the structural breaks, because the song unfolds with such subtlety and melodic tenderness. The piano part mostly provides an accompaniment of slowly lapping chords. Yet there is also a dialogue between the melody and the bass line in the left hand of the piano part, not a constant dialogue but a captivating one. In a way, the bass "voice," to call it that, honors the sublime emotions of the melodic line by sometimes lingering on a harmonic pattern and deferring to the words.

That Schubert had an instinctively dramatic feeling for harmony comes through moment by moment in his songs: a pungent chord will stab a crucial word; an aching harmony will cushion a sighing melodic phrase. But his harmonic daring works structurally as well by bringing sectional definition to the segments of a song.

So far I have presented Schubert as the last of the Viennese Classical masters, the last of the Vienna Four. But he was also in the vanguard of the new Romanticism of his time, the movement that broke down Classical traditions and genres, found common ground with literature and philosophy, and explored the infinite while valuing deeply personal expression. Romantic fervor and experimentation abound in countless Schubert songs.

Take his terrifying rendering of Goethe's "Erlkönig." This is the chilling tale of a father furiously riding his horse home on a windy night, bearing his young son, trying to reach his farm, though who awaits him there is not clear. The son seems to see and hear the Erl King, a supernatural being, who calls to the boy, inviting the "dear child" to come and play beautiful games amid colorful flowers on the shore. The scared boy asks his father if he hears the Erl King too. The father reassures the boy. What he sees is just a streak of mist, his father explains; what he hears is just the trees rustling. But when the father finally arrives home, the boy is dead in his arms.

The dark, demonic music is run through with obsessively repeated right-hand octaves and chords (a notoriously difficult challenge for a pianist). Schubert dramatically fleshes out the three characters in the tale, four, really, including the narrator, giving each his own musical characteristics: the narrator's lines are midrange, in minor keys and ominously cool; the confused, susceptible boy is higher up, in pleading tones; the steadfast father has low-set phrases, sometimes switching to major mode as if to demonstrate solidity and calm; and the eerie Erl King, in an inspired touch, beckons the "handsome boy," as he calls him, in inviting major-key phrases. This harrowing song is a triumph of dramatic ambiguity. The seductive Erl King sounds almost more fatherly than the father, until, in a chilling turn, feeling rebuffed, the Erl King threatens to take the boy by force if need be.

There is another crucial reason that Schubert may have been drawn to lieder. Structuring large-scale works, like sonatas and symphonies, did not come easily to him. A poem provides a composer with a ready-made structure. You can mimic it closely by writing music that follows the verses of the text, or you can boldly play against the structure, by, for example, setting a poem with flowing music that does not adhere to the stanzas, what is called a through-composed approach.

Schubert's public profile as a song composer was enhanced considerably when he won a champion in the Austrian baritone Johann Michael Vogl, one of the most successful singers of his day. In 1813 Schubert had been deeply impressed to hear Vogl sing the role of Orestes in Gluck's *Iphigénie en Tauride*. They finally met in 1817. Though nearly thirty years Schubert's elder, Vogl took to Schubert and deeply admired his songs. Besides introducing them on his Vienna programs (his performance of "Erlkönig" created a sensation in 1821 and fostered its publication), Vogl took Schubert on several recital tours of upper Austria. Schubert had to indulge Vogl in his penchant for adding embellishments to the melodies and delivering crucial lines with expressive liberties, such as nearly speaking a word. "Vogl is here," Schubert wrote to Schober in 1824, "and interests himself almost exclusively in my songs." He adds that Vogl "rewrites the melodies and makes, so to speak, a living out of it." Still, Schubert was tolerant; and the collaboration benefited them both.

To add fodder to the speculation over Schubert's sexuality, it's interesting to note that Vogl did not refrain from singing Schubert songs with poems written in a first-person female voice. Also, Vogl seems to have been a dandy. Playing on Vogl's surname ("Vogl" means "bird" in German) and his interest in ancient Greek classicism, Schubert described him in one letter as "the Greek bird who flutters about in Upper Austria." Solomon points out that Schubert's friends routinely describe Vogl as an "old bachelor" and that his marriage at fifty-eight was a subject of grand merriment among Schubert and his circle.

For generations, Schubert's symphonic scores, sonatas, and chamber works, however remarkable the music, were thought to be ineffectively structured, too long, and repetitive. In comparison with Beethoven's inexorable-seeming structures, Schubert's sonatas and symphonies can come across as lacking cohesion and developmental thrust.

Yet over time, Schubert's structures, if unconventional, were seen as offering a different template for extended development. In 1838, a decade after Schubert's death, Schumann visited Vienna and was shown the manuscript for Schubert's Symphony No. 9 in C by Schubert's brother Ferdinand. The piece had languished, unperformed, since it was written in 1825. Schumann, overwhelmed by the score, soon celebrated it in a review for a journal he edited, famously speaking of the music's "heavenly lengths." Some readers have seen veiled criticism in that comment. I think that Schumann, a perceptive critic, vividly captures the essence of the piece. When a Schubert symphonic movement enters into a repetitive episode, it's natural to wonder whether some tightening might have been in order. Yet just try to come up with an expendable passage. The pieces somehow do seem to accord with "heavenly" pacing.

I was fascinated to hear Philip Glass, a pioneer of Minimalism, single out Schubert as a crucial influence on his own music. Glass did not mean that Schubert was some sort of proto-Minimalist. Yet there can be a ritualized aura, a transfixing quality, to Schubert's sonata-form movements. Often Schubert will take a theme that might already be rather long and put it through its paces during an extended development section. He will repeat it, without much trimming or concision, over and over as it goes through sequences and moves through different keys.

This aspect of his work really impressed me when, with two colleagues, I performed Schubert's Trio No. 2 in E-flat for Violin, Cello, and Piano, a long, challenging, and ultimately astonishing piece. During the development section of the first movement, the cello and violin trade melodic phrases based on, but slightly different from, the opening main theme. As this dialogue spins out, the piano plays passage after passage of downwardly cascading figures. This goes on, through various keys, for several minutes. For me, Schubert is saying: Okay, let's take some time to really ponder the inner qualities of that melodic phrase, not by picking apart its component motifs, but by letting it wander through harmonic realms and expressive planes. It's not at all Philip Glass Minimalism, which usually involves fixating on thematic or rhythmic repetitions. But the spellbinding effect in Schubert can feel similar.

Schubert's idiosyncratic way of handling symphonic structure may have been out of step with the composers of his day. But it powerfully influenced composers of later generations, especially Mahler and Bruckner, two Austrian late Romantics whose careers were centered in Vienna.

Beethoven's towering importance in the Vienna of the 1820s both inspired and intimidated not just the composers of his day, like Schubert, but those who followed him. Beethoven was the most famous and successful composer of his time; Schubert struggled continually to establish a career, with bouts of success alternating with long periods of financial stress. Beethoven knew of Schubert's work, especially his songs, and admired the young composer. Did they actually meet? The record, from my reading, is unclear. They were certainly not colleagues. I can imagine, though, that there were occasions when Schubert and his friends, sitting at some cafe, would see Beethoven—deaf, eccentric, a composer titan—passing by on the street, taking another of his self-absorbed walks, as was his habit. Conversation at Schubert's table would stop. He would point and tell his buddies, "Look, it's Beethoven."

Given Schubert's output and his high regard within musical circles, it's terrible that Schubert had limited opportunities to hear his large-scale works performed in public concerts by professional ensembles. He heard performances at Vienna's musical societies, of which there were many, but that was not the same. And then there were the Schubertiades.

The first documented one took place in early 1821. These informal gatherings were held at the homes of wealthier music lovers, with anywhere from a dozen to, at times, more than a hundred people in attendance. Naturally there would be dancing, drinking, socializing, and lots of high-minded, opinionated artistic conversation. The setting was especially conducive to singing songs and playing four-hand piano pieces. But ambitious Schubert compositions, including chamber pieces, serenades for instrumental ensembles, and excerpts from stage works were tried out as well.

These gatherings provided a place of refuge from the post-Napoleonic, Metternich-sponsored repression throughout the German Confederation at the time, including the Hapsburg-ruled Vienna that artists of Schubert's day had to endure. This atmosphere is described vividly by Ian Bostridge in his fascinating 2015 book, *Schubert's Winter Journey: Anatomy of an Obsession*, about *Winterreise* (Winter Journey), Schubert's wrenching cycle of twenty-four songs that trace a jilted young man's snowy trek into isolation and despair. Bostridge contextualizes the cycle in this book, which blends a song-by-song guide with an exploration of politics and wide-ranging topics, from the treatment of syphilis in 1820s Vienna to the allegorical history of the linden tree.

Schubert, like other artists in his circle, lived under a government that put ensuring domestic security above all else. There were crackdowns on liberal thinking, purges of reform-minded professors from their posts, and investigations into suspected revolutionary activities, including immoral behavior, often resulting in severe punishments. So, if Schubert set to music a poem espousing independence, however metaphorically, the song could be performed amid safety, and relative privacy, at a Schubertiade.

Though no radical, Schubert had his brush with the law because of his friendship with Johann Senn, a poet who harbored liberal ideals and openly supported Tyrolean independence. Senn, who had long been on a secret police list of suspicious individuals, was arrested in a raid at his lodgings in 1820, where he made matters worse by denouncing the government as "too stupid" to be able to penetrate his secrets. A few of Senn's friends, including Schubert, were there that night and also taken in. Schubert was released, Bostridge reports, with "a black eye and a severe reprimand." Senn was imprisoned for fourteen months and then exiled from Vienna. His friends regarded him as a hero.

If four-hand piano pieces were popular items at Schubertiades, there were also pragmatic reasons for Schubert's devotion to the genre. For generations, Schubert lore has held that the composer endured a lifelong financial struggle, from crisis to crisis, constantly dependent upon friends for both money and places to live. His energy and spirit, it was thought, were bludgeoned by the indifference of publishers and, for the most part, the public.

It's true that Schubert faced periods of near-poverty and that publishing houses mostly passed on his most ambitious works. His final years were particularly tough. "It is impossible for me to come either to Gmunden or anywhere else," Schubert wrote to a friend in 1826, "for I have absolutely no money, and everything else is going very badly with me too."

Still, he did enjoy some periods of professional success, including strong sales of published songs like "Erlkönig," and in 1821, acceptance into the main Viennese composers' society. His ebullient Fifth Symphony became something of a hit in town. And he made decent money from the publication of pieces aimed at the growing market for amateur music making: lighter songs, vocal duets and quartets, choral pieces for singing groups, solo piano waltzes and other dances, and, of special value, his four-hand piano pieces, which he produced in volumes.

The practice of writing compositions for two people seated at one piano did not really get going until the 1780s. With four hands available, the genre proved ideal for arrangements of overtures and symphonic works. Mozart composed a number of original pieces for piano four-hands. Schubert was the first major composer to embrace the genre eagerly.

Several aspects of the art form enticed him. Two pianists playing together, even amateurs, could produce quite a sound and dispatch lots of notes. So even a play-through of a jaunty little march could create a big impression in a living room. Also, Schubert made sure to include passages here and there where the hands of the two pianists overlapped. This compelled a moment of physical intimacy very appealing to a young man courting a young woman.

Schubert composed batches of four-hand pieces full of engaging touches and flourishes, but simple enough to be read at sight by dedicated amateurs. Other pieces were more elaborate, so that even professional pianists partaking in a Schubertiade surely had to practice beforehand, at least a little. Of this group one of my favorites is Schubert's Grand Rondo in A Major, an eleven-minute piece that begins with a wistfully beguiling melody over an accompaniment of flowing sixteenth notes and goes through all manner of dreamy, quizzical, and intense episodes.

Schubert wrote quite a few extremely complicated works for piano four-hands, notably one of his masterpieces: the haunting, episodic, often knotty Fantasie in F Minor. The theme, long-lined and elegant yet jumpy and anxious, is one of Schubert's most astonishing melodies. But this is no piece for sight-reading.

Nothing in Schubert's professional life frustrated him more than his inability to make his way in the world of Viennese music theater. He wrote his first works for the stage as an ambitious adolescent, to no avail. "The fact that the management of the Opera House in Vienna is so stupid and produces the finest operas but none of mine makes me pretty furious," Schubert wrote to Schober in 1818. In 1820, at twenty-three, he managed to have two light operatic works presented at Viennese theaters, to scant attention. During his short life he embarked on some twenty theatrical projects, many never completed. Even the few that made it to production were essentially failures.

How could a composer with such a dramatic sensibility and feeling for ambiguity, attested to by countless songs, not have been a natural for the stage?

For one thing, Schubert often wound up having subpar librettos to work with. There were many able librettists in Vienna, but the best were in high demand, and Schubert, with his record of failure, would not have been a good prospect for collaboration. He also made some bad calls. Choosing friendship over pragmatism, he teamed with Schober on a three-act comic romance, *Alfonso und Estrella,* both of them working hastily. The piece was rejected.

Also, only through pragmatic experience in the theater, and lots of it, can any composer learn the opera business. You simply have to get pieces produced and see how they work on stage and how audiences react in order to learn the ways of the genre.

These days, certain Schubert operas get performed now and then, sometimes even in full productions. The problems come through, including the shortcomings of Schubert's music. For all the beguiling tunes and effervescence of Schubert's score to *Alfonso und Estrella* and other stage works, the music seems dramatically one-dimensional. That covert language I detect in so many of Schubert's instrumental pieces and songs? It's mostly absent from his stage works. The music is awkwardly obvious.

The defining crisis of Schubert's life came at twenty-five, when he contracted syphilis. At that time in Vienna, the disease was rampant. Some records suggest that one in five people in the city carried this infection. The sexually promiscuous were inviting trouble, and whatever Schubert's orientation, he was known among friends for his insatiable sexual appetites. He may have contracted the disease from visits to prostitutes. The prognosis at the time was grim. Those infected might last from three years to a decade. In an awful way, an earlier death from comorbid conditions was merciful since mental breakdown and delusions were common in the late stages of syphilis.

You only need read a letter Schubert wrote in 1824 to his friend Leopold Kupelwieser—his most often-quoted letter—to understand the devastating impact of his illness:

> *To be brief, I feel myself to be the most unfortunate and the most wretched man in the whole world. Picture to yourself someone whose health is permanently injured, and who, in sheer despair, does everything to make it worse instead of better; picture to yourself, I say, someone whose most brilliant hopes have come to nothing, someone to whom love and friendship are at most a source of bitterness, someone whose inspiration (whose creative inspiration at least) for all that is beautiful threatens to fail, and then ask yourself if that is not a wretched and unhappy being.*

He kept working, composing being his best therapy. Schubert spent some weeks in a Viennese hospital in 1823 undergoing treatment. Amazingly, while there he began composing a masterpiece that would shape the remainder of his creative life and forever alter the genre of lieder: the song cycle *Die schöne Müllerin*.

In 1821 the young German lyric poet Wilhelm Müller, three years older than Schubert, published a group of twenty poems refashioned from an informal song-play he and some friends had created in a Berlin salon. *Die schöne Müllerin* (The Lovely Mill Maid) was intended by Müller to be either spoken or sung by a single performer, like a dramatic monologue. The poems tell a story, though crucial details are left to the imagination.

A young journeyman miller wanders the countryside in search of a mill to work at. Extolling the joys of carefree wandering, he follows a trail near a babbling brook, which he speaks to like a nature boy confiding in a friend. He comes upon a mill, where he secures work and immediately develops a crush on the miller's lovely daughter. At first he thinks his feelings are reciprocated, which sends him into bursts of delirious joy. But soon he realizes that the young woman has become infatuated with a hunter. The journeyman's fury devolves into despair and depression. He resolves to kill himself. At the end, he asks his friendly brook to give him rest beneath its water and sing to him as he dies.

Müller might be all but forgotten were it not for Schubert's interest in his poems. This monologue inspired Schubert to write what is really the first great song cycle with a compelling narrative structure. Other composers had done musical settings of groups of related poems by a single poet, notably Beethoven, who in 1816 wrote *An die ferne Geliebte* (To the Distant Beloved), a cycle of six songs on poems by Alois Jeitteles, a twenty-year-old medical student, that explore themes that preoccupied Beethoven: the sublimation of erotic longing into art and the power of song to form a spiritual union with a "distant beloved." Beethoven linked the songs musically by writing connective piano transitions. Still, the cycle does not really tell a story.

Die schöne Müllerin does. In this cycle, Schubert demonstrates gripping dramatic flair, psychological insight into human nature, an uncanny ability to convey emotional ambiguity, a knack for depicting scenes and settings in music—all the qualities so bafflingly absent from his operas.

In the first song, "Das Wandern" (Wandering), our young miller salutes the joys of wandering, likening his passage through the countryside to the constant flow of water and the continuous turning of wheels at mills. The music is hearty and evocative of a folk song, with a gently rollicking piano accompaniment. The second song, "Wohin?" (Where To?), would seem simple enough at first: the lad comes upon a babbling brook and, captivated, speaks to it. "Is this, then, my path?" he asks. Schubert inventively conveys the flowing waters through rippling piano accompaniments, a recurring device in the cycle's later songs. But already, in just the second one, Schubert suggests the psychological fragility of this seemingly hearty lad. When the young man questions the brook, the subdued music turns subtly intense, harmonically complex, and strangely serious. In the next song, the impetuous "Halt!" ("Stop!"), the wanderer sees a gleaming, inviting mill and thanks the brook for leading him to it.

From this point on, Schubert seizes on images and implications in Müller's poems to write music that suggests this lad may be inwardly troubled, even unstable. In "Danksagung an den Bach" (Thanksgiving to the Brook), having seen the lovely mill maid, he wonders whether it was the brook's plan all along to bring him together with the sweet young woman. "Is this what you meant?" he asks the brook, quite seriously. The guileless quality and yearning lyricism of the song are beguiling, yet a little weird.

As the cycle continues, it becomes clear through Schubert's settings of the poems that the lad is swept up in self-delusion. Clearly the mill maid has been nice to him. But you can imagine that he is conflating a few friendly exchanges into an expression of affection. He keeps turning to the brook for advice on what increasingly seems his pathetic love life. In "Ungeduld" (Impatience), convinced that the young woman has feelings for him, the lad wants to carve a declaration of love on every nearby tree. On the surface, the song is an insistent strophic setting of an exuberant poem, each verse proclaiming the young man's breathless joy, enforced by rippling rhythmic triplets that run through the right-hand piano part. Yet there is something obsessive, nearly unhinged, about the music.

Knowing that she loves the color green, the lad gives her a green ribbon. But when the hunter enters the picture in "Der Jäger" (The Hunter), the miller fires off an accusatory song directed at himself, in which riffs suggestive of hunting horns in the voice and piano become like battering rams. In the most psychologically exposed song, the lad sings with bitter irony of "Die liebe Farbe" (The Beloved Color): green! The green of weeping willows, of the merry hunt, of the grass covering the grave he now imagines for himself. The melody of this hauntingly slow song is complemented, most of the time, by a mimicking lower voice in the piano part; but the right hand becomes fixated on a repetitive single note, a numbing musical effect that reflects the young man's obsessive state of mind. You are not surprised when in the final song, "Des Baches Wiegenlied" (Of the Brook's Lullaby), the brook sings (or is the dying man imagining this?) a lullaby, assuring him that a cushioning bed awaits him beneath the gurgling waters.

The cycle was published in 1824 and won some admirers, but never caught on with the public. Schubert's friends, though, thought the work a breakthrough.

Schubert now lived and worked under the assumption that he would soon die. Not surprisingly, he entered even darker realms of feeling and experience in his work. That year, 1824, he produced two remarkable string quartets, his last in that genre: the String Quartet in D Minor, known as *Death and the Maiden* because Schubert used the melody of one of his most sorrowfully beautiful songs as the theme for the second movement, written in a theme and variations form. The String Quartet in G Major followed soon after. Though never publicly performed in Schubert's lifetime, the piece is today considered one of the most sublime, and demanding, works in the chamber music literature.

Four years after *Die schöne Müllerin,* Schubert set to music another cycle of poems by Müller, *Winterreise.* Schober had stumbled upon the texts, which had been published in two groups of twelve, and passed them along. This was not Schubert's final work; but with its combination of utter bleakness and staggering inspiration, it might as well have been.

Bostridge, as I've indicated, has written an insightful study of this work. The narrative of the story is not entirely clear. In the first song, "Gute Nacht" (Good Night), a young man has left the town where his sweetheart lives, seemingly rejected by her parents, who have lined up a better prospect for their daughter. Bostridge, like actors who make up backstories for characters they play when a script leaves out details, has come up with a more fleshed-out, rather Byronic one for *Winterreise.* He imagines that the young man was a tutor in the young woman's house, but overstepped his bounds and became too attached, forcing her parents to take action.

The first song, in D minor, sets the mood for the cycle and the course for the unfolding tragedy. The piano plays a downward-arching melody over a steady pattern of walking chords that never stops. The singer enters, saying "I arrived a stranger, a stranger I depart." The girl has spoken of love, he says; her mother of marriage. But now, rather than being driven out, he has chosen to find his own path. "Let stray dogs howl," he sings, as he begins a solitary journey through snowy woods, past distant houses, on a chilly road. Here is a prime example of the minor-to-major key phenomenon in Schubert that I discussed earlier. As the last verse of the song begins, when the wanderer says to his distant beloved that he will not disturb her as she dreams, the song slips into D major. But the turn toward harmonic tenderness, far from providing comfort, makes the music, and the wanderer's dilemma, seem even sadder.

During this daunting eighty-minute cycle, longer than most symphonies, the songs uncannily, sometimes horrifically, depict graphic images in the text: the young man's frozen tears on his cheeks; his footprints in the snow; the crackling ice of the frozen stream; the eerie image of the wanderer's hair turned prematurely white from the snow; the sounds of barking dogs as he passes by while their owners slumber. In one of the last songs, "Das Wirtshaus" (The Inn), the wanderer comes upon a graveyard. But he sings of it in a gently entreating melody over warm, inviting chords, likening the place to an inn for tired travelers. He is weary to the point of collapse, he says. Needing rest, he asks whether all the rooms are taken in this house, addressing no one, of course.

The only other person who appears in the cycle comes in the final song, when the wanderer chances upon a pathetic organ grinder ("Der Leiermann") standing beyond the village, playing the best he can with numb fingers. No one listens to this old outcast; no one sees him. We listeners know he is there, though, because we hear the man's bare-bones music in the piano, which slowly plays repeated iterations of a slippery open fifth (the most elemental interval) while the wanderer sings a despairing melody all the more powerful for its simplicity. Avoiding obvious melodrama, this wanderer does not commit suicide, at least from what we know; instead, at the end of the cycle he asks the organ grinder: "Shall I go with you? Will you play your hurdy-gurdy to my songs?"

By this point, 1827, Schubert was in poor health and continuously depressed. He clearly identified with Müller's wanderer; he must have worried that he would soon be experiencing delusions and near-madness. He tried out the cycle at Schober's place for a group of friends, who, according to Spaun's recollections, were shocked by the pervasive bleakness of the cycle. Schober said that only one song, "Der Lindenbaum" (The Linden Tree), had pleased him. Schubert reportedly replied that these songs pleased him more than all his others, and in time "you will get to like them too."

Schubert spent his last days at the apartment of his brother Ferdinand. His symptoms—fevers, vomiting, swollen joints—suggest he may have had typhus, or been suffering from mercury poisoning, since mercury was then deemed a treatment for syphilis.

On November 12, 1828, he wrote to Schober: "I am ill. I have had nothing to eat or drink for eleven days now, and can only wander feebly and uncertainly between armchair and bed." I have had a soft spot for James Fenimore Cooper ever since I read this letter, in which Schubert tells Schober how much he enjoyed *The Last of the Mohicans* and other Cooper adventure novels, and asks his friend if he might have "anything else of his." A week after writing this letter, Schubert died.

During the last few months of his life, Schubert also wrote his final three piano sonatas, all published posthumously. These have long been staples of the repertory. It's not uncommon for a pianist to perform them in order on a single, formidable program.

I had a touching experience with the last one, the Sonata in B-flat. I was making some videos with Gabriel Johnson, who was then a video reporter at the *New York Times*. I would sit at my piano in my apartment, playing and explaining music. This particular video was one of a series I did on the topic of moments in music that take you by surprise.

One of the most disturbing surprises in music comes in the opening movement of that final Schubert sonata. It begins with a songlike melody, calming and steady yet slightly wistful, played in warm chords by the right hand with the left hand playing the repeating bass notes, but also an inner voice of lapping eighth notes that lend the music a gentle impetus. The melody comes to a natural resting point over the dominant chord of the key.

Then, as that chord and the melodic note linger, the left hand drops out: it's like the floor of the music has vanished. Out of nowhere, deep in the bass register, the piano plays a long, ominous, unnerving trill.

Then, as if nothing has happened, the main theme starts up again, calm, a little sad, but familiar. This time, though, you don't trust it at all. What on earth was that disturbance about? you wonder. The melody takes a turn, as melodies do, and then settles down, but again, a different ominous low trill intrudes, this time taking us, almost dragging us, into the next section of the movement.

This movement has often been described as a premonition of death. Indeed, scary things—messages from the dark side, especially low trills—keep breaking into the music.

Gabe had his own perceptive way of describing this sonata. He was not a particular fan of classical music and didn't know much about Schubert. But in earlier videotaping sessions I had played other Schubert pieces, and Gabe had always felt the music strongly.

When we finished up the session on this late sonata movement, Gabe said that all the music I had played that day was neat, but especially the Schubert.

"Wow," Gabe said. "Schubert, he was like an alien."

I knew just what he meant, which was that Schubert was like some uncanny outsider, some hypersensitive outcast (a gay outcast?), who could zap down from wherever and zone right into our deepest, inarticulate feelings, even while seeming to mingle with us.

An alien. I never would have thought of that. It seemed right.

CHAPTER NINE

AN UNFORGETTABLE
DAY IN 1836

FRYDERYK FRANCISZEK
(FRÉDÉRIC FRANÇOIS) CHOPIN
(1810–1849)

ROBERT SCHUMANN
(1810–1856)

I f I could zap myself backward in time to hear just one legendary composer in performance, whom would I choose? The obvious temptations would be Bach at the organ in Leipzig, or Mozart introducing a piano concerto in Vienna, or maybe Beethoven tearing through the *Waldstein* Sonata followed by one of his audacious improvisations. Imagine hearing Liszt play his awesome Transcendental Études, or perhaps even more revealing, tackling Beethoven's daunting *Hammerklavier* Sonata, a score widely considered incoherent and unplayable when Liszt championed it. After attending Liszt's performance of the sonata in Paris in 1836, Berlioz wrote that this profound artist had solved the "riddle of the Sphinx" and revealed himself "the pianist of the future."

Yet I would pick Chopin, for sure. Perhaps the time he played his be-guiling, brilliant Piano Concerto in F Minor for an audience of some nine hundred in Warsaw a couple weeks after turning twenty, the triumph of a hometown boy; or later, at any one of Chopin's intimate salon performances for select audiences in Paris, a period when he largely avoided giving public concerts.

Why Chopin? Well, I can sort of imagine the formidable Bach at the organ. From all reports, Bach's playing effortlessly conveyed the mix of rigorous musical construction and bold imagination in his extraordinary organ works. And we have vivid descriptions of Mozart bringing uncommonly crisp articulation and lyrical lilt to the fortepiano. Beethoven? In my mind I can almost hear him, seized with inspiration, playing a piano of the day with such powerful intensity that his fortissimo chords would snap strings within the instrument. I even have an idea of how Liszt must have sounded, with his uncanny blend of staggering virtuosity, utter command, and superstar charisma.

But what was it like to hear Chopin? The reports we have are tantaliz-ingly elusive. Of average height for his day (about 5 feet, 6 inches) and very slender, Chopin was frail well before tuberculosis started weakening him in his thirties. From what we know, his playing had matchless beauty of sound and affecting refinement. He brought uncanny clarity to the inner voices of a multi-layered piano piece and dispatched long-spun melodic lines with the grace of a fine opera singer.

Writing to his family in 1829 from Vienna, where he had just given a successful concert, Chopin complained that "it is being said everywhere that I played too softly, or rather, too delicately for people used to the piano-pounding of the artists here." Yet in that same letter he reported that his improvisation on a Polish theme had "electrified the public." His per-formance of his Variations for Piano and Orchestra on "Là ci darem la mano" (from Mozart's *Don Giovanni*) was equally triumphant. After each variation, Chopin wrote, the "applause was so loud that I couldn't hear the orchestra's *tutti*" (meaning the orchestral introduction to the next varia-tion). So his playing can't have been overly delicate.

Also, a pianist who could rivet audiences with performances of formidable pieces like his *Heroic* Polonaise in A-flat, which bursts midway into a stirring episode driven by thunderous left-hand octaves, or the episodic Ballade in G Minor, which builds to a hell-bent coda, must have been able to summon flinty sound and ample power.

Chopin's reputation as a pianist was based on some thirty public performances he gave during his thirty-nine-year life. Still, his renown spread through the network of select salons in Paris. And the stream of published Chopin works, for which there was steady demand in Europe, must have suggested what his playing was like to buyers who could not hear him live.

If Chopin's keyboard pianism was enigmatic, so was his character, and in many ways, his music.

The son of a French immigrant to Poland who became a teacher at the Lyceum in Warsaw and of a devoted Polish mother, Chopin by nature was reserved, though he seems to have cultivated this quality as a protective device. He could be the epitome of graciousness with his perfect manners and impeccable dress. Yet conflicted emotions churned within him and he had a capacity to sting, as he let on in an 1839 letter from Marseille to his devoted Parisian friend Julian Fontana, who became Chopin's copyist and all-purpose assistant. "It is not my fault," he wrote, "that I am like that fungus which looks like a mushroom, but poisons those who pull it up and taste it, mistaking it for something else. I know that I have never been any use to anyone—but also not very much to myself."

That dichotomy applies to a great deal of Chopin's music, which has long been a little too popular for its own good, too readily loved for its surface charms and elegance. Take the celebrated waltzes, both the ones that swirl with captivating playfulness and those that sigh with melancholic lyricism. These are not waltzes for dancing, but Chopin's musical ruminations on the mystique of the waltz. Tucked within their appealing veneers are intrepid harmonic progressions, subtly complex inner voices, and hints of Chopin's radical streak. The fiery Waltz No. 14 in E Minor (Op. Posthumous) unfolds with nerve-wracking breathlessness and ends in a demonic torrent.

Consider the Fantasie in F Minor, composed in 1841, a substantive score of nearly fourteen minutes. By calling it a fantasy Chopin was emphasizing the work's formal freedom, and the music does seem generated by unbridled imagination. An opening section, like a solemn march, shifts between a theme played in low unison octaves and choralelike responses of almost poignant richness. Then the piece breaks into an improvisatory section of impetuous runs that keep stopping abruptly on tense chords. Wildness erupts, leading to an urgent theme over restless left-hand figures in triplets. Then, just when the music crests into seemingly triumphant chords, the swirling intensity returns. Finally there comes, out of nowhere, a pensive episode played mostly in yearning, subdued harmonies.

After more moody turbulence, the Fantasie drifts into A flat (the relative major key) and ends quizzically with undulant spinning figures that waft softly away. Almost as an afterthought come two solid fortissimo chords (in an unconventional IV-I harmonic cadence), making for a curious conclusion, stirring but a little blunt.

So is this piece a fantasy? In some ways, absolutely. Yet however elusive it may seem, the Fantasie is a strategically plotted composition employing an intricate network of themes and motifs in an overall structure at once fantastical and inexorable.

Chopin is often linked with Robert Schumann, born the same year, 1810. Though considered pillars of the Romantic era, they were quite different and had little direct contact. Schumann, born in Zwickau, Germany, lived and worked mostly in German cities, especially Leipzig. A bookish young man, he was raised in a literary household where music was cherished but not considered a pragmatic career path. Initially Schumann felt drawn as much to literature as to music. He would become a journal editor and critic, one of the most original and influential critics in Germany. Chopin, by contrast, was quite inarticulate when describing music, including his own.

Schumann was a failed pianist, owing to a lame right-hand finger, an injury or a condition Schumann may have exacerbated by using a chiroplast, a mechanical device for practicing. The actual cause remains uncertain. He was blessed to marry Clara Schumann (formerly Wieck), one of the greatest pianists of her day. Clara, who outlived Robert by forty years, became the most important champion of her husband's works.

Schumann was fired with enthusiasm for the Romantic currents in literature and the arts, ideals that embraced overt emotion and individualism, glorified nature, and extolled the past, especially medieval lore and myths, a rediscovery that took hold in Germany at the time. To some degree, Romanticism challenged the rationalism of the Age of Enlightenment, though Schumann, who valued craft in composition and worked hard to gain skills in counterpoint, sometimes spoke of "enlightened" Romanticism, a vague term that seems a typical critic's hedge.

Chopin placed much less value on aesthetic and philosophical movements, including Romanticism. In essential ways he kept himself apart from the larger world and its ideas, though his Polish identity was central to his being. George Sand, the novelist and proto-feminist with whom Chopin had a life-defining nine-year relationship, used to quip that Chopin was "more Polish than Poland."

Yet at twenty, Chopin left Warsaw to further his career and never returned. The outbreak of the November uprising in Warsaw in 1830 provoked Russia to crack down on Poland. Chopin made his way to Paris and spent most of the rest of his life in this city, where there was a large, active community of Polish expatriates. The failure of the avowedly liberal French constitutional monarchy to provide support to Poland incited intense pro-Polish demonstrations in Paris.

Both Chopin and Schumann had fervid musical imaginations. Yet the whimsical, innocent aspects of Schumann's fantastical side were not to Chopin's taste. These qualities run through Schumann's early works, like *Papillons* (Butterflies). This enchanting piano suite unfolds as a series of short, epigrammatic pieces, some of them practically fragments. The Schumann scholar John Daverio aptly described *Papillons* as "a gossamer tissue of premonitions and recollections."

Schumann's life and work were defined by emotional problems and mental illness that began in his youth, a subject I'll return to. Even in early letters and diaries he described hearing music and voices, experiences that both enthralled and overwhelmed him. Schumann described himself as having two personalities, two complementary internal characters: Florestan, who was impetuous, passionate, and hotheaded; and Eusebius, who was dreamy, wistful, and tender. He wrote important critical pieces in the form of dialogues between the two. Though this division within his psyche originated as a literary conceit, it can be seen as an early manifestation of mental disorder that would eventually cause Schumann misery and drive him to attempt suicide.

The best way to understand what links and separates Chopin and Schumann as composers, I think, is to view their work through the prism of Beethoven.

Even before he died, in 1827, Beethoven had established a paradigm of the composer as titan, a philosopher-hero striding across his time, across all times, creating monumental, enduring works, bringing symphonic heft not just to the symphony but to sonatas, string quartets, and other larger forms. Like many composers of his generation, Schumann held Beethoven in awe. This towering master was inspiring, yes, but intimidating. How could anyone write a symphony after Beethoven? Yet every aspiring composer felt compelled to try.

Not Chopin. As a young man he studied and admired Beethoven's works, naturally. But that whole Beethovenian symphonic imperative meant nothing to Chopin. He just wasn't interested. He loved Mozart and, after immersing himself in Bach's Preludes and Fugues, became a Bach devotee. And he adored opera, especially the Italian opera of his day. Chopin was entranced by flowing operatic lyricism, by great voices put at the service of long-spun melodic lines. He also loved the dances and character pieces of his homeland, like the polonaise and mazurka.

Yet Chopin was quite content during most of his life to compose for the piano, except for a few early works with orchestra, a handful of chamber pieces, and songs. He was never tempted to write a symphony, and even his three piano sonatas have unconventional, un-Beethovenian structures. He resisted the entreaties of his most beloved teacher from home to write the great Polish opera.

But Schumann lived under the shadow of the Beethoven symphonic imperative. For the most part, he effectively balanced his fantastical and intellectual dimensions, writing teeming piano suites and rhapsodically beautiful songs by the dozen, but also composing four ambitious symphonies, three string quartets, numerous sonatas and chamber works. These demanding projects compelled Schumann to channel his vibrant imagination into architectonic sonata-form structures. There are awkward aspects to his symphonies. The orchestrations, even after Schumann made extensive revisions, can seem thick and heavy. Some twentieth-century maestros actually adjusted the orchestrations. Leonard Bernstein, an influential Schumann champion, conducted these works as written, and through his performances and recordings made a compelling case for Schumann's skill with large musical structures. The scores have been embraced in recent decades by a new generation of conductors. I love the Schumann symphonies.

Still, for me and for many others, Schumann's very greatest works are those in which he could unleash his fantastic imagination through unorthodox forms that achieve compelling narrative sweep, especially his major solo piano works, like the Fantasie in C or the astonishing suite *Kreisleriana,* scores that have long been central to the piano repertory. Master pianists and young virtuosos alike immerse themselves in these fervent pieces precisely because they can seem so unwieldy.

The two composers first met briefly when Chopin passed through Leipzig in late September 1836 en route to Carlsbad. Then, on October 9, they shared an "unforgettable day," in Schumann's words. Schumann was thrilled to hear Chopin play his new Ballade in G Minor. Chopin may have tried out a version of the Second Ballade, in F, a work he would later dedicate to Schumann, an intriguing choice: you could describe the ballade as having a split personality. A tender, pastoral theme keeps getting interrupted by vehement outbursts. It concludes with a demonic, near-crazed coda that cuts off at a climactic high point and, after an eerie moment of silence, returns to a traumatized remnant of that tender theme. Was this dedication a coincidence? Or was Chopin intuiting something about his colleague's emotional character?

FRYDERYK CHOPIN

Mikołaj Chopin, a Frenchman from Lorraine, an enterprising and restless young man, found work in Poland as tutor to the son of Countess Justyna Skarbek on an estate in Żelazowa Wola, about thirty miles west of Warsaw.

There he met Justyna Krzyżanowska, who had been sent to the estate in her youth to be an attendant and companion to the countess, a distant relative. The couple married in 1806.

According to official records, Fryderyk Chopin, the second of four children, was born on February 22, 1810, but throughout his life he gave March 1 as the date of his birth. Seven months later the family moved to Warsaw because Mikołaj had secured a post as a teacher at the new lyceum, located in the Saxon Palace. The family resided in a comfortable apartment in a wing of the palace. When the lyceum moved to a different palace, near the university, the Chopins took an apartment in an adjacent building.

The family mingled with professional people and educators, taking part in intellectual and cultural circles that prefigured the Parisian salon milieu Chopin would later find so commodious. At school he mixed with the children of well-born, even aristocratic, families. So despite the relative modesty of his own background, Chopin grew comfortable early on among the elite.

As a boy he performed at these salons, where his prodigious gifts astonished listeners. He was soon receiving invitations from Belweder Palace. Some early public performances also spread word of his emerging genius.

It's interesting that neither of Chopin's main music teachers during his youth was primarily a pianist. The Czech-born Wojciech Żywny, an accomplished musician who began working with Chopin when he was six, introduced the boy to Bach (the Preludes and Fugues from *The Well-Tempered Clavier*) and the Viennese masters. At around eleven, Chopin began lessons with the mentor who would shape him as a musician, Józef Elsner, the rector of the High School for Music in Warsaw, where Chopin eventually enrolled. Elsner oversaw Chopin's study of harmony and gave him thorough training in composition. During this period Chopin had organ lessons from a noted pianist at the school. Still, he would later claim to be largely self-taught as a pianist.

When Chopin graduated in 1829, Elsner's final report concluded: "Chopin F., third year student, exceptional talent, musical genius." But this young genius sensed scant opportunity for artistic growth and patronage in Poland. So he ventured to Vienna, where he experienced an epiphany and realized that his future lay elsewhere. He gave two auspicious public concerts. At one he played the Variations on "Là ci darem la mano" from Mozart's *Don Giovanni,* for piano and orchestra, which I mentioned earlier.

Chopin was not instinctively drawn to composing for orchestra. Still, a composer-pianist seeking to make his name had no choice but to write concertos, or at least concertolike pieces for piano and orchestra. These variations, utilizing the charming, coy theme of the duet during which Giovanni attempts to seduce the foolishly trusting young country girl Zerlina, last about eighteen minutes. The orchestration, if lacking subtlety, does the job. The piano writing is fluid, lyrical, and brilliant.

The piece begins with a mysterious introduction, with dark stirrings in the strings. The piano enters playing a kind of rumination on Mozart's melody. The whole introduction, which lasts almost five minutes, is a kind of tease: If you didn't know in advance that the piece was going to consist of variations on "Là ci darem," you might not pick that up from the hints of the tune Chopin drops in. Finally we hear Mozart's melody played straightforwardly, though with some playful tweaks. Then, after a passage for orchestra that becomes a recurring bridge between sections, come Chopin's series of variations. In the first, the piano spins out brilliant runs in double thirds. In another, the left-hand piano part has an agitated accompaniment in chords while the right hand plays a breezy filigree. The most dramatic departure is a minor-mode variation, where the music turns pensive and Chopin's love of Italian opera, with its long-lined melodic writing, comes through. For an animated coda, Chopin turns Mozart's tune into a feisty polonaise.

The variations are beholden to the taste at the time for showy piano pieces. Still, Chopin folds surprising harmonic twists and tender lyrical tunes into the music, even during passages of overt virtuoso display. If hardly a great work, the variations hint at the Chopin to come. Schumann, in his inaugural review as a critic, writing two years after the premiere based on his study of the published score, went overboard with praise. In the review, Schumann's Eusebius persona, having come upon the piece, lays it on a piano rack and declares, "Hats off, gentlemen, a genius!"

I was privileged to study the original manuscript of this early Chopin work at the Morgan Library and Museum in New York, which has one of the world's finest collections of historical music manuscripts. It's charming to see Chopin's mix of fastidious and freewheeling penmanship. On the last page of the bound volume, among random musical sketches, there's a kind of cartoon, a drawing of a bewigged man in a coat with epaulets next to a monument with a missing statue, clearly a caricature, a good one, of Mozart. From the reports of friends, Chopin was also a skilled mimic.

While in Vienna, Chopin took every chance to attend opera performances. In later years, when this lifelong opera buff began teaching piano in Paris, he urged his students to spend fewer hours practicing and more going to hear fine opera singers in order to learn how to shape and express a lyrical line. Chopin lived in the era of bel canto opera. The period and the term demand some explanation.

During a conversation with friends in Paris in 1858, Gioachino Rossini, sixty-six at the time, wealthy, portly, and retired from the opera business for some thirty years, lamented the decline of Italian singing. "Alas for us," he said, "we have lost our bel canto."

With this comment he was mostly referring, it would seem, to the heritage of singing as practiced in Italy from around the mid-1700s onward. But the term "bel canto," which can be translated as "beautiful singing" or "beautiful song," has also been used to describe the era of Italian opera that thrived through the first decades of the nineteenth century.

The bel canto vocal practice valued smoothness of vocal production (that is, "even" legato) throughout the entire range of the voice. Ideally, one did not want to hear a singer shifting gears, in a sense, from low to middle to high registers, exposing what are deemed "breaks" in the voice. The practice also demanded an ability to execute fleet runs, sustained trills, and various ornaments routinely employed to embellish a vocal line.

A trinity of masters stood atop the roster of early nineteenth-century composer-practitioners of bel canto opera: Rossini, Gaetano Donizetti, and Vincenzo Bellini. Actually, the term "bel canto" did not come into fashion until midway through the nineteenth century, employed as an expression of nostalgia for a fading tradition. So Donizetti, best known for *Lucia di Lammermoor*, did not really know that he was a bel canto composer.

Still, if beautiful singing in the Italian manner carried the day in the bel canto era, then it was natural for composers to write music that would showcase such vocalism. For me, and for Chopin, the most enticing element of the practice involved the approach to writing melody.

Catchy tunes in all styles of music share certain qualities: they are usually laid out in symmetrical phrases with simple melodic bits that are often repeated. A perfect example would be "Twinkle, Twinkle Little Star." Rossini and company wrote their share of catchy tunes. But the hallmark of the bel canto operatic style involved melodies spinning out in long, flowing lines where phrase demarcations were almost disguised. Of course, melodies were written this way long before the nineteenth century (think of medieval chant) and long afterward (songs like Burt Bacharach's "Alfie" and Paul McCartney's "Yesterday" have poignantly elongated, long-spun phrases). But during the bel canto era this approach to melodic writing was pushed to entrancing extremes.

Perhaps the purest, most elegant bel canto melodist was Vincenzo Bellini. Born in Sicily in 1801, he died tragically young in Paris, in 1835. The epitome of a bel canto aria might be "Casta diva," from Bellini's *Norma*. The title character, a druid priestess, has, against her sacred vows, secretly given birth to two children, by an officer of the Roman occupation. In this aria Norma calls upon her people to embrace peace, not war. The ornamented melodic phrases of "Casta diva" sensitively elongate crucial syllables of the Italian text to form a haunting melody that seems to hover above an undulant but respectful accompaniment pattern in the orchestra.

By the mid-1850s, when Rossini was mourning the languishing heritage of bel canto, the Romantic era had taken hold and fostered the public's taste for heatedly dramatic opera, works that demanded more intense and powerful singing. Tenors like Gilbert Duprez, born in Paris in 1806, who had been a prized "tenore di grazia," a light lyric tenor whose agility and lyrical elegance were ideal for roles like Count Almaviva in Rossini's *Barber of Seville*, followed the shift in taste by developing a weightier sound and more carrying power. He is thought to have been the first tenor to sing a high C not with the typical, lighter "head voice" but with a full, powerful "chest voice." Opera audiences went wild. Duprez created a sensation in a revival of Rossini's *William Tell*, the composer's final opera (after which he inexplicably retired from opera in his late thirties, at the height of his fame and wealth). But Rossini compared the sound of Duprez's high C to "the squawk of a capon with its throat cut." Tastes had changed.

The element of bel canto practice that significantly shaped Chopin's musical voice was the long-lined approach to melodic writing as exemplified by Bellini, whom Chopin got to know during his first years in Paris.

Earlier, in Poland, after writing the "Là ci darem" Variations, Chopin felt under pressure to produce a concerto, an obligatory early step on the standard composer's career path. He wrote two in quick succession: the Piano Concerto No. 1 in E Minor (which was actually the second one completed, though it was published first); and the Piano Concerto No. 2 in F Minor. Both were composed and performed, with Chopin as soloist, in Warsaw in 1830, the year he turned twenty. These large-scale works, lasting some forty and thirty-four minutes, respectively, represent an enormous leap of confidence and originality over the Variations.

If a pianist-composer intent on making his way in the field at the time had to write a concerto to showcase his own virtuosity, that's not exactly what Chopin did. There are passages galore of brilliant runs, improvisatory-sounding episodes where the piano breaks into spiraling figures, and bursts of keyboard-spanning arpeggios. Still, concertos by other composers of this period, like Johann Nepomuk Hummel and Sigismond Thalberg, were more overtly virtuosic and dazzling. Chopin's concertos present intricate difficulties that require pianists to elicit refined textures and clarify inner voices—those quasi-melodic strands in between a melody and accompaniment (or bass line), somewhat like the alto and tenor parts in pieces for chorus.

These concertos have been faulted, fairly, for merely passable orchestration. During passages where the orchestra dominates, the scoring is dense, unvaried, and heavy with strings. In long stretches when the piano takes charge, the orchestra retreats almost too much into the background, though there are some lovely moments where solo instruments, especially woodwinds, trade phrases with the soloist.

I've never been bothered by the inadequate orchestration in these scores because the music is so eloquent, ingenious, and personal. In the Concerto No. 2 in F Minor, my favorite, the main theme for the piano in the first movement begins with a sighing yet insistent melody, almost a wannabe march, cushioned by poignant chords that slink downward. A vehement burst tries to shift the mood. But soon the piano takes off on a long melodic extenuation of the theme, music that breathes and yearns with sadness, drenched in bel canto lyricism. Even as the music spins captivating lyrical lines, Chopin, a devotee of Bach by this point, folds inner voices into the right-hand part, subtle complexities that make this piece so challenging.

During this extended episode, the piano takes a phrase from the theme and puts it through harmonic and melodic turns that sound like ruminations, as if Chopin were exploring every emotional implication of the music, at first nervous, then resigned, now slightly panicked, now somberly determined to push on. In its subdued, elegant way, the music comes across as intensely revealing, like the musical equivalent of intimate confessions from Chopin's diary. You almost feel like you're prying.

The slow second movement, a Larghetto, is like a bel canto aria transfigured for the piano. A dreamy theme sings and glides through melodic arcs over a gentle accompaniment of broken chords. But the melody, though inspired by the operatic style, goes through elaborate embellishments that no soprano could execute. And the accompaniment is not merely supportive but interactive.

The vibrant finale has the feel and rhythmic character of a mazurka, at once wistful and playful. During one episode, the pianist must play several pages of nonstop runs for the right hand, a whirlwind of triplets that keep spinning through every imaginable harmonic progression, over an accompaniment of jumpy left-hand chords. This was Chopin's way of showing off his virtuosity. No Lisztian fusillades of notes and octaves here, though the most overtly brilliant piano writing comes during the movement's giddy coda.

Following their auspicious premieres, these concertos became calling cards for Chopin as he ventured from his hometown to explore opportunities elsewhere. He even fashioned solo piano versions he later played in Paris salons.

Chopin had no clear grand plan when he left Warsaw in the fall of 1830 other than to make a European tour and see what resulted. A good friend from the lyceum, Tytus Woyciechowski, accompanied him. Chopin's complex, veiled relationships with women, including his long liaison with George Sand, are a little hard to fathom. But he maintained a circle of male, mostly Polish soul mates. He would not have left Warsaw without Tytus. In a typical letter to Tytus while Chopin was performing in Vienna earlier that year, addressing his friend as "My dearest life!" Chopin wrote: "I have never missed you as I do now; I have no one to pour things out to, I have not you. One look from you after each concert would be more to me than all the praises of the journalists." Increasingly, another school friend, Jan Matuszyński, then a medical student in Warsaw, became an intimate.

Just a week after arriving in Vienna, the young men learned of the Warsaw uprising, the armed revolt within partitioned Poland against Russia, whose czar, Nicholas I, had crowned himself King of Poland in 1830, an action that instigated the Polish-Russian War. The valiant Tytus, rushing home to take part, persuaded Frédéric (now using the French spelling of his first name) that he could serve Poland better by sticking to his artistic destiny. Still, Chopin was now stranded in a city where Poles were viewed with suspicion.

He wound up remaining in Vienna for eight months, with ups and downs in his career ambitions. The crisis in Poland clearly deepened his feeling about conveying Polish character and culture in music. In his youth he had written some showy polonaises and lilting, lightweight mazurkas. He turned to the mazurka again, but this time with renewed seriousness and depth. While in Vienna he wrote the first nine of the fifty-eight mazurkas he would sanction and publish.

The mazurka is a Polish folk dance, often of a lively character, though sometimes wistful, written in triple meter with an idiomatic, elusive rhythmic gait. The emphasis usually goes on the third beat of the measure, though sometimes it goes on the second. But there is a characteristic pull on the second beat, a kind of slight, suspenseful accentuation, before the strong third beat. And, typical of most folk dance forms, there is usually lots of repetition, including whole sections.

Chopin kept some of these basic characteristics in most of his mazurkas. But from the first one he published, the Mazurka in F-sharp Minor (Op. 6, No. 1), he makes this genre his own, lending it musical and emotional complexity. A jumpy, somber, yet sinewy theme goes through a couple of sequential statements, then crests on aching chords and slips back down in four descending measures full of melodic figurations and piercing harmonies. Even a contrasting middle section, with a Slavic tint and tinkling intervals evocative of tambourines, has darkness and near-obsessive repetitions.

This is the first of four mazurkas in Op. 6. Chopin mostly published the dances in groups of three or four. It's not clear that the mazurkas in any group were meant to go together, as in a suite, though when played that way the groups do make sense. Even in many hearty, rustic mazurkas (like the third in Op. 6), the mood is usually ambiguous and the music has a dark side.

I think some of Chopin's greatest, most exploratory, and tragic pieces are found among the later mazurkas, like No. 35 in C Minor (Op. 56, No. 3), a folk dance transformed into a searching and profound rumination. Whenever I play it I can barely get through it emotionally. Yes, many mazurkas are vibrant and cheerful. But even these can seem eerily melancholic.

The challenge for pianists is to reveal the musical complexities of a Chopin mazurka while somehow conveying its character as a dance. It makes sense that Polish pianists have had an advantage in playing these works convincingly. The great Arthur Rubinstein recorded Chopin's fifty-one mazurkas (a complete survey but for the youthful works that were published later) three times: first in the late 1930s, then in the early 1950s, and finally during five sessions over eight days, ending on January 3, 1966, shortly before turning seventy-nine. I grew up with the three-LP album from the late 1950s, but came to love the final survey the most. Here is a great Polish artist proudly, humbly, yet with utter assurance, recording pieces he had played for seven decades, in performances that sing and sigh, that dance and yet go deep.

Todd Welbourne, a pianist friend, has an interesting theory about the Chopin mazurkas. Chopin became a dedicated teacher and wrote many pieces that were popular in his time and remain so with student and amateur pianists today. But almost every mazurka, however straightforward and technically approachable it might seem at first glance, has at least one thicket of real difficulty, either some virtuosic bursts of chords or some finger-twisting tangle of lines. Todd suspects that these mazurkas were such personal pieces for Chopin that, in truth, he didn't want too many amateurs performing them. He intended the mazurkas for more mature artists; he couldn't accept that they would be played superficially or carelessly, even in private settings.

In the summer of 1831, having had difficulty procuring a passport from Russian officials, Chopin finally left Vienna for Paris via Germany, wracked with doubt and upset to be dependent upon money provided by his father. In Stuttgart that fall, feeling miserable, news came that the Polish resistance had collapsed under the superior force of the Russians. In an agonized, near-incoherent entry in his diary, Chopin, stuck in Germany, brooded on the fate of his homeland, assuming the worst: "My poor father! The dear old man may be starving, my mother not able to buy bread? Perhaps my sisters have succumbed to the ferocity of Muscovite soldiery let loose!" Referring to his dead sister Emilja, he writes: "Poor suffering Mother, have you borne a daughter to see a Russian violate her very bones!—Mockery! Has even her grave been respected?" This long entry ends: "Alone! Alone!—There are no words for my misery; how can I bear this feeling—"

Given the turmoil in Poland, it now would have been impossible for Chopin to return home. He kept on to Paris and arrived there in

November, and almost immediately found the bustling city, with its sizable community of Polish expatriates, culturally stimulating and suited to his mostly amiable, if mercurial, manner. At the start of this period he shared an apartment with Jan Matuszyński, his medical student friend from home.

"Paris is whatever you choose," Chopin writes in a letter to his friend Tytus that December. "You can amuse yourself, be bored, laugh, cry, do anything you like, and nobody looks at you; because thousands of others are doing the same as you, and everyone goes his own road. I don't know where there can be so many pianists as in Paris, so many asses and so many virtuosi."

Though he arrived with few introductions, Chopin made his way steadily, hearing the sensational violinist Paganini perform, attending operas, and meeting luminaries like Rossini, the composer Luigi Cherubini, and the German-born pianist Friedrich Kalkbrenner, who mightily impressed Chopin ("If Paganini is perfection, Kalkbrenner is his equal"). He was befriended by Liszt, at the time living in Paris with his mistress, Countess Marie d'Agoult, who had left her husband. Marie, who would later write novels (and a three-volume history of the Revolution of 1848) under the pen name Daniel Stern, had three children with Liszt, his only ones, born during the 1830s: Blandine, Daniel, and Cosima, who would marry the German conductor and pianist Hans von Bülow and then leave him to live with, bear children to, and eventually marry Wagner.

During my Top Ten Composers project at the *Times* I never really considered Liszt as a contender to make the cut. But if I had played a different intellectual game, to determine the top ten all-around musicians in history, Franz Liszt (1811–1886) would not only have made it, but would have been a plausible candidate for the top spot.

As a pianist, Liszt pushed the existing boundaries of technique, texture, and sound. From all accounts, his performances were not just stunningly virtuosic but mesmerizing, mystical, white-hot, almost sexual. His leonine mane, stern visage, and lean physique, with long, thin fingers able to encompass what seemed impossibly wide-spaced chords, added to his allure. As we learn from the scholar Alan Walker's definitive three-volume biography of Liszt, between 1839 and 1847 Liszt gave some one thousand public performances. During a ten-week period in Berlin, he played some eighty different works on twenty-one recitals, fifty of them from memory, an uncommon practice in his day.

Driven by his ecstatic fans, the phenomenom of "Lisztomania," a term coined by the poet Heinrich Heine, swept Europe during the 1840s. Well-born women scooped up his coffee dregs and cigarette butts and carried them in necklace vials.

Liszt invented the concept of the piano "recital," as he described it, purposefully borrowing a literary term to suggest that a piano program should be not just an offering of various pieces, but more like a recitation, with compositions arrayed to develop a theme. He championed sonatas by Schubert and Beethoven that baffled his contemporaries. He played the works of colleagues and competitors almost always better than they could. Still, in 1847, at thirty-five, burned out by the touring routine and sufficiently wealthy, he retired from the concert stage to devote himself to composition. In later years he played in public on occasion, but accepted no fees.

As a composer he produced some thirteen hundred scores, not just dazzling and poetic piano pieces, but organ works, austere sacred choral compositions, rhapsodically lyrical songs, and much more, including some thirteen orchestral tone poems, a genre Liszt essentially invented. Also called symphonic poems, these free-form, descriptive, single-movement orchestral works were inspired by tales from classical mythology, romantic exploits, fantasy, or even historical figures. The diaphanous textures in many of Liszt's milky piano pieces anticipated the Impressionism of Debussy and Ravel.

The large body of piano transcriptions and paraphrases that Liszt composed—solo piano versions of everything from Schubert songs to scenes from Mozart and Verdi operas—are often misunderstood today. In these works Liszt uses the piano to take listeners deep into the music without the distraction, in a sense, of orchestra instruments or operatic voices. During the only interview I had with the legendary pianist Vladimir

Horowitz, in 1988 (a year before his death at eighty-six), he told me that Liszt's ingenious piano transcriptions of the nine Beethoven symphonies were the "greatest works for the piano, tremendous works," but, he added, "they are 'sound' works," meaning pieces that draw upon the piano's full coloristic possibilities. Horowitz played them for himself all the time, but never in concert, fearing audiences would not "understand them," he told me. "We are such snobs," he said.

Of course, Liszt's output also includes many flashy, superficial pieces. Yet his reputation as a pioneering and accomplished composer continues to grow. Liszt's exploration of chromatic harmony and daring dissonance influenced Wagner. And though perhaps it's too much to say Liszt "made" Wagner, he certainly provided a powerful endorsement at a crucial point in Wagner's career by conducting the 1850 premiere of *Lohengrin* in Weimar. Liszt also left volumes of musical-literary writings: essays, critical pieces, even an insightful, if ostentatious, biography of Chopin (whom Liszt survived by thirty-seven years), not to mention some six thousand letters.

Over his life, Liszt taught more than four hundred piano students, many of whom achieved greatness, like Carl Tausig, Hans von Bülow, and Arthur Friedheim (who would teach the mother of Van Cliburn). Because he believed in "génie oblige" (the obligation of genius), Liszt never accepted payment for lessons, much to the chagrin of his rivals. In 1861 his period in Rome began, when Liszt went on religious retreats and eventually took minor orders, and was thereafter known as the Abbé Liszt.

On the downside, he was a terrible father. Financially, Liszt supported his three children generously. But he left them to be raised, mostly in Paris, by others. Initially he entrusted them to his kindly mother, but later put them under the supervision of governesses who were steeped in archconservative French Catholic thinking, and who embraced strict forms of discipline. As his relationship with Countess Marie deteriorated, he fought to keep her from the children, though to some degree (the story is confusing) Marie, a leftish intellectual, benefited professionally by not having the children under her direct care. Months, even years went by when Liszt did not see them.

Liszt and Chopin had a close and admiring but testy relationship. Liszt's extravagant personality and abundant energy smothered Chopin. Chopin respected Liszt's comprehensive musical skills and was in awe of his pianism, though he objected when Liszt introduced embellishments into Chopin's music when he played it. The proudly robust Liszt grabbed Chopin tightly by the arm and took him all over Paris to foster introductions with major musicians and potential patrons.

With increasing self-awareness, Chopin clarified his personal vision for a creative life. In 1831, writing to Elsner, his beloved teacher in Warsaw, who had been agitating for his student to undertake large-scale orchestral compositions, even a Polish opera, Chopin respectfully demurred. He described the challenges that even established composers in Paris faced in getting productions of their operas and performances of symphonic pieces. Instead, Chopin argued, "I must think of clearing a path for myself in the world as a pianist, putting off till some later time those higher artistic hopes which your letter rightly puts forward." To be a "great" composer, Chopin states, requires "enormous knowledge." In the cultural climate of the day, Chopin argued, "a man is fortunate if he is at once a composer and an actor," meaning a composer who could perform his own works. Nothing would interfere, Chopin promised, with "my perhaps overbold but at least not ignoble desire to create a new world for myself," that is, as a pianist.

This was a turning point, a crucial self-revelation. If "greatness" as a composer involved writing operas and symphonies, so be it. Chopin would not strive for that kind of greatness. But he had an inkling of his own path. Music history has been forever grateful that he stuck to it.

One problem remained: Chopin's increasing discomfort with performing in public. In his biography of Chopin, Liszt quotes his then-deceased friend as saying, "I am not suited for concert giving; the public intimidate me; their looks, only stimulated by curiosity, paralyze me; their strange faces oppress me." Chopin mostly made his name through the network of intimate salons in Paris, winning patronage and gaining the attention of the bigger publishing firms. Yet to make a good living he increasingly turned to teaching. And unlike Liszt, from the start Chopin charged the heftiest fees he could command.

His pupils included many aristocratic young women and dedicated amateurs. His most prodigious talent, Karl Flitsch, a Hungarian, died tragically at fifteen. Some contemporaneous reports suggest that Chopin found teaching onerous. But this view was countered by his most prominent student, Karol Mikuli, a Polish pianist and composer, who maintained that Chopin devoted himself to teaching for hours a day with deep involvement. True, Mikuli conceded, there were many stormy lessons and "many a lovely eye left the high altar" of Chopin's studio "in tears"; and, to be sure, Chopin demanded "ceaseless repetition" and could show "feverish vehemence," in lifting his students to the standards he demanded. But, for the most part the beloved master was patient and encouraging, Mikuli affirmed. For the rest of Chopin's life, teaching would be his main source of income.

The balance Chopin brought to his professional life allowed ample time for composition. That he was determined to have an impact on the understanding of technique, sound, and color at the piano is clear from his 24 Études, pieces he worked on for years starting in his late teens. The 12 Études, Op. 10, were published in 1833; the follow-up volume, 12 Études, Op. 25, in 1837. These works remain touchstones for every aspiring concert pianist. If you can play the Chopin études comfortably, you should be able to handle anything written for the piano from Chopin's time to the present.

Études, as their name attests, are study pieces, usually focused on developing a specific aspect of technique for whatever instrument the pieces are written. Most composers try to write études that rise above the level of exercises and contain musical substance. Liszt pushed this approach to the extreme with his visionary *Transcendental Études*. Chopin, for the most part, stuck closer to tradition by writing varied works, each of which intricately explored a specific technical challenge. Still, in his own more elegant, less Lisztian way, Chopin transcended the technical issues addressed in his études to compose some ravishing music.

Take the first: Étude No. 1 in C Major, a study of arpeggios for the right hand that ripple up and down the keyboard in fleet sixteenth notes, as the left hand supplies a firm bass line in stolid octaves. The arpeggios pass through bold harmonic progressions and key areas far removed from C major. In a good performance a pianist should exude such effortless command of the scintillating arpeggios that listeners become swept away by the harmonic journey the music leads them through.

With the Étude No. 2 in A Minor, Chopin was being a little cute. The piece seems innocent enough on the surface. The right hand makes its creepy-crawly way up and down the keyboard playing chromatic scales (that is, all the black and white keys), while the left hand plays a simple *oom-pah* accompaniment of lightly staccato chords. But Chopin also requires the pianist to buttress these chromatic scales with a couple of notes at the start of each beat to make a full chord. This means that the creeping scales must be played mostly with the outer (weaker) fingers of the right hand: the middle one, the ring finger, and the pinky. That's terribly difficult, though only other pianists in the audience would understand this.

In the Étude No. 5, the *Black Key* Étude, Chopin chooses a key (G-flat major) comprising mostly black notes on the piano and then keeps the music's spiraling, perpetual-motion triplets for the right hand as much as possible on those black keys. There are études that explore other specific technical issues: large rolled chords, bursts of double octaves, breathless spans of double thirds, leaping chords for both hands. The so-called *Revolutionary* Étude (No. 12 in C minor) is a vehement and stormy piece in which the left hand is continually tested with roiling runs, and the right hand plays a defiant theme in chords. In a few études Chopin can't restrain himself from writing a halting lament, or a melancholic song without words. Yet even these soft-spoken études at some point break out in a bout of chords, a patch of runs, or some other technical feat, however briefly.

During his productive early years in Paris, rather than heeding his old teacher's advice to compose ambitious sonatas and symphonies, Chopin continued to write mazurkas and polonaises, and gravitated to more free-flowing genres like impromptus, scherzos, and, a Chopin specialty, nocturnes. John Field, an Irish composer of the previous generation, essentially invented the genre of the piano nocturne, a dreamy, lyrical piece suffused with the aura of nighttime. Chopin adopted Field's idea but took it further, composing pieces that often begin with melancholic, lapping lyricism but inevitably turn complex and agitated, even dangerous.

Perhaps feeling pressure to do so, Chopin wrote three sonatas. The first, essentially a student work, is seldom heard today. The latter two are repertory staples, though unconventional in design and content. Sonata No. 2 in B-flat Minor, from 1837, has long been dubbed the *Funeral March* owing to its grim, profound slow movement. The shocker, though, is the fourth, and final, movement, a short, experimental, demonic piece. The hands, in parallel octaves, play an onrushing, eerily hushed, and murky line that twists and weaves continually, going through bizarre harmonic realms until it sputters out at the end, when the piece slams shut with a fierce fortissimo chord. If the slow movement is a funeral march, the final one has long been described, aptly, as the wind whooshing over a grave. Schumann the critic, who should have known better, was mystified by this finale, writing that it "resembles mockery more than any kind of music." He confesses, though, that "from this joyless, unmelodious movement an original and terrifying spirit breathes on us . . . so that we listen fascinated and uncomplaining to the end—though not to praise; for this is not music."

In his Sonata No. 3 in B Minor, from 1844, Chopin wrestles on his own terms with the Beethovenian imperative and writes a commanding, intricately structured work. For me the great achievement of this sonata is the sublime slow movement, which has the character of an episodic, noble nocturne.

Still, unlike the majority of his contemporaries, Chopin was simply not engaged by the principles and imperatives of sonata form as passed down from Haydn and amplified by Beethoven—that whole thesis-antithesis thing, where over several movements the inherent possibilities of small motifs and themes are explored, developed, and somehow reconciled. His answer to the challenge of Beethoven was to pose the question differently.

Instead of an argument, Chopin created narratives, with discourses among various themes and episodes, which are either left unresolved or brought to a head in some heroic, or horrific, final outburst. The real equivalents in Chopin to Beethoven's sonatas were pieces like his four

Ballades, a title Chopin chose because of its literary connotations, suggesting a poetic narrative. My first immersion in these original and powerful works came during college, when I performed the Ballade No. 1 in G Minor in my senior recital at Yale, an intimate concert that took place in the dining hall of my residential college, Branford.

The recital was the culmination of my undergraduate education: a music major's equivalent of a senior thesis. So my teacher, Donald Currier, whom I revered, had encouraged me to think big. I opened with a grand Haydn sonata, then played Beethoven's Sonata No. 31 in A-flat (Op. 110), my first crack at one of the intimidating "late" Beethoven sonatas. Indeed, learning that masterpiece, with its complex final fugue, consumed me. I also dared to take on Schoenberg for the first time: the Five Pieces, Op. 23 (though I only played the first three). These forbiddingly complex yet intensely expressive atonal works were tremendously hard for me. It took a year to learn them. But once I knew them I played them confidently from memory.

To end, I paired a Chopin nocturne with that first ballade. The Ballade in G Minor, composed over several years, completed in 1835, opens with an elusive rising line in parallel octaves that sort of traces a quizzical harmony (what's known as a Neapolitan sixth chord). It drifts off. Then the right hand plays a sighing three-note melodic gesture over two questioning chords, the second one bitterly sweet, spiked with a dissonance. There is no resolution. Instead, after a moment of silence, the main matter of the piece, it seems, begins, with the saddest theme imaginable accompanied by poignant chords.

The ballade builds in intensity and breaks into tumultuous fury. But a soothing second theme arrives to calm things down. The music continues to unfold, shifting between agitated, fleetingly joyous settings of those two themes, with some frenzied episodes along the way, until a demonic coda wipes away memory of everything that came before.

Though this ballade contains virtuosic flights, technically thorny passages, and that hell-bent coda, the music is effectively conceived for the piano. What really made it so difficult for me, however, was less the

FIORI POETICI
Raccolti nel Funerale
DEL MOLTO ILLVSTRE:

The only certain portrait of Claudio Monteverdi, from the title page
of *Fiori Poetici*, 1644, a book of commemorative poems for his funeral.
During the last phase of his long career, while holding down the
prestigious post of maestro di cappella at the Basilica of St. Mark in
Venice, Monteverdi was galvanizing the city with his late operas.

Johann Sebastian Bach, 1748, in the portrait considered to be the closest likeness to him. Though renowned throughout Germany as a master organist and musician, Bach was considered somewhat old fashioned as a composer in his day. One son affectionately dubbed him "Old Wig."

George Frideric Handel, date unknown. Cosmopolitan, entrepreneurial, and a born theater composer, Handel, a German, had an improbable three-decade run writing popular Italian operas for English-speaking audiences in London.

Franz Joseph Haydn, 1791, while in London, where, to his surprise and delight, he was greeted as a celebrity by a public that couldn't get enough of his music.

The Mozart family, around 1780, with Wolfgang Amadeus Mozart at the keyboard; his sister, Maria Anna (Nannerl), to his right; his father, Leopold, standing; and his deceased mother, Anna Maria, depicted in a portrait on the wall. The next year Mozart made a break with his domineering father, as well as his hometown of Salzburg, by moving to Vienna to make it on his own.

Ludwig van Beethoven, around 1870. Beethoven, who cultivated the mystique of the composer as colossus, was widely considered a living genius, even when his daring compositions confounded fellow musicians and audiences.

Franz Schubert, date unknown. Though he struggled professionally throughout his short life, Schubert enjoyed the support of a devoted circle of friends who were in awe of his gifts.

Frédéric Chopin, 1849, the year of his death at age thirty-nine. Uninterested in writing symphonies or operas, indifferent to conventional assessments of greatness, Chopin devoted himself to playing, teaching, and composing visionary pieces for the piano.

LEFT Robert Schumann, date unknown. As a composer and an influential critic, Schumann tried to reconcile the fantastical and the intellectual realms of music.

RIGHT One of the finest pianists of her time and a gifted composer, the young Clara Schumann became a devoted wife to Robert Schumann and a caring mother to their children, nursing her husband through periods of mental instability and then surviving him by forty years. This photograph shows the widow Schumann in her later years.

Richard Wagner, 1861, in Paris. To his acolytes, he heralded "the music of the future." With support from patrons, he designed and saw through construction an opera house made to order for his own music dramas: the iconic theater in Bayreuth, Germany, site of the annual summer Wagner Festival.

Giuseppe Verdi, 1886, the year he turned seventy-three. He rose from humble origins to become the dominant figure of Italian opera in the nineteenth century. His works remain staples of every opera house.

Johannes Brahms, around 1866, at the time he was immersed in composing his longest, most ambitious, and most personal work, the German Requiem. He still looks like the "young eagle" that Robert Schumann dubbed him when Brahms appeared at the Schumann home in Düsseldorf in 1853.

LEFT Giacomo Puccini, looking dapper, prosperous, and self-satisfied, around 1900, the year his opera *Tosca* premiered in Rome.

RIGHT Claude Debussy, around 1900, in Paris.

LEFT Arnold Schoenberg, 1948, in Los Angeles. With his invention of the twelve-tone system of composition, Schoenberg believed he had taken music to the next exciting stage in its evolution.

RIGHT Claude Debussy (left) and Igor Stravinsky, friends and allies, 1910, in Paris. In 1912, they played a four-hand piano version of Part I of Stravinsky's *The Rite of Spring* for a gathering of acquaintances in Paris, a year before the ballet caused a near riot at its premiere.

Béla Bartók (center left) using a phonograph to record folk songs sung by Slovak peasants in the village of Darázs, 1908. Besides being a modernist master, Bartók was a pioneer in the field today called ethnomusicology.

technical challenges than the emotional tug. Even in places where the ballade bursts forth with virtuosic brilliance the music dips into deep reservoirs of feelings, both sadness and passion, often at the same time; it dissects every facet of those contrasting themes and explores every implication of the wrenching harmonies. The late Beethoven sonata took me to a spiritual place; the Schoenberg engaged my intellect, challenging me to find beauty in complexity. But that Chopin ballade exposed me, while also demanding that I dispatch a formidable piano piece. There I was, just turned twenty-two, still sorting out being gay, full of longings, including for a few friends sitting in the first row at this recital. Chopin allowed me no secrets when I played his ballade.

Though Chopin's relationship with George Sand was central to his life, it did not start well. He met her at a soirée at Marie d'Agoult's in 1837 and was taken aback, as he commented to a friend. "What an unattractive person La Sand is. Is she really a woman?"

Born Amantine Lucile Aurore Dupin, she chose the pseudonym George Sand for her career as a writer, a prolific and successful writer, with dozens of novels, travelogues, plays, stories, and memoirs. Six years older than Chopin, Sand had legally separated from her husband in 1835 and was raising their two children, Maurice and Solange. Short (barely five feet tall), with a dark complexion and bulging eyes, Sand was a proto-feminist and liberal partisan. She moved with equal certainty in aristocratic and bohemian circles, blithely having affairs, smoking cigars, and often adopting male attire.

In the spring of 1838, she and Chopin met again, and romantic feelings immediately stirred between them. By June they were lovers. Sand could not quite fathom the attraction she felt toward the pale, retiring, almost asexual Chopin. Given her heartiness and self-confidence, Sand set about shaping Chopin up and restoring his health. She insisted that a stay in Majorca would help him, though the trip was also motivated by her determination to escape the attentions of a possessive former lover. Alas, the Majorca sojourn during the cold, damp winter of 1839 was a disaster. The townspeople, upon discovering that the couple were unmarried, were affronted and unfriendly; and finding good accommodations proved difficult. Chopin even had to wait for a proper piano to arrive from the Pleyel company in Paris.

Sand would later admit to friends that Chopin brought out maternal instincts in her. As their relationship continued she seems to have become less like a lover (some biographers question the length of their sexual intimacy) and more like a nurse. She would call him "my third child," her adored "little corpse." Sand could not abide Chopin's absurd jealousies and tantrums. He never felt comfortable around her eccentric artist friends and shared nothing of her fervor for socialist ideals. Still, they clearly had powerful romantic, artistic, and emotional bonds, however inexplicable.

In 1846, as their relationship frayed, Sand began writing *Lucrezia Floriani,* a novel easily read as a thinly veiled portrait of her affair with Chopin. The title character is a famed, worldly thirty-four-year-old actress who has left the stage and is raising four children from three different fathers in Italy. She meets and falls in love with the introspective and sickly Prince Karol, who is traveling with a devoted friend, Salvator. Karol, overcome with love for Lucrezia, becomes possessive and jealous, even over minor matters in her life.

It may have been mean for Sand to vent feelings about Chopin in the guise of a novel. Yet her descriptions of Prince Karol shed light into darker, self-absorbed, even self-pitying corners of Chopin's character: "Karol had no small defects. He had only one—large, unintentional and fatal: mental intolerance. He was incapable of opening the floodgates of compassion fully, in general charity, when judging things human."

In another passage, Sand writes that Karol, believing poor health would cause his early death, resigned himself with "something of a mixture of bitterness and pleasure." Lucrezia thinks that Karol's health is not actually threatened by any serious decline. Still, as the narrator explains, "In this conviction he detached himself more and more each day from humanity, of which he believed he no longer formed part. All the wickedness that existed on this earth became remote to him."

The next year, 1847, the book was published, and for accumulated reasons the couple separated, never to meet again.

But during the better years, they enjoyed warmth, devotion, and mutually supportive life routines, sharing adjacent houses in the Pigalle neighborhood of Paris for some years, and spending most summers at the estate of Sand's grandmother in the village of Nohant, in central France. Even during that sorry trip to Majorca, Chopin managed to be productive, completing, among other pieces, his twenty-four Preludes.

Chopin had reimmersed himself in the study of Bach's Preludes and Fugues when he composed this seminal work. In homage to the master, he composed twenty-four preludes in each of the major and minor keys, though he never considered coupling them with fugues. Chopin's fascination with counterpoint rarely took the form of writing exclusively contrapuntal pieces (as Schumann did). Inspired by the fanciful, inventive qualities Bach brought to many of his preludes, Chopin wrote his own richly varied preludes. Some unfold in restless bursts; some are exquisite miniatures. A few are downright radical, especially the Prelude No. 2 in A Minor, with a gnarly, slow theme, like the grim song of a Slavic bass folk singer, over an accompaniment of hulking, weighty, strange intervals and chords. There are delicate preludes with dancing rhythms and gossamer filigree, and curt, curious preludes that seem almost fragments. Students have played the simpler ones for generations. But only accomplished pianists perform the complete set, since some of them are among the hardest Chopin pieces, like the crazed Prelude No. 16 in B-flat Minor, which should go as fast and fiery as possible.

Chopin never fully recovered from his breakup with Sand, which likely further undermined his declining health. He continued to teach, to play in salons, and even to travel, though a temporary departure from Paris was prodded by the February Revolution of 1848, which in France brought forth the Second Republic. Jane Stirling, a devoted Scottish piano student, arranged for Chopin to visit London, where, despite feeling so ill he kept to his room for eighteen days, he gave a few concerts and mingled in artistic and aristocratic circles. He continued to Scotland, where his health worsened. Back in London, in a letter to his sister, he complained about the "kind Scottish ladies" who were boring him again, including one seemingly determined to make him a Protestant and save his soul. "Why should

God kill me this way," he wrote, "not at once, but little by little and through the fever of indecision."

Finally, back in Paris, with financial assistance from Stirling, he took new rooms at the Place Vendôme and was visited by Ludwika, his despondent sister, and her husband and daughter, providing rare family intimacy. He had last seen his parents during a brief reunion in Carlsbad.

Having been persuaded to take the final sacrament, Chopin died on October 17, 1849.

ROBERT SCHUMANN

The town of Zwickau, in Saxony, was a tumultuous place when Robert Schumann was born there in 1810, the fifth and last child of August Schumann, a Romantic novelist and translator, and his wife, Johanna Christiana. That year Napoleon began his campaign to subjugate Eastern Europe, and hordes of his soldiers kept passing through. Zwickau endured chaos and a typhus epidemic. Robert's mother took ill when he was three. The boy was sent to live with another family for a couple of years, a traumatic disruption, though he later described his caretaker as a second mother.

The Schumann household maintained its comfortable ways as best as possible. His mother had a lovely singing voice. Though August, who made his real income from translating Walter Scott and Byron into German, was no musician, he loved music. So when Robert showed early talent his father encouraged it, purchasing a fine Viennese piano and providing the boy piano lessons from the town organist. Once Robert started playing the piano with facility, his father showed him off to houseguests, taking special delight in the boy's improvisations.

Still, August, the son of a minister, ran a disciplined home. Robert's childhood turned more austere when, at nine, he entered the local *Gymnasium,* where the curriculum was rigorous. But his music studies continued.

From his first years, Robert was a dreamy child with a vivid imagination who wrote stories, poems, and dramatic scenes. At the *Gymnasium*, he formed a reading club with fellow students.

A double family tragedy struck when he was fifteen. His sister, older by fourteen years, died of what seems to have been suicide; ten months later his father died suddenly while his mother was out of town at a health spa. The trauma sent Robert into an emotional crisis, provoking fits, depression, and suicidal thoughts. He would endure a lifelong struggle with mental instability.

In his will, August Schumann had made Robert's inheritance conditional on his completing a three-year course of university studies. Though unenthusiastic about it, Robert, at eighteen, settled in Leipzig to study law. An indifferent law student, he was still swept up in passions for music and literature.

The work of two authors increasingly claimed him. The first was the novelist known as Jean Paul, who wrote tales of romance and chivalric exploits in which paired characters, complementary or opposites, made frequent appearances. Schumann described Jean Paul as "interwoven with my inner being." Some years later he discovered E. T. A. Hoffmann, the Prussian Romantic author of fantasy and horror tales, best known for "Nutcracker and Mouse King" (which inspired the ever-popular ballet with music by Tchaikovsky). Three of his stories of impossible loves became the basis for Offenbach's opera *Tales of Hoffmann*, whose leading tenor role is the idealistic, delusional Hoffmann in a highly fictionalized portrayal.

Within a few months of arriving in Leipzig, Robert arranged to study with the noted piano teacher (and piano seller) Friedrich Wieck, who was impressed with Schumann's potential. However, Wieck's professional and personal life was focused intently on Clara, his daughter, who was nine when Schumann met her. Clara's mother had left her husband for another man when the girl was four. Upon Clara's turning five, Wieck obtained legal possession of her, and "possession" describes the manner of his control driven by determination to turn this prodigiously gifted child into a major touring pianist. During lessons he could be bullying and belittling, calling her lazy and disobedient, even untidy. Wieck had remarried, and Schumann reported his shock at seeing Friedrich physically abuse Clara's young half brother, Alwin, after the boy bungled a performance.

Around the time Schumann entered the Wieck circle, Clara began thorough studies in composition and orchestration. Her father arranged concerts, prepping Clara for the rigors of life on the road and instilling in her a desire to please audiences. The cultural historian Anna Beer, in her book on the forgotten women of classical music, argues that Wieck accepted the prejudices Clara would encounter in a male-dominated society and culture. A female performer might attract special sympathy through the combination of musical brilliance and girlish innocence, a combination of traits Wieck tried to foster in Clara.

Within a year or so, Schumann was bored with law and restless. In a diary entry, he wrote that his talent for music and poetry was about the same. But music won out. His fretful mother, convinced her son was ruining his professional life, wrote to Wieck for an assessment of Robert's musical potential. Wieck assured her that Robert could thrive if he would submit to a rigorous six-month program of daily studies in piano, theory, and composition.

Schumann moved into the Wieck home, but over time grew impatient with his teacher, who seemed single-mindedly focused on Clara. Also, Wieck may have started to develop doubts about Robert, as he observed the young man's mood swings. He might even have detected stirrings of attraction between Robert and Clara, though years later, in a joint diary, the couple dated their first kiss to the night of Clara's sixteenth birthday, in 1835, outside the door to the Wieck house. At the party that evening, Felix Mendelssohn, their friend and colleague, who was enthralled with Clara's playing and admired her compositions, danced heartily and joined the festivities. He had just accepted the directorship of the important Leipzig Gewandhaus Orchestra, a post he held until his death in 1847.

In 1831, while studying with Wieck, Schumann endured the stiffening of the middle finger of his right hand that I mentioned earlier. He tried all manner of treatments, including animal baths (in which the lame hand was inserted inside an animal carcass). Nothing worked, ending his hopes for a career as a pianist.

In 1833 he suffered another crisis when malaria took the lives of a brother and a sister-in-law. He sank into a severe depression, from which his recovery was fitful. It is also thought by many, perhaps most, biographers that during this period Schumann contracted syphilis, the disease that could have caused his final mental breakdown. A close friend, Ludwig Schunke, an aspiring pianist and composer, took a room next to his in a boardinghouse and helped Schumann through this crisis. By late the following year, Schunke was dead of tuberculosis; he was twenty-three.

Many romanticized portraits of Schumann have entwined his music and madness. However glib, it's tempting to see wellsprings of wild-eyed imagination in Schumann's volatile emotions and inner demons. In a landmark 1985 book, *Schumann: The Inner Voices of a Musical Genius,* Peter Ostwald, a psychiatrist and musician, examined all available evidence, including an incomplete autopsy. In his probing and sympathetic psychological biography, Ostwald reasoned that though Schumann's deterioration could have been the result of syphilis, other neurological conditions and illnesses could have caused these symptoms as well. That Schumann suffered severe psychiatric problems is certain. As Ostwald asserted, Schumann had severe depression, extremes of sadness and irritability, episodes of sleeplessness and panic, guilt and self-accusatory behavior, even delusions and hallucinations. The most comprehensive diagnosis, Ostwald suggested, would be a major affective disorder, though some later scholars, notably John Daverio, questioned Ostwald's conclusions, maintaining that from the accumulated evidence it seems "reasonably certain" that Schumann contracted syphilis.

In any event, Schumann's mood swings and episodes of debilitating depression started early in his life, as reported by family, friends, and colleagues who revered him, including Clara well before the couple married in 1840. Within Schumann's circle, the composer's intense emotions and unbridled imagination found outlet in his music and made him endearing, except during the worst of times.

If Schumann could not be a composer-pianist, he set about becoming a composer-critic. With Schunke and Friedrich Wieck, who was still supportive at this stage, Schumann founded *Neue Zeitschrift für Musik* (New Journal for Music), which first appeared in April 1834. The following year, after Wieck quarreled with the journal's editor at the time, Schumann found a new publisher, making him sole owner and editor. All the latest music was reviewed and discussed in its pages, with reports from foreign critics. From the start, the journal served to counter the prevailing popularity in Germany of music rife with empty virtuosic display and the influence of ostentatious Italian opera. To Schumann's dismay, Rossini continued to reign in German opera houses. Recalling the mission of the journal, Schumann later wrote that he and his musical brethren would lend a hand to "bring the poetry of our art into honor once again."

The enterprise was animated by another band of composers, a society, though a secret one, "since it never existed anywhere save in the imagination of its founder," Schumann wrote. This was the Davidsbündler (the Davidites, or David's Club), named for the valiant young biblical slayer of Goliath. Schumann's society was populated by the "antithetic artist-characters" he had invented, his two personalities, the dreamy, poetic Eusebius and the impetuous, fiery Florestan, moderated by Master Raro (a stand-in for the academic Wieck). "Like a scarlet thread," Schumann wrote, "this society of Davidsbündler ran through the entire journal, mingling 'Truth' and 'Poetry' in humorous fashion." Though the humorous, extravagantly Romantic tone of many articles was not for all readers, the *Neue Zeitschrift* gained followers and influence, and would be a primary source of Schumann's livelihood for a decade.

The same year that Schumann started the journal he meet Ernestine von Fricken, a charming young piano student of Wieck's from the village of Asch. Schumann was smitten and the feeling was mutual, so the couple entered into an engagement. In the summer of 1835, however, Schumann learned that Ernestine was the illegitimate daughter of an army captain and his feelings altered, surely motivated in part by concern that the match would bring social disadvantages. In any event, Schumann's feelings were increasingly directed at Clara, to the severe displeasure of her father.

Schumann tended to compose in phases, sticking to a genre until he had almost exhausted it. During the 1830s he channeled his inspiration into piano works, including several scores that for many, including me, represent his greatest achievement. Harkening to the Beethoven tradition he composed three sonatas, including the breathless, impetuous Sonata No. 2 in G Minor and the Sonata No. 3 in F Minor, so epic that he subtitled it "Concerto without Orchestra." In homage to Bach he composed a series of pieces in the "form of fugues," as he put it. For his contribution to the étude tradition he wrote his majestic Symphonic Études, which ends with an exuberant, technically daunting march.

Schumann's most original works were his idiosyncratic piano suites, collections of character pieces, dances, portraits, and fragments. Don't be misled by the fanciful titles of these piano suites, like *Carnaval* and *Davidsbündler Tänze* (David's Club Dances). These are formidable and ambitious compositions. Yes, the music abounds in fantasy, fervor, unbearable sadness, suspense, terror, and childlike innocence. Yet structural rigor and contrapuntal intricacies run through the idiosyncratic scores. It's this sometimes uneasy yet bonded blend of emotional wildness and compositional precision that makes these works so astounding. Every great performance of one of Schumann's suites is like a search operation, an attempt to unravel the elusive strands of the music, while still conveying the myriad moods, however capricious, menacing, or dizzy.

Despite the freedom implied in its title, the Fantasie in C Major, a thirty-minute piece in three movements, may be Schumann's most astutely structured piano work. He began the first movement, originally called "Ruines," in 1836, when Clara's father was standing in the way of her burgeoning relationship with Schumann, and described it as a "deep lament for Clara." Hewing loosely to sonata-form structure, the movement is interrupted with episodes of contemplation and bouts of flinty rage. But it ends tenderly with a quotation from Beethoven's song cycle *To the Distant Beloved.* The second movement is an episodic march, at once playful and dangerous; during the finale, a tender and aching slow movement, time seems to disappear into the ether.

Schumann's masterpiece, I think, is *Kreisleriana,* a thirty-minute suite of eight contrasting movements inspired by an E. T. A. Hoffmann character: Johannes Kreisler, a moody composer, a genius who does not fit in, whose work is inhibited by his extreme emotional sensitivity. Overflowing with music and ideas, Schumann composed the piece in a rush of inspiration in April 1838. As he wrote to Clara, "You and one of your ideas play the main role, and I will dedicate it to you . . . then as you recognize yourself you will smile fondly." (Actually, the published score would be dedicated to Chopin.)

The first piece begins with a breathless, almost fiendish whirlwind of spiraling right-hand passage-work, prodded forward with jumpy octaves and chords in the left hand. But listen more closely and a hint of a melodic line, maybe more than one, seems to be trying to break through the rush of right-hand notes; and the rising octaves and chords of the left hand are going through a complex, almost tortured harmonic journey. And that's just the first section of the first piece in this suite.

The Schumann piece that was central to my development, not just as a pianist but as a person, was *Carnaval*. My guide was Donald Currier, my professor of piano at Yale.

Tall, balding, always in a tweed sports coat and tie, Don was a decent, kindly man and an elegant pianist, a modest master. In pieces like Chopin's frenzied Scherzo in B Minor he could draw upon demonic intensity that surprised you, since his overall approach was so refined. His restraint, taste, and vitality made him a consummate interpreter of staples like Beethoven's Third Piano Concerto. He brought the lyricism of a true opera buff to his performances of Mozart.

And he had an uncanny connection to Schumann, which was a little curious, since so much of Schumann ripples with fury, despair, and passion. Don came from a traditional, rather uptight New England family and avoided talking openly about himself. He seemed a man of secrets. Though he had morose periods, he could be wonderfully affable and charming.

As I got to know Mr. Currier (which is what I called him until I left

Yale and we became friends), I understood better. For many years he had felt yearnings for men and had his share of youthful involvements. But he was a product of his times, and could not fully act on his feelings. I was coping with the same issue when I showed up that first day at his studio, something he soon figured out. We sort of talked around it, not about it, until much later.

I think he identified with Schumann powerfully but also understood him intellectually. One summer, while he was preparing *Kreisleriana* for a recital, he wrote to me about its difficulties: "It is so complicated and contrapuntal that one has to be aware of what every finger is doing at every moment." His performance that fall at Yale was magnificent. Clearly Mr. Currier connected to the teeming emotions and roiling undercurrents that can make passages in this music seem almost unhinged. But the probing musician in Mr. Currier, the reserved New Englander, understood that all Schumann needed, to make the balance right in this episodic piece, was some intellectual intervention to calm things down, just a little, even as the heart was racing. In a way, Mr. Currier took the same approach to "performing" his own life.

During my junior year, with Mr. Currier's support, I took on Schumann's virtuosic *Carnaval*, a piece I loved but feared, given its formidable technical challenges. Schumann wrote this thirty-minute suite in 1834–1835 while courting Ernestine von Fricken. It consists of twenty-one short pieces that lightly suggest masked revelers at a carnival before Lent. Schumann gave the piece a curious French subtitle, "Scènes mignonnes sur quatre notes" (Little Scenes on Four Notes). Those notes come from the letters of Asch, Ernestine's hometown, which in German correspond to specific pitches. (In Germany and some other countries, the note a semitone below C is called H instead of B.) From these Schumann derived three musical cryptograms, or motifs: A, E-flat, C, B (A-Es-C-H); A-flat, C, B (As-C-H); and E-flat, C, B, A (Es-C-H-A). Schumann also found four letters from his own surname in "Asch."

Each piece in *Carnaval* has a theme or melody built from at least one of these motifs. Now, this may seem like a cryptic compositional game. But in its fanciful way, the technique is rather close to the sophisticated technique of motivic development that Beethoven used in his most ambitious sonatas and symphonies. In any event, you can enjoy the music immensely without knowing the riddle of the four notes. Yet for all its constant variety, *Carnaval* comes across as musically integrated, due in part to Schumann's embedding of the motifs in the score.

Carnaval opens with a "Préambule," a stirring flourish of heroic chords that segues into a breathless chase, like some manic waltz. From this point on, the suite becomes a series of character portraits: a clumsy Pierrot followed by a flippant Arlequin; a noble waltz that reminds us we are at a masquerade with dancing. A tender portrait of Eusebius is paired with a hotheaded Florestan. So it continues, with a spiraling evocation of butterflies; a chirpy waltz that celebrates the letters of Asch; a beguiling yet highcharged depiction of "Chiarina" (Schumann's nickname for young Clara); a poetic evocation of Chopin; and "Estrella," a romantic portrait of Ernestine. More portraits slip by, culminating in a triumphant, almost feverish finale: a March of the Davidsbündler against the Philistines of music.

If it sounds enchanting, it is. But the music is technically and emotionally demanding in complex, awkward ways. The pieces that should dance and skip have buried intensities and finger-twisting passages.

I didn't have the technique to toss off *Carnaval*. As a junior in college during the fractious late 1960s, I identified with the emotional complexities of the music. That undertow sucked me right in. Still, I remember giving a mistake-prone but vibrant and deeply felt performance. At the end of the feisty final march, the audience (admittedly full of friends) gave me a standing ovation. I've played tougher houses since. Among those standing and beaming was Mr. Currier.

In 1979, at the age of sixty, Don married his wife, Charlotte, a gifted poet, a valued writing teacher, and a warm, affirming person with two sons from a previous marriage. At the lovely ceremony, Charlotte read a poem she had written for the intimate occasion, "Not to Look Back Is the Rule," which she recited, her words mingling with music, a recording of Don performing—naturally—Schumann: the pensive slow movement from the

Second Piano Sonata. (Their marriage lasted thirty years, until Don died at ninety-one. Charlotte survived him by seven years.)

As a panicked Friedrich Wieck watched romantic feelings between young Clara and Robert intensify, he took action. He denounced Schumann to his daughter and tried to separate them, sending Clara in 1836 to Dresden, where Schumann covertly visited her. After a period of silence between them lasting eighteen months, they began corresponding in the summer of 1837. With a yes from Clara, the couple considered themselves pledged.

Throughout this period, Clara continued performing to acclaim, including a triumphant Viennese tour. Her celebrity was such that a dessert, "Torte à la Wieck," was named for her. Friedrich Wieck remained implacably opposed and sought legal recourse, which proved futile. The couple had to wait for Clara to come of age. On September 12, 1840, a day before Clara turned twenty-one, they were married in Leipzig. Clara moved from her family's commodious home to her husband's modest place farther from the city center. By this point, Friedrich, defeated, was living in Dresden.

From a certain perspective you can understand Wieck's opposition. The Schumann marriage is often portrayed as one of the great love stories in music. The reality was more complicated. Robert insisted that his emotional and creative being depended upon Clara's faithfulness. "Just love me a lot, do you hear—I ask a lot because I give a lot," he wrote to her. "Your radiant image, however, shines, through all the darkness, and I can bear things more easily."

Though it's hard to fathom, Clara embraced the role as Robert's savior. Complete happiness, Clara wrote before their marriage, would come when she could fall into Robert's arms and say, "Now I am yours forever—my music and I."

Yet how did her music develop while being Robert's wife? Clara would bear him eight children, losing her first son in infancy and enduring other pregnancies that resulted in miscarriages. She was expected to be the primary caregiver of the family. She certainly compromised her work as a composer. Time and again, Robert praised Clara's creative skills, used melodies she had written as themes for variations, and encouraged her—to a point. Robert was of his era in his attitudes toward women. Men "stand higher" than women, he wrote; and composition, his art, was a loftier endeavor than performing.

Clara tried hard to keep composing, mostly writing chamber works, songs, and piano pieces, music distinguished by lyrical grace, skill at handling counterpoint, and a penchant for daring harmonic turns. It's sad to read her self-critical comments about her own Piano Trio in G Minor (Op. 17), in which she acknowledges the score's "nice sections" and "rather well-executed" form, but concludes that the piece "remains the work of a woman."

However, she curtailed her ambitions regarding larger forms and genres, something that would have happened, no doubt, even if she had not been married and a mother. Why would a nineteenth-century woman composer attempt a symphony or an opera when there was little chance of a performance from established orchestras and opera companies, all bastions of male control?

Robert even tried to get Clara to limit her concertizing so that she could stay home and tend to him and their children. To her credit Clara refused, even when it meant bringing an infant along on tour. Besides, the family needed the income she earned. Clara had to cope with Robert's chronic depressions, including a severe mental breakdown in 1844 that included insomnia, body tremors, and a raft of phobias.

In anticipation of his marriage, Schumann had had a burst of creativity, focused on vocal composition. Between 1840 and 1841 he composed nearly one hundred and forty songs, including cycles that are staples of the repertory, especially the elaborate *Dichterliebe* (A Poet's Love), settings of sixteen poems by Heinrich Heine. There may have been a pragmatic element to this shift of concentration, since there was a steady market for lieder in Germany; and composing songs was less demanding than attempting symphonies and other large-scale works. But romantic bliss inspired him. The song genre also allowed Schumann to combine his feelings for poetry and music.

For me, Schumann's most affecting song cycle from that year of song is *Frauenliebe und -leben* (A Woman's Love and Life). Schumann chose eight poems by Adelbert von Chamisso that offer a woman's first-person narrative of her relationship with a man. In each song Schumann sensitively captures his female protagonist's inner life and emotional journey: her first crush; her near-disbelief over his love for her; her contentment upon gazing at her engagement ring; the fluttering excitement as she prepares for the wedding, aided by sisterly attendants; the bliss of marital affection; the joy of motherhood; and finally her bitter, stunned grief over his untimely death.

Melting, wayward chromatic chords in the piano part animate the poetic images and emotions of the texts. In several songs the piano part has striking independence, as if commenting upon the woman's story. At the very end, instead of driving home the tragedy of the husband's death in wrenching music, a piano epilogue provides a sad benediction by simply repeating the beautiful, contented music of the opening song without the voice.

Schumann continued, almost systematically, to move from genre to genre. In 1841 he wrote two of his four symphonies, the works that would later be published as No. 1 (*Spring*) and No. 4, a bold experiment in cyclic structure. The next year saw an outpouring of chamber music. Then, in 1843, his first German oratorio.

Schumann's mental breakdown in 1844 may have prompted the family's move to Dresden, where Wieck was then living. Schumann's Leipzig career was essentially stuck. He thought that the burgeoning theatrical scene in Dresden might offer fresh opportunities to write dramatic works.

In subsequent years, given his chronic emotional problems and periods of mental instability, Schumann's composing grew erratic. He sometimes voiced his state of mind with eerie lucidity. In a letter to Clara, relating a dream, he describes calling out to her and hearing her answer "really loud," but reassuringly. "A sort of horror fell over me," he writes, "like the ghosts that traffic with each other over the flatlands. I won't do it again, this calling; it really wears me out."

Even so, in 1850 Schumann was gratified to win the post of municipal music director in Düsseldorf, which necessitated a major move for the family. His regard in German cultural circles was such that his arrival was greeted by a dinner and ball in his honor and serenades from town musicians. This welcome phase in his career, and new start for the Schumann family, was short-lived. He proved a technically inadequate conductor. Disgruntled players voiced their complaints to the authorities and Schumann's contract was terminated in 1851.

For Robert and Clara, the great event of 1853 was the appearance of a twenty-year-old composer and pianist from Hamburg, a "young eagle," as Schumann wrote: Johannes Brahms. With a letter of introduction from the great violinist Joseph Joachim, a Schumann friend and colleague, Brahms entered the household at a point when Robert's health was taking an ominous turn. Still, after hearing Brahms play some of his own works, including the exuberant, symphonic-size, Piano Sonata No. 1 in C Major, Schumann recounted the event in an article titled "New Roads."

He had long awaited, he wrote, a talent to appear, a "musician who would reveal his mastery not in a gradual evolution, but like Athene would spring fully armed from Zeus's head. And such a one *has* appeared; a young man over whose cradle Graces and Heroes have stood watch."

The young Brahms stayed with the Schumanns for several weeks, forging a bond that would remain for both of their lives, a story I tell more fully in the chapter on Brahms.

The final crisis came just months later. Ostwald begins his book with a harrowing description of what happened.

On February 27, 1854, a cold and rainy day, Schumann, dressed in a thin robe and slippers, and sobbing, left his house in Düsseldorf, walked unsteadily to the Rhine River four blocks away, brushed past attendants at the tollgate to the crossing bridge, and halfway across, leapt into the icy waters.

For days Schumann had complained of evil spirits haunting him. The day before his suicide attempt he played the piano for a student composer, feeling strangely joyous, though he was sweating profusely. He told Clara that he had to go to an insane asylum, because he was no longer able to control his mind. But that night he seemed calm.

Fishermen rescued Schumann from the river. Doctors argued that he should be separated from Clara and his family and placed in an asylum. Almost placidly, Schumann agreed. He was sent to a small, private facility in Endenich, a suburb of Bonn. There, for more than two years, he went through treatments, with good days and bad. There were periods when he could compose and play the piano. Clara wanted to see him but the doctors and staff ruled against it. Brahms was a devoted and regular visitor. When he was up to it, Schumann, still under the spell of the great Beethoven, took walks into Bonn to pay respect at the Beethoven memorial statue.

Only when Robert's condition seemed dire did doctors sanction a visit from Clara. She made one trip, but was dissuaded from going into Robert's room at the last minute by the doctors, and by Brahms, who feared the experience might shock her. On July 27, 1856, on her third attempt to see her husband, Clara was admitted. The emaciated composer embraced her and smiled. But he was nervous and twitchy. The next day, Clara gave him a little tea, some jelly, and wine. "He slurped up the wine from my fingers— ah, he knew it was me," she wrote in her diary.

On July 29, while Clara was picking up their friend Joseph Joachim, the great violinist, from the train station, Schumann died alone in his room.

Clara survived Robert by nearly forty years, composing little but performing extensively. She was regarded as one of the finest pianists of her time and was a sought-after teacher. Naturally, the widow Schumann made a specialty of her husband's works.

THE ITALIAN REFORMER AND THE GERMAN FUTURIST

GIUSEPPE VERDI
(1813–1901)

RICHARD WAGNER
(1813–1883)

I t's handy for music history that Richard Wagner and Giuseppe Verdi, the dominant figures in the parallel realms of nineteenth-century German and Italian opera, were both born in 1813: Wagner in Leipzig on May 22 and Verdi in Roncale, a small town in the Duchy of Parma, on October 9 or 10 (the baptismal record is imprecise). In another coincidence, each achieved a breakthrough triumph in 1842, Verdi with the premiere of *Nabucco*, in Milan, and Wagner with *Rienzi*, in Dresden.

They did, however, pursue different artistic aims. Though Verdi reformed and experimented with the Italian opera tradition, he never really moved beyond it, nor wanted to. By contrast, the brash, young Wagner espoused "the artwork of the future," a concept hailed by his acolytes and disparaged by his enemies. Wagner would later clarify his thoughts, writing that the phrase was too vague and inadequate to explain his visionary aesthetic.

Verdi and Wagner never met, which was probably just as well. Wagner avoided commenting on Verdi publicly, though he didn't mind when his offhanded put-downs were circulated. Taking a different tack during an 1899 interview with a German newspaper when he was eighty-six, Verdi described Wagner as "one of the greatest geniuses," who left us "treasures of immeasurable and immortal worth," though he qualified his praise by explaining: "I, as an Italian, do not yet understand everything." The savvy Verdi may have been playing the press.

As a young piano student and emerging opera buff, I fell quickly under Verdi's spell. In 1964, just sixteen, I heard the legendary soprano Renata Tebaldi as Desdemona in a production of *Otello* at the Metropolitan Opera—twice! The first time I sat way up in a balcony seat, the guest of a former elementary school teacher. But I just had to hear Tebaldi's Desdemona again. So I persuaded three musician friends to go. We got standing-room tickets right near the stage, though off to one side. I will never forget the sheer, plummy gorgeousness of Tebaldi's voice during Desdemona's final scene, when this wrongly suspected wife sings the unbearably sad "Willow Song" and then says her prayers, the sublime "Ave Maria," and goes to bed for what turns out to be the last time. During the final ovations at the Met that night, Tebaldi was called back so often she finally appeared with a light coat over her costume to signal that she truly had to leave.

In high school I couldn't quite fathom Wagner. An epiphany was forced on me during my junior year at Yale when I took a yearlong survey course titled "History of 19th-Century Music" geared toward music majors. The professor was Robert Bailey, a lanky, middle-aged musicologist and Wagner scholar, who stood out during this period of sixties rebelliousness for his conservative political views and bookish manner. The first day of class, with straight-faced seriousness, Professor Bailey divided nineteenth-century music into three periods: Pre-Wagner, Wagner, and Post-Wagner. This meant that Schubert and Schumann were lumped among the Pre-Wagner figures, while Brahms and Bruckner were Post-Wagner composers. My beloved Verdi rated only a passing mention, which Professor Bailey delivered with barely concealed condescension. Several weeks of the course were devoted to a detailed analysis of *Tristan und Isolde.*

Even at the time, though just a student, I found Bailey's take absurdly slanted. Still, explaining the musical century through Wagner's impact on it was a fascinating exercise, and not invalid. I certainly emerged from this academic indoctrination with an appreciation for Wagner's staggering genius that has only increased over the years: at last count I had fifteen recordings of the complete *Ring* cycle.

GIUSEPPE VERDI

In later life, a dramatist to his core, Verdi somewhat dramatized the story of his humble, rural upbringing, presenting himself as almost a self-taught anomaly. In truth, he did take an unlikely path to operatic greatness.

He was the first child of Carlo Verdi, an innkeeper of modest means in the small town of Roncale, and Luigia, listed on Giuseppe's birth certificate as a "spinner." Their younger child, a daughter, would die at seventeen. Both parents, as the scholar Roger Parker has pointed out, came from families of landowners who valued betterment and schooling. The instruction Verdi received from village priests likely involved some music. As Giuseppe's gifts became clear, his parents bought him an upright piano. The boy took lessons from the organist at the local church. Before long, he was substituting for his teacher during services. Following the organist's death, Giuseppe, just nine, inherited this paid position.

To advance his education, the boy was enrolled as a boarder in the upper school in Busseto, several miles away. Giuseppe returned every weekend to play at Sunday services. By twelve he began more rigorous training in Busseto under Ferdinando Provesi, whose official job was maestro di cappella at the town church.

Provesi was basically Busseto's Mr. Music: he ran the local music school and co-directed the amateur orchestra, the Società Filarmonica. Busseto was actually a "little fortress of culture and commerce," the scholar Mary Jane Phillips-Matz emphasized in her comprehensive Verdi biography, and the amateur orchestra at its peak had upward of seventy players. The ensemble's other director was Antonio Barezzi, a successful grocer and passionate musical amateur who would become the central figure in Verdi's early professional and personal life.

According to an autobiographical sketch he later dictated to a publisher, Verdi said that during his teenage years he composed all manner of marches, concertos, piano pieces, and cantatas, works that were played in concerts or used in church, most of which have been lost. His involvement with the local orchestra was not formalized until he was about sixteen and became its leader.

In 1831, then eighteen, Verdi moved into the Barezzis' house, where he gave lessons in singing and piano to the kindly man's daughter, Margherita. Later that year the couple became engaged, to the delight of Barezzi, who believed in Verdi's promise.

The next step was obvious: Verdi had to go to the conservatory in Milan, the cultural capital of the north, with its renowned La Scala opera house. With a strong recommendation from Barezzi, Verdi won a municipal scholarship to further his education, though the award did not kick in immediately. So Barezzi pledged to personally fund his future son-in-law's first year at the conservatory.

Full of gratitude, Verdi traveled to the city and auditioned, but was turned down. One factor may have been his age: at eighteen, he was a few years older than most entering students. Apparently the faculty found his piano technique unconventional. Whatever the reason, this rejection would sting for the rest of Verdi's life.

Barezzi came to the rescue, offering to support private lessons for Verdi in Milan. Years later, after Barezzi's death, the composer hailed his benefactor in a letter to a friend, saying that he owed Barezzi "everything, everything, everything." He wrote, "I've known many men, but none better!" Barezzi "loved me as much as his own sons, and I loved him like a father."

Verdi began rigorous studies in Milan with Vincenzo Lavigna, a composer and teacher who had just retired as a coach at La Scala. Lavigna encouraged Verdi to attend the opera and introduced the young man into Milanese musical circles.

In 1835 Provesi died. Verdi applied to succeed him as Busseto's music director. Though denied the appointment as organist, Verdi was given the secular component of the post, which involved directing the orchestra and teaching. He moved to Busseto and, now a professional musician, married Margherita Barezzi in the spring of 1836. He seems to have adored her. They had two children, first a girl, then a boy. Though losing infants to illness was a sad reality of life during this era, what happened to Verdi is unimaginable. In less than two years, between 1838 and 1840, he lost his entire family: first the girl, then the boy, and finally Margherita, who succumbed at twenty-six to rheumatic fever, according to civil records.

Yet these years also saw his entry into opera. He had been struggling for some time to compose his first, originally called *Rocester*, to a libretto by Antonio Piazza, a journalist. A reworked version called *Oberto*, with the libretto fixed up by the experienced Temistocle Solera, was accepted for production at La Scala. It opened in the fall of 1839, earning encouraging reviews and a decent run. The opera is a stern drama set in thirteenth-century Italy about an exiled count's reconciliation with his daughter, who had been seduced by a nobleman, and the father's attempt to avenge her wrong. Verdi's score, beholden to Donizetti and Rossini, was strong enough to impress Bartolomeo Merelli, the impresario of La Scala. Sensing Verdi's potential, Merelli offered a contract for three more operas.

Merelli, hoping to include a comedy in the fall season of 1840, showed Verdi several options, none of which enticed him. Verdi reluctantly agreed to have a go at an adaptation of a libretto by Felice Romani that had fizzled more than twenty years earlier, now titled *Un giorno di regno* (King for a Day). It was while working miserably on this score that Verdi took ill and was nursed back to health by Margherita, only to then watch his devoted spouse die. The opera was a dismal failure. Now a childless widower, Verdi threatened to retire from music completely.

The persistent Merelli showed Verdi the libretto of *Nabucco*, also by

Solera, a biblical drama about the King of Babylon, who, having ruthlessly conquered a band of Hebrews in Jerusalem and dragged them into captivity in his homeland, comes to accept Jehovah. A more experienced composer had rejected the libretto. Merelli found the text distinguished and urged Verdi to set it.

Verdi wearily took the manuscript home. In a later account, surely exaggerated, he tells of flinging the thing on the floor, and how it fell open to the page where the Hebrews, captive in Babylon, sing a chorus, "Va, pensiero, sull'ali dorate" (Go, my thoughts, on golden wings). Though the Hebrew people are enchained, no oppressor, they assert, can restrain their thoughts of home and freedom. Transfixed by these lines, so Verdi claimed, he read on and finally agreed to write *Nabucco* for Merelli.

Verdi described the composition process as tortured: "One day a verse, the next day another, at one time a note, at another a phrase. Little by little the opera was written." This part of his account rings true.

Though not Verdi's first masterpiece, *Nabucco* has flashes of emerging genius. There are some pro-forma, stiffly structured arias and ensembles. But the score is rich with rousing episodes, magisterial melodic writing, and compelling choruses, especially "Va, pensiero," all the more moving for the directness and elegance of Verdi's music.

The Scala premiere in the spring of 1842 was a sensational success. An extended revival played that fall. Within a few years *Nabucco* played in Vienna, Berlin, Paris, Lisbon, even Buenos Aires. Verdi was hailed as a young giant of Italian opera. Over the next twelve years alone he would compose sixteen operas, not including a couple of revisions, for houses in Naples, Rome, Venice, Milan, Paris, London, and elsewhere. In no time he was earning big fees from productions and publications. In 1844 he started buying property in the Busseto region: some farmland with a country house as a home for his parents; a palazzo on Busseto's main street; and, in 1848, some fields and houses in the village of Sant'Agata, where, over many years, he built the complex that came to be known as Villa Verdi. He essentially lived there from 1851 until his death.

Nabucco marked another life-changing encounter for Verdi. The vocally punishing role of Abigaille, believed to be Nabucco's daughter, though actually born a slave, was sung by the soprano Giuseppina Strepponi, who earned gratitude from Verdi for dispatching the music's jagged runs and leaps with intensity while bringing warmth to lyrical lines. By the next year, she and Verdi had begun a relationship.

Verdi set up house with Strepponi, who had retired from singing, when he moved to Paris in 1847 to pursue career opportunities there. Two years later the openly unmarried couple settled in Busseto, which incensed its churchgoing residents. Whatever Verdi's private spiritual ideals, he was a religious agnostic, fiercely anticlerical and contemptuous of moralistic posturing. Throughout his life Verdi had a built-in hypocrisy detector. He and his partner would find their own way through life, thank you.

In 1852 he even had to defend himself to Barezzi, who questioned his lifestyle in a fretful letter. Writing from Paris, Verdi reminded Barezzi that he lived in a district that "has the bad habit of continually interfering in other people's affairs, and disapproving of everything which does not conform to its own ideas." This is why there has been gossip and whispering, Verdi continues. But, he asks, what harm has he done? He had never been secretive: "In my house there lives a lady, free and independent, who, like myself, prefers a solitary life, and who has a fortune capable of satisfying all her needs. Neither I nor she is obliged to account to anyone for our actions. But who knows what our relations are? What affairs? What ties? What rights I have over her or she over me? Who knows whether she is my wife or not?" And finally, "She has every right, both because of her conduct and her character, to that consideration she habitually shows to others." He concludes by stressing that he has always considered Barezzi his benefactor, that this is "an honour and I boast of it."

It's an extraordinary letter, the tribute of a powerful man to a woman he reveres for her goodness and character. How could Barezzi not have felt ashamed? In 1859 Verdi and Strepponi finally chose to marry, privately, traveling to a village in Piedmont, with no friends or family in attendance.

Throughout the next years, the busiest of his career, he accepted commissions from houses in Venice, Rome, Naples, Florence, even London, and enjoyed burgeoning success. Yet, in creating his works he had to contend with two ongoing and often annoying challenges: operatic conventions and government censorship.

Audiences for Italian opera in the first decades of the nineteenth century had grown accustomed to long-standing conventions of the art form, particularly regarding matters of structure. Take, for example, the standard double aria. In the first part, a character would sing a cavatina, usually a reflective aria in a moderate tempo expressing some contentment, or yearning, or cautious expectation of a lover's coming, or perhaps sadness over some loss. Then, typically, something happens: someone bursts in with good news, or a warning, delivered in agitated recitative. This leads the character who sang the cavatina to break into a cabaletta, a faster and usually more ornate and showy aria, expressing resolve to take action or joy over some desired outcome. Of course, master composers like Donizetti and Rossini found ways to personalize this convention and introduce subtle variety.

Verdi came of age artistically during a period when the conventions of Italian opera were pervasive. Even after being proclaimed a bold new voice, he was expected to honor the heritage and not shake up things too much. As his success spread and his confidence grew, he expressed frustration with the outmoded conventions that he feared were inhibiting his work and the whole genre of Italian opera.

In a letter to the librettist Salvatore Cammarano about the in-progress *Il Trovatore* (The Troubadour), Verdi espoused a radical vision of what sounds like through-composed musico-dramatic structure. "If in the opera there were no cavatinas, duets, trios, choruses, finales, etc.," he wrote, "and if the whole work consisted . . . of a single number I should find that all the more right and proper."

These were fleeting thoughts, a busy composer venting his restlessness. Mostly Verdi was content to adapt the conventions to his personal artistic aims and tweak the forms from within. For all his complaining, Verdi benefited by taking these conventions into account, by channeling his inspiration into time-tested structures. He found ways to refine and adapt the conventions of his day without abandoning them completely. Verdi's career can be seen as a gradual but steady effort to transform traditional structures and forge fresh ways to create music drama.

Even in his earlier works, Verdi took standard forms, like the double aria, and brought such keen dramatic insight and musical sophistication to bear that you almost don't notice a scene is basically hewing to convention. Take the double aria in Act I of *Macbeth*, when we first meet Lady Macbeth.

Verdi's tenth opera but first truly great one, *Macbeth* was written for Teatro della Pergola in Florence, where it premiered in 1847. (Verdi revised it significantly in 1865.) A lifelong devotee of Shakespeare, Verdi had already considered a *King Lear* opera, but in 1846 *Macbeth* seemed more doable. Verdi was so eager to turn "one of the greatest creations of man," as he described the play, into an opera that he wrote his own prose libretto and sent it to Francesco Maria Piave, who was quickly becoming his preferred librettist, to make adjustments and turn it into verse.

In his depiction of Macbeth—a formidable baritone role—Verdi compellingly conveys the fatal passivity that runs through Shakespeare's character. In scene after scene Macbeth's music somehow strives to be regal and willful, but is undercut by halting complexities, as in Macbeth's recitative-arioso "Mi si affaccia un pugnal?" ("Is this a dagger I see before me?"). Alone on stage, he contemplates what he is about to do with the weapon in his hand and imagines the awful sight of King Duncan's blood staining its blade. You can hear his doubts and remnants of a conscience in the melodic twists and harmonic tugs of the music.

Verdi's finest achievement in this opera is the soprano role of Lady Macbeth, who even more than in Shakespeare's play dominates and drives the drama to its horrific climax. This comes through from her first entrance, a double aria in Act I.

As the orchestra plays a series of agitated flourishes, Lady Macbeth enters reading a letter she has received from her husband relating the predictions of the witches, who in this opera are not an eerie threesome but a female chorus. In a daring dramatic touch, the soprano actually reads the letter, speaking the words softly, turning them over in her mind. Then Lady Macbeth launches into a blazing stretch of dramatic recitative. Sensing the throne at hand, she wonders whether her husband, who is ambitious in his soul, will have the ruthless fortitude to follow the obvious steps to power. She then sings a dramatically charged equivalent of a cavatina, "Vieni, t'affretta!" ("Come, get you hither!"), in which she goads her absent husband: So the prophetesses promised you the throne of Scotland? Well, don't hold back. Take it!

Then a messenger rushes in and announces that King Duncan, accompanied by Macbeth, will be arriving that very night; the king will stay at the home of his valiant general and Lady Macbeth. At this news, the soprano dispatches a vehement cabaletta, "Or tutti sorgete" ("Arise now"), calling upon all the ministers of hell, those spirits that spur mortals on to bloody deeds. In a demonic line that Verdi sets to chilling music, she says, "Let the knife not know whose heart it strikes." Macbeth, it's clear, will have to man the knife; but the indomitable Lady Macbeth will embolden him with her amoral ambition.

As his career advanced, Verdi increasingly immersed himself in the casting and staging of his works. He had particularly strong feelings about Lady Macbeth, as he wrote to Cammarano, who was overseeing a staging in Naples the year after the opera's premiere in Florence. Verdi had heard that the soprano Eugenia Tadolini was slated to sing Lady Macbeth. Though Verdi admired Tadolini's artistry, he thought her too refined for the role. He wanted Lady Macbeth to be "ugly and evil," Verdi wrote. "Tadolini has a wonderful voice, clear, flexible and strong, while Lady Macbeth's voice should be hard, stifled and dark," he insisted, even "diabolic."

Surely he was exaggerating a little to get his way. Some of the greatest exponents of Lady Macbeth, especially, for me, Shirley Verrett, demonstrated how to convey malevolence and blinding ambition by cushioning crucial phrases with seductive allure.

The other persistent challenge to Verdi's creativity during the decades when he grew to dominate opera in his homeland came from the struggles for Italian unification, the matrix of political movements known as the

Risorgimento (meaning resurgence or revival). After Napoleon's fall, the Congress of Vienna (1814–1815) restored the prerevolutionary jumble of independent states in Italy, most of them under the dominion of the Austrian Empire. This Risorgimento campaign, dedicated to uniting the states and principalities of the Italian peninsula into a single Kingdom of Italy, played out over decades, with underground movements and regional wars. The struggle lasted until 1871, when Rome became the capital of a unified nation. And the arts, including opera, were swept up in the movement.

Starting with *Nabucco,* many of Verdi's works were seen as espousing Italian nationalism, however metaphorically. In time, "Va, pensiero," the chorus of captive Hebrews in *Nabucco,* was embraced as practically a Risorgimento anthem. During the 1840s, operas like *I Lombardi* (the full title translates as "The Lombards on the First Crusade") and *La battaglia di Legnano* (The Battle of Legnano), about northern Italians who join an alliance to battle occupying Germans, were received as overt contributions to the cause of unification. Verdi was a feisty patriot who would accept election to the first Italian parliament in 1861, though he served only briefly, mostly as a figurehead, and attended few sessions.

By the late 1850s, the slogan "Viva VERDI" was shouted as a popular acronym for "Viva Vittorio Emanuele Re D'Italia" ("Long live Victor Emmanuel King of Italy"), referring to Victor Emmanuel II, who in 1861 became the first king of a united Italy since the sixth century. The slogan had a double-edged meaning: "Long live the king" and "Long live Verdi."

Naturally, before unification the states under foreign control, especially Austrian, had to contend with restrictions and censorship. For Verdi the worst years of interference were the 1850s, perhaps his most productive decade.

Given the fraught political climate, Verdi should have anticipated the official backlash when he announced his intention to compose an opera based on Victor Hugo's play *Le Roi s'amuse* (The King Amuses Himself). The play had been banned by the French government the day after its 1832 Paris premiere. Verdi's opera was slated for the 1851 season of Teatro La Fenice, in Venice.

The resulting opera, *Rigoletto,* would set Verdi on an impressive career roll. Over the next two years he produced *Il Trovatore* and *La Traviata,* sometimes working on both scores simultaneously. *Trovatore* opened in Rome in January 1853; *Traviata* in Venice less than two months later. So over a short period he wrote three great and enduringly popular operas that still form the core of the nineteenth-century Italian repertory at opera houses around the world. For me, *Rigoletto* seems the watershed work in Verdi's career and merits some detailed analysis.

Set in Paris in the 1520s, Hugo's play examines the escapades of Francis I of France, presented as a despotic and profligate womanizer. The tragic hero is Triboulet, the court jester, a hunchback who harbors bitterness toward the king, the courtiers, and entitled French society. The jester keeps secret that he has a young adult daughter essentially restricted to their house.

In Piave's libretto, the opera was to be called *La Maledizione* (The Curse), making a focal point of a crucial early moment when the aristocratic father of a young woman who had been seduced by the king comes to court to denounce the monarch. Triboletto (as he is called in the initial libretto) mocks the impotent father's outrage. The incensed man places a curse on the king and his jester for ridiculing a father's grief. Triboletto reacts with horror, since curses are very real to him, and this specific one cuts close to home.

Piave had blithely assured Verdi that the Austrian censors would present no obstacles. He was wrong. An official rejection letter expressed profound regret that the noted poet and celebrated maestro had lavished their talents on a libretto of such "revolting immorality" and "obscene triviality" as *La Maledizione.* You can understand the sensitivities of the censors. Like Hugo's play, the opera depicted a monarch as debauched and violated religious precepts by showing characters in thrall to a superstitious curse. And to have a deformed hunchback as the opera's central character was deemed coarse.

Discussions to resolve the impasse began while Verdi waited in Busseto. Having looked at the changes that had been forced on Piave, Verdi pushed back in a letter to the director of La Fenice. Of course the locality could be shifted, he wrote, and the king could easily become a duke or a prince.

Still, he had to be an "absolute ruler," entitled to behave as he pleased; he must be a "libertine," Verdi insisted. The old man's curse, so "terrifying and sublime in the original," here "becomes ridiculous," Verdi wrote, because the motives for uttering it were now too vague. The worst for Verdi was that the modified libretto avoided making Triboletto an "ugly hunchback." Verdi wrote: "I thought it would be beautiful to portray this extremely deformed and ridiculous character who is inwardly passionate and full of love. I chose the subject precisely because of these qualities and these original traits, and if they are cut I shall no longer be able to set it to music." In a revealing phrase that applies to all of his work, Verdi wrote: "I say frankly that my music, whether beautiful or ugly, is never written in a vacuum, and that I always try to give it character."

In this case, Verdi and Piave mostly prevailed. Hugo's French king became the Duke of Mantua in the sixteenth century. Triboletto, now Rigoletto, remains a hunchback, and is one of the richest roles for baritone in Italian opera. Some details that amplify the plot were removed, leaving a few holes in the narrative. Still, all in all, Verdi wrote the opera he had imagined. *Rigoletto* was a tremendous success at its 1851 premiere.

It opens not with an overture but an orchestral prelude that conveys the dark, oppressive mood of the story and introduces the grim theme associated with the curse. When the curtain goes up, festivities are under way in a splendid hall of the ducal palace, with obsequious courtiers and fair ladies carrying on, while the orchestral music evokes a background dance band in the hall. The preening Duke (a tenor) soon launches into an almost aggressively ebullient aria, in which he brags about his life of pleasure with this woman or that ("Questa o quella"), however many he wants.

Rigoletto's function within the palace is immediately established in his interactions with the courtiers. Naturally he is the butt of jokes; it goes with the job, though his physical handicap invites especially cruel barbs. But he counters the contempt, and, even worse, the pity, of the courtiers by laughing at himself first and turning jokes back at his mockers. He can even be a little jocular with the Duke, though he has learned the boundaries well.

When old Monterone breaks into the party to accuse the Duke of seducing his daughter, his chilling music stops the action cold. That this is a man of great personal dignity, a suffering father who somehow blames himself, all comes through in Verdi's stern phrases. Rigoletto mocks Monterone by mimicking the father's accusations in a whining voice. Outraged, Monterone intones the curse, hammering the words syllable by syllable, capped by a shuddering chord from the entire orchestra.

The next scene begins with an ingenious dramatic stroke. Walking home at night on a dark lane near the courtyard to his house, Rigoletto, haunted by Monterone's curse, is approached by a mysterious man who introduces himself as a hired assassin and, curiously, offers his services should Rigoletto need them. The two men converse in nearly naturalistic vocal lines over the hushed, eerie orchestra as a strangely innocuous yet ominous theme is played by a solo cello and bass. Terrified, Rigoletto shoos the assassin, Sparafucile, away. This leads not into an aria, the expected convention, but a powerfully original soliloquy ("Pari siamo") in which Rigoletto realizes that, after all, he and the stranger are not so different: Sparafucile wounds with a dagger; Rigoletto with mocking words.

A long scene follows between Rigoletto and his daughter, Gilda, a role for a coloratura soprano who can spin lyrical phrases adorned with embellishments, suggesting that beneath her demure exterior stirs a restless young woman. Indeed, as we soon find out, on her visits to church accompanied by her nurse, the only outings her father has allowed, Gilda has become smitten with a young student of no means but great charm: the Duke in disguise bent on another conquest.

As in many Verdi operas, the relationship between parent and child comes through with extra layers of attachment and emotion, given Verdi's personal experience of losing his daughter and son so young. For me, *Rigoletto* is also an insightful exploration of the unintended catastrophe that can result by keeping secrets within a family.

The libretto suggests that Gilda, having been schooled away from home, has only been back with her father a brief time. She is full of questions. Rigoletto believes he is protecting his daughter by keeping her in the dark about their family background. He won't even speak of Gilda's dead mother other than to say she was an angel from heaven. It's too painful. His deepest fear is that the courtiers would find it a trifling amusement to see the daughter of a hunchbacked jester seduced. As a result, he has turned into an overbearing, almost paranoid, parent. It's not surprising that Gilda, so curious about the outside world, becomes an easy target for the dashing Duke in his student guise.

The courtiers do, in fact, know that Rigoletto is keeping some woman at his house. Assuming she's his mistress, they kidnap her, with the duped Rigoletto's inadvertent help, and deliver her to the Duke. In a shattering scene, Rigoletto appears in jester's garb at court, near delirious with shock, singing a broken "*la-ra, la-ra*" ditty. He has come to find (he hopes) and rescue Gilda. Finally, Rigoletto lets loose. He demands to see his daughter— yes, his daughter!—and denounces the courtiers in an impassioned, nobly wrenching aria that transcends all conventions.

Rigoletto has its share of arias and ensembles that hew close to operatic norms of the day. In the final act, which takes places in a seedy inn on the outskirts of the city, run by Sparafucile and his sister, Maddalena, the Duke sings the famous aria "La donna è mobile" (Women are fickle). He lays out his case that, given the flightiness of the fair sex, rather than trusting them you might as well go with it. Verdi was so sure he had a hit tune with this aria that he kept it under wraps until the night of the premiere.

The remarkable quartet that comes later, before the final tragedy that results in the guilt-ridden Gilda's sacrificial death, is a classic example of Verdi showing his skill by sticking with (or, you could say, sticking it to) the conventions of the genre. Rigoletto has hired Sparafucile to kill the Duke and brought the disgraced Gilda to the inn so she can see for herself what this lecherous monarch is actually like. The voices of the four characters mingle in a soaring, intricate ensemble, each one expressing his or her thoughts.

The Duke flirts shamelessly with Maddalena, who flirts right back. Peeking through the window from outside, Gilda listens, stunned, recognizing in the Duke's seductive words the very lines he used on her. Rigoletto tells Gilda that weeping will do no good, that he will right everything and then take her away. As a musico-dramatic device, this quartet demonstrates what opera can do in the hands of a Verdi that spoken theater cannot match: present four simultaneous expressions in overlapping melodic strands, mingled yet musically distinctive.

After these three milestone works of the early 1850s, Verdi's pace slowed down. Depending upon how you count the works he later revised (and retitled), Verdi wrote some nineteen operas over the fourteen years from 1839 to 1853; but he composed the remaining eight (not including significant revisions of earlier works) over a period of nearly forty years. After *Traviata,* he had less patience with the fickle world of Italian opera and found increasing satisfaction as a landowner and farmer in Sant'Agata.

Some of the great works of these later years came from unusual commissions that Verdi could not resist. A generous invitation from the Paris Opera resulted in *Don Carlos,* a stunning Verdi masterpiece loosely based on Schiller's play about Carlos, Prince of Asturias (1545–1568), the eldest son and heir to King Philip II of Spain. On the surface this work offers a Verdian take on the French grand opera genre: it's written in five acts, complete with a requisite ballet and an enormous choral ensemble: a spectacular and chilling auto-da-fé. But *Don Carlos* is a profoundly complex work, the *Hamlet* of nineteenth-century Italian opera in the way it explores the tragic confusions of consequential people caught between their private feelings and public responsibilities. The opera becomes a multi-layered exploration of each character's emotional ambiguities.

No moment reveals Verdi's piercing insights as a musical dramatist more profoundly than the scene in Act IV, when we see Philip alone in his study. The king is now fully aware that Elisabeth, the young wife who was compelled by duty to marry him, still has powerful feelings for his son, Carlos, who loves Elisabeth helplessly. The king sings the most soul-searching, weightily sad aria in all of Verdi. That this scene begins with a mournful solo cello somehow reflects Philip's inner torment. He is so isolated and alone. Elisabeth never really loved him. Why should she? Philip has kept a mistress on the side, the swarthy Princess Eboli. He may be king, but he, like all the people of Spain, is beholden to the dictates of the church. The Grand Inquisitor appears to him in this scene as an old, blind, unyielding monk demanding the death of the rebellious, liberal-minded Carlos, a father's bond be damned.

Five years after the 1867 premiere in Paris, the opera was presented in an Italian revision in Naples. Verdi would revise it twice more, cutting out the ballet and, in one, eliminating the first act in Fontainebleau. So what's the "true" version of this masterpiece? In recent decades, the original French version has been gaining hold in opera houses. But the complete five-act score with the libretto in Italian is probably the standard, and it's magnificent.

An unusual commission came to Verdi from the Khedive (Viceroy) of Egypt for an Italian opera to celebrate the opening of the new opera house in Cairo. The khedive was a progressive-minded leader who wanted to modernize his country. Working with the librettist Antonio Ghislanzoni, Verdi fashioned a work set in ancient Egypt at a time of war with Ethiopia. *Aida* has long been identified as lavish grand opera, famous for its Triumphal Scene, with rows of Egyptian heralds trumpeting the victory of their army over the enemy, as soldiers march past cheering throngs of choristers trailed by exotic dancers and carriages full of war booty. Companies for generations have tried to outdo each other by staging this crowd scene with rows of supernumeraries and glittery spectacle. Even horses!

Actually, *Aida* is mostly an intimate personal drama dominated by scenes for one, two, or three characters. Wanting to give his commissioners something traditional, Verdi wrote a score that in places might seem a throwback to his earlier style, with set-piece arias and ensembles. But whole stretches of *Aida* offer music of refinement, mystery, and gossamer textures.

The drama turns on conflicts between romantic love and patriotic duty. Aida, an enslaved Ethiopian princess, serves as a personal maid to the alluring and manipulative Amneris, the daughter of the King of Egypt, who loves the valiant young Radamès, the captain of the guard. But Radamès has been carrying on a secret affair with Aida, who has kept her royal background secret.

The Aida of my youth, one of the greatest Aidas of all time, was Leontyne Price. I'll never forget hearing her at the Metropolitan Opera (the old

Met!) when I was in high school, especially the inspired aria "O patria mia" (O my country), the turning point of the entire drama, when Price's soaring, achingly sad and urgent phrases seemed to envelop me even in my upper-balcony seat.

Aida's noble father has appeared among the new batch of captured Ethiopians. When he discovers her romantic alliance with Radamès, he implores her, shames her, really, into taking advantage of the captain's love and finding out the battle plans of the Egyptians for their next campaign against the Ethiopian forces.

At the end of opera, Radamès, as punishment for his betrayal, has been entombed alive. As he voices his despair, he is horrified to see Aida crouching in the darkness. She has secretly hidden in the tomb, choosing to join her lover in death.

Many years after attending my first *Aida,* I was honored to spend time with Leontyne Price for some *New York Times* stories. As an African American artist who grew up in segregated Mississippi, Price understood prejudice and injustice. In 1955, when NBC Opera Theatre, a television series that broadcast live, staged operas, chose Price to sing the title role of Puccini's *Tosca,* many network affiliates in the South, including her home state, refused to show a program featuring a black Tosca and her white lover. So Price brought a personal connection to music that depicts a character torn between duty to her oppressed people and an illicit love for an enemy of her nation.

In 2000 I accompanied Price on a visit to a group of schoolchildren in Harlem, where she read a storybook version of *Aida* she had written, and in a surprise, sang before an assembly. Afterward she took some questions. One youngster asked why Aida was her favorite role. Price answered: "When I sang Aida, I used the most important plus I have. You have it; I have it. This beautiful skin. When I sang Aida, my skin was my costume."

Another comment Price made to those children in Harlem seemed especially revealing. She was asked if there was something about the story of the opera that she might change if she could. Yes, Price said. Rather than sacrificing herself for her lover, she would have wanted Aida to sacrifice her love and return to her country with her father to fulfill her duty. I have a hunch that Verdi would have been intrigued by that twist on the story.

Verdi did not attend the 1871 premiere of *Aida* on Christmas Eve 1871. But he carefully supervised the European premiere at La Scala in Milan in February 1872, a triumph that over the next two years alone led to productions in Italy, Germany, Spain, Austria, Argentina, New York (at the Academy of Music), and elsewhere. Having completed this major project, Verdi retreated to Sant'Agata to tend to his farmlands.

Then he met Arrigo Boito.

Born in 1842, Boito was a gifted poet, critic, librettist, and composer. In his twenties he was a firebrand who considered Verdi old hat and urged his generation to radicalize Italian opera. Then he wrote one, *Mefistofele,* based on Goethe's *Faust,* and learned that this business was harder than it looked. A failure at its 1868 premiere, the opera was revived successfully in 1875. By then, Boito had matured and considered Verdi a genius.

In 1879 Verdi and Giuseppina had dinner in Milan with Giulio Ricordi, from his publishing house, and the young conductor Franco Faccio, a close friend of Boito's. Ricordi brought up the idea of an opera adapted from *Othello.* Verdi's passion for Shakespeare was stoked. The next day Faccio brought Boito to Verdi's hotel. Their talk was cautious but encouraging. Three days later, Boito sent the composer a scenario for an *Othello* opera. Despite himself, Verdi was hooked.

For a long while Verdi dithered. He went through periods of doubt about his own stamina and Boito's sincerity. Once engaged, he wrote to Boito with detailed reactions to his libretto, while praising the text overall. By early 1884, Verdi, then seventy, was composing the score.

Shakespeare's elaborate play had to be condensed drastically, with the central story given more focus. The playwright's first act, in Venice, where Othello and Desdemona have clandestinely married, was eliminated. *Otello* begins on the shore of a coastal city in Cyprus as a storm at sea rages.

The first sound we hear is a gnashing, dissonant fortissimo chord from the orchestra, which immediately incites frantic runs among scattered instruments, to convey the heaving waves and wailing winds. A chorus of Cyprians trade terrified phrases, then break into desperate pleas for Otello's safe landing. Finally the boat manages to dock. The general enters triumphantly, and in one of the grandest, most vocally daunting entrances in all of opera, the tenor in the title role sings the declaration, "Esultate!" (Rejoice!). The "Muslim pride" is buried in the deep waters, Otello sings, and the very heavens seem to acclaim the glory of Cyprian arms. The music is a heroic, full-voiced proclamation. If a tenor singing Otello can pull off this daunting entrance as Verdi wrote it, the fortitude and charisma of the character is instantly established.

In a later scene, the malevolent Iago plots with Roderigo, a Venetian gentleman who has a secret yearning for Desdemona and cannot abide that she is married to a Moor, a former slave. Iago, jealous of Otello's newly appointed captain, the wholesome and honorable Cassio, proceeds to get the young officer drunk at a public celebration of Otello's victory.

Fights break out, just as Iago has planned. Cassio, out of control, wounds the noble Montano, who was trying to restore order. Otello rushes in, silences the crowd with a chilling command, and then, upon learning what happened, reluctantly strips Cassio of his rank. Roused from her marital chamber, Desdemona arrives, and we have something rare in Verdi: a love duet with a soprano and tenor who, at the moment of their intimacy, seem to have no complicating issues to inhibit their bliss. Though the duet has a self-contained structure, it unfolds as a series of rhapsodic avowals between an enraptured couple, ending with Otello's almost ritualized gesture when he adoringly kisses his wife three times, to the music of the "Un bacio" (A Kiss) motif.

In a telling scene in Act II, Cassio, shamed by his conduct and suffering from Otello's dismissal, goes, at the manipulative Iago's urging, to Desdemona to humbly ask her advice. Iago has begun to plant doubts in Otello's mind about his wife's virtue. When Desdemona pleads Cassio's case and asks her husband to forgive the crushed young man, the plaintive phrases she sings are so lush and romantic that subliminally you wonder whether there might be some truth to Iago's charge that Desdemona secretly loves Cassio.

At one point, in place of an important Shakespeare soliloquy for Otello, the opera presents a curiously light choral episode, when a delegation of townspeople and children bearing flowers serenades Desdemona with songs and mandolins. But as Verdi knew, intensely dramatic music can clobber you quickly. Just prior to this scene, as Iago sows doubts in Otello's mind, the music builds, moment to moment, with seething intensity. Verdi had to cool things down—hence the lapping, lyrical choral serenade. The scene also presents the townspeople as character witnesses for their new first lady. Before long, Iago is back at work manipulating his boss, and the music drives to a chilling final duet in which Otello, crazed with jealousy, vows to take bloody revenge.

In the final act, as Desdemona prepares to go to sleep in her bedchamber, Verdi gives her the wistful "Willow Song" followed by the angelic "Ave Maria." Sometimes, even in a good performance of Shakespeare's play, as the moment of Desdemona's death approaches it's hard not to see Othello as a weak-willed fool, for all his heroic deeds and legacy of suffering. But when a great soprano sings this scene in Verdi's opera, I'm always left concluding that, alas, raging jealousy may just be an inevitable part of the human condition. How could a husband as experienced in the world doubt a woman whose devotion and goodness come through so beautifully in Verdi's music?

On the day of the Scala premiere, February 5, 1887, the streets around the opera house were crowded with Milanese who had no tickets but at least wanted to be part of the scene. During the final ovations, Verdi, then seventy-three, and Boito were called back and back to the stage. Afterward, when Verdi and his wife got into their carriage, men in the streets detached the horses and dragged it to the Grand Hotel as crowds cheered.

After *Otello*, Verdi, pleased with his work, turned his attention to farming and philanthropy. He had long been involved with the planning of a badly needed charitable hospital in the vicinity of Sant'Agata, and that facility, built in nearby Villanova, opened in November 1887. All of its beds were immediately filled.

But Boito was eager to collaborate again and came up with the one idea Verdi could not resist: not just another Shakespeare project but a comedy. He sent Verdi a synopsis for an opera about the character Sir John Falstaff, the dissolute, portly, lovably boorish old knight, adapted from Shakespeare's *The Merry Wives of Windsor* and in scenes from *Henry IV, Part 1* and *Part 2*. Verdi was delighted.

"Excellent! Excellent!" he wrote to Boito. "One could not do better than you have done." This new work, "which just two days ago was in the world of dreams, now takes shape and becomes reality! When? How? . . . Who knows?"

When Verdi received Boito's completed libretto, he saw almost no need for alterations. The comic complications start in the opening scene, when we learn that the self-deluded Falstaff, who gets through life by mooching, has sent an identical love letter to two respectable women of Windsor, hoping to entice at least one of them into a tryst. Though Verdi wanted to keep the project secret, he began composing immediately, working in spurts, slowly and with difficulty.

For me the most revealing comment Verdi made while composing *Falstaff* came in a letter to Giulio Ricordi. "I am more convinced than ever," Verdi wrote, "that the huge size of La Scala would ruin its effect." In conceiving this opera, he explained, he had given no thought to theaters and singers. "I have written it on my own behalf to please myself, and I believe that, instead of La Scala, it ought to be put on at Sant'Agata."

Indeed, with this miraculous opera you sense Verdi disregarding general expectations about what an opera is supposed to be and finally, truly indulging himself. Inspired by Boito's snappy adaptation of Shakespeare's comic verse, Verdi wrote music that responded minutely to the verbal patterns and jaunty flow of the text. The score is like a rich fabric stitched together from hundreds of musical snippets. When the dramatic moment compels characters to break into a lyrical phrase, Verdi supplies some beautiful melodic lines, as when the young Nannetta—the daughter of the socially ambitious Ford and his sensible wife, Alice—and her adoring Fenton share avowals of young love during a mostly bustling comic scene. Yet though beguilingly lyrical, the tender exchanges between the young lovers are fleeting, like a series of melodic teases. Then Verdi gets us right back to the gurgling comedic music that prevails.

In its structure, *Falstaff* is as close as Verdi came to writing a through-composed opera, without set pieces and arias. There is an almost-aria for Fenton, a short but ardently lyrical ode to love, in the final scene, set in Windsor Park at night. The merry wives have concocted a scheme to humiliate Falstaff by luring him to an oak tree where, at midnight, he will be pricked and terrified by a chorus of goblins and spirits (the children and townspeople of Windsor are in on the plot). He needs to be taught a lesson. And later, Nannetta, disguised as the Queen of the Fairies, sings an enchanting quasi-aria with chorus, gorgeous music with floating melodies for soprano and delicate choral refrains. Otherwise *Falstaff* is mostly a continuously unfolding, wondrously lithe ensemble piece.

What Boito and Verdi convey so effectively in *Falstaff* is that this supposed comedy is not that funny when you really consider it. The merry wives play some mean tricks on Falstaff, a tubby old loudmouth. But all he's done to warrant their annoyance is circulate an absurd love letter.

Yet Verdi's Falstaff has a dark side. Having squandered his nobility and whatever money he had, Falstaff carries a bellyful of resentments in his beer-engorged paunch. The opera invites us to enjoy Falstaff's humiliation, which feels a little uncomfortable. At the end, having been exposed and ridiculed, Falstaff turns to the townspeople and asks what they would do without a character like him in their midst. A good point, the citizens admit. He then leads the ensemble in an everyone-on-stage final fugue, "Tutto nel mondo è burla" (All the world's a jest), a complex, ingenious piece, at once the ultimate comic-opera finale and Verdi's slightly satirical send-up of that most august of musical forms, the fugue.

Falstaff did open at La Scala after all, in February 1893, another triumph. Verdi was seventy-nine. After this he really did retire. He continued his philanthropic projects, including the construction of a retirement home in Milan for musicians who had come on hard times. Called Casa di Riposo per Musicisti, the building was completed in 1899. Verdi didn't want it to open until after his death, which came on January 27, 1901, when he was eighty-seven.

The Casa di Riposo continues to house needy musicians.

RICHARD WAGNER

I'll never forget the chill I felt when I first came across a disturbing full-page photograph in Frederic Spotts's engrossing 1994 history of the Wagner Festival in Bayreuth, Germany. Taken at the festival in the mid-1930s, the photo shows Hitler looking out from a second-story window of the annex that was added to the opera house in 1882 for King Ludwig II, Wagner's most important patron.

An excited throng has gathered in the plaza outside the annex. Everyone in the crowd is facing the Führer with their right arm raised in a Nazi salute.

During the summer of 2006, I attended a new production of Wagner's *Ring* at Bayreuth. And every time I stood in that plaza I thought about that unnerving photo. Looking up to that window, I realized how close Hitler would have been, how almost touchable he would have seemed.

As Führer he attended every festival between 1933 and 1939. In his book Spotts argues that no other head of a modern state was so obsessed with the arts. "Wars come and go," Hitler said. "What remains are cultural values alone." Inspired by Wagner's concept of opera as the ultimate *Gesamtkunstwerk,* an art form uniting poetry, music, theater, visual design, philosophy, even architecture, Hitler thought of himself, Spotts suggests, as an epic impresario with all of Germany as his opera house.

Historically, Hitler's enthusiasm for Wagner exacerbated complicated issues that tainted the composer's works and essays long before the rise of the Third Reich. Even during an era when anti-Semitism permeated European cultural and political circles, especially in Germany, Wagner's strident prejudices stood out. For him, all of what he viewed as superficial, ostentatious elements in contemporary music were attributable to the influence of Jewish musicians. Even a composer as skilled as Mendelssohn, Wagner felt, produced pieces spoiled by a facile, almost fawning quality, as if the composer were some interloper trying to speak a foreign musical language. In his essay "Das Judentum in der Musik" (Judaism in Music), Wagner argued, in the words of the scholar and critic Barry Millington, that "the rootlessness of Jews in Germany and their historical roles as usurers and entrepreneurs" have "condemned them, in Wagner's view, to cultural sterility." Wagner believed that German art had to be protected from this corrupting Jewish influence.

Yet while I had moments of eerie discomfort in the plaza at Bayreuth that summer, I was swept away by a thoughtful new production of the *Ring* and the probing, exhilarating performance that the German conductor Christian Thielemann drew from the superb festival orchestra. Beyond Wagner's case there has long seemed a paradox within all the arts: that certain narrow, petty, even warped people have somehow transcended themselves and touched the sublime in their work. Leaving the Bayreuth house after the inspired performance of *Die Walküre* that week, I was overcome more than ever by this profoundly human and deeply moving opera.

In *Walküre* the god Wotan must face up to the hash he has made of things. A power-grabbing patriarch, Wotan has broken the covenants he was bound to uphold and bungled his responsibilities as a father. From a godly distance he watched his stalwart son Siegmund grow into a heavy-hearted and homeless young man. Wotan hopes to manipulate Siegmund into rectifying the mistakes he himself has made. He turns for help to his favorite daughter, Brünnhilde, the spirited Valkyrie maiden, who adores him. Alas, it's too late. The downfall of the gods has been set in motion, as Wotan despondently understands. Still, the willful Brünnhilde acts not as her father reluctantly commanded but according to what she thinks he really wants.

The last twenty minutes of *Die Walküre,* when Wotan places Brünnhilde under a sleeping spell atop a mountain surrounded by impenetrable fire, is a portrait of a father punishing himself by punishing his child. This transfixing scene has some of the most sorrowfully beautiful music ever written. No one can convince me that the man who composed this opera, whatever his failings, did not understand the mystery of life, the sadness of human frailty, the tragedy of ambition, the cycles by which mistakes of one generation are visited upon the next.

Looked at from the cold perspective of financial soundness and artistic growth, Hitler's patronage of the festival during the 1930s was actually harmful. Jews had made up a significant proportion of the opera-loving German public. As Hitler's true intentions became clear, foreigners stayed away. Before long, attendance plummeted so steeply that Hitler ordered government agencies to buy blocks of tickets and compelled military officers, even those with scant interest in opera, to attend.

Worst of all, Jewish artists—singers, orchestral musicians, choristers, conductors—were purged from the festival. Many of them were forced into exile, with careers terribly disrupted, sometimes ruined. Others never made it out of Germany alive.

Since its founding, the festival has been run by members of the Wagner family, who in the decades after World War II tried to muddy the record of Wagner's anti-Semitism and the family's complicity with the Nazis, especially the role of the British-born Winifred Wagner, the wife of the composer's son, Siegfried. Winifred, who took charge of the festival in 1930, the year of her husband's death, was besotted with Hitler. When he came to Bayreuth, Hitler often stayed at Wahnfried, the Wagner family home, where he became beloved "Uncle Wolf" to Winifred's four children.

The entire orientation of the festival changed in 2008, when the half sisters Eva Wagner-Pasquier and Katharina Wagner, great-granddaughters of the composer, became its co-directors. From the start they pledged to make the festival less elitist. They also promised to unearth family links to the Nazi era in time for the Wagner centennial in 2013. The result was the 2012 outdoor exhibition, "Silenced Voices: The Bayreuth Festival and the Jews from 1876 to 1945," a series of some forty gray panels in the park adjacent to the opera house, next to the old bronze bust of Wagner. Each panel has a photograph and the history of a Jewish artist who took part in the festival at Bayreuth only to be purged or exiled or worse. The exhibition is now on permanent display.

In 2015 Katharina Wagner became the sole director and the renovated Wagner Museum at Wahnfried opened with a new, modern structure added. The house where Siegfried once lived has been repurposed as a museum with detailed displays and short films offering a brutally honest examination of the Wagner family's involvement with the rise of National Socialism.

R ichard Wagner was the ninth child born to Carl Friedrich Wagner, a clerk in the Leipzig police agency, and his wife, Johanna, the daughter of a baker. Yet there will always be some confusion over Richard's parentage. Carl Friedrich's friend Ludwig Geyer, an actor and playwright, was a frequent guest at the Wagner house. In November 1813, six months after Richard's birth, Carl Friedrich died of typhus. The next year Geyer and Johanna probably married, though documentation is sketchy. Geyer became Richard's official stepfather and, once settled into family life, proved a devoted parent. Wagner appears to have thought Geyer to be his biological father. The truth is unclear. As Millington suggests, it's not surprising that in choosing subjects for operas Wagner was often drawn to rootless characters who crave knowledge of their parents.

Geyer moved the family to Dresden, where he had work opportunities at the Hoftheater. Richard shared his stepfather's love of theater, and as a young boy was inspired by a production of Weber's *Der Freischütz,* a story of magic, romance, and adventure, conducted by the composer. Still, Richard's studies in music were minimal. When Geyer died in 1821, Richard was enrolled in a boarding school on the outskirts of the city. He imagined becoming a playwright and wrote a drama he intended to set to music. He never did.

When his family returned to Leipzig in 1828, Wagner neglected his academic studies to pursue theater and music. Proper music training did not begin until he enrolled at Leipzig University and took a concentrated tutorial with the cantor of St. Thomas Church. While at university Wagner composed a Beethoven-inspired Symphony in C and began work on an opera, *Die Hochzeit* (The Wedding), never completed.

In 1833, when Wagner was twenty, his brother Albert pulled strings to get him his first real job, as choirmaster at a theater in Würzburg. That year he wrote his first opera, *Die Feen* (The Fairies), a fanciful work in the style of Weber that was never produced in Wagner's lifetime. He would continue to write both the librettos and the music for all his operas.

Wagner went through stretches of his life mired in financial troubles, evading creditors and indulging in spendthrift habits. In 1834 he took what seemed a promising post as music director of the traveling theater company based in Magdeburg, made his debut as an opera conductor, and wrote his second opera, *Das Liebesverbot* (The Ban on Love), loosely based on Shakespeare's *Measure for Measure,* with a score that reveals a striking debt to Bellini's bel canto lyricism. The opera was produced at the Stadttheater in Magdeburg in 1836 but was deemed a failure and withdrawn after a single performance, leaving Wagner strapped again.

During this shaky period he fell in love with Minna Planer, one of the company's leading actresses, a beauty who seems to have returned Wagner's affection. Though of average height for his day (about 5 feet, 5 inches), Wagner had a commanding presence, even as a young man. He followed Minna to a theatrical engagement in Königsberg, where she helped him secure a position as music director, if only briefly. They married in November.

Wagner clearly adored "my dear sweet girl," as he called her. In a letter from Berlin he writes: "I shall never be happy, never enjoy even a single moment of happiness until I can again enfold you passionately in my arms once more." Marrying Wagner must have been an impulsive act for Minna, who left him briefly for another man the next spring. Their relationship would remain turbulent.

Minna rejoined Richard in 1837 after he secured a responsible post as music director of the theater at Riga, Latvia. True to form, Wagner mismanaged his household, provoked contractual wrangles with the company, accrued debts, and wound up having to flee.

En route to London in secret, the couple took a ship during a severe storm, a frightening experience that would later inspire the sea-storm music in *Der fliegende Holländer* (The Flying Dutchman). They eventually settled in Paris, where Wagner, professionally frustrated, made his living arranging operas by other composers for publishing firms.

But he composed steadily, completing *Rienzi* and *The Flying Dutchman* by 1842. That year he traveled to Dresden for the premiere of *Rienzi* at the Hoftheater. Set in fourteenth-century Rome and loosely based on the life of a populist crusader against unjust nobility, *Rienzi* is a five-act epic, rich with choruses, crowd scenes, a compelling depiction of a mob, stirring arias, and lavish orchestration. Within a month of the triumphant premiere, Wagner was appointed kapellmeister at the King of Saxony's court, with chief conducting duties at the theater.

The opening music of *The Flying Dutchman* certainly evokes a treacherous sea storm. You can almost hear rainy squalls and choppy waves in the turbulent strings and gnashing brass, driven by an ominous theme, like some desperate horn call. Choral exclamations convey the shouts of the crew echoing off the stony bluffs of a Norwegian fiord. The story, adapted from Heine, is the nautical legend of a defiant Dutch sea captain who one day swore to navigate the Cape of Good Hope, even if the Devil tried to stop him. For his rash words the Dutchman is condemned (By the heavens? The fates? Satan?) to roam the seas eternally, allowed just one brief stop ashore every seven years to try to seek redemption through a woman's love. The time has come for another docking, this one in a Norwegian village, where Senta, the daughter of a sea captain, lives. A serious and self-absorbed young woman, Senta has become obsessed with a picture of the Dutchman and the legend of his fate. She imagines herself the vehicle of his redemption.

The score contains some distinct arias, a rousing sailor's song, and a spinning chorus for the women of the village who mend sails and nets. Even so, Wagner made progress toward his concept of through-composed music drama, especially with the long, churning monologue for the Dutchman as he makes his heavy-footed way to the dock. Wagner originally composed the opera to be performed in one continuous swath lasting some two hours and twenty minutes. But after its 1843 Dresden premiere, bowing to pragmatic concerns, he revised it into a three-act version. Most companies today opt for the original.

During the remaining years of this decade Wagner produced the next two of what he himself dubbed his three *romantische* (romantic) operas, referring to their story lines and musical styles.

Tannhäuser, which had its premiere in 1845 at the Hoftheater in Dresden, presents a somewhat heavy-handed dichotomy between sacred and profane love. To explore this theme Wagner combined two unrelated medieval German legends: the tale of Tannhäuser, a knight crusader from Franconia who willingly succumbs to the allure of Venus, the goddess of love; and the story of the song contests held at Wartburg castle, in Thuringia, where knights and minstrels competed for prizes that often included the hands of young women.

There are two sets of characters with contrasting styles of music in this long, episodic opera. The opening scene depicts a bacchanal at the Venusberg, the hideaway of Venus, alive with bathing maids, dancing sirens, and cavorting nymphs. Wagner's restless, skittish music, harmonically unsettled, reaches a pitch of orgiastic abandon, until finally it settles down and we hear alluring, soothing choral refrains. Act II introduces us to the knightly realm in the Hall of Song at Wartburg, where Elisabeth, the winsome niece of the honorable Landgrave of Thuringia, sings a joyous greeting to the glorious hall ("Dich, teure Halle"), a set-piece aria that has long been a concert favorite. Elisabeth, who had fallen in love with Tannhäuser earlier when she heard him excel in a song contest, awaits his return and anticipates a blissful reunion.

When he arrives, Tannhäuser readily enters the song contest. But hearing Wolfram, a good-hearted contender, sing an idealized paean to love (which the savvy Wagner conveys in earnest but somewhat stiff and square music), Tannhäuser cannot help scoffing at this tepid love ode. He launches into an ecstatic song, a graphic tribute to burning desire. Everyone in the hall is shocked; Elisabeth is crushed with disappointment. Tannhäuser must leave.

There is no real synthesis between sacred and profane love. Sacred love prevails. The spiritually bereft Tannhäuser, transformed by Elisabeth's death from grief, finds salvation amid lofty choral stirrings of pilgrims returned from Rome. Though the juxtaposition of styles can be awkward, *Tannhäuser* certainly provides the "romantic" fervor Wagner promised on its title page.

His third "romantic" opera, *Lohengrin*, introduced in Weimar in 1850, is a more integrated and assured work in its dramatic shape and musical character. Still, you must take a leap into melodramatic mysticism to go along with the story, set in tenth-century Antwerp, based on medieval German romances about Lohengrin, a knight of the Grail. Yet with Wagner's radiant, multi-layered score this magical tale turns into a spiritual parable.

Wagner suffuses the story with elegance from the first strains of the transfixing orchestra prelude, which conveys the aura of the Grail through high floating strings. The music unfolds in an ethereal span of slow, shimmering beauty. In this prelude, and throughout the opera, Wagner moves decisively into the realm of a richly chromatic and wayward harmonic language.

Lohengrin also represents an advance in Wagner's extensive use of what came to be called leitmotifs (leading motifs), though this term did not originate with Wagner. It was first applied to his works by a music historian in 1860 and didn't really come to Wagner's attention until the *Ring* was produced in 1876. Previously, Wagner had employed more general terms, like "melodic moment" and "thematic moment."

Wagner may have had reservations about the term, but it's long been a useful tool for analyzing his works. A leitmotif is simply a theme, musical idea, or harmonic progression that is associated with a character, locale, action, object, supernatural force, or any other significant element of an opera. An important example in *Lohengrin* is what's called the forbidden question leitmotif, associated with Lohengrin's admonition that he must not be asked his name or background, even by the noble, trusting Elsa, whom he defends and marries. After establishing the musical association with this facet of the story, Wagner invokes it, for example, when the question later burns in Elsa's mind.

In crucial dramatic moments of an opera, Wagner's invocation of a leitmotif can be forceful and explicit—for example, the knightly sword motif that runs through the *Ring*. Yet for the most part, Wagner weaves subtle or slightly transformed evocations of a leitmotif into the orchestra. As listeners we may not consciously pick up these veiled references. But our ears have better musical memories, as Wagner knew. So the near-disguised invocation of a leitmotif can still accomplish its psycho-musical aim.

The lead tenor role of *Tannhäuser* presents formidable vocal challenges. Wagner made unprecedented demands upon singers. Still, the idea that it takes a barrel-chested heldentenor (heroic tenor) to sing Tannhäuser and Tristan, or a super-sized dramatic soprano to sing Brünnhilde, is an unfair caricature.

Yes, a Wagner singer must have a voice with plenty of carrying power in order to be heard over a Wagner orchestra, as well as enough stamina to last through these works: the running time of *Tannhäuser* is about three and a half hours; *Götterdämmerung* is four and a half!

Yet Wagner respected the basic precepts of the bel canto approach to singing, which valued evenness throughout the vocal range, flexibility, and a smooth legato. Brünnhilde's famous, and much parodied, Valkyrie call of "Hojotoho!" includes a sustained trill before the final high note—a vocal embellishment right out of Rossini.

The outstanding Wagner singers of my early experience, especially Birgit Nilsson and Jon Vickers, had enormous voices but also lyrical elegance, and never sounded like they were forcing or shouting. Singers who try to muscle their way through Wagner roles usually wind up having short careers.

W agner could not attend the premiere of *Lohengrin*, which took place at the Staatskapelle in Weimar in August 1850, arranged and conducted by Liszt, a steadfast supporter. Politics had intervened. Wagner was hiding out in Zürich.

He had long been sympathetic to left-wing causes and the progressive Junges Deutschland (Young Germany) movement, which found inspiration in utopian socialism. During the late 1840s, Wagner made his Dresden home a gathering place for German nationalists and foreign radicals. When an insurrection broke out in 1848, Wagner got involved. During a crackdown by Prussian troops the next year, arrest warrants were issued, and Wagner, now a prominent target, was forced to flee, first to Weimar, and finally to Switzerland. He would spend twelve years there in exile, without steady employment or an official post.

During these first years in Zürich, Wagner wrote a series of significant essays, including "The Artwork of the Future" and "Opera and Drama," the two that most fully explained his concept of opera as a *Gesamtkunstwerk*. He advanced populist principles for music drama. Theaters, he argued, would have to be redesigned to eliminate social hierarchies, without the upper classes seated in rarefied special sections, so that the entire space could better serve the communal artistic experience.

He also asserted that music, like other components of his total work of art, had to support the drama, the implication being that music's role was subordinate. This notion has always confused me. If all Wagner meant was that music should serve the words, then opera composers from Monteverdi to Mozart to Britten would agree. But if he meant that music should be in any way subordinate to the overall drama, then I disagree. Thankfully for music lovers, Wagner's own music dramas are driven and defined by his music.

During this Zürich period Wagner also began working on the *Ring* cycle, an operatic venture of unprecedented scope. It would take him some twenty-five years to complete the *Ring*, from initial concept to final composition, though in 1857, having finished nearly three-quarters of the cycle, Wagner set it aside for eleven years. He was hardly idle during the break: he wrote *Tristan und Isolde* and *Die Meistersinger von Nürnberg*, two staggering masterpieces.

He finally finished the *Ring*, in 1874. The pragmatic challenges of this four-part music drama were unprecedented. The complete cycle was not premiered until 1876, in a production that inaugurated the house at Bayreuth. The *Ring* still challenges any opera company. Even so, no company today considers itself a player in the field until it comes up with its own *Ring*.

One curiosity about the creation of the *Ring* is that Wagner wrote the librettos in reverse order. Inspired by tales of Norse mythology, he sketched out a libretto for an opera to be called *Siegfried's Death*. Naturally, he had to include scenes and passages about his hero's life prior to the events surrounding his death. Then he decided to flesh out more of that life in a prequel. He wound up going back even further, then added a prologue, until finally he had a chronological series of four operas: *Das Rheingold* (The Rhinegold), the prologue; *Die Walküre* (The Valkyrie); *Siegfried;* and *Götterdämmerung* (Twilight of the Gods). When he started composing, however, he set the texts to music in the proper order.

In the *Ring* Wagner comes much closer to achieving his ideal of a *Gesamtkunstwerk,* a through-composed dramatic form integrating all the arts. This mythic tale perfectly suited his ambitious aesthetic aim. And what a tale!

The title of the entire cycle, *Der Ring des Nibelungen* (The Ring of the Nibelung), alludes to Alberich, a smithy of a downtrodden race, the Nibelung dwarfs. Alberich seethes with long-nursed resentments and stifled ambitions. *Das Rheingold,* the prologue, lasting some two and a half hours and performed without break, opens with a wondrous scene set below the swirling currents of the Rhine, where we meet the three Rhinemaidens, who guard a lump of magical gold near the riverbed. Legend holds that anyone who renounces love and crafts a ring from the enchanted gold can become master of the universe. This symbolism is crucial. The *Ring* can be taken as a metaphorical tale about the relationship between power and love. Real love, not just lust or sex, but deep, emotional love, involves relinquishing some power.

In the opening scene, Wagner's undulant orchestral music evokes the river, starting with a primordial sustained low E-flat, over which a motif of rising notes from an E-flat chord linger and then diffuse into lapping arpeggio figurations, all to convey the rippling currents. This shimmering, shifting prolongation of an E-flat harmony lasts for the first 136 measures of this engrossing orchestral introduction.

Alberich comes upon the Rhinemaidens and, with nothing to lose, starts flirting with them. Of course they find him odious, though at first they amuse themselves by flirting back, only to end by mocking and rebuffing him. But they let slip the secret of the gold. So Alberich decides to renounce love, steal the gold, and use his smithy skills to make a ring. He easily escapes with his prize, leaving the Rhinemaidens stunned by his greed and humiliated by their own irresponsibility.

The next scene opens atop a mountain where Wotan and his wife, Fricka, are asleep as daybreak beckons. While full of contradictions, Wotan should be recognizable to any political junkie. Though he heads an extended family of gods, Wotan is not all-powerful. His authority is restrained by a system of checks and balances through a cabinet of sub-gods. Even Wotan's immortality is dependent upon the goddess Freia, Fricka's sister, who tends to the golden apples that keep the gods eternal. Wotan's main responsibility involves enforcing the covenants engraved in ancient runes on the spear he carries with him at all times.

Prior to the events of *Das Rheingold,* Wotan had hired the giants Fasolt and Fafner to build Valhalla, a glorious castle, as a home for the gods. Wotan seems to have thought that if only he could get all the gods under one roof, like some imperial White House, he might better control them. The castle will also be a fortress for their protection. But as payment for their labor Wotan promised the giants something he cannot deliver: the goddess Freia. He figured that when the time came he would finagle the terms of the contract.

That time has arrived. The giants appear, holding the terrified Freia, to demand the payment they were guaranteed. In a bind, Wotan calls upon Loge, a demigod of fire and trickery, who arrives with news and a possible rescue plan.

Loge tells Wotan about Alberich, who has returned to Nibelheim, the underworld where the dwarf race resides. Having made a ring of the stolen gold, Alberich is using its magical power to coerce the Nibelungen workers into mining a hoard of gold. Loge leads Wotan to this lower realm, where they find the gloating Alberich.

Among Alberich's new possessions is a magic Tarnhelm, a thin golden helmet that allows its wearer to turn himself into any other person or creature, or even become invisible. Alberich shows it off, briefly becoming first a monstrous serpent, and then a small frog, at which moment Wotan and Loge pounce. They seize Alberich, who returns to his dwarf form, now a captive.

The intruders command Alberich to instruct his minions to cart all the newly mined gold to Valhalla. Wotan also claims the Tarnhelm and, most important, the ring—but not before Alberich places a sneering curse on it, a leitmotif ominously fortified by the snarling orchestra.

Back at the mountaintop, the giants, though reluctant to surrender their claim to Freia, agree to accept the stash of gold along with the Tarnhelm as a substitute payment. Intrigued by the ring that Wotan is wearing, the giants demand it. Wotan, bored in his loveless marriage and hungry for more power, refuses to relinquish the ring.

Then, in arguably the most important episode of the entire cycle, Erda, the earth goddess, ascends from her underworld with a prophecy. Intoning her vocal lines over mysterious orchestral music (an ingeniously subtle, slowed-down and minor-mode transformation of the leitmotif associated with the swirling waters of the Rhine), Erda warns Wotan to give up the ring. He has broken the covenants he swore to uphold, undermining his authority, she explains. The ring is cursed, its power now useless to Wotan.

Reluctantly Wotan surrenders the ring. Sure enough, its curse kicks right in. The giants start fighting over the gold, especially the ring. Fafner kills his brother Fasolt and then coldly stalks off with his booty.

But Wotan's curiosity has been aroused. Erda is the source of all knowledge, and, as Wotan knows, knowledge is power. The gods and goddesses march with renewed dignity up a rainbow bridge into Valhalla, their new home, as the orchestra enshrouds them in celestial music based on the majestic leitmotif of Valhalla. From this point on, the *Ring* becomes a battle of wits between the lordly Wotan and the lowly Alberich, played out by their surrogates over generations.

Die Walküre takes place many years later. During that interim much has happened.

Wotan indeed paid a long visit to Erda, who bore him nine daughters, whom Wotan raised to be Valkyries, a sibling posse of warrior maidens tasked with bringing heroes fallen in battle to Valhalla, where they will be revived and pressed into service as defenders of the gods. Wotan also fathered twins, a boy and a girl, from a mortal woman, in an effort to foster a new race of Volsungs that might undo his mistakes and somehow reclaim the ring. Things have not worked out as he had hoped, however, as we discover during the first act of *Die Walküre*.

An orchestral prelude evokes a harrowing storm, with a sustained string tremolo that menacingly swells and subsides in volume, a hard-driving motif in the lower strings that shifts up and down the steps of a D minor scale, and brassy bursts of the thunder motif from *Rheingold*. That obsessive riff, now calmed down, returns as the curtain rises to reveal a rough-hewn dwelling place deep within a forest. A tall tree in the midst of the house protrudes right through its roof.

A young man (Siegmund) comes through the door looking tattered and exhausted. The orchestra plays a forlorn slow motif that dips and rises, a transformed version of the pelting rain riff. The man collapses in a faint, which rouses a young woman (Sieglinde) from an inner chamber. She assumes that her husband has returned. Instead, the fearful woman finds a pitiable stranger.

The orchestra plays the Sieglinde motif, which is melodically yearning and inquisitive. The man startles awake and asks for water, which Sieglinde fetches. Quenching his thirst, he asks who it is that revived him. Looking into each other's eyes, these young people feel an instinctive connection, something Wagner conveys beautifully by having the orchestra mingle their poignant motifs.

The approach of Hunding, Sieglinde's husband, is announced by a leitmotif, a menacing brass fanfare, though a fleeting flourish of triplets makes it seem a little pompous.

Hunding calls for his evening meal and, bowing to protocol, grudgingly invites the stranger to sit with him. In time the young man, who calls himself "Wehwalt" (meaning the Woeful One), tells his story, which Sieglinde seems greedy to hear, as her husband notices.

He was born with a twin sister, Siegmund says; his father was called Wolfe. One day, when just a young boy, he and his father returned from hunting to find their wolf's nest home burned to the ground, his mother killed, and his sister abducted. For some time afterward he roamed the woods with his father, until a tribal band attacked them and they were separated. At this moment in the story the orchestra, playing the Valhalla motif, tells us what Siegmund does not know: that Wolfe, his father, is the god Wotan.

Siegmund continues his tale. He arrived at their home in desperation, he says, having lost his weapons, and nearly his life, in an attempt to rescue a young woman who was being forced into marriage. Hunding now understands that this stranger is the intruder who tried to stop the wedding ceremony he just attended. This means his enemy is sitting before him at dinner. Following the customs of his clan, he permits the stranger to stay the night, but tells him to arm himself and prepare to fight in the morning.

Left alone, Siegmund calls in despair to his long-absent father, who promised that in a time of need he would find a powerful weapon. Sieglinde appears and, looking frantic, explains that she slipped a sleeping potion into Hunding's drink so that the stranger can escape.

As Sieglinde tells her story in wistful, aching phrases, the orchestra gently sounds the Valhalla motif, which is prolonged lyrically and keeps shifting into higher, more lofty-sounding key areas, until it transforms into a consoling phrase that supports Sieglinde's sighing vocal lines. Here is Wagner using a leitmotif to convey an essential message to the audience, something that Sieglinde does not realize: that her father is a powerful god; that she is not the orphaned nobody she has been made to believe; and that the noble young stranger is her long-lost brother.

All this comes out in time during the long subsequent scene between these two affecting characters. Wagner's music shifts from episodes coursing with sensuality and desire, to stretches of tenderness and relief. Unable to resist their stirred-up emotions, they embrace the inevitable, that they can be brother and sister as well as a loving couple

It's a crucial metaphorical point, and strangely touching, that in the *Ring,* where most marriages and couplings seem to result from pacts between clans or even magic potions, the one union of pure love is the incestuous relationship between Siegmund and Sieglinde.

The dramatic climax of the act (a moment that also suggests sexual arousal and potency) comes when Siegmund, calling upon his father, straining with athletic effort, pulls a sword from the tree in the middle of the house and waves it over his head as Sieglinde looks on in ecstasy. The lover-siblings rush off together as the orchestra explodes with frenzied jubilation.

A brief orchestral prelude in Act II depicts the unseen lovers fleeing Hunding and arriving at a wild, rocky place. From this stormy passage the orchestra segues into a full-blown statement of what will later become the Ride of the Valkyries music. Wotan wants Brünnhilde to shield Siegmund and help him prevail.

Brünnhilde, excited to carry out this order, sings her famous *hojotoho* warrior cry, and then slyly gives her father a warning. Fricka is approaching and she looks really angry, Brünnhilde says. In this brief moment we glean much about her relationship with Wotan. Though he is a stern, ferocious father, Brünnhilde dares to have fun with him, joking that while she herself, being a warrior maiden, knows nothing about marital spats, Fricka seems ready to provoke one. After another war cry, Brünnhilde rushes off.

Fricka arrives and castigates her husband for hiding himself in the mountains to avoid his wife's notice. As the godly guardian of marriages, Fricka has heard Hunding's call for revenge against those who have wronged him.

Wotan asks what their offense was. Love's magic bewitched them, he argues. Calling her husband stupid and deaf, Fricka lays out her case in what may be the most convincing depiction of a marital argument in opera.

Not only have these impulsive young people violated Sieglinde's wedding vows, Fricka charges; they have entered into an incestuous bond. In shock she asks: "When did it ever happen that brother and sister are lovers?"

Wotan seems unperturbed. Things that never occurred can take place spontaneously, he explains. The gist of his reply, really a stinging putdown, is: So, Fricka, you've never heard of such a thing? Well, you've heard of it now.

Fricka then begins a long litany of Wotan's failings. He thinks nothing of his noble family and his sacred vows; he rips apart bonds he himself had made to gratify the pleasure of these "monstrous twins." But who is she to protest, Fricka says in despair, when her own husband has strayed so often during his marriage?

Wotan patiently tries to explain the larger context to Fricka. He has been engaged in a long-term effort to raise a hero who, free of divine protection, can take independent action to do the deed upon which the very future of the gods depends. What he means, of course, is that Siegmund can steal back the ring.

But Wotan realizes, just as Erda had warned him, that he himself set in motion the grim fate of the gods, and that the curse upon the ring remains. His controlling hands, from afar, would be all over Siegmund's heroic actions. Fricka's argument is unassailable.

Wotan, defeated, asks Fricka what she wants of him. Wotan must not just abandon Siegmund in his coming fight with Hunding, Fricka insists, but remove the power of Siegmund's sword and cause him to be killed. Despondent, Wotan accedes to her wishes. In leaving, she attempts a moment of loving reconciliation, as the orchestra swells with an arching, tender melodic line. Wotan remains stiff and remote.

Returning to the scene, Brünnhilde finds her father troubled. "I am the least free of all men," he says, almost to himself, "the saddest." "Confide in me," Brünnhilde urges. In a wrenching moment, Wotan asks whether by expressing his thoughts aloud he would release his grip on his own will. Brünnhilde gently replies that in speaking to her, Wotan is speaking to his will.

So begins the long episode known as Wotan's Narrative, in which he tells Brünnhilde the whole, sorry story of his restless wanderings, his theft of the ring, and Erda's prophecies. This scene should affect anyone who has felt deep love for a fearsome, patriarchal father who, in a rare confessional moment, unburdens himself to a devoted child.

Wotan orders Brünnhilde to defend the sacred vows of marriage by aiding Hunding. Knowing her father's true heart, Brünnhilde begs him to take back this awful command. But Wotan is vehement. Sadly, she promises to obey and heads off.

In the next scene, Siegmund and Sieglinde arrive at a rocky pass in the forest. Brünnhilde mysteriously appears, as the orchestra plays a solemnly rising melodic line cushioned by rich, ebbing chords, a leitmotif signaling the annunciation of death. Struck by her gravely spiritual presence, Siegmund asks who she is. Only those fated to die can see me, Brünnhilde replies. She is here to take him to a special place for heroes, Valhalla. "Will I find my father there?" Siegmund asks. "Your father will be there to greet you," Brünnhilde assures him. "Will I be welcomed by a woman?" he asks. "Wotan's daughter will serve you drink," Brünnhilde replies. Siegmund now recognizes who this immortal stranger is. "Will Siegmund embrace Sieglinde there?" he asks hopefully. No, Sieglinde must remain behind.

Then, Siegmund insists, he will not follow Wotan's daughter. Rather than leave Sieglinde he will kill her, he says, then kill himself. As he hoists his sword Brünnhilde shouts for him to stop.

Brünnhilde has never seen a man and woman in love, certainly not her thunderous father and his quarrelsome wife. Deeply moved, she tells Siegmund that she will protect him after all. As she leaves, Hunding approaches.

A brutal fight ensues. But at the moment when Brünnhilde appears and shouts to Siegmund to trust his sword, Wotan, furious, intervenes and takes away the sword's power, allowing Hunding to smash it in two and stab Siegmund fatally. As the Valsung dies, his grieving father cradles him for a bitterly brief moment. In the background, Brünnhilde gathers the sword pieces and ushers the horrified Sieglinde away.

Act III opens with the best-known music of the *Ring*, the Ride of the Valkyries, though those who know it only from its version as an orchestra piece may be thrilled to hear it as originally conceived: a rousing ensemble for eight female Wagnerian singers whose voices soar over a glorious orchestral din. The warrior maidens see Brünnhilde approaching on her flying steed. She has a young woman with her. No Valkyrie has ever brought a woman to Valhalla.

Brünnhilde pleads with her sisters to protect her and Sieglinde from Wotan, who is furious with them both. In despair, Sieglinde wants to join her beloved in death. But Brünnhilde explains that Sieglinde must live for the sake of the son she now carries. Sieglinde, feeling exultant, sings the soaring redemption motif, a theme that will return at the conclusion of the entire *Ring* cycle.

As Wotan approaches, the Valkyrie sisters form a flank of bodies to hide Brünnhilde. But their father promises to visit Brünnhilde's fate on any Valkyrie who protects her. She emerges to accept her punishment. After all, how bad can it be?

Very bad. Unhinged with anger, Wotan declares that he will remove Brünnhilde's godly powers and place her in a sleeping spell atop this mountain. The first man who finds her will claim her as his wife.

Her sisters are horrified. But lest they suffer the same fate, they must leave this place forever, Wotan decrees. The rest of this long act is devoted to one of the most complex father-daughter interactions ever written.

Brünnhilde tries in numerous ways to make the same point: that in disobeying Wotan's instructions she was following his heart, his true will, which she is privileged to know. She tries to blame Fricka for coercing Wotan to act against his instincts and love for the twins. The real cause of his fury, though, seems obvious: in defying her father, Brünnhilde also defied Fricka, while he, Wotan the god, caved to his moralistic wife's demands. As a husband, let alone a god, he's ashamed. In punishing Brünnhilde he is punishing himself.

Brünnhilde would rather die than suffer such defilement. But if Wotan's punishment must be imposed, she says, may she make one adjustment? While she is under the sleeping spell can her mountaintop be protected by, say, a wall of fire, so that only a heroic man deserving of her will make his way to her? Wotan breaks down and agrees, and they share a final father-daughter embrace.

With a haunting series of sustained chords that touch on a cyclic harmonic progression, chords written in two lines, one descending, the other ascending, Wotan removes Brünnhilde's godhood. To me, this transfixing music suggests what is taking place metaphysically: Brünnhilde is descending into sleep and shedding her godly nature while ascending into a transformed state of ordinary mortality, which has its pluses, as she will learn.

Wotan calls upon Loge to whip up some fire. Soon the mountaintop is surrounded by impenetrable flames, as high woodwinds and strings flicker with the Magic Fire Music over an orchestral undertow dominated by the fate motif that was heard when Brünnhilde appeared to Siegmund to announce his death. But it's Brünnhilde who has sunk into a deathlike sleep. For now.

The battle between Wotan and Alberich is carried on through their descendants during the last two operas in the cycle. *Siegfried* tells the story of the child of Siegmund and Sieglinde. He has been raised in the forest by the wily Mime, Alberich's bullied brother, who found the desperate Sieglinde in the forest and cared for her until she died in childbirth. Mime hopes to twist this boy to his own ends and gain the ring, which would teach his brother a lesson. The motherless Siegfried has grown to be strong and impulsive, and has never known fear.

Siegfried is like the scherzo of a four-movement Wagnerian operatic symphony. Still, the title character has two consequential encounters on the path to his destiny with Brünnhilde.

In the first, he confronts the giant Fafner, who, thanks to the Tarnhelm, has taken the form of an enormous, sleepy dragon, guarding the cave where the gold is stashed. Siegfried handily slays Fafner and claims the magic ring, having been alerted to its baffling powers by a forest bird. The second encounter occurs when Siegfried comes upon a sullen man in a gray cloak carrying a spear who calls himself the Wanderer. It's Wotan, now a remnant of the powerful god, who has taken to roaming the forest, waiting for the inevitable. The Wanderer attempts to persuade this restless young man to take the ring back to the river. When that fails, he tries to block Siegfried's way. But Siegfried lunges at the Wanderer, smashing the old man's staff—the symbol of Wotan's authority—in two. The Wanderer walks dejectedly away—the last appearance of Wotan in the *Ring*.

This leads to Siegfried's ultimate encounter, atop the mountain surrounded by fire. He discovers what he assumes to be a sleeping warrior. When he removes the breastplate and horned helmet, he is stunned. He has never before seen a woman. For the first time ever, Siegfried experiences fear. All the previous certainties of his life have been rattled.

He kisses Brünnhilde, awakening her. She, too, is stunned and confused. Her godhood is gone. In a good performance, this moment is overwhelming. As Brünnhilde senses her changed nature, halting remnants of her Valkyrie cry rustle in the orchestra, trying to lift off but too fractured to do so. New sensations of human vulnerability stir within Brünnhilde, along with intimations of joy and relief. Thus begins one of the great love scenes in opera, music that mingles helpless desire, strange fear, and mystical ecstasy.

In *Götterdämmerung,* back at the mountaintop, Brünnhilde and Siegfried are blissfully enjoying their love. Yet Siegfried has grown restless and yearns to continue his manly manifest destiny—pursuing adventures. Wearing the ring as a token of Siegfried's love, Brünnhilde is certain he will return. So off he goes.

Then humans enter the *Ring* fully for the first time. Hagen, Alberich's illegitimate son, who has become his father's instrument for retribution against Wotan and his descendants, has been accepted into a landed family, the Gibichungs, headed by the brother and sister Gunther and Gutrune. Hagen has come up with a labyrinthine scheme to entice the renowned Siegfried to the castle, and then spike his drink with a drug that will cause him to lose all memory of Brünnhilde and fall in love with Gutrune.

When he shows up, Siegfried proves an easy mark. He accepts the drink and falls helplessly for Gutrune. Now he will do anything to serve the family. Hagen tells him about a woman on a mountain and persuades him to abduct her and deliver her to Gunther as a bride. That woman, of course, is Brünnhilde.

Though there are myriad complications, Siegfriend delivers the shocked, betrayed Brünnhilde to the Gibichungs. In the penultimate scene, after Hagen's plan to kill Siegfried and make it look like a hunting accident, has succeeded, the dying man is restored to reason just long enough to invoke the name of his beloved Brünnhilde. When she learns that she and Siegfried were victims of a conspiracy, Brünnhilde takes apocalyptic revenge.

During the magnificent Immolation Scene, she places Siegfried's body on a funeral pyre and then rides her horse into its flames, which grow wildly. The unearthly fire engulfs Valhalla and the gods cowering within, guilty of corruption and overreaching. The river overflows its banks, douses the flames, and carries the ring back to the Rhinemaidens. The world order will be restored. The "twilight" of the gods slips into never-ending night. For better or worse, man is going to have to get along with the gods.

At least that's my take. Few works are as rich in interpretive possibilities as the *Ring*. For me, though, one given cannot be toyed with. I'll go along with any production concept—stage it as a *Star Wars* saga, portray Wotan as the powerful CEO of the Valhalla Corporation—as long as the gods come across as members of a big dysfunctional family. I think Wagner intended for us to see ourselves in the gods. Whether they seem mythical, contemporary, or futuristic, the gods should look, more or less, like us.

A s Wagner worked feverishly on the *Ring*, he increasingly comprehended the production demands this epic work would entail. No theater he knew of could stage the *Ring* as he conceived it: a four-part, fifteen-plus-hour music drama presented on consecutive nights. What company had the resources and personnel? If he couldn't find the house he needed, well, he would have to build one, tailored to his visionary conception of opera as drama.

Beyond these frustrations, there was Wagner's unceasing frustration with Minna, his unhappy wife, whom he was beginning to think of as an emotional invalid. These combined stresses probably caused him to break off composition of the *Ring* in 1857, after completing Acts I and II of *Siegfried*. He needed a fresh creative jolt. He had an idea he'd been pondering for years.

I n the fall of 1854 Wagner immersed himself in the writings of the philosopher Arthur Schopenhauer, especially his 1818 work *The World as Will and Representation*, as he explained in a letter late that year to Liszt.

Schopenhauer's "principal idea, the final denial of the will to live, is of terrible seriousness, but it is uniquely redeeming," Wagner wrote. "When I think back on the storms that have buffeted my heart and on its convulsive efforts to cling to some hope in life," against his better judgment, Wagner explained, "I have now found a sedative which has finally helped me to sleep at night," namely, "the sincere and heartfelt yearning for death: total unconsciousness, complete annihilation, the end of all dreams—the only ultimate redemption!"

At the time, though still working on *Walküre* and "dreaming" on *Siegfried,* as Wagner reported to Liszt, he had another work in mind. Since he had never in his life "enjoyed the true happiness of love," he wrote, "I intend to erect a further monument to this most beautiful of dreams, a monument in which this love will be properly sated from beginning to end: I have planted in my head a *Tristan and Isolde,* the simplest, but most full-blooded musical conception."

Something else was causing Wagner to experience insatiable will: an infatuation with Mathilde Wesendonck, a poet and writer, the wife of a silk merchant, both of them loyal supporters of Wagner. In 1857 the couple placed a cottage on their estate in Zürich at Wagner's disposal. Wagner wrote song settings for voice and piano of five poems by Mathilde, a cycle known as the *Wesendonck Lieder.* Two of them, Wagner said, were "studies" for *Tristan und Isolde* in which he tried out themes that would become crucial to the opera. It is not known whether there was actually an affair, but in 1858 Minna found a compromising letter from Wagner to Mathilde, resulting in a bitter showdown. Minna left for Germany; Wagner sought peace and quiet in Venice. He had already finished the libretto for *Tristan,* and by August 1859 he had completed the composition. He seized on the legend of Tristan and Isolde to explore love as an overwhelming force leading to metaphysical transfiguration.

In Wagner's version, set in the Middle Ages, Tristan, a noble knight from Brittany, orphaned in youth, is the adopted heir of Marke, King of Cornwall, his uncle. The story begins aboard a ship, navigated by Tristan, who is taking Isolde, a young Irish princess, to Cornwall to be the wife of his honorable king. The first voice we hear is a young sailor singing a solo song about some "wild Irish maid." Assuming she is being mocked, Isolde curses her "degenerate race" for not resisting the tyranny of their enemies in Cornwall. She directs particular fury at Tristan. In a long, heated scene known as Isolde's Narrative and Curse, which she pours out to her devoted maid Brangäne, we learn why.

Sometime earlier, Tristan, having been provoked into combat, killed Isolde's betrothed, Morold. Suffering a poisoned wound himself, Tristan, calling himself "Tantris," was found by Isolde, famed for her practice in the herbal arts. She nursed him back to health. When she realized who this Tantris really was, Isolde resolved to kill him. Yet something in his eyes, she tells Brangäne, softened her; something passed between them and she dropped her sword on the ground.

Tristan returned to seek her hand not for himself, but for his childless king. Now, utterly humiliated, Isolde is being brought "like a chattel," she tells Brangäne, to be Marke's joyless bride. That Tristan has avoided her during the trip stokes her bitterness. She has resolved to take action.

Sending word through his devoted servant Kurwenal, Isolde has asked Tristan to share a drink of reconciliation with her. But she instructs Brangäne to prepare a death potion: Tristan and Isolde will die together. Brangäne is horrified. The only way she can think of to subvert Isolde's chosen path is to substitute secretly a love potion.

Tristan, who values duty above all else, reports to Isolde as requested. When she proposes a drink, he suspects what she is up to, but does as asked.

What is this love potion in Wagner's telling of the story? Does it have any actual effect? Perhaps it is a kind of truth serum that makes it impossible for Tristan and Isolde to repress their mutual feelings any longer. In another intriguing interpretation, by drinking what they both believe to be poison, Tristan and Isolde enter into Schopenhauer's realm of love as an insatiable yearning that can only be resolved through death. Or maybe the potion is essentially a placebo that allows them to give in to their passion.

After sharing the drink, Tristan and Isolde feel shocked and panicked. What have we done? What now? They are soon seized with uncontrollable desire.

The core of Act II involves a long, complex love duet for the couple, who meet illicitly at night. When Tristan appears, the lovers overflow with ecstasy, though their feelings slowly calm as the mellifluously lyrical duet begins, "O sink hernieder, Nacht der Liebe" (Descend, O night of love). Metaphorically, the opera—this scene most of all—equates self-abnegating love with darkness and night. Daylight represents intrusive, almost leering reality and must be shunned.

The first section of the duet unfolds in pliant lyrical exchanges, music of gently undulant and serene beauty. But as passion builds, Wagner folds in jabs of dissonance, wayward harmonic passages, and hints of rhythmic turbulence; Tristan and Isolde's vocal lines break into breathless bits and start overlapping. Phrase by phrase the music becomes more fitful and intense, pulsing and seething until the duet reaches an orgasmic climax brutally cut off when Marke arrives, devastated by the betrayal of his trusted heir. In all of music there is no more visceral a depiction of coitus interruptus.

Marke has been brought to the scene by Melot, a courtier, who has grown suspicious of his friend Tristan's feelings for Isolde. Now the king can see the sad truth. Rather than defend himself, Tristan invites Isolde to follow him into the realm of night. A fight ensues with Melot, but Tristan drops his sword and allows himself to be grievously stabbed.

In the final act, the wounded Tristan has been brought to his family's castle in Brittany by the stalwart Kurwenal. Worse than his fatal injury is Tristan's unquenchable yearning. A shepherd pipes a forlorn tune as Tristan sleeps fitfully, now exposed to hateful day. When Kurwenal says that Isolde is en route, Tristan is swept away with frenzied expectation. Then, in a vocally punishing scene for a heldentenor, Tristan first once, then again thinks that some distant ship carries Isolde, only to be crushed with disappointment. His music shifts through long stretches of hysterical exclamations and delirious outbursts.

Finally Isolde's ship arrives and she comes rushing to Tristan. The lovers have just a brief embrace before Tristan dies. Alas, Marke, having heard about the potion from Brangäne, had come to bless the couple. The opera ends with Isolde singing the great Liebestod (love-death), though Wagner actually called this radiant soliloquy Isolde's Transfiguration, the more precise way to describe her entrance into death. Does she alone, Isolde wonders, hear the music that sounds from within Tristan's body? She will join him in the "world-breath," Isolde sings, to drown, to founder, where unconsciousness becomes rapture.

Wagner's score, some four hours of music, remains a milestone of music history. For one thing, the musical language represented a breakthrough into bold, new regions of chromatic harmony, an elusive harmonic idiom that makes whole stretches of music seem almost unmoored from tonal (major and minor) grounding points. Wagner's experiments in *Tristan* prefigure Schoenberg's radical move into atonality.

If the harmonic language of *Tristan* is often so wayward, how did Wagner achieve musical coherence and narrative sweep? Through his sophisticated use of leitmotifs, and not just as identifying thematic tags. Wagner's integrated use of motifs is analogous to Beethoven's technique of thematic development, but pushed to new reaches of complexity. A lifelong devotee of Beethoven's works, especially the late string quartets, Wagner closely studied the way the master generated an entire multi-movement work from a few melodic (and often rhythmic) motifs in the opening phrases. Wagner put this technique to work in opera, especially in *Tristan*.

The orchestral Prelude to *Tristan und Isolde*, one of the most analyzed works of music history, begins with the cellos playing a soft, yearning unison line that rises achingly from a midrange A up a sixth to F, and then slides down chromatically to E, and then D-sharp, at which point woodwinds and horns land on a harmony: the four-note so-called Tristan chord. At that moment the oboes begin a four-note rising chromatic motif, sort of an inverse of the descending one.

This is a theoretically complicated business. The harmonically ambiguous Tristan chord still rivets both listeners and music theorists. The takeaway, though, is that within these few measures, Wagner introduces crucial motifs that will run through, drive, and lend shape to the entire opera, no matter how fraught and impetuous any episode of music turns. Other crucial motifs are soon heard in the Prelude. Still, it's amazing how much of this score is derived from Wagner's intricate manipulations of those initial ascending and descending motifs and that famous chord.

Though Wagner completed *Tristan und Isolde* in 1859, the first performance did not take place until 1865, at the Nationaltheater in Munich. In the interim, two people forever altered his life.

In 1857, then twenty, Cosima Liszt, one of Franz Liszt's three illegitimate children, who was living in Berlin, married the German conductor and pianist Hans von Bülow, seven years her senior and one of her father's most impressive and devoted students. A troubling sign for the marriage came during the couple's honeymoon, when, joined by Liszt, they visited Wagner in Zürich. Cosima found herself in the presence of a charismatic figure, like a "vain peacock" who both "enchanted and appalled her," according to her biographer Oliver Hilmes. During that stay her obsequious husband, already a Wagnerite, seemed "paralyzed by Wagner's overpowering genius." Yet one night, when Wagner read his completed libretto for *Tristan* to his guests, the experience caused Cosima to burst into tears. This genius had already gotten to her.

Over the next few years the von Bülows had two children: Daniela, named in memory of Cosima's brother, Daniel, who had died at twenty; and Blandine, named for Cosima's sister, who had died in 1862, shortly after giving birth. (So Liszt lost two of his three children.) The von Bülows made periodic visits to Wagner, whose marriage to Minna had long been in shambles. Their attraction proved undeniable. If we can believe Wagner's account, in late 1863, during a long coach ride in Berlin, Richard and Cosima sealed their bond with "tears and sobs," as he later wrote in his autobiography. Extricating themselves from their marriages would take some doing.

In 1864, almost simultaneously, an eighteen-year-old devotee of Wagner's music became King Ludwig II of Bavaria. In short order Ludwig summoned his hero to Munich, settled his debts, and placed him in a fine house near the palace. At Wagner's suggestion, the king appointed von Bülow royal pianist. Cosima came with her husband and two daughters to Munich. Nine months later she gave birth to a daughter, Isolde, by Wagner. Von Bülow was so singularly devoted to Wagner that he legally accepted the child as his own.

King Ludwig was homosexual. Given the religious values and cultural ways of that era, let alone his public duties, Ludwig was strikingly open about this aspect of his nature. Though his enthusiasm for Wagner's art was genuine, he was also enthralled with Wagner the man, something Wagner seems to have manipulated to his advantage, as this 1864 letter to the king makes explicit:

> *My dear and gracious King,*
> *I send you these tears of the most heavenly emotion in order to tell you that the marvels of poesy have entered my poor loveless life as a divine reality! And this life, with its final outpouring of verse and music, now belongs to you, my gracious young King: dispose of it as you would of your property!*
> *In the utmost ecstasy, faithful and true.*

Describing a visit with Ludwig in a letter to a close friend, Wagner wrote: "Our meeting yesterday was one great love-scene which seemed as though it would never end."

But Wagner, ever the radical, could not resist trying to influence Ludwig's policies and appointments, which rankled the king's ministers. Realizing that he was losing the support of his government, and the public, Ludwig caved. He insisted that Wagner leave Bavaria, though he kept providing some financial support. Minna, sadly, died in early 1866 of a heart attack. Wagner did not attend the funeral.

He moved to a home near Lake Lucerne, now joined by Cosima. In 1867 the couple's second child, Eva, was born. Cosima started agitating for a divorce from von Bülow, who resisted.

Even as his wife pursued a scandalous relationship with Wagner, von Bülow conducted the premiere of *Tristan und Isolde* in 1865 and *Die Meistersinger* in 1868, both in Munich, with crucial support from Ludwig. When Cosima's third child with Wagner, Siegfried, was born in 1869, von Bülow finally agreed to a divorce. It would not be sanctioned by a Berlin court until 1870. Soon after, Cosima and Wagner, now the parents of three children, were married.

The difficulty of finding adequate singers for the punishing title roles of *Tristan und Isolde* had been a major obstacle in getting the work to the stage. Wagner auditioned Ludwig Schnorr von Carolsfeld, a very stocky, bushy-bearded tenor, then twenty-eight, and his Danish-born wife, Malvina, and, very pleased, urged their casting. Clearly, the tenor's powerful, ringing voice and stamina trumped his unprepossessing physique in Wagner's mind. Just a few weeks after the last of four performances he took ill and died. His demise entered opera lore as evidence that the role of Tristan was not just a voice killer, but worse. Actually, the overweight von Carolsfeld seems to have contracted what was termed "rampant gout," which progressed to delirium.

Though the Munich premiere fortified the convictions of Wagner devotees who saw him leading music and drama into the future, *Tristan* was met with widespread bafflement and outright hostility in many circles. The influential, if conservative, critic Eduard Hanslick, already a noted Wagner detractor, wrote in 1868 that the Prelude to *Tristan* reminded him of "the old Italian painting of a martyr whose intestines are slowly unwound from his body on a reel."

Ludwig continued to encounter opposition from his ministers over his support of Wagner. Still, he fostered the premiere of the composer's next work, *Die Meistersinger von Nürnberg* (The Master Singers of Nuremberg), a warm and wise comedic tale, though with lingering controversial elements.

Set in mid-sixteenth-century Nuremberg, the story presents a community that above all else values the art of song, that is, the craft of mingling poetry and music. The collective heroes of the tale are a group of everyday craftsmen, including a tinsmith, a baker, a furrier, a soap maker, and a stocking weaver. But these essential citizens have also gained entry into a select guild of master singers, open only to those who have demonstrated thorough knowledge in the honored tradition of song writing. The most revered master singer is the self-effacing cobbler Hans Sachs, who has lost his wife and children.

One day, Walther von Stolzing, a knight from Franconia, arrives in Nuremberg. A restless youth in search of something (he doesn't seem sure of what), Walther notices a lovely young woman as she sings a hymn with the congregation at church. He's instantly smitten.

She is Eva, the only child of Veit Pogner, a goldsmith and a proud master singer. Walther dares to speak to Eva, who is aflutter with feelings for him. But her father has promised her in marriage to the winner of this year's annual song contest, which is about to take place. This we learn when the scene shifts to a regular meeting of the master singers. Eva may refuse the winner, her father says. But if she does, he will not permit her to wed anyone.

Though Walther has his lyric poet side, he's no master singer. He decides to audition for the guild and enter the contest, but the song he delivers rattles the masters, with its freewheeling combination of romantic poetry and impassioned melodic lines. That Walther is an aristocrat also counts against him: here is one area of life where tradesmen can achieve superiority.

Walther's most severe critic is Sixtus Beckmesser, the middle-aged town clerk and the guild's designated keeper of the rules, who hopes to win the song contest and Eva's hand. Hans Sachs, however, is strangely affected by Walther's song. Yes, the young man has bent some rules. But the song hints at new modes of expression.

Sachs takes Walther under his wing and tutors him, not just in song writing but in the art of courtship. The character of Beckmesser could well be Wagner's satirical depiction of his critic nemesis Hanslick, another stickler for rules. One of the most winning descriptions of this great opera was written by Virgil Thomson, an admitted "anti-Wagnerian," in a 1945 review of a Metropolitan Opera performance. Thomson described *Meistersinger* as "the most enchanting of all the fairy-tale operas." It is "enchanting musically," he wrote, "because there is no enchantment, literally speaking, in it." In fact, "There is no metaphysics at all. The hero merely gives a successful debut recital and marries the girl of his heart. And Wagner without his erotico-metaphysical paraphernalia is a better composer than with it. He pays more attention to holding interest by musical means, wastes less time predicting doom, describing weather, soul states, and ecstatic experiences."

Everything turns out for the best. Beckmesser, who has tried to cheat his way to winning the contest by singing a song he assumes to be the creation of Sachs, garbles the performance and is publicly humiliated. That song had actually been written by Walther, with some guidance from Sachs. When Walther steps up and sings it properly, the townspeople are beguiled. Even the masters are swept away by the freshness and integrity of Walther's artistry. When Pogner tries to drape Walther with the master singer's chain, the knight impetuously declines it. This leads Sachs to deliver a homily that has long been pointed to by critics as evidence of anti-Semitic themes that run through this entire work.

"Scorn not the masters, honor their art," Sachs sternly tells Walther. Our masters have cared for this art in their own ways, cherished and nurtured it, kept it "genuine," "German and true," Sachs sings.

So far, you could argue, Sachs has simply stood up for his country's cultural heritage. But then his comments become disturbing. Beware, "evil tricks" threaten us, he tells Walther. Should the German people and kingdom decay under a "false, foreign rule," no prince would understand his people; foreign "mists" and foreign "vanities" would plant "in our German land." So honor the German masters, Sachs urges. For even if the Holy Roman Empire dissolves in mist, for us there would yet remain "holy German art."

Many historians see this homily as an operatic version of Wagner's screed about the Jewish corruption of German culture, a theme that runs through the opera, in this view. That it comes from the mouth of a character so otherwise humane just makes it worse.

Still, this opera also exudes humanity and glows with Wagner's affection for the characters, even, in a way, the unappealing Beckmesser, who knows that his only regard in town comes from his standing as a master singer, and who certainly gets his due.

Wagner had initially lied to Ludwig about his affair with Cosima. Partly to mollify the monarch, Wagner gave in when Ludwig insisted that the first two *Ring* operas be introduced in Munich; both were given shaky performances. Wagner knew that he had to create a theater tailored to his aesthetic ideals.

He had already laid out his vision in the preface to the full published text of the *Ring* in 1863. He wanted a smaller town in Germany, accommodating to visitors, and with no competing opera enterprise. The theater would be a temporary structure suitable to a summer festival. He visited the town of Bayreuth to check out the Margravial Opera House, an exquisite Baroque theater built in the 1740s, but, Wagner felt, unsuited to the *Ring*. Town officials, realizing Wagner's festival house would draw attention to Bayreuth, offered an appealing site on top of a grassy hill in the north side of town for free. At his own expense, Wagner bought a family home adjacent to a park off the grounds of the former margrave's palace. This would become Wahnfried, the Wagner home, today the Wagner Museum.

The foundation stone for the Bayreuth opera house was laid in 1872. But funds were not forthcoming. Wagner conducted a rush of concerts to raise money. Architectural plans kept getting scaled down, not in the size of the theater but in the quality and permanence of the materials. When Ludwig realized that the project was foundering, he lent Wagner the required funds to finish construction. (He could no longer risk making outright gifts.)

The materials may have been simple—wood walls and a canvas-covered wood ceiling—but the theater fulfilled Wagner's vision. The auditorium, originally with 1,645 seats and some rear boxes, is built like an amphitheater, on a single raked, fan-shaped level. During the 1930s the building was fortified and the seating area slightly expanded. But the house remains much the way Wagner envisioned, and is still a summer-only facility (without air-conditioning).

There is a double proscenium, which, to the audience, gives the impression that stage action takes place at some mystical distance, even though the space is intimate and the singers quite close. The most striking feature is the sunken orchestra pit, nearly covered by a hood that curves over the rows of instruments tilting toward the stage. So the orchestra is invisible to the audience, which enhances the musical magic. Also, the sound is directed first back toward the stage, where it mingles with the singing of the cast and chorus, and then flows into the house. The acoustics have a completely distinctive quality: the sound of the orchestra seems to be coming from no fixed place; it enshrouds you.

But to achieve this effect, the pit had to be built with a series of six descending narrow wood rows, rather like huge descending steps, with the strings on the top ones and the brass and percussion lower down.

I was once given a tour of the pit—a discombobulating experience. The sound heard by the orchestra players in that covered space is a drastic distortion of what the audience hears in the hall. So conductors must balance things according to how they think the sound will resonate in the theater, not according to what they are actually hearing. With an adaptable conductor in charge, though, a Wagner score at Bayreuth sounds mellow, rich, and extraordinarily clear.

Also, because of the hood over the pit, it's much easier for singers to project their lines over the orchestra without pushing their voices. Wagner's concept of opera as music drama comes through viscerally.

After some delays, the first Bayreuth festival took place in the summer of 1876, featuring the premiere production of the entire *Ring* presented over five (not Wagner's originally intended four) days. The finest German musicians were recruited to perform in the orchestra. Hans Richter conducted a strong, committed cast. The stage designs, awash in Germanic Romanticism, did not entirely please Wagner, who thought that future productions should scenically match his visionary concept of music drama, though he was vague about what this would entail. Still, the *Ring* premiere was worldwide news. The *New York Herald* gave extensive coverage to each opera, with timely articles sent via transatlantic cable, starting on page one and continuing on page two (including reproductions of full pages from the score). This suggests the high level of musical literacy among general readers in New York in the 1870s. The articles include enthusiastic subheads: "Opera as it should be given"—"A revelation in opera"—"An assured success."

Back in Bayreuth, though, the effort exhausted everyone involved. (The

Ring was not presented again there until 1896.) Six years passed before Wagner and his supporters could afford to present a second festival at Bayreuth. For this occasion he composed his final opera, a work intended from its conception to be performed only at the Bayreuth house: *Parsifal.*

Every aspect of this enigmatic and multi-layered opera has been a source of debate and contention, starting with the designation Wagner gave it: *Bühnenweihfestspiel,* a "festival play for the consecration of a stage." Wagner was just thirty-two when he read the story of Parsifal as told by the medieval German poet and singer Wolfram von Eschenbach. He had been nursing the idea of an operatic Parsifal for thirty-five years.

The opera has been extolled as a sublime sacred work, appropriate for performance at Easter time because of the long scene in Act I when the knights of the Grail perform their version of a Holy Communion ritual. Yet *Parsifal* has been denounced in other Christian quarters as a sacrilegious travesty. As many scholars have noted, the theme of gaining enlightenment through compassion and renunciation relates as much to Buddhism (a philosophy that fascinated Wagner) and Schopenhauer as it does to Christianity. The irreligious Nietzsche, who had once venerated Wagner and saw the character of Siegfried as the epitome of the *Übermensch* (superman), considered the compassionate Parsifal a dismaying regression.

To me, the most compelling aspect of *Parsifal* seems not at all enigmatic: the universal theme of the often circuitous ways in which wisdom is passed from generation to generation, from sage to seeker. This theme plays out constantly in popular culture, from the *Star Wars* saga to the adventures of Harry Potter.

The sage in *Parsifal* is Amfortas, the leader of the knights of the Grail in a remote region of northern Spain, probably in mythological times. Amfortas thinks himself a failure, an unworthy leader who wandered into the realm of the sorcerer Klingsor, succumbed to the temptations of a seductress, and lost the sacred spear of Christ in a fight with the sorcerer, who gave Amfortas a wound on his side that will not heal. Guilt now wracks Amfortas even more than the constant pain. According to prophecy, a holy fool will appear, a young man who knows compassion, someone who can restore leadership to the suffering knights.

One day, a passerby kills one of the knight's cherished swans with a bow and arrow. The culprit is Parsifal, a seemingly clueless and rootless youth. Could this be the holy fool? Parsifal is chastised for his rash killing of an innocent bird by Gurnemanz, the eldest knight, a good-hearted man who despairs for the anguish Amfortas suffers. Gurnemanz invites Parsifal to witness the Holy Communion ritual. The young man is affected but baffled. Gurnemanz comes to the conclusion that Parsifal is not the prophesied holy fool, just some young fool. He tells the boy to head off, with a warning to "leave our swans alone!"

Wagner takes a minor player in the myth and turns her into a fascinating central character: Kundry, an ageless, wild-eyed woman in perpetual torment with herself. She is essentially Wagner's invention. We first encounter Kundry in Act I bringing healing balms for Amfortas to the knights, who accept her but treat her warily. Kundry regularly disappears into the realm of the sorcerer Klingsor, who knows how to incite the seductive passion coursing within her. All she wants is to be released from the curse of life through spiritual death. Parsifal wanders into Klingsor's realm, where Kundry helplessly tries to seduce him. It's very suspicious that she seems to know so much about his dead mother. Wagner leaves you hanging.

Parsifal resists Kundry's aggressive attempts at seduction and vanquishes Klingsor, gaining back the holy spear. When we encounter him next in Act III, he has been wandering for years, pondering existence, lost and confused. He comes upon Gurnemanz, who senses the change within him. The old knight performs a baptismal rite upon Parsifal, who now sees the role he has been intended for. In a final scene, he places the spear on Amfortas's wound, which miraculously heals, and blesses Kundry, who in a state of spiritual exaltation finally dies. Parsifal will now assume his place.

This story inspired Wagner to write a score of diaphanous beauty and transfixing spirituality. During the second act, in Klingsor's realm, complete with a chorus of seductive flower maidens, the music segues from deceptively lyrical sweetness to a cauldron of seething sensuality. In this score Wagner continues his exploration of bold chromatic harmony, with passages almost untethered to tonality.

But the most radical element of the score involves its treatment of rhythm and time. From the spacious prelude that seems to hover in place to the shimmering final chords, stretches of this opera move with almost static timelessness. Yet if these passages lack pulse, they convey supple movement from phrase to phrase, section to section.

As part of Ludwig's loan to Wagner to complete work on Bayreuth, the king could insist that musicians from the national theater in Munich present the premieres of Wagner's future works. At the time, the Jewish conductor Hermann Levi was music director in Munich. Wagner was affronted, Cosima even more so: she completely shared her husband's prejudices against Jews. Yet Wagner admired Levi's musicianship and grew to depend upon him. Reports suggest that Levi conducted marvelously.

Wagner was ill—he had suffered a series of angina attacks—during the premiere run of *Parsifal* in August 1882. The family thought it wise to head to Italy for the winter, and settled in Venice. Wagner died on February 13, 1883, at sixty-nine, in a palazzo on the Grand Canal. A funeral gondola carried his body along the canal. He was then brought to Germany for burial on the grounds of Wahnfried. It would be forty-seven years before Cosima joined him there.

When asked about how one can reconcile Wagner the genius with Wagner the man, I often think of Paul Heller, the father of Tom Heller, my roommate and good friend at Yale. During those years I became close to Tom's family in Evanston, Illinois, especially his father. Dr. Heller, a noted research hematologist and a revered teacher at the University of Illinois's medical school, was a survivor of Nazi concentration camps. He grew up in a region of Czechoslovakia where German was the dominant language and attended medical school in Prague. Though not musically trained, he was a passionate music lover with vivid memories of attending concerts and operas in his youth. He loved Verdi, but he was especially affected by Wagner.

Tom became a doctor, moved to Seattle, and raised a family there. Once, when I was reviewing a new production of *Tristan und Isolde* that inaugurated the renovated house of the Seattle Opera, I brought Dr. Heller, who was visiting Tom's family, with me. He was very grateful for the invitation and deeply moved by the performance.

It's a testimony to Wagner's work that Paul Heller—a Holocaust survivor, who was liberated from Buchenwald when American soldiers arrived and personally guided the war correspondent Edward R. Murrow through the camp—could see through the nastiness of Wagner the man to the beauty of his art.

THE SYNTHESIZER

JOHANNES BRAHMS (1833–1897)

M y favorite story about Brahms comes from the memoirs of the master Austrian pianist Artur Schnabel. The book is actually a collection of freewheeling autobiographical talks that Schnabel gave in 1945 to an audience of music students at the University of Chicago. In the second one, he recalls meeting Brahms during several informal excursions outside Vienna. Schnabel was about twelve at the time, which means these encounters would have been between 1894 and 1895, just a couple of years before the composer died, of cancer, in 1897, a month shy of sixty-four.

During this period in his life, Schnabel recalled, the portly, bearded Brahms was in the habit of taking Sunday trips to the "lovely hilly woods surrounding Vienna" accompanied by a group of friends, mostly musicians. One regular was Eusebius Mandyczewski, a musicologist and composer with whom the young Schnabel was then studying theory and composition. Mandyczewski worked for years as Brahms's amanuensis. The time had come, Mandyczewski thought, for young Artur to join these Sunday jaunts with Brahms. Schnabel describes the experience charmingly.

The group would board a horse-drawn tram in Vienna around 8:00 a.m., drive through the suburbs to the destination terminal, and then complete the trek on foot. "On all these occasions," Schnabel wrote, "Brahms treated me in the same manner: before a meal he would ask me whether I was hungry; after one, whether I had had enough. That was all he ever said to me. Why, after all, should he talk to a child?"

He also saw Brahms indoors, Schnabel continues, when Mandyczewski brought him to gatherings at the homes of Viennese families, "music lovers whose intimacy with Brahms seemed their greatest pride." These occasions were mostly devoted to playing chamber music. One family, the Conrads, regularly hosted a private choir for which Artur was pressed into service as accompanist. Though usually present for these musicales, Brahms tended to sit a few rooms off in the library reading. But the doors were kept open and apparently he could hear everything. Some thirty or forty years later, Schnabel wrote, he learned to his astonishment that Brahms had not only heard him performing as a child at these gatherings but "had praised what I did at the piano." Brahms clearly had felt no reason to compliment a mere boy, however precocious, directly.

Our impressions of Brahms the man have been dominated by images and tales from these later years. A well-known painting of the composer from that period by Willy von Beckerath shows Brahms playing the piano: leaning back, eyes shut, with thick arms extending over a sizable belly, his hands crossed on the keyboard. The stump of a cigar dangles from Brahms's mouth, its ashes poised to fall into his long gray beard. Though venerated as a living master and eventually quite wealthy, Brahms lived modestly, retained a common touch, and wore cheap suits. He was known to go about Vienna now and then without socks. He could be prickly and sarcastic, but also loyal and generous to his friends.

The young Brahms who arrived on the scene in the 1850s, however, was a dashing, slender figure with delicate features, long sandy hair, penetrating blue eyes, and a soft, high speaking voice. In a series of private introductions, Brahms staggered some formidable musicians with his commanding pianism and bold compositions. One was the renowned violinist and composer Joseph Joachim, just two years older, who would become one of Brahms's closest colleagues. They first met in Hanover when Brahms, then twenty, fresh from Hamburg, played through some of his piano pieces. "Never in the course of my artist's life have I been more completely overwhelmed," Joachim recalled decades later.

As I related in the chapter on Schumann, both Robert and Clara were awestruck when the young Brahms appeared at their home in Dusseldorf in the fall of 1853 bearing a letter of introduction from Joachim, their mutual friend. To Clara the young Brahms was like a divine apparition. In his diary Robert described Brahms as a genius, a young eagle, and, intriguingly, a "demon." Perhaps Schumann thought only some dark force could explain such a prodigious young artist.

In an effusive article titled "New Roads," Schumann anointed Brahms "a chosen one." He excitedly described the compositions Brahms had played, pieces that took him and his wife to "enchanting spheres," piano sonatas that were "veiled symphonies," songs "the poetry of which would be understood even without the words," chamber works, and more, each so different "it seemed to stream from its own individual source" yet "all united by him into a single waterfall." Musing on the future, Schumann wrote that should Brahms "direct his magic wand" to the realms of chorus and orchestra, "we can look forward to even more wondrous glimpses of the secret world of spirits."

In truth, rather than feeling exhilarated by this testimony from an influential composer and critic, Brahms was embarrassed. How could any emerging musician merit such praise or meet such expectations? Brahms was intensely self-critical, a trait he retained throughout his life. He claimed to have destroyed some twenty string quartets before he finally composed the three he saw to publication—the only ones we have. Over many years, he consigned countless manuscripts to various fireplaces, including almost all the early works he composed prior to those he played for Schumann. Inherent insecurity alone does not explain Brahms's severe self-assessments. He truly thought an enormous quantity of his efforts were simply subpar. He may have been right.

That said, Schumann, Joachim, and other admirers of Brahms were onto something. In those first sonatas and piano pieces they heard a genuinely new voice, a young man attuned to the Romantic ethos of his time yet steeped in the Classical heritage. That heritage, however, had reached a crossroads.

The standard forms of the sonata and the symphony depended upon the clear delineation of key areas by means of traditional tonal harmony. When a first movement of a Haydn symphony stated a theme in a stable (tonic) key, then went through a patch of harmonic wandering to arrive at a second theme in a related (dominant) key, the music took listeners on a dramatic journey to a temporary destination. But the Romantic harmonic language of Brahms's day placed a premium on ambiguity, on disguising key areas and milking instability for all its expressive potential. This worked great for Wagner in his music dramas, but presented vexing challenges to Schumann, Brahms, and subsequent composers who kept trying to write structurally cogent sonatas and symphonies.

From his early years, Brahms set about adapting the Romantic language, including its embrace of often ambiguous chromatic harmony, so as to bring Romantic fervor to the honored forms of the Classical era.

How did he do it? Of all people, Schoenberg offered insight into this question in a much-debated 1947 article titled "Brahms the Progressive" (originally a 1933 radio talk). Schoenberg astutely analyzed Brahms's way of generating long structures from short, concentrated motifs. In this Brahms was following Beethoven's technique of motivic development. But Brahms took it further, to Schoenberg's thinking, relying on brief, almost cell-like collections of pitches that would permeate a score. Brahms also jostled everyday expectations of symmetrical phrasing by using bold irregularities of line and rhythm, another way he coaxed a sonata or a piano quartet movement into seeming quite daring.

In Schoenberg's last completed book, *Structural Functions of Harmony*, he went even further, claiming Brahms as a proto-modernist who anticipated the loosening of tonality and the coming of atonality. Schoenberg pointed to several late works in particular and analyzed what he called Brahms's penchant for "enriched harmony" that moved boldly through remote, unrelated harmonic regions.

Now, Brahms did not like to think of himself as progressive. He got

burned from his one venture into musical politics in 1860, when he joined
with Joachim and some other composers in a collective takedown of what
was called the "New German School," led by Liszt and like-minded composers who considered Classical forms spent, embraced the symphonic
poem along with other freer genres, and pushed harmony to extremes of
ambiguity. A leaked draft of the article generated a backlash from forward-
looking musicians, who ridiculed Brahms and his co-authors as hopelessly
conservative. Brahms the polemicist promptly retired.

But Schoenberg was right about the searching, even radical, progressiv-
ism of Brahms's harmonic language in his last years, especially in the late
piano pieces. Take the Intermezzo in E-flat Minor (the last of a collection
of six short pieces published as Op. 118, composed in 1893).

The Intermezzo begins with an elusive theme, if you can call it such,
which hovers within a narrow band of a few notes, like some haunting
chant, until it halts for a moment, tellingly, on F (the note a whole step
above the tonic E-flat), at which point, underneath the theme, a strange,
hushed, slow arpeggio (an ambiguous diminished-seventh chord) rumbles
way low in the piano and ripples up the keyboard. As the suspended melodic F slips down to the tonic note, E-flat, this mysterious low arpeggio
keeps rising, then turns around and descends again to the depths. The
theme moves an octave lower and this murky business essentially repeats,
but even more eerily. The Intermezzo eventually builds to an episode of
vehement agitation, with bouts of fearful octaves and chords. Then the
haunted opening of the piece returns, this time pounded out with terror,
until, at the end, the music drifts off, like some lacy premonition of
twentieth-century challenges to the existing musical order. Forget Wagner.
With its use of bold harmony, enigmatic motifs, and elusive emotional
undercurrents, this Intermezzo anticipates Expressionism—the Schoenberg of *Erwartung*, the Berg of *Wozzeck*.

So we have competing takes on this giant's achievement: Brahms the
Classicist, Brahms the Romantic, Brahms the Progressive. I'm persuaded
the most, however, by those who see Brahms as a synthesizer.

Brahms had an enormous knowledge of, and reverence for, early music.
If not quite an official musicologist, he collected autograph scores of the

Viennese masters and edited (or co-edited) works by François Couperin and other Baroque composers. He mastered the old art of counterpoint and wrote dozens of pieces in neo-Baroque styles: intricate choral works, chorale preludes, and fugues for organ.

Yet he also loved folk songs and all kinds of dance music, from elegant waltzes to wild Hungarian czardas. He gratified his creativity, while making some money, composing music for amateur performance, including four-hand piano pieces and works for community choirs.

He also, however, took on the challenge, the burden, really, of the symphonic imperative as laid down by Beethoven. Brahms worked at least fourteen years on his First Symphony before he finally dared to introduce it to the public. Admirers dubbed the piece "Beethoven's Tenth," in part because the steadfast theme of the finale (following a dark, wary introduction) resembles the "Ode to Joy" theme from Beethoven's Ninth, an homage Brahms surely intended.

In another admirable aspect of his career, Brahms was a thoroughly pragmatic composer and performer. He gladly took on periodic directorships of nonprofessional choirs, local orchestras, and high-quality music societies, believing that composers should move among the music-loving public and work with dedicated amateurs. He absorbed this hands-on approach early from his enterprising father, a musician for hire in Hamburg and a colorful character.

Johann Jakob Brahms, who came from a long line of craftsmen in lower Saxony, bucked family pressure in becoming a musician. At twenty, in 1826, he settled in Hamburg, the North German city that maintained remnants of its mercantile past. Johann found work playing flute, horn, violin, and double bass in dance halls and cafes. In time he became a regular bass player with the city's state theater and philharmonic society. If not exceptionally gifted, Johann was a resourceful, multi-skilled musician. His career would be familiar today to any freelance player getting by in an American city.

In 1830 he married Johanna Nissen, a kindly seamstress seventeen years his senior, an unconventional move even within Johann's open-minded artistic circle. At the time she was living in the home of her married sister. Johann took a room with the family and proposed to Johanna after a week.

Johannes Brahms was the couple's middle child, born on May 7, 1833. An older girl, Elise, endured shaky health throughout her life. Fritz, the youngest, also a musician, seems to have been the black sheep of the family. In search of opportunities and adventure he moved to Venezuela, a defensive reaction, in part, to his brother's burgeoning success. When Fritz returned to Hamburg, he became a music teacher and provoked periods of alienation from his siblings.

When the children were young, financial insecurity strained the parents' marriage and caused the family to change residences often, whenever the rent proved too steep or, after a run of lucrative work, Johann decided to upgrade their quarters. Still, the Brahms boys attended solid private schools and were given lessons in piano, cello, and horn. After young Johannes expressed his clear preference for the piano, his father found him a top-notch teacher, Friedrich Wilhelm Cossel.

In the most fortunate turn of Johannes's childhood, Eduard Marxsen, a respected pianist and composer, heard the ten-year-old boy perform in a chamber music program and was duly impressed. Before long Marxsen took over Johannes's instruction, teaching him piano and music theory for free. By his early teens, Johannes was giving well-received piano recitals, programs that included such formidable works as Beethoven's *Waldstein* Sonata.

Like his father, Johannes was expected to earn money as a musician even during his adolescence. He played for private social events, took gigs in pit bands at theaters, and wrote four-hand piano arrangements for publishers. There have long been stories that during these impressionable years Johannes was compelled to play piano in places of ill repute, like waterfront bars where obliging women were available. In recent years some scholars have cast doubt on these reports. Still, Brahms spoke of the experiences bitterly in later life. Jan Swafford, a perceptive Brahms biographer, finds the evidence and the anecdotes fairly persuasive.

Popular with sailors, these places "integrated the services of dancehall, bar, café and whorehouse," Swafford writes in his 1997 Brahms biography. The "fair and pretty" Johannes was "surrounded by the stench of beer and unwashed sailors and bad food," and between dances singing girls "would sit the prepubescent teenager on their laps and pour beer into him," and worse, Swafford suggests. Though the composer just hinted at what took place, he raged about it for the rest of his days. Swafford vividly reports one incident many years later when Brahms, having drunk too much, broke up a party with a sordid condemnation of the female character. Defending himself to the friend, he reportedly said: "You tell me I should have the same respect, the same exalted homage for women that you have! You expect that of a man cursed with a childhood like mine!"

Whatever the truth, Brahms never married and had only passing involvements with a few women, including one intense but short-lived engagement. In later years, like many professional men in the Vienna of his day, he readily obtained the services of prostitutes.

A career break came when, around the age of fifteen, Brahms met the feisty, somewhat older Hungarian Jewish violinist Ede Reményi, who had been forced to flee Hungary for participating in the 1848 uprising against Austria. They began giving recitals together, including a momentous (for Brahms) tour of Germany in 1853. Reményi introduced Brahms to gypsy music and dance, though what Reményi played was probably not the raw, earthy Hungarian folk music of the Magyar tradition but a stylistic hybrid. Brahms developed a lifelong fondness for this "gypsy" music. Several of his most popular, and profitable, works were steeped in the idiom, like his sets of Hungarian Dances, which appear in versions for solo piano, piano four-hands, and orchestra.

That 1853 tour took the duo to Weimar, where Reményi introduced Brahms to Liszt, who, curious to know Brahms's music, played through the young composer's virtuosic Scherzo (later published as Op. 4) at sight. Brahms was duly impressed. Reményi eventually broke off from Brahms, in part, as he later claimed, because the young composer dozed through Liszt's performance of his own Sonata in B Minor during their stay in Weimar, though how anyone could have slept while the galvanic Liszt played that astonishing piece is impossible to imagine.

The tour also brought Brahms to Düsseldorf, where he met the Schumanns and became practically a member of the household. Among the many pieces Robert Schumann reported hearing during that visit were Brahms's first two piano sonatas, "veiled symphonies rather," as Schumann described them, and it's easy to understand that impression.

Brahms's Piano Sonata No. 1 in C Major (actually composed after his second sonata but published as the first) has a symphonic structure of four movements and lasts some thirty minutes. The vigorous opening theme is a fanfarelike flourish of chords that recalls in its rhythmic character the opening of Beethoven's mighty *Hammerklavier* Sonata. After some intricate manipulations of that motif, the second theme, with its nostalgic lyricism and dreamy harmonic wanderings, provides a pronounced contrast. Intriguingly, the long middle section (the development) becomes almost fixated on the melancholic second theme, though bustling eruptions of those opening chords keep popping up.

The slow movement, in C minor, is a theme and variations, a form that would become a Brahms specialty. The theme is a sorrowful folk song under which Brahms prints the German lyrics in the score. There's a gutsy Scherzo, then an impetuous Finale, full of runs in triplets for the right hand, phrases that keep sputtering forth in short bursts, like an athletic young man who keeps catching his breath.

This ambitious sonata may nod to Beethoven. Still, here is the music of a composer from a new generation claiming the Beethovenian sonata heritage on his own bracing terms, making the form less dense (if consequently less deep), yet instilling it with a fresh, brash kind of clearheaded intricacy. During this extended visit, Brahms completed his sternly majestic Sonata No. 3 in F Minor (which would be his last), an even more symphonic-size composition, written in five movements, with a wistful, Romantic-style Intermezzo inserted between a snappish Scherzo and hurtling Finale, and lasting nearly forty-five minutes.

Brahms shared other piano pieces with the Schumanns, along with songs and chamber works, all of them revealing "superabundant fantasy, most intimate feelings and mastery of form," as Clara recalled in her diary. She also found it moving to see Brahms sitting at the piano, with his "interesting, youthful face which is completely transformed as he plays, his beautiful hands which achieve victory over the greatest difficulties with the greatest ease." Clara was doubly enchanted by this young artist because her husband's increasing instability had been creating such stress for the family. She was also pregnant with her seventh child, which meant pulling back on some remunerative concerts at the worst possible time.

With Robert Schumann's intercession, Brahms secured the publication of his three sonatas and a few other pieces. He thrived in the company of these dazzling new friends. When Joachim came to visit he found Johannes "a better and nobler man," as he recalled, more gregarious and confident, "often bubbling over with mirth."

But life in Hamburg beckoned. Brahms returned home for Christmas of 1853.

Everything changed on the awful day in late February 1854 when Robert Schumann, confused and delusional, jumped into the Rhine just blocks from his home and within days was committed to an asylum in Endenich. Brahms hastened to Clara's side, essentially basing himself in Düsseldorf for the two years of Schumann's confinement, until the composer's death in July 1856. Brahms occupied a "charming and comfortable" bedroom, as he described it, on a separate floor in the Schumann house, became a surrogate father to the children, managed the family finances, tended to Robert's publications, and even watched over the household when Clara resumed concert tours. During Robert's confinement, it was Brahms who visited the asylum periodically, not Clara, whom doctors kept away until just before the end. Brahms's devotion to the Schumanns impeded his own career at a crucial point. Why did he do it?

Because of Clara. From the moment he met her, as a wife, mother, and musician, Clara become Brahms's ideal of womanhood. He increasingly developed powerful romantic feelings for her as well. Clara reacted confusingly. Though this young man's devotion filled a void during the worst crisis of her life, she clung emotionally to her suffering, absent husband and treated Brahms with motherly affection. The truth was clearly more complicated.

Yes, Clara was fourteen years older. But Brahms grew up with the model of his father's marriage to a woman seventeen years older. During this period, Joachim, though impressed by Brahms's selfless dedication to the Schumann family, was dismayed to see how his gifted friend neglected his own art and career.

Even during Robert's final months Brahms wrote to Clara, who was concertizing, with undisguised yearning: "I wish I could write to you as tenderly as I love you, and give you as much kindness and goodness as I wish for you. . . . I constantly want to call you darling and all kinds of other things, without becoming tired of adoring you."

But were Johannes and Clara ever lovers? Following Robert's death in July 1856 they took a trip along the Rhine and stayed some time in Switzerland to take stock. Afterward they essentially went their separate ways. Clara returned home and rededicated herself to concertizing, work that earned her a good living and provided therapeutic relief.

Brahms's romantic yearnings clearly lingered. For more than four decades he and Clara remained friends, and exchanged countless letters, most of which Clara destroyed before she died. No definitive evidence exists that their relationship ever went beyond the platonic, though some think it did. I tend to side with the biographers who argue that refraining from sexual involvement would have been appropriate to the protocols of the era and in keeping with their individual characters: Clara, the honorable, long-suffering widow Schumann; and Johannes, the increasingly irascible and aloof composer and pianist.

The trip to Switzerland with the newly widowed Clara had left Brahms frustrated and perplexed. Back in Hamburg he nursed his feelings, found some work conducting, and composed some works for women's chorus. He was also hired for a seasonal post during winter months as a musician in the court of Detmold. Still, his friends, especially Joachim, worried that Brahms was neglecting his career. For the next few years he published nothing. But he was hardly idle.

Earlier, in 1854, while still swept up with the Schumann household, Brahms had started toiling over an ambitious work that would consume him for five years, a score that took several forms before reaching the final one: the Piano Concerto No. 1 in D Minor. Brahms had felt compelled to put everything on the line in a breakthrough piece.

His first idea had been to write an expansive piano sonata. Realizing that a single piano was inadequate to his vision, he recast the score as a three-movement sonata for two pianos. But, as he wrote to Joachim, "not even two pianos are really enough for me." Admitting his "confused and indecisive frame of mind" to his trusted friend, he sent along sketches and asked for an honest appraisal. That year, 1854, he traveled to Cologne and heard a performance of Beethoven's Ninth Symphony (also in D minor) for the first time. This overwhelming experience actually inhibited him from attempting his own symphony. (It would be twenty-two years before the premiere of his first one.) But hearing Beethoven's masterpiece prodded Brahms into confronting his inexperience with orchestration and turning that two-piano sonata into a concerto for piano and orchestra.

As he worked obsessively on the concerto, especially during 1856 and 1857, Brahms sent drafts to Joachim, who, though excited by the juxtaposition of magisterial and turbulent elements in the music, had reservations about the episodic structure of the overall work. In an 1856 letter Joachim singled out stretches in the first movement that he felt were too fragmentary, "not flowing enough—restless rather than impassioned." He explained that after the "significant opening, that wonderfully beautiful song in minor," he missed "an appropriately magnificent second theme." Joachim acknowledged that "something commensurably elevated and beautiful in major, something that competes in breadth with the opening idea, must be hard to find." But he was not blind, he assured Brahms, to the "many glories of the movement."

From the published concerto as we know it today, the unconventional structure of the piece—what Joachim found "fragmentary"—seems the inspired music of an audacious young composer bent on imbuing the Classical concerto with the free-ranging fervor of the Romantic age. When completed, this weighty, hurtling piece, lasting some fifty minutes, was the longest concerto that had ever been written.

I'm struck by Joachim's description of the first movement's "breadth." If there is one word that gets at the core of Brahms's music for me it's breadth. Whether the mood of a piece is stormy or sunny, tortured or majestic, Brahms's melodic lines and phrases—all the horizontal elements—tend to be long-arched and expansive. And Brahms's music also exudes breadth vertically. His piano chords seem chock-full of notes and are widely spaced; outbursts of octaves, chords, and runs typically span the keyboard. When the piano partners a violin in a Brahms sonata, the piano writing often has orchestral range and depth, with undulant patterns that enshroud the violin in rippling arpeggios or buttress it with dense, thick harmonies. Instruments in Brahms's orchestral works routinely blend highs and lows into thick sonorities. Breadth comes through even in the attitude that Brahms often conveys. In the midst of some fraught episode, the music somehow maintains an Apollonian overview of the turmoil, a slight distancing from the angst and intensity that provides some emotional perspective. Call it breadth.

You can imagine how this unruly, symphonic piano concerto confounded audiences in its day.

A long orchestral exposition begins the first movement, with the ominous peal of a sustained low D in the basses, fortified by a timpani roll and a blast of horns. A grimly assertive theme immediately breaks out, led by the first violins, a theme that unfolds in segments, like a chain of concentrated thoughts, full of leaps and thrashed-out trills. The music builds to a climactic point, then the incessant low D in the basses and rumbling timpani plunges dramatically down a half step to C-sharp, and this opening passage plays out again in a more unsettled harmonic cast.

Eventually the music gives way to an undulant, wide-spaced arpeggio in the lower strings over which a lyrical theme, carried by the violins, tries to calm things down. The fitful opening music returns and seems to find its way out of the stress with a combative flourish that becomes almost a heroic theme, though it doesn't last long enough to establish that mood.

Still, the tension subsides and the orchestra turns quiet as the piano readies itself to speak. When it does, the piano takes up not the lurching opening theme but that quasi-heroic passage and starts to explore it, as if to look deeper, to ponder the implications of the music, which now seems almost pensive. The orchestra mostly stays in the background, listening, but slowly becomes more involved. This piano introduction builds and builds until finally it breaks out with a steely piano rendition of the agitated opening theme. Then the movement truly digs in and takes off.

At one point, when the music has calmed, the piano, in a long solo passage, introduces a noble new melody: here's that "magnificent second theme" that Joachim had said he missed in Brahms's earlier sketch of the movement. And it is magnificent. It unfolds in chords like a stately chorale, except that each phrase is first played by the right hand, then echoed lower down by the left, almost like a Bach canon. The theme then opens up into a refrain of an earlier passage in the orchestra, a melodic line that keeps leaping higher and higher, as the left hand plays wide-spaced chords in slow arpeggios. After a majestic climax, the piano becomes more reposed, almost delicate, and the orchestra, seemingly entranced by the melodic magic, takes over.

The movement goes through intense episodes, especially an extended development section, which begins with a valiant blast of double octaves in the piano but segues into a battle with the orchestra; concentrated fragments of the stormy opening theme serve as weapons in this clash. During the concluding section, the piano and orchestra, though both defiant, seem in sync, and the effect is almost glittering. Yet in no way have the tensions been resolved.

The second movement, a slow, solemn Adagio in wistful D major, has a long-lined theme that epitomizes the breadth Brahms can bring to melody: Brahms described it as a "gentle portrait" of Clara. There are dreamy passages for the piano, where lines expand high and low, as if trying to pin down the strands of some elusive, mystical music.

The finale, a spirited Rondo in D Minor, begins with a dark theme that has a touch of gypsy music to it. But the left hand plays a string of steady sixteenth notes, like some homage to a Bach toccata. It goes through contrasting major-mode episodes that become burly yet playful. The long final coda is full of frantic piano cadenzas and dizzying interactions with the orchestra that Joachim would describe as "awakenings." Indeed, there is a counterintuitive quality to the conclusion: it's as if, amid all the hurly-burly and shouting, the concerto, rather than capping a journey, is jumpy to set off on a new one.

The first public performances took place in Hanover and Leipzig in early 1859, with Brahms as soloist. The reception in Hanover was poor; the reaction to the performance in Leipzig by the Gewandhaus Orchestra, with Julius Rietz (who disliked the piece) conducting, was downright hostile. A conservative critic proclaimed the concerto three-quarters of an hour of "rooting and rummaging," with nothing to offer but "waste, barren dreariness," a desert of "the shrillest dissonances and most unpleasant sounds." Brahms could be philosophical about critics, but not about the reception by the audience. At the end, "three hands attempted to fall slowly one into another," Brahms wrote to Joachim, but "a quite distinct hissing from all sides forbade such demonstrations."

In spite of this, the concerto will please someday, Brahms assured Joachim, adding, stoically, that this entire experience was the best thing that could have happened to him: it "forces one to collect one's thoughts appropriately and raises one's courage."

Shortly afterward Brahms performed the piece at home, in Hamburg, with Joachim conducting, and this time the reception was better. The performances were sold out, attracted attention, and earned Brahms some desperately needed money.

Yet Brahms had to face reality: he was a struggling composer with no real following and few solid prospects. The setback had a life-altering impact on his personal life.

In the summer of 1858, staying in the bustling city of Göttingen, Brahms had become infatuated with Agathe von Siebold, the attractive, dark-eyed, and spirited daughter of a respected professor at the university. Joachim had been sweet on Agathe too. But Brahms fell for this cultured young woman, who had a warm voice and sang his songs beautifully. By the next year, they were engaged.

However, after the fiasco of the concerto, facing career uncertainty, Brahms needed personal space. He rushed to see Agathe but after the reunion wrote a confusing letter, effusive yet blunt. "I love you! I must see you again! But I cannot wear fetters," he declared. "Write to me, whether I am to come back, to take you in my arms, to kiss you and tell you that I love you." It would seem that, for now, Brahms wanted a lover, not a wife. Agathe, crushed but clear-eyed, broke things off.

But the next couple of years proved productive for Brahms. He composed two serenades for the court orchestra in Detmold, where he still held a winter post. In writing his piano concerto Brahms had had to overcome trepidation about his skills at orchestration. These genial serenades, however, are deftly conceived for orchestra.

In the early 1860s Brahms went on a tear, turning out a number of masterful chamber works. His Piano Quartet No. 1 in G Minor, composed in 1861, represented a breakthrough. In general, Brahms had a penchant for overloading his chamber music in an effort to achieve symphonic depth and musical breadth. The instruments can seem to be straining for maximum passion and expressivity; textures can become thick and muddy. Performers who play these pieces must try hard to highlight crucial voices in a given passage and bring balance to the overall musical textures. Brahms's three string quartets, though alive with engrossing music, can be particularly challenging to realize in performance.

But the three piano quartets are, to me, more effectively conceived. Brahms complained continually about the difficulty of blending the percussive, metallic sound of the piano with the warmth and richness of string instruments in chamber works. But he mostly solved those problems in these quartets for piano, violin, viola, and cello. In agitated episodes the piano seems excitingly pitted against the three strings to riveting effect; in restrained, lyrical passages the piano shifts moods and cushions wafting strings to achieve glowing equanimity of sound.

The teeming Piano Quartet in G Minor is especially effective. The first movement starts with the piano playing a beckoning theme in bare triple octaves, as if stating a proposition. The three strings, one by one, pick up the theme as the piano steps back, providing harmonic support jolted with subtle syncopation. The piano replies with a yearning phrase in parallel sixths for both hands, which sounds almost like a fleeting duet. But something stirs within the strings. Sure enough, that initial proposition returns in the piano, now in fierce fortissimo octaves. The strings join the fray.

Then the piano stirs up trouble through ominous grumblings. And this movement suddenly seems to take off on a long, fitful adventure.

An Intermezzo movement follows, with a lilting yet curiously fretful melody over a repeated-note cello riff and a playful middle section offering a beguiling contrast of mood. The subsequent slow movement is noble and expansive, interrupted by an animated, sputtering-march episode of a heroic cast. The finale is a wild-eyed, breathless gypsy Rondo, which the piano keeps trying to dominate through bursts of brazenly virtuosic brilliance. It ends in a mad rush by all four instruments, though they seem forcibly bound together because there is no other choice.

The young Brahms wrote his first important set of variations during his time in the Schumann household, appropriately, his Variations on a Theme by Robert Schumann (1854). Within three years he had composed his Variations on an Original Theme, and Variations on a Hungarian Song.

Brahms's penchant for using small motifs to generate whole movements of larger-scaled works served him well in writing variations. He could tease out various little motivic bits of a theme and spin them into boldly diverse variations. Brahms found this genre liberating. He did not have to structure an architectonic sonata movement. Instead, he could write a long work that unfolded as a series of short, contrasting episodes, which he organized into an inexorable arc of drama.

His next major work in this genre was a breakthrough for the young Brahms, and also for me as a young pianist.

When I was a Yale undergraduate Rudolf Serkin concluded a piano recital at the university with a Brahms piece I knew about but had never heard: Variations and Fugue on a Theme by Handel (written during the composer's burst of creativity in the early 1860s). This thirty-minute work, a set of twenty-five variations on a frilly theme taken from a Handel keyboard suite, ending with a staggering fugue, at once awed and rattled me.

The *Handel* Variations show another side to Brahms: not the tortured soul, but the cocky showman; not just the pioneer of Romantic fervor but the devotee of old music, especially Baroque. The work confirmed that the variation genre ideally suited him.

But Brahms had to have a juicy theme to work with, like this beguiling melody taken from one of Handel's keyboard suites. Structured in two four-measure phrases (each one repeated), the melody is at once puckish and stiffly ornate. It seems intent on simply ascending the first five steps of the B-flat major scale, but keeps circling around on itself, sort of two steps forward and one step back. Progress is also slowed because certain notes are adorned with elaborate trills and melodic turns.

Brahms begins in the first variation by turning the tune into a sort of jaunty peasant dance, with a bumptious bass pattern and comically exaggerated ornamental flourishes. The second variation spins out in strands of four-part counterpoint employing a two-against-three rhythmic device that is a hallmark of Brahms's style in all his works. (Two against three involves overlapping lines of three notes per beat in one voice and two notes per beat in the other. The effect conveyed is as if two lines, though in duet, are going their own ways in terms of rhythmic flow. Lots of earlier styles of music, and composers both before and after Brahms, use this two-against-three device, but Brahms was almost obsessed with it.)

The third variation is a tease, with the right and left hands trading sly three-note gestures. So the fourth one comes as a shocker: a fusillade of fortissimo octaves and thick chords that surge along with perpetual-motion relentlessness.

After this the listener realizes that anything is possible. Brahms does not disappoint, as the variations keep coming: a mysterious minor-mode canon for two voices, played in octaves; a sputtering fanfare; a sizzling Hungarian dance in which each phrase spans the keyboard from top to bottom; a gentle variation that suggests little birdcalls in the flowing right-hand part. One slowish variation slinks stepwise up and down the keyboard in thick chords: here is Brahms the explorer of bold chromatic harmony. A variation that evokes the tinkling of a cuckoo clock leads to a linked pair that turns dark and determined, driven by resolute triplets that break into whiplash runs for both hands. A final, heroic variation is a triumphant fanfare of leaping chords and octaves: if a pianist's hands do not blur while dispatching it, the tempo is not fast enough.

And then that fugue, which starts diligently with a theme that unfolds in two clipped four-note spurts, a little evocative of Handel's theme. The fugue builds to four voices, but soon everything splits apart as those voices expand into double thirds and sixths and steely octaves. At one point, the music turns inward and seems almost constrained. But this is just a ploy, setting us up for a colossal conclusion, when three strands of fearlessly exhilarating music happen at once: cascading octaves and double thirds in the right hand; steadily chiming octaves in the left hand; and somehow an inner voice with that obsessive four-note motif. When I heard Serkin's performance it seemed as if he had three hands.

Years later, I dared to take on the *Handel* Variations. I played it for a degree recital in my doctoral program at Boston University. Ideally, you don't just perform the *Handel* Variations, you don't just get through the piece. It should seem as if you've utterly conquered the technical challenges; there should be no sense of struggle. The only way I could convey that sense was to let go, notes be damned. I can barely listen to the recording I have of that performance, since it's marred by too many clinkers. Still, a lot of the playing is exuberant and colorful. I sure remember enjoying myself in the moment.

In September 1862, at twenty-nine, Brahms made his first trip to Vienna, the city that would in time become his home. Relocating to this cultural capital had been urged on him by friends and colleagues, especially Clara Schumann and Joachim. This visit was a trial run. The affability of Viennese life charmed Brahms, not to mention the proliferation of stylish Viennese ladies. He quickly made musical connections, including the pianist Julius Epstein, who was impressed with Brahms's pianism and overcome by his compositions. Epstein introduced Brahms to the members of the Hellmesberger Quartet, who immediately engaged Brahms for a concert introducing his Piano Quartet in G Minor, a performance that won him critical praise and public buzz. Emboldened, Brahms started arranging his own concerts, playing his chamber works, the *Handel* Variations, and piano pieces by Bach and Schumann—again with encouraging success, and this just a couple of months after his arrival. From the letters Brahms sent home, his parents assumed their son was conquering the city.

Actually, Brahms had not yet committed to relocating. He had pinned his career hopes, and personal pride, on winning a post that had become open as leader of the singing academy and philharmonic orchestra in Hamburg. Shortly after his arrival in Vienna he learned that he, a native son, had been passed over in favor of a popular baritone, Julius Stockhausen, who was also a friend. Though losing the job may have wounded Brahms badly, the early Brahms biographer Karl Geiringer argued that "posterity is much more inclined to view this setback as providential and beneficial to his art." The atmosphere of Vienna enlivened Brahms's stolid character and spurred his creativity.

He returned to Hamburg in time to spend his thirtieth birthday with his family. There he found his parents going through the last stages of enmity that soon caused them to separate. The elderly Johanna's health had weakened; years of financial struggle and marital stress had left their mark on Johann. Brahms had to help his parents settle into separate residences. He took the breakup badly, but tried to understand, encouraging them to remain in touch and providing financial support.

Back in Vienna in 1863, Brahms secured a modest appointment as the director of the Vienna Singakademie. He took the job seriously and programmed music by early masters like Heinrich Schütz and Bach, along with more recent works by Beethoven and Mendelssohn, and new scores, including his own. He resigned after a year, finding the duties too constricting upon his time for composition.

But this reimmersion in serious choral music inspired him. Ever since the death of Robert Schumann in 1856, Brahms had been contemplating a major sacred choral work. In early 1865 he was shaken by the death of his mother at seventy-six. The combination of these experiences may have led him to conceive, and, over three years, complete, a work that brought him wide renown, the German Requiem.

The formal title of the work is in effect a statement of purpose: *Ein deutsches Requiem, nach Worten der heiligen Schrift* (A German Requiem, to Words of the Holy Scripture). The heritage of choral requiems was long and rich. But Brahms never considered setting the standard Latin liturgy of the Catholic requiem mass to music. His aim was to write a humanist, rather than strictly Christian, requiem. To this end he selected scriptural passages from the German Lutheran Bible for his text. In every sense, this is a "German" requiem, written in the language of its target audience, although in a letter to the music director of the Bremen cathedral Brahms revealed that he would gladly omit the word "German" and instead call it a "Human" requiem.

Whereas traditional requiem masses are focused on prayers for the dead and thoughts of their salvation, Brahms's German Requiem is directed to those left behind, who mourn and search for comfort. In his requiem Brahms wanted no trace of Christian dogma, all the familiar pieties about the redeeming death of our Savior. Though there are moments when the Lord is indeed invoked as a source of comfort, the overall message comes through clearly: in facing loss, we humans must love and comfort one another.

Originally the requiem, which was scored for chorus, baritone and soprano soloists, and orchestra, had six movements, beginning with a setting of a passage from Matthew, a beloved beatitude: "Blessed are they that mourn; for they shall be comforted." This version received its first performance at the Bremen Cathedral on Good Friday in 1868, with Brahms conducting a chorus of two hundred and a large orchestra. At the end, Clara Schumann, who had been escorted to her seat by Brahms, sobbed quietly, as others cheered. Swafford writes that the audience appears to have left "in an atmosphere of awe and grace."

Soon afterward, Brahms added a movement, "And ye now therefore have sorrow; but I will see you again," which he dedicated to his mother. This would become the fifth of seven movements in a score lasting some seventy minutes, making it Brahms's longest work. A restrained, contemplative quality pervades the requiem, though the score has flashes of anger and episodes of distress.

The opening movement, "Blessed are they that mourn," begins with a softly resonant pedal tone in the string basses that at first seems ominous. Immediately gently pliant melodic lines rise and mingle in the higher strings, though intriguingly Brahms eliminates the violins from this movement to enhance the dark, deep cast of the music. Voices in the choir enter, calmly blessing those who mourn. The movement segues into sections of resolute affirmation, and the choir and orchestra break into a fleeting passage of sturdy counterpoint.

The second movement, "For all flesh is as grass, and the glory of man as the flower of grass," seems at first forbidding, with a heaving theme that unfolds in short phrases and a softly throbbing motif in the lower strings and timpani. Steadily the music gains in activity and uplift. The stern message—"For all flesh is as grass"—is emphasized in chilling choral outbursts, yet the music builds to an intricate contrapuntal ensemble of pulsing certitude, proclaiming that the "ransomed of the Lord shall return, and come to Zion with songs and everlasting joy upon their heads." This is, after all, the natural cycle of life. We're going to be fine. That's the message here.

The gravely beautiful "Lord, make me to know mine end" begins with a pleading melody for solo baritone, soon answered by the chorus in assuring phrases over a walking line in the string basses. No whole movements are given over to the solo baritone and soprano in this requiem; instead, their lines emerge from and engage with the chorus. Here for a moment, though, is a hint of what a subdued aria from a Brahms opera might have been like had he written one.

The requiem continues with comparable inspiration in every movement. The fourth movement, a setting of the psalm "How amiable are Thy tabernacles, O Lord of Hosts!" is tenderly beatific. The added fifth movement, "And ye now therefore have sorrow," is graced by a wafting, heavenly theme for soprano solo and maintains consoling loveliness through shifts of mood and text. The most terrifying episodes come during the sixth movement, when the chorus, in battle mode, declares that "Death is swallowed up in victory. O Death, where is thy sting?" The requiem ends with a stirring setting of "Blessed are the dead," invoking the Spirit's promise that they may rest from their labors and that their works "do follow them."

The first performance of the complete seven-movement requiem by the Leipzig Gewandhaus Orchestra and Chorus in early 1869 was widely acclaimed, and marked a turning point in Brahms's career.

Brahms continued to spend long periods away from Vienna on tour as a pianist, or visiting colleagues, and taking stretches of his summers relaxing in Baden-Baden. But Vienna was claiming him. In 1872, with his reputation growing, he was appointed director of concerts of a prominent music society, the Vienna Gesellschaft der Musikfreunde. Taking a reformist approach, he made sure that only professional musicians could be appointed to the orchestra, and expanded the repertory to include early works by Bach and those composers who were not of the Wagner-Liszt circle, including Schumann, Joachim, Max Bruch, and, of course, himself.

He settled on permanent lodgings, an apartment near the Musikverein, the acoustically splendid concert hall of the Vienna Philharmonic, which opened in 1870 (and remains in operation). He would live there for the rest of his life. As before, Brahms found that the duties of a professional post left him too little time for composition. He stepped aside in 1875, after three years. Now in his forties, his days as a slender, shy youth behind him, he let his beard grow and put on weight. Thus began the period of Brahms's maturity, producing masterpiece after masterpiece and becoming a living legend in Vienna.

After working intermittently for at least fourteen years on his Symphony No. 1 in C Minor, he finished it in 1876 and allowed the premiere to take place in November of that year by a fine orchestra in Karlsruhe. This is the work I mentioned earlier that was sometimes dubbed "Beethoven's Tenth" owing to the similarity between the affirming theme of the last movement and the "Ode to Joy" melody in the stirring finale of Beethoven's Ninth. In a speech following the premiere, a representative of the orchestra hailed the master for having proved that the last word in symphonic writing had not yet been written. Still, the piece also provoked doubting criticism and incomprehension.

For Brahms, seeing this piece to its premiere was like getting a monkey off his back. After having struggled so long to complete his First Symphony, Brahms wrote the Symphony No. 2 in D fairly quickly during the summer months of 1877, while staying in a charming Austrian village in the province of Carinthia. The joy he drew from spending time in a friendly rural setting comes through in the sunny, glowing music. This is thought to be Brahms's pastoral symphony. The scoring is delicate; the textures translucent. In a letter to Fritz Simrock, his publisher, however, Brahms suggests that this symphony is "so melancholy that you can't stand it," that he had never written anything "so sad," and that the score should be published "with a black border."

Surely the composer was being impish. Yet in truth, the music is run through with forlorn undercurrents and episodes of intensity, especially in the first movement. The finale bustles along with almost aggressive high spirits: Swafford aptly describes it like "Brahms on a Prater merry-go-round." For me, the best performances dig below the sunny surface of the symphony to expose the music's piercing heat rays.

The outstanding work of this period, Brahms's most titanic score, is the Piano Concerto No. 2 in B-flat, a piece many pianists regard as the most technically difficult of the standard repertory concertos. The great Alfred Brendel wrote of its "unsurpassable pianistic perversions."

Brahms started sketching the piece during a pleasant spring trip to Italy and Sicily in 1878, completing it in 1881. In a letter to a musical confidante, Brahms slyly described the finished work as a "tiny, tiny piano concerto, with a tiny, tiny wisp of a scherzo." Actually, written in four movements, with a dark, fervid scherzo as a second movement, the concerto lasts some fifty minutes.

The first movement begins with a theme—calm, lyrical, a little pensive—introduced by solo horn. The piano answers in an elegant, almost courtly way, with gently lapping chords that ascend more than five octaves on the keyboard (that Brahms breadth thing) before ending with an echo of the final turn of the horn's lyrical theme. The pattern repeats for the theme's second phrase: with the horn answered by the piano. The orchestra picks up the melody, ponders it, and leaves it a little hanging, harmonically.

Then the piano takes over with a vehement, stormy cadenza of roiling arpeggios and leaping chords, massive and terrifying. Until finally it shifts into a majestic mode, eventually taking up the initial theme and shaping it into something triumphant yet a little scary. This emboldens the orchestra to burst forth with a stirring marchlike statement of that theme.

The first movement, though basically hewing to a sonata form, unfolds with episodes that are alternately heroic, suspenseful, and vehement, especially a passage where the piano breaks into leaping, relentless, pummeling chords. That "wisp" of a scherzo? It's actually restless music with a hint of Slavic sadness, propelled by a rippling rhythmic riff that sets off a dialogue of short, heaving phrases between piano and orchestra. Its middle section (the trio), in contrast, is almost festive and celebratory. You can imagine church bells chiming manically, at first, anyway. The suspicious piano answers this outbreak with a spectral passage of scurrying chords until, in time, having voiced its wariness, the piano, now on its own terms, joins the festivities. Then the Slavic storminess returns.

The majestic slow movement opens with an arching, noble theme for a solo cello, cushioned by the orchestra. Rather than take up the theme, the piano mostly offers lyrical and developmental passages of commentary upon it. The finale, perhaps the movement most redolent of Brahms's trips to Italy, is joyful and sunny, though with episodes of slashing intensity and a daringly breathless, almost dizzying coda.

Brahms had largely ceased activity as a touring pianist by the time he played the public premiere of the Second Concerto in Budapest in 1881. He had to have been a little rusty technically. Yet he not only played to acclaim, but took the piece on tour with the Meiningen Court Orchestra and its conductor, Hans von Bülow, visiting twenty-two cities over three months.

Like most of Brahms's mature works, the Second Piano Concerto met with significant pockets of resistance. No doubt the music provoked many genuinely baffled reactions. But some of the pushback was due to ongoing enmity between opposing compositional camps, what has been called the War of the Romantics, during the second half of the nineteenth century.

Leipzig, where Mendelssohn had earlier been a major presence, was the headquarters of the camp thought to be conservative, a value unabashedly embraced by its adherents, especially Clara Schumann, Joachim, Brahms, and their later followers, including Antonin Dvořák, a Brahms devotee who was championed by the older master. Weimar was the mission control center of the Wagner-Liszt camp, the "New German School," self-described radicals who advocated pushing exploration of chromatic harmony into new realms and valued freer-formed "program music" over more structured "absolute music," with its adherence to Classical-era forms. The Leipzig composers kept trying to extend the symphonic heritage. The Weimar adherents composed symphonic tone poems and literary-inspired works with sui generis structures. Wagner, a Beethoven disciple, thought the proper way to honor that towering German master was to write epic, mythical operas.

In truth, Brahms was intrigued by Wagner's music, though he tended to keep this to himself. Nevertheless, he was thrust into this polemical battle and seen by the traditionalists as a like-minded opponent to the fervid followers of Liszt and Wagner. For me, the pointlessness of this standoff is crystalized by the story of Tchaikovsky's first meeting with Brahms. Tchaikovsky, who lived far off in Russia, was largely isolated from this stylistic battle. He met Brahms in 1888 in Leipzig while in the midst of a three-month European tour—a rare opportunity for musicians in the cultural capitals of the West to hear the works of a significant Russian composer. The meeting took place at the home of a mutual friend, Adolph Brodsky, a Russian-born violinist. At the time Brahms was fifty-five, with most of his major compositions behind him, and Tchaikovsky was forty-eight.

Prior to this meeting, Tchaikovsky, after hearing Brahms's First Symphony, bluntly dismissed him in his diary as a "giftless bastard." It annoyed him to see such a "self-inflated mediocrity . . . hailed as a genius."

Upon meeting him, Tchaikovsky fell under the sway of Brahms's strong, genial personality. Still, he was put off by the music, which he found cerebral and complex. (He attended a performance of Brahms's Double Concerto.) Though in person he showed deference toward the renowned German composer, Tchaikovsky dared to share some of his reservations during their conversation. In his diary he told the whole truth.

There was something "dry, cold, vague and nebulous in the music of this master that is repellent to Russian hearts," Tchaikovsky wrote. Brahms's pieces were admirably serious, with no showy effects or trivialities, he explained. But in spite of this, "the chief thing is lacking—beauty!" In a revealing statement he saluted Brahms's "firm, proud renunciation of the tricks that solemnize the Wagner cult, and in a much less degree the worship of Liszt." But, he added, "I do not care for his music."

Two years later they met for the second, and last, time, in Hamburg, where Tchaikovsky conducted his own Fifth Symphony, a performance Brahms made a point of attending. Brahms didn't much like the piece. Their lack of sympathy for each other's music seems baffling today. How could Tchaikovsky, the composer of *Swan Lake* and the molten Fourth Symphony, not have responded to Brahms's intense, majestic First Symphony? And how could Brahms, the composer of that teeming symphony, a piece that takes us on an emotional journey through torment, dissension, grim acceptance, and ultimate triumph, not have been excited by Tchaikovsky's impassioned, militaristic, and finally exalted Fifth Symphony?

Looked at in historical context, this War of the Romantics made as little sense as more recent stylistic hostilities in the arts—for example, the polemical grumblings between mid-twentieth-century playwrights who variously championed lyrical or absurdist or bleakly realistic theater.

During this productive period, when not preoccupied with writing large-scale scores, Brahms continued to compose lighter fare—songs, four-hand piano duos, waltzes galore, as well as two volumes of ebullient pieces that combine all of these genres: his *Liebeslieder-Walzer* (Love Song Waltzes), scored for four vocal soloists and four-hand piano duet. Brahms was an ardent fan of Johann Strauss Jr., the Viennese "Waltz King." In the late 1880s, at a festive party hosted by Strauss at his summer villa, Strauss's wife Adele (his third, and last) asked Brahms, who was attending, to autograph her fan. The obliging composer wrote out the first notes of Strauss's "Blue Danube" waltz, and the words "Leider nicht von Johannes Brahms" (Unfortunately not by Johannes Brahms), a splendid compliment to an admired colleague. As H. L. Mencken wrote about this story, "Brahms had written plenty of waltzes himself, and knew that it was not as easy as it looked."

Brahms completed his Symphony No. 4 in E Minor in 1885, a work that nods to his love of early music by ending with a stirring passacaglia movement (based on the Baroque variation form, with a repeated theme that can appear in any voice or line). When the next year he wrote his unusual Double Concerto for Violin, Cello, and Orchestra, he started telling friends and associates that he was retiring as a composer. That resolve didn't quite hold.

Between 1892 and 1893 Brahms composed four groups of piano pieces, published under four opus numbers, a total of twenty individual works. These were relatively short pieces, most of them lasting just several minutes. He titled these pieces either "intermezzo" or "capriccio," with one "romance," one "ballad," and one "rhapsody" among them These terms suggest lighter, lesser fare: "intermezzo" historically denotes a diverting shorter work played between acts of an opera or a ballet; "capriccio" implies a little caprice, no big deal.

Actually, these are among Brahms's most searching, harmonically pathbreaking, visionary pieces, including certain ones that Schoenberg pointed to in making his case for "Brahms the Progressive."

The seven pieces published as Op. 116, also called "Fantasien" (Fantasies), come across as an integrated set, with subtle linking motifs that several scholars have detected. I first learned and played them in college. It always felt as if I were performing some otherworldly thirty-minute epic. The set starts with the dark, slightly crazed Capriccio in D Minor, followed by the forlorn Intermezzo in A Minor, which has a delicate, mystically strange middle section. The bombshell is the fifth piece, the slow, mysterious Intermezzo in E Minor. At least it's officially designated as being in E minor. In fact, it's like an experiment in breaking down the boundaries of tonal harmony. The first section of this eerie intermezzo is a series of abrupt two-chord gestures in which the first chord, already a little ambiguous, bleeds into some murky, unresolved dissonance, each gesture more intense and harmonically unstable than the previous.

Brahms was further tempted out of his inclination to retire by his excitement over the German clarinetist Richard Mühlfeld, at the time first clarinetist of the orchestra in Meiningen, from which Hans von Bülow had recently retired as director. An impressively accomplished musician, Mühlfeld had entered the orchestra in 1873 as a violinist, though after three years he was appointed principal clarinet, having essentially taught himself the instrument.

In 1891 Brahms heard Mühlfeld, thirty-five at the time, as a soloist in Weber's Clarinet Concerto in F Minor and also some chamber works. Extraordinarily impressed, Brahms immediately began writing pieces for Mühlfeld to play, his first chamber works featuring clarinet, resulting in four major scores, a project hailed by generations of grateful clarinetists ever since.

That summer, in a burst of inspiration, Brahms composed the sublime, intricately textured Quintet in A Minor for Clarinet and Strings, which Mühlfeld introduced with the Joachim Quartet in Berlin in December, a performance so successful that the audience demanded that the melancholic Adagio movement be repeated. Brahms also wrote his compellingly mercurial Trio for Clarinet, Cello, and Piano in A Minor, which he eagerly performed with Mühlfeld and a cellist colleague. He affectionately called Mühlfeld "his dear nightingale," because the clarinetist's tone, while dark and rich, was so sweet and clear.

Brahms discussed every aspect of the instrument and its capabilities with Mühlfeld. In 1894 Brahms was so excited that Mühlfeld was coming to visit him in Vienna that he started composing two major works: the Sonatas for Clarinet and Piano in F Minor and E-flat Major. "I wish you could be with us," Brahms wrote to Clara in anticipation of the visit, "for he plays very beautifully." Describing his new works with self-deprecating humor, Brahms added: "If you could extemporize a little in F-minor and E-flat major you would probably chance on the two sonatas." Not only did Brahms try out the pieces with Mühlfeld, he took them on the road in a series of concerts with this stellar musician.

Still, Brahms did curtail his compositional activities. One momentous event, however, compelled him to take up manuscript paper: the death of Clara Schumann in May 1896, at seventy-six. Brahms was devastated.

He turned to the organ and, paying homage to early music, wrote eleven Chorale Preludes for Organ, short, contrapuntally elegant treatments of, for the most part, Lutheran chorale tunes. Several of these works convey peaceful serenity, with a touch of steadfast affirmation. Yet a feeling of solemn loss pervades the set. It was surely deliberate that Brahms composed two settings of the final hymn tune, "O Welt, ich muss dich lassen" (O World, I must leave you).

This was Brahms's last completed composition. About six months later, on April 3, 1897, he died in Vienna at sixty-three.

It would be suitably romantic to think that he died of grief over the great love of his life. But prior to Clara's death Brahms had been experiencing symptoms of jaundice. In time, a Viennese doctor told Brahms he had cancer of the liver, the disease that had taken his father in 1872.

During his illness friends paid visits; admirers sent gifts, food, and whole caskets of wine. Representatives from the music capitals of Germany and from Paris and London attended Brahms's lavish funeral in Vienna. In his native city of Hamburg flags were flown at half-mast on all the ships in the harbor.

I wouldn't have imagined it, but Brahms helped New York come to terms with the trauma of September 11 in 2001. A week after the horrific terrorist attacks, the New York Philharmonic had been scheduled to open its season with a gala concert. Kurt Masur, then the orchestra's music director, canceled those plans. Instead, he announced that the Philharmonic, joined by the New York Choral Artists, the American Boychoir, and two vocal soloists, would perform Brahms's German Requiem as a benefit for the families of first responders. I initially wondered whether a German maestro conducting a "German" Requiem to honor fallen New York heroes was the most appropriate response. Masur was convinced that Brahms's requiem, a piece directed at those left behind, could offer comfort to a grieving, shattered city. He was right, as I acknowledged at the start of my *New York Times* review: "Kurt Masur's unabashed belief in the power of music to make big statements and foster healing has sometimes invited kidding. No longer. If ever there was a moment when Americans, particularly New Yorkers, needed musical inspiration and healing it is now."

The magnificent performance conveyed the expansive breadth of the music, the uncanny melding of sadness and mystery. It was Masur's finest hour and, in a way, Brahms's too.

THE REFINED RADICAL

CLAUDE DEBUSSY (1862–1918)

I n every era various catchy terms have been coined to describe entire art movements, styles, and aesthetics, often to the dismay of the actual creators. Many of these terms, however handy as reference tools, are reductive at best, misleading at worst.

Schoenberg hated having his musical language described as "atonal," a word that, he wrote, "can only signify something that does not correspond to the nature of tone." Duke Ellington had very mixed feelings about "jazz," a slanglike word that never lost its early associations with "New Orleans bordellos," as Ellington ruefully noted. Philip Glass has long debunked "Minimalism" as a description of his style. It's easy to understand why, since his early detractors deployed the term as a pejorative. He prefers "music with repetitive structures," which is certainly more accurate, if cumbersome.

"Impressionism" is another one of these problematic words. Claude Debussy, even during his lifetime, was routinely described as the premier "Impressionist" composer. That tag lingered for generations in music appreciation books and program notes. More recently this term, which was initially applied to painting, has been losing its hold on Debussy, which would have pleased him: he disdained the association, though he was inconsistent in his protestations.

Debussy hated dogma but understood that evocative terms can be helpful to the general public. He looked the other way when program notes for an important performance of *La Mer* (The Sea)—three symphonic sketches for orchestra—described the piece as, "in a word, musical impressionism." Sometimes Debussy tried to fudge things. The titles of his twenty-four Préludes for Piano, released in two books of twelve each, could not be more impressionistic: "Footsteps in the Snow," "The Girl with the Flaxen Hair," "The Sunken Cathedral," "Mists," "The Wind in the Plain." But in the published editions Debussy put the titles at the end of each prelude, in lowercase letters within parentheses.

He vented his true feelings, not just about the term itself but about its application to all the arts, in a 1908 letter to Jacques Durand, his publisher, explaining what he was attempting in *Images pour orchestre,* a set of pieces he was working on at the time. "I'm trying to write 'something else'—*realities,* in a manner of speaking—what imbeciles call 'impressionism,' a term employed with the utmost inaccuracy, especially by art critics who use it as a label to stick on Turner, the finest creator of mystery in the whole of art!"

"Realities" might seem a curious way to describe Debussy pieces that entrance you with milky textures, alluringly ambiguous harmonies, and time-stands-still flow. Yet Debussy's choice of that word, "realities," reveals much about his aims.

The term "Impressionism" had indeed been stuck on painting, starting with a sardonic 1874 review of an exhibition of modern art in Paris by the critic Louis Leroy, who appropriated the title of Monet's *Impression, soleil levant* (Impression, Sunrise) to mockingly dismiss the painters as "impressionists."

During the 1860s the conventions of French painting—valuing distinct images, precise brushstrokes, and historical subjects—were upheld by the Académie des Beaux-Arts in Paris. A rebellious group of young artists, including Monet, Renoir, and Frédéric Bazille, who met regularly in a cafe, embraced daring new concepts and techniques. They used short, loose brushstrokes and washes of pure, unblended colors to suggest spontaneity. They often painted outdoors, seeking to capture the shifting qualities of sunlight and shadow, and the way images seemed to vibrate. Their works explored a different mode of perception: to portray *how* we see subjects and scenes.

Naturally the old guard, along with most critics, abhorred all radical art and kept it out of the Paris Salon, the prestigious juried show. The young renegades formed their own society and, in time, presented their own exhibitions. Cézanne's works received notably stinging reviews. The pan that lingered, though, was Leroy's takedown of Monet's *Impression, Sunrise,* a seascape depicting the harbor of Le Havre. Since the painting was titled "Impression," there had to be some impression in it, Leroy speculated. To him it seemed a mere sketch. "Wallpaper in its embryonic state is more finished than that seascape," he wrote.

Still, as this new art gained adherents, the term acquired currency. The painters lumped together as Impressionists were stylistically wide-ranging. Yet in time they tolerated, even puckishly embraced, the label, much the way Andy Warhol and his fellow travelers did not much mind when critics dubbed their works "Pop Art," especially if it helped to brand their pieces for the art market.

Debussy, an astute and lifelong lover of the visual arts, had little use for the term "Impressionism." But he was inspired by the actual paintings. Its application to music came later, at the dawn of the twentieth century. Even in Debussy's earlier compositions, both admiring and mystified critics discerned elements that seemed musically analogous to Impressionist currents in painting. Those elements, however you label them, are unmistakable. They run through the works of the other ingenious composer long deemed an Impressionist, Maurice Ravel, with whom Debussy had a polite but cool relationship and rivalry. He wrote to his friend the musicologist Louis Laloy: "I agree with you that Ravel is extraordinarily gifted, but what annoys me is the attitude he adopts of being a 'conjurer,' or rather a fakir casting spells, and making flowers burst out of chairs."

In music this aesthetic placed a high priority on color, that is, the actual qualities of sound (timbre, in musical terminology) that could be produced by sensual, diaphanous approaches to writing for the orchestra, and fluid, tremulous techniques of writing for the piano, involving generous use of the sustaining pedal to prolong and mingle sounds and chords. The rippling runs, washes of passage-work, and spiraling figurations in piano works by Liszt and especially Chopin (a composer Debussy revered) anticipated Debussy's experiments. But his stunning innovations shattered the existing conception of what was possible on the piano.

Take the opening of "Reflets dans l'eau" (Reflections on the Water), the first of his *Images,* Book I, for piano. The music may sound gracious on the surface: a beckoning theme, emerging in the piano's midrange, is ensconced, in a way, within floating chords that rise and fall in delicate patterns. But as sonorities linger and blend, the harmonic tensions between these chords, which drift here and there, come through. When the piece breaks into rippling, watery right-hand arpeggios, the effect is too extreme to be merely pretty. It's like arpeggio madness.

Debussy stood out among composers of his generation in exploring new realms of harmony. Striving for ambiguity through myriad procedures, he used thick, unresolved chords (so-called extended harmonies) with intervals of the seventh, ninth, and eleventh added to basic chords (triads) to convey open-ended, expansive qualities—the kinds of chords that run through composers from Gershwin to Bill Evans to Sondheim. Moving beyond the standard tonal (major and minor) scales, Debussy adapted medieval modes (their precursors) and experimented with exotic scales that allowed for freer roaming.

The word "Impressionism" inadequately describes what Debussy was up to in other ways as well. By artistic and intellectual inclination, he was a refined and precise craftsman, a typically "French" characteristic, many would say. (I do.) With Debussy, every note in the watery passages of a piano piece, or in a series of cloudy orchestra chords, has been carefully chosen. The telling detail meant everything to Debussy.

To pursue both ambiguity and precision in one's art might seem a contradiction, but not with Debussy, given his contrarian, enigmatic nature. Though he came from humble origins, as he rose within artistic circles and accrued sophisticated patrons, Debussy coveted the trappings of high society and a successful career—while also disdaining them. Though he intensely needed relationships, that very need left him feeling compromised.

Recollections of Debussy describe him as mercurial, at once deeply sensitive, yet quick to take offense. The slightest thing could turn him sullen and angry.

Edward Lockspeiser, a music historian and critic who wrote an influential biography of Debussy, first published in 1936, suggests that one of the keys to the composer's personality was a curious combination of "irony and sensuousness—the one eating into or attempting to override the other." Little by little throughout his life, Lockspeiser writes, Debussy "obscured himself from the outside world by a screen of bristling irony."

Debussy almost purposefully enshrouded himself in mystery, a quality reflected in his compositions. Beneath all the hazy (if precisely rendered) and sensual surfaces of Debussy's works, the music surges with undertows, subliminal emotions, and eerie implications.

So it makes sense that while resisting links with Impressionism, Debussy identified strongly with Symbolism, the late nineteenth-century movement in poetry and the arts. Edgar Allan Poe, who died at forty in 1849, was regarded as a proto-Symbolist by the movement's adherents. Poe's stories were notably translated into French by the poet and essayist Charles Baudelaire, who died in 1867, and whose own works greatly influenced experimental poets of the next generation, especially Stéphane Mallarmé (1842–1898) and Paul Verlaine (1844–1896).

The Symbolist movement emerged during the mid-1880s in opposition to naturalism, realism, and standard forms and genres. Its practitioners cultivated imprecision and mystery, with a feeling for the occult and the macabre. The movement's informal headquarters was Mallarmé's salon. Debussy, who became the poet's friend, often attended these Tuesday gatherings.

Lockspeiser emphasizes that the Symbolist writers saw poetry as insufficient before the power of orchestral music. Symbolist poetry valued the assonance and sounds of language. The musicality of a poem was, in a sense, more important than its subject. Everything in this poetic art form was allusive. Lockspeiser quotes revealing comments from the notebooks of the critic and poet Paul Valéry, a Mallarmé disciple. We Symbolists, Valéry wrote, "were nourished on music," and "our literary minds dreamed only of extracting from language the same effects, almost, as were produced on our nervous systems by sound alone."

Mallarmé's intoxicatingly musical and elusively erotic poem *"L'après-midi d'un faune"* (The Afternoon of a Faun) was hailed a watershed of Symbolism when it was finally published, after years of revision, in 1876. Nearly two decades later the poem inspired Debussy to write a breakthrough orchestral work, *Prélude à l'après-midi d'un faune* (Prelude to the Afternoon of a Faun), first performed in Paris, in 1894. Looking back from the mid-twentieth century, the French composer Pierre Boulez asserted that "modern music was awakened" by Debussy's *Faun*.

The piece is not actually a prelude to anything, but rather a complete, intricately organized ten-minute composition, though the music has an improvisatory quality. Mallarmé was initially distressed that Debussy had based a musical work on the poem, which he considered already suffused with poetic music. He arrived at the premiere "looking like a soothsayer, with a Scotch plaid over his shoulders," and listened nervously, Debussy later recalled. Mallarmé was completely won over. He told Debussy that the music "prolongs the emotion of my poem and conjures up the scenery more vividly than any color."

The poem is written in the voice of a sensual faun, who awakens from an afternoon nap and starts playing his panpipes alone in the woods. He sees nymphs and naiads passing by, becomes aroused, and chases after them; but they elude him. Tired and frustrated, he gives himself over to sleep, a sleep filled with visions of nymphs and erotic stirrings.

The lines are flush with passages that seem at once graphically sexual and ambiguously metaphysical, as when, spying a pair of nymphs, the faun says:

> I run, when, at my feet I see enlaced
> Two girls, each in the other's arms embraced,
> Both wounded by the pain of not being one.

The faun speaks of lips on fire, of the secret terror of the flesh. In a note about *Faun*, Debussy emphasized that it is a very free illustration of Mallarmé's poem, not a synthesis of its contents.

This era-changing music, which seems so atmospheric, lush, and evocative on the surface, is actually a carefully structured (you might say cagily structured) composition. It opens—the scene is set—with the most famous flute solo ever written. The melody begins with a soft midrange C-sharp that slinks down and lands on G before turning around and crawling back up, skipping a couple of notes. The high and low endpoints of this miniphrase trace the interval of the tritone, which in the medieval era was heard as diabolic (though in time it became the activating element of the everyday dominant seventh chord). Still, for all the drowsy mindlessness of the moment, this faun's melodic piping already seems irresolute, in need of relief. The flute plays this phrase again, but then continues with a rising, deceptively calming melodic turn suggesting that a moment of repose is coming. Then the melody lands on an unexpected note: A-sharp.

At that instant, other woodwind instruments undergird that eerie melodic note with a slightly tense chord as a harp plays a silken, sensual, rising and falling glissando outlining an ambiguous seventh chord. A clarinet, trying to calm things down, plays what could be a little three-note tag to the melody, supported by a plush harmony in the strings, which have been in wait until now. Yet everything feels unsettled. Suddenly there's silence—for a whole measure. You wonder, Did I hear this right?

You did, Debussy answers, by repeating those responsive measures with the woodwind chords and harp. Then the faun's piping returns, this time with tremulous strings and, buried inside, a needling figure in a single horn, soon joined by another.

In less than a minute, we are both captivated by the colors and beauties of the music and left confused. The key signature indicates the piece is in E major, but the music sounds elusive. It's as if this initial episode wants to be in E major, but some lurking force within is determined to prevent such an ordinary yearning. And is there a pulse? Not really. Also, what to make of all the tense silences?

Soon the flute and the other instruments try to get along. Harp chords and arpeggios seem more benign and supportive; the strings loll about blithely. But the flute becomes aroused and skittish (the faun chasing after the nymphs?). Another flute joins in for a restless exchange, sort of catch me if you can, until the two flutes entwine in unison and settle down.

A lurking clarinet creeps in and pounces, setting off frenzied reactions among the flute, clarinet, and harps. Various characters could be ducking for cover in the woods. Then we hear a variant of the flute theme that initially seems animated and breezy, until the music swells with Wagnerian opulence.

Just as the chase seems to arrive at a standoff, a new theme emerges in the woodwinds, a spacious, descending melodic line that dips low, then rises to a higher starting point and descends again. For all the languorousness, it's hard to discern the true nature of this melodic phrase. Is it forlorn, contemplative, or waxing romantic? There's a slightly edgy rhythmic quality to the theme because crucial notes keep coming on off-beats. I prefer performances that emphasize this jagged aspect. But with each reiteration of the melody it becomes more insistent, restless, and elaborate. The strings throb as if they're panting, then take over the line and almost turn it inward, making the phrase calmly expressive, even as the rest of the orchestra seems to bustle nervously.

By the end, when two flutes play elaborations of the faun's theme and the strings tremble, the music seems not calm, but spent. There is one more statement of the main theme, this time played in hushed, rich chromatic chords, as if the forces of tonal harmony are entrapping the faun's dreamy melody. Then, finally, amid delicate flecks in the orchestra, the prelude ends with a clear, stable E major chord—what we have been waiting for, in a sense. Yet after what Debussy has put us through, you don't trust the calm one bit.

Prelude to the Afternoon of a Faun may be Debussy's most performed piece. It's often placed at the beginning of an orchestra program, considered a good mood-setter, rich with gorgeous orchestral sonorities and surging melodic lines. By now we like to think we know and love Debussy's beautiful *Faun* and his other evocative pieces, just as we think we know and love Impressionist paintings. Ah, look at the splashes of color in Monet and Renoir. And *La Mer* by Debussy? Why, you can just hear heaving waves coursing through the orchestra.

Yet the surface beauties of these very popular Impressionist paintings can distract us today from the utter radicalism of these works. The same holds true with Debussy, one of the most radical composers in history.

Think of his use of rhythm, his approach to time. After hundreds of years of pulsing music, along comes Debussy writing pieces that for long stretches can seem pulseless, near-static, almost beyond time. Even Debussy's popular "Clair de lune" (Moonlight), from his early *Suite berga-masque* for piano, has daring elements of rhythmic writing. The music is rightly beloved for its dreamy harmonies and lilting lyricism. But each segment of the well-known melody is stated in a mini-phrase that stops short, so the harmonies can linger, before the next mini-phrase picks up the thread, which injects a hint of tension and momentary confusion.

Vaslav Nijinsky certainly understood the churning eroticism of Debussy's *Faun*. In 1912 he performed the title role in a ballet to the piece that he choreographed for the Ballets Russes. A year before Stravinsky's *Rite of Spring* incited a near-riot at its Ballets Russes premiere, Nijinsky's *Afternoon of a Faun* was nearly as controversial. He and the dancers used jerky, unorthodox movements. At the end, as the faun, having given up his chase, slowly succumbed to dream-filled sleep, Nijinsky stroked himself in languid ways that suggested masturbation, to the shock of many. But what exactly did these disturbed audience members imagine was on the mind of the still-horny faun? Nijinsky sensed exactly what was smoldering below the lovely surface of Debussy's music.

Though Debussy's ancestors were mostly farmers in the Burgundy region of France, his immediate predecessors resettled in the larger region of Paris around 1800. The composer's grandfather, a wine seller, later became a carpenter. His father, Manuel-Achille Debussy, a hearty man, served for seven years in the marine infantry before marrying Victorine Manoury, moving to Saint-Germain-en-Laye, a suburb to the west of Paris, and opening a china shop. Though Manuel had scant education, he fancied himself a music connoisseur and enjoyed going to Paris playhouses, despite chronic financial strains on his marriage.

Achille-Claude Debussy, born on August 22, 1862, was the first of five children (a younger brother died at seven) and would always be his mother's favorite. Friends and family later recalled that the uncommunicative young Achille-Claude, who often kept to himself, had an instinctive fondness for small ornaments, intricate engravings, and delicate treats from the pastry shop. He also liked collecting butterflies.

In 1870, with the outbreak of the Franco-Prussian War, which humiliated France, and the siege of Paris, the family took refuge in Cannes at the home of Manuel's sister. (Debussy first went by Achille, then, flipping the order of his names, Claude-Achille, until, around the time he turned thirty he began calling himself Claude for the duration of his life.) In Cannes, even amid dislocation and hardship, Claude soaked up atmosphere and local color. "I remember the railway in front of the house and the sea on the distant horizon," he recalled in a 1908 letter to Durand, "which sometimes gave the impression that the railway came out of the sea, or else went into it (as you pleased)."

The war, which resulted in a unified German nation-state claiming most of the French Alsace and Lorraine regions, ruined Manuel's china shop business. He joined the revolutionary Commune, but was arrested by the regular French army in 1871 and sentenced to four years in prison. After a year in detention the remainder of the sentence was commuted, though Manuel lost his civil rights.

In Cannes, Claude's aunt arranged for him to have piano lessons with a local Italian musician. He immediately showed talent and musicality. Back in Paris, through a family friend, he was brought to the attention of Antoinette Mauté de Fleurville, a pianist who had studied with Chopin, or so she claimed. Recognizing the boy's potential, she prepared him for entry to the Paris Conservatory. Manuel, who had thought of coaxing his firstborn into the navy, now imagined him becoming a successful virtuoso.

Following auditions, the ten-year-old Claude was admitted to the Paris Conservatory in 1872 and remained there for eleven years. Actually, he never stood out as a pianist. From the start he excelled in solfège class and ear training, and won a prize for his skill at accompanying singers. When he started writing, his proclivity for experimental harmonies disconcerted his teachers.

In the summer of 1880, when almost eighteen, Debussy came to the attention of Nadezhda von Meck, a Russian businesswoman and amateur musician who was Tchaikovsky's tenacious patron. Her husband, who had died in 1876, made a fortune as an engineer in Russia's burgeoning railroad industry. Madame von Meck had a curious relationship with Tchaikovsky, providing him a sizable stipend but insisting that they not meet, lest, it would seem, her inflated image of him as a lofty, visionary artist be sullied. They communicated extensively through letters.

But the young Debussy, though just a musician whom von Meck engaged to teach her many children piano and play duets with her, became almost a member of her family, spending time first in a seaside town in southwest France and then in Florence. There he wrote his first mature pieces for piano, including a trio that he performed with a young violinist and a cellist in von Meck's circle. During the next two summers Debussy made his first trips to Moscow and Vienna while working for von Meck, from whom he obtained a glimpse of worldly, cultured life.

After that first summer Debussy returned to his studies in Paris and, to support himself, secured a job accompanying the students of a prominent voice teacher. In that class he met Marie-Blanche Vasnier, a woman of thirty-two married to a building contractor. She became Debussy's first love. Marie-Blanche had musical sensitivity and a sweet voice: Debussy wrote a group of short songs, or *mélodies,* for her. Her daughter would later recall Debussy spending long days with the family, working on songs with her mother, taking long walks, and slipping into a funk at night when he lost at card games. The affair was serious and lasted several years.

At the time, like all aspiring French composers, Debussy attempted to win the prestigious Prix de Rome, an annual state-sponsored scholarship that awarded winners in various artistic fields a coveted residency of three to five years at the French Academy in Rome. Ravel submitted works for consideration five times and never won. In 1884, on his third try, Debussy won for his cantata *L'Enfant prodigue,* a "lyric scene" for three singers and piano (with sections written for piano four-hands), a retelling of the parable of the prodigal son. Debussy's score won the votes of 22 out of 28 jurors, including that of Charles Gounod, who thought it a work of genius. In writing this piece Debussy, at the advice of his composition teacher, may have reined in his progressive tendencies. I'm closer to the opinion of my former colleague Bernard Holland, who in a *New York Times* review of the later orchestrated version deemed it a student effort, "an untroubling, wanly Romantic exercise with few adumbrations of the important work to come."

Almost immediately after being chosen for this coveted tenure at the Villa Medici in Rome, the chronically ambivalent Debussy regretted it, anticipating boredom, the vexations of being in a foreign locale, and the stifling effect of professional expectations.

Upon arriving, his fears were realized. "Here I am in this abominable Villa and I can assure you my first impression is not a good one," he wrote to M. Vasnier (the husband of his adored Marie) in February 1885. He complained about Italy's terrible weather. Rome lacked the friendliness of Paris, he added; he had overheard fellow musicians "running each other down." He admitted, "I've been so lonely I've cried."

One telling phrase in the letter to M. Vasnier stands out. "I'll never forget," Debussy wrote, "all you have done for me, or how welcome you made me inside your family circle." Did the husband of the woman he loved know about his wife's affair? It seems possible. After completing the minimum two-year residency, Debussy returned to Paris in the late spring of 1887.

Contentedly back home, Debussy entered what's often described as his bohemian period, when he lived like Henri Murger's (later, Puccini's) Latin Quarter bohemians, hanging out at cafes, frequenting artistic confabs, mingling with Symbolist writers, and befriending composers, including Paul Dukas (*The Sorcerer's Apprentice*) and, by 1890, Érik Satie.

It was during this period that Debussy's love-hate obsession with Wagner came to a head. In his youth, he was a "Wagnerian to the pitch of forgetting the simple rules of courtesy," as Debussy recalled much later. He earned some money from publishers by preparing piano reductions of

Wagner operas. Friends during those years remember Debussy playing whole acts of *Tristan und Isolde* on the piano from memory.

It's not hard to understand what attracted Debussy to Wagner. The German composer's rich harmonic language, so evasive of major-minor moorings, offered a template to Debussy, who also strove to break down "tonal fences, walls of formality," while still managing to "contain the rampage of chromaticism," as Leonard Bernstein put it in his Norton Lectures at Harvard. Wagner's orchestrations often radiate with a sensuous glow that strongly influenced Debussy. And Wagner's experiments with time-stands-still rhythmic pacing decisively impacted Debussy.

Wagner's operas can be taken as an early exploration of the Symbolist aesthetic. They're full of glaringly obvious symbols, each with its own distinctive leitmotif: the magic gold, Wotan's spear, Siegfried's sword, Alberich's curse, Amfortas's wound. Still, Wagner's symbolism comes loaded with metaphysical baggage that Debussy increasingly saw as mumbo-jumbo. Wagner's self-importance, Debussy began to feel, seeped into his music and weighed down the scores. In time he perceived the so-called Wagner revolution as a fallacy and saw Wagner's ideas as having "a bad influence on a lot of music and a lot of countries," as he wrote in 1910 to a Hungarian impresario. Wagner was "a beautiful sunset who has been mistaken for a sunrise." But Debussy himself had once held that "mistaken" view.

In the summers of 1888 and 1889 Debussy made pilgrimages to the Bayreuth Festival, the headquarters of Wagnerism, where he came to terms with this towering, suffocating figure. Finally, the Wagnerian spell began to lift for Debussy. Or so he tried to convince himself.

Though his sojourns in Bayreuth were pivotal to Debussy's development, his attendance in 1889 at the Universal Exposition in Paris, with its extensive offerings of Asian arts and culture, may have influenced him more profoundly. For the first time, he heard Javanese gamelan music in performance and experienced a creative epiphany. Many aspects of this music must have fascinated him: the exotic instrumental sounds, at once sinewy and delicate; the circuitous lyrical strands; the way bustling rhythms played out over sustained spans of time. Most of all, Debussy was affected by the allure of non-Western scales and modes. Recalling the exposition in a letter to the poet and writer Pierre Louÿs some years later, Debussy wrote: "Remember the music of Java, which contained every nuance, even the ones we no longer have names for. There tonic and dominant had become empty shadows of use only to stupid children."

During these years Debussy was also fascinated by the Russian music Madame von Meck had introduced him to, especially Mussorgsky's opera *Boris Godunov,* which he studied from the score. (In 1908 Debussy attended performances of Russian opera Sergei Diaghilev brought to Paris, including *Boris Godunov,* starring Feodor Chaliapin.) That opera gripped him, with its spare vocal writing mimicking the patterns of the Russian language, and its harmonic language steeped in unusual scales (the whole-tone scale, the octatonic scale). These alternative scales to the tonal (or diatonic) major and minor ones are hard to describe without getting very theoretical. But at least a couple of them—the whole-tone scale and the pentatonic scale—demand some explanation.

The scales common to Western music mostly involve tones separated by either half steps or whole steps. The chromatic scale, as I explained in the chapter on Bach, is all half steps, comprising all twelve standard pitches between, say, middle C and the C an octave higher. The major and minor scales use seven tones in various patterns of whole and half steps. Except for two half steps—between the third and fourth tones, and the seventh and final one—the major scale consists of whole steps.

Those half steps, because they rub so close together, have some innate tension: they almost demand resolution. The seventh tone is formally called the leading tone, a name that makes explicit its character: it wants to "lead" to the final note.

The whole-tone scale, in contrast, comprises only whole steps. So on the piano, starting with that middle C, the notes of that whole-tone scale would be C, D, E (all white ones), then F-sharp, G-sharp, A-sharp (all black), ending, after one more whole step, on the higher C.

What matters is the sound, the effect of the whole-tone scale. The avoidance of half steps gives this collection, or series, of tones a more open-ended character: no single tone stands out; no relationship between two neighboring tones seems to cry out for resolution of some kind.

Prior to the mid-nineteenth century, whole-tone scales in Western music mostly showed up fleetingly, usually just in a passage that turned whole-tone for a bit. A famous example is the German chorale tune "Es ist genug," which Bach harmonized and used to end a great cantata, "O Ewigkeit, du Donnerwort." The first four notes of the melody ascend four whole steps in order. It's a bold, even strange opening to a chorale melody, and Bach harmonized it in a way to maximize the strangeness. It sounds like the chorale is attempting to burst out of all harmonic boundaries in the space of four melodic notes.

Liszt used whole-tone scales in extended passages of certain works, especially later experimental pieces. The scale turns up often in Russian music, not just Mussorgsky but Glinka and Scriabin.

Debussy latched on to it eagerly when he was in the mood to evade the "empty shadows" of tonic and dominant harmony. He deploys a whole-tone scale, using it with a bold lack of harmonic direction, in his piano prelude *Voiles* (meaning veils or sails). It begins with a motif of descending parallel thirds (and then parallel fourths), written in a whole-tone scale. The lacy, elusive music conveys a floating quality, or billowing veils.

Debussy knew about whole-tone scales before he started incorporating them into his pieces. But the pentatonic scale, so common in Asian music, may have been almost a revelation when he attended the exposition.

The purpose of this scale (similar, in a way, to the whole-tone scale) is to avoid, in a sense, those tense half steps. True to its name, the basic pentatonic scale has five tones: on the piano, one such scale would be C, D, E (two whole steps), and then G and A (another whole step), but the distance between that E and G is three half steps (call it a step and a half). That gap is a defining quality of the scale. Again, sticking more or less to those tones, a melody can spin along and along and along. The pentatonic scale has appeared in many world cultures, especially in folk music. As it happens, the first two phrases of a very familiar tune, Stephen Foster's "Oh! Susanna," use only the five notes of the pentatonic scale ("I come from Alabama with a banjo on my knee" and so on).

Puccini used the pentatonic scale to evoke Asian settings in his operas, especially *Turandot*. Indeed, in that work he actually borrowed pentatonic Chinese tunes he found in a book.

Several aspects of pentatonic scales appealed to Debussy: the way music employing these scales represented a challenge to tonal orientation; the rich aura that came from sounds rooted in ancient musical cultures; the profusion of parallel perfect fourths and fifths, a use of intervals historically frowned upon in traditional Western practice. He mostly drew upon the pentatonic scale in fleeting passages, or for a touch of the exotic. The perpetual-motion toccata from the *Pour le piano* suite starts in bustling C-sharp minor (the natural minor version of the scale). But fragments of a punchy pentatonic tune break through here and there. "Serenade of the Doll," from *Children's Corner,* begins with a gently dancing figure that bounces along on a perfect fifth. A cute tune with grace notes breaks in, sort of riding over the perfect fifth, suggesting a playfully jumpy pentatonic theme. Is this an Asian doll serenading us?

Writing to Eugene Vasnier in 1885 from Rome during his residency, Debussy described his emerging, and unconventional, ideas about music drama. "I would always rather deal with something where the passage of events is to some extent subordinated to a thorough and extended portrayal of human feelings," he explained. Debussy's former composition teacher recalled the young musician specifying early on what he ideally wanted in a librettist: a poet who "would merely hint at things and allow me to graft my thought on his," someone whose characters "belong to no time or place."

In 1890 Debussy started on his first opera when the noted French poet Catulle Mendès, convinced that Debussy was destined to be a composer of the future, approached him with a project. Mendès had written a libretto,

Rodrigue et Chimène, based on the adventurous Castilian folk legend of El Cid. The story and poetic language were ill-suited to Debussy. Still, thinking he could not afford to turn down such an opportunity, Debussy persevered for some two years. "My life," he would complain to a friend, "is hardship and misery thanks to this opera."

Debussy's personal life had gained stability after meeting Gabrielle Dupont, called Gaby, a forceful young woman with blond hair and piercing green eyes, whose father was a tailor in Normandy. Not much more is known of her background or how the couple met. But Gaby became Debussy's partner during his often impoverished bohemian years. He took her to cafes, to the circus (which he loved), to occult meetings, and on boulevard walks, but, the French musicologist François Lesure reported, "did not risk being seen with her in middle-class drawing rooms."

Then, in May 1893, he attended the Paris premiere of Maurice Maeterlinck's Symbolist play *Pelléas et Mélisande,* a mysterious love triangle. Debussy had read the published version the previous year. Here was a play that seemed made to order for Debussy's fantasy of a drama of no time and place that merely hinted at things. Set in the mythical kingdom of Allemonde in an unspecified, vaguely medieval time, the play taps into the subliminal tensions among the members of a sullen royal family living under some psychically oppressive cloud.

Debussy was so excited by the possibilities of Maeterlinck's play that he decisively abandoned the Mendès project and turned to *Pelléas.* He knew he would need the author's permission to write an operatic adaptation. Debussy's friend Pierre Louÿs reached out to Maeterlinck through an intermediary, who arranged for a meeting in Ghent, the playwright's birthplace. Louÿs accompanied Debussy on the trip to Belgium in November 1893.

The meeting could not have gone better. When Maeterlinck talked theater, Debussy found him fascinating. The playwright granted Debussy permission to make whatever cuts he wanted, and even suggested "some important ones—*extremely useful ones even!*" as he wrote in a letter to his friend the composer Ernest Chausson

Maeterlinck, who was just one week younger than Debussy, professed a poor understanding of music. When Debussy thanked the playwright for his consent, Maeterlinck replied that it was he who should be the grateful one. At least that's how Debussy described their encounter. Years later, Louÿs had a different recollection: that he had to do most of the speaking for the new collaborators since Debussy was shy and Maeterlinck shyer still.

Capping a promising professional year for Debussy, his String Quartet in G Minor was given its premiere in Paris late that December by the eminent Ysaÿe Quartet. This masterfully written and fearlessly original work, completed when Debussy was thirty-one, is like his calling card, an announcement that he had found his voice and honed his aesthetic—evoking the distant past, nodding to current trends, and taking intrepid steps into the future, all at once.

Debussy employed a cyclic thematic structure in this four-movement score, a technique pioneered by Liszt and utilized by, among others, César Franck, whose own quartet had been given its premiere in 1890. The process involved fashioning a mottolike theme that, in slightly altered or tweaked versions, would run through an entire score, as opposed to the standard concept of contrasting themes. The quartet's motto comes right at the dark, vigorous start of the first movement. The modernist elements of the piece result as much from Debussy's inventive writing for strings—to produce startling sound effects and lush, veiled colorings—as from the actual musical materials of the score.

I love the second movement, a deceptively playful scherzo. It opens with pizzicato chords for all the instruments except the stubborn viola, which sounds stuck, repeatedly playing a fidgety yet slightly ominous riff. As the other strings begin what could be an every-which-way pizzicato dance, that stuck viola does not budge! Finally, it relents and joins in. But then the first violin takes up, almost triumphantly, the cantus firmus, until, in a while, the fun subsides and the strings segue into a middle section, a plush, shimmering episode with a lofty violin theme (another tweak on the motto that runs through the piece).

The sublimely lyrical, harmonically radiant Andantino that follows might seem on the surface a straightforward slow movement written in essentially an ABA structure. Musician friends of mine had a string quartet play this slow movement for a reflective moment during their wedding ceremony—perfect music to convey a couple's contemplative feelings at the start of a life together, including the unknowns that lie ahead. The finale begins with recapitulated bits and transitional elements from the earlier movements, before breaking into its powerful main section. For all the impetuous energy of the music, it's easy to miss that Debussy shows off his skills, putting that motto theme through all manner of treatments, inversions, and twists.

Though the critical reception was mixed, this premiere represented Debussy's first real professional success in Paris. The next year would see the eventful premiere of his *Prelude to the Afternoon of a Faun*. But to make his living Debussy still depended upon routine work, including accompanying vocal classes and choruses. His spirits were "leaden," he wrote to Chausson in early 1894, adding: "All my hopes now are centered on *Pelléas et Mélisande* and God alone knows whether this hope is any more than just a puff of smoke!"

Debussy first fashioned the play into a libretto. As he started composing, he felt encouraged. Soon, however, he complained to Chausson, late in 1893, that the "old ghost of Klingsor" (referring to the evil sorcerer in *Parsifal*), "alias R. Wagner," to be precise, as he wrote, kept "appearing in the corner of a bar" on the manuscript, forcing Debussy to tear up pages and start over.

By late 1895 Debussy had completed a musical draft of the entire opera, though he kept tinkering with it until its 1902 premiere, in Paris, nearly a decade after he'd begun. Even more than Maeterlinck's milestone play, Debussy's operatic adaptation may be the most important single work of the Symbolist movement. It's certainly the first, and one of the greatest, masterpiece operas of the twentieth century. And what's really going on does not take place on stage.

The opera, called a "lyrical drama" on its title page, opens with the orchestra setting the scene: a thick, forbidding forest. Bare, subdued block chords, rich with deep strings, play a motif hinting of medieval sacred music, with parallel fifths, almost like a fragment of harmonized plainchant. An ominous two-note theme breaks out in a flustered dotted rhythm, activated by surging chords and hints of a whole-tone scale. Then the opening motif returns, still embedded with those medieval-sounding parallel intervals, but this time more plaintively harmonized.

This music is associated with Golaud, a prince, probably in early middle age, who is a widower and a grandson of the aged King Arkel of Allemonde. Golaud has lost his hounds, and his way, while hunting boars in the forest. A delicate, almost fragile melody plays over fluttering textures in the orchestra as Golaud first appears. He will never find his way back to the castle, he frets; even his hounds won't find him, he fears. He'll have to retrace his steps.

Golaud sees a young woman weeping at a well and cautiously approaches her.

"Ne me touchez pas, ne me touchez pas!" ("Don't touch me!"), she says, looking frightened. Debussy sets these first words of his troubled heroine like sputtered recitative, at once terrified and threatening.

Golaud tells her not to be afraid. "I won't do you any . . . ," but instead of completing his thought by saying "harm," Golaud can't help commenting, "Oh! You are beautiful." Again the woman tells him not to touch her, or she will throw herself in the water.

Cautiously, he tries to find out more. She answers evasively. "Who has hurt you?" he asks. "Everyone," she replies. She has run away, fled, she says. But from where? From what? "I am lost," is all she answers.

Every reluctant reply the young woman gives to Golaud just raises more questions. Golaud sees something shining in the water of the well. "It's the crown he gave me," she explains. He? Did she drop it? Toss it away? She says it fell in while she was crying. Golaud is sure he can retrieve it, but she doesn't want it anymore. She would rather die, she says. Perhaps, it seems, she tossed it away. It's not clear.

She admits to being cold. With prompting, the woman tells him her name, Mélisande. Almost passively, she follows Golaud, who will lead her, he hopes, to his grandfather's castle.

While working on the opera in early 1894, a frustrated Debussy wrote to Chausson that he had spent days trying to capture "the 'nothing' that Mélisande is made of." Even during this introductory scene, the music Debussy wrote seems uncannily revealing of hidden strands within this troubled young woman.

Sometimes Debussy's method is musical understatement, as when Mélisande sobs at the well and the agitated orchestra thins to a solo melodic fragment followed by two sighing chords, consoling yet slightly wary. When Mélisande complains of the cold, the vocal line is oddly blunt—a monotone statement of the bare facts of the matter. Yet the orchestra seems to be listening to Mélisande, wondering about her, as that earlier restless two-note motif reappears, now prolonged and rhythmically smoothed out into a calmly oscillating figure over pungent sustained harmonies. Is the chill Mélisande feels a harbinger of doom? Or is it some guiding fate ushering her into the protective realm of Golaud? The music leaves you guessing.

Six months have passed. In a room in the castle, Geneviève, the mother of Golaud from her first marriage, is reading a letter he has sent to Pelléas, the son from her current marriage, who is much younger than his half brother. Listening closely is Arkel, the nearly blind king, who had asked the normally obedient Golaud to wed a well-connected princess. But, as Golaud explains in the letter, after meeting the sobbing Mélisande, who was like a child, he married her. He has stayed away for fear that Arkel will be disappointed. He asks in the letter for Pelléas to break the news and prepare their grandfather.

Debussy's music makes Geneviève's reading of the letter sound like the forlorn pronouncement of that fate. Her phrases are direct, almost affirmative, as if she were trying to convince herself that there may be some good purpose in Golaud's impulsive marriage. Yet the vocal lines, passing atop weighty, forlorn orchestral sonorities, still seem grounded and fretful.

Pelléas appears, and, as with Mélisande, when we first encounter him he's crying. This emotional, impressionable young man has received a letter from a beloved friend who is mortally ill, and wants to go to him before he dies. But Arkel sternly reminds Pelléas that his own father (who does not appear in the opera) is also seriously ill, and needs his son at his side. So even before Pelléas and Mélisande meet, Debussy's music for each of their introductory scenes suggests that this emotional young man and the fragile, secretive young woman are fated to fall in love, as soon happens, a bond that both overwhelms and frightens them.

For me, the most telling scene, fraught with symbolism and feeling, comes a little later, at the start of Act II. Pelléas, having decided to put off his intended departure, takes Mélisande to a well in the park. Legend has it that this well once had magical powers to cure the blind. Mélisande leans over the shadowy depths of the water, trying to touch the surface. She can't reach it, but the long strands of her hair tumble down and get wet.

She then starts to play with her wedding ring, tossing it in the air and catching it in her hands, like a willful child. Both her sputtered vocal bursts and some spiraling figures in the orchestra seem manically playful. Pelléas's warnings that Mélisande should be careful lest she drop the ring come across as effete and inadequate. When the ring does slip through her hands, as she almost seemed to intend, the orchestra illustrates the moment with a simple descending, cascading line. Mélisande, now terrified, wonders what she can tell Golaud. "The truth," Pelléas answers, even though Mélisande has come across so far as a compulsive liar—not that the oblivious Pelléas would know. It's only a ring, he says, trying to calm her. It's much more, Debussy's music at the end of the scene suggests, churning with harmonic density and darkness that sound Wagnerian. Indeed, at the very moment Mélisande lost the ring, we soon learn, Golaud was thrown off his horse and injured.

Debussy was pleased with his work in the scene showing Mélisande and Pelléas in a cave, where she has told Golaud she lost the ring. They know this search is pointless since the ring is at the bottom of the well. But Mélisande needs to be able to report details of the cave to convince Golaud she tried to find it.

"I've finished the vault scene," Debussy wrote in the summer of 1894 to his friend Henry Lerolle, a painter and an amateur violinist. "It's full of implacable terror and mysterious enough to make the most well-balanced listener giddy." A revealing romantic encounter between Pelléas and Mélisande comes a little later. Mélisande is combing her hair by a castle window when Pelléas appears below. He says he must leave the next day and asks Mélisande to reach her hand down to his. She will do so, she says, only if he agrees to put off his departure. He does.

But her hand can't reach his. So he tells her to drop her long locks out the window. As Pelléas envelops himself in Mélisande's hair, delirious, Debussy's music—rapturous and sensual, with blooming string sonorities, panting crescendos, and radiant orchestral chords spiked with shards of bright piercing dissonance—suggests what's really taking place.

Golaud comes upon them and, though suspicious, dismisses their behavior as child's play. Still, he warns Pelléas to stop and not to bother Mélisande, who is now pregnant. But his jealousy, stoked by his young wife's annoying evasiveness, inevitably builds. In an eerily subdued, deeply troubling scene, Golaud forces Yniold, his sweet young son from his first marriage, into spying on them, hoisting the boy up the castle wall to peer through the window of Mélisande's room, where Yniold says they have often been together. He tells his father that he sees Uncle Pelléas and Mélisande caressing. In a poignant musical-verbal touch, Yniold addresses his father as "petit père," which translates literally as "little father." Throughout this tense scene the frightened boy's term of endearment seems forced. In his letter to Lerolle, Debussy wrote that he was trying to make this scene terrifying, that "it has to be profound and absolutely accurate!" There's one utterance of "petit père," Debussy added, "that gives me nightmares."

The opera moves to the inevitable final catastrophe. In a fit of jealous rage, Golaud attacks Pelléas with his sword, killing his brother and wounding the nearby Mélisande. In the final scene (a short Act V), as Mélisande lies dying, Debussy's music has the quality of a dirge, tinged with an ancient cast, less restrained than curiously refined and precise, "accurate," to use Debussy's revealing adjective, music in which every note tells. As Mélisande dies, the orchestra hardly murmurs. She has given birth to, it is implied, a premature girl. The child must now live in Mélisande's place, Arkel says. It's this poor little one's turn.

Over several years, attempts to stage the opera stalled, to Debussy's frustration. During this period, feeling confined in his relationship with Gaby, Debussy began an affair with Thérèse Roger, a salon singer who had performed some of his songs at the Société Nationale de Musique with the composer at the piano. To the surprise, and, in time, dismay, of his friends, Debussy announced his engagement to Thérèse, though it was short-lived. Relations with Gaby ended badly. In July 1899 Debussy fell passionately in love with Rosalie Texier, called Lilly, who was twenty-five and a model with a fashion house. "I yearn for the blush of your red lips," he wrote in an 1899 letter. "You've made me love you more than a man is allowed to, perhaps." In this letter he sounds like Wagner's Tristan in the throes of fatalistic love. "The need to destroy myself for your greater joy becomes so violent, at times it resembles a death wish."

Lilly threatened to break off the relationship if they did not marry. Debussy agreed; the couple wed that October.

In 1901, following the model of Berlioz and other composers before him, Debussy became a critic, starting with a regular column in *La Revue blanche*, at first employing a pseudonym, Monsieur Croche. With this platform, he championed his unusual areas of interest, like Mussorgsky; wrote elegantly of early French masters, especially Rameau; critiqued the French musical establishment; and advocated for emerging composers to liberate themselves from conventional forms.

That same year, he finally received a written commitment from Albert Carré, the director of the Opéra-Comique in Paris, to stage *Pelléas et Mélisande* in 1902. Demands from Maeterlinck almost sank the plan.

The playwright wanted his mistress, Georgette Leblanc, to have the role of Mélisande. Leblanc wrote a recollection of the time, toward the end of 1901, when Debussy came to play through the score of his opera for her and Maeterlinck. Her vivid, self-aware account rings true.

The position of the piano forced Maeterlinck to have his back turned to Debussy, allowing the poet to make desperate signs of impatience to Leblanc. At first the score's beauties escaped Leblanc. But by the point of Mélisande's death scene she was entranced and wanted badly to have the role. Maeterlinck urged it and Debussy was delighted, Leblanc reports. Rehearsals began.

Then Maeterlinck read in the paper that the Scottish soprano Mary Garden had been engaged to sing Mélisande. Feeling betrayed, he referred the case to the Society of Authors. But Debussy had a written agreement from Maeterlinck that gave precedence to the composer over matters of casting and the final shape of the libretto. Leblanc recounts a scene in which Maeterlinck, who "did not like musicians any more than music," threatened Debussy, brandishing a cane. Two weeks before the April 30, 1902, premiere of the opera, a letter appeared from Maeterlinck in *Le Figaro* claiming he had been excluded from his own work, which was now in "the hands of the enemy." He denounced "arbitrary and absurd cuts" from his play that had made the libretto incomprehensible. Maeterlinck ended by wishing for the opera's "immediate and decided failure."

Rehearsals had spread over fifteen weeks, starting in January. The dress rehearsal turned rowdy. Attendees had been handed a written parody of the libretto, with lascivious spins on the story and mocking descriptions of Garden's Scottish-accented French. Though the premiere went well, the initial reception was decidedly mixed. The uncomprehending reviews were to be expected. One critic bluntly described the music as "vague, floating, without color and without shape, without movement and without life."

But many composers, especially Dukas, along with some progressive writers, playwrights, and adventurous music lovers, were transfixed by the work. By the fifth performance, Garden later recalled, the house "had become a cathedral." *Pelléas* reached the milestone of one hundred performances at the Opéra-Comique in 1913, a significant run. Even at the time of the premiere, the novelist and essayist Romain Rolland described the opera as one of the three or four outstanding achievements in French musical history.

The immediate period after the premiere of *Pelléas* brought to Debussy another dramatic turn in his personal life and a musical milestone. In 1904 he met Emma Bardac, whose vitality, intelligence, and musical sophistication (she was a gifted singer) contrasted with his wife Lilly's naïve charms and lack of refinement. Emma, who was forty-two, the same age as Debussy, had been married at seventeen to a banker and had two children (her son had studied composition with Debussy). That summer he and Emma, now a couple, traveled together to the isle of Jersey, off the coast of Normandy, and then the coastal town of Dieppe, staying away for nearly two months. Upon returning, Debussy wrote to Lilly to explain that their marriage was over. A desperate Lilly attempted suicide by shooting a pistol at her chest but survived. As talk of the scandal spread and reports appeared in the press, many of Debussy's friends abandoned him.

Debussy and Emma took a pleasant house in the Bois de Boulogne in Paris, where, in late October 1905, their daughter, Claude-Emma, known as Chouchou, was born. (She would be Debussy's only child.) Lawsuits related to the divorce from Lilly impacted Debussy for years. The couple eventually married in 1908. Though their relationship went through difficulties, they remained together. Mary Garden, Debussy's Mélisande, later recalled him as "a very, very strange man" who may not have "ever loved anybody really."

As the turmoil of his break with Lilly and the attendant crises played out, Debussy composed *La Mer,* which had its premiere in Paris two weeks before the birth of Chouchou. For a composer so touchy about being labeled an Impressionist, Debussy almost invited listeners to hear *La Mer* as musical picture painting. He had always loved the sea and kept a Japanese woodblock print of Hokusai's *The Great Wave off Kanagawa* on a wall in his study. He gave evocative titles to the work's three movements, which he called "symphonic sketches": "From Dawn till Noon on the Sea," "Play of the Waves," "Dialogue of the Wind and the Sea." Still, as he wrote in a letter to a fellow composer, this music was born of his *memories* of the sea; the depictions were indirect and filtered through his creative imagination.

To be sure, this influential Debussy work begins with what sounds like a subdued, atmospheric depiction of the sea at dawn: softly rumbling timpani, murmuring low strings, flecks of harp, woodwind lines that try to peek through the musical mists. Still, in 2018 I heard the dynamic Finnish conductor Susanna Mälkki lead a performance of *La Mer* with the New York Philharmonic so detailed, incisive, and exciting that I forgot all about cresting seas, splashing waves, and hooting gulls. I was too engrossed with the way this performance highlighted piercing elements of Debussy's harmonic language and revealed its churning rhythmic impetus, even during long stretches that may have seemed placid on the surface. In the final sketch, during passages of tumultuous frenzy, Mälkki drew out the music's symphonic majesty, and drove the piece headlong to its brassy climax, which in this coolly urgent account seemed more terrifying than triumphant.

I prefer performances, like Mälkki's, that treat *La Mer* first and foremost as an audacious symphonic composition. Debussy the critic urged fellow composers to liberate themselves from traditional forms and genres. In *La Mer* he put that recommendation into action: Debussy offers a model of how to write a de facto symphony for the twentieth century.

As usual, the reviews of the premiere were mixed. But by this point a significant contingent of musicians, artists, and the public had identified Debussy as a pioneering modernist. References to "Debussyism" circulated within contemporary music circles and appeared in the columns of sympathetic (and unsympathetic) critics.

During these years Debussy focused increasingly on the piano. Even seemingly modest works offered bracing and radical approaches to writing for the instrument. The *Children's Corner* suite, composed for Chouchou and completed in 1908, begins with an impish piece called "Doctor Gradus ad Parnassum," a reference to a standard text on counterpoint by Johann Joseph Fux. More specifically, the piece evokes a student pianist practicing his Czerny exercises, those boring teaching pieces full of sequential arpeggios and figurations meant to build finger technique. The music starts off with a charming evocation of rudimentary white-key piano studies, all perpetual-motion sixteenth notes. But as the student's imagination wanders, the music takes mischievous side trips into far-off harmonic regions and erupts with spurts of wild, jagged passage-work. Finally, with the practice hour coming to a close, the student races to finish the "exercise" and the practice session. The piece ends with onrushing swirls of runs and some final thumping chords.

In the sixth and last piece, "Golliwog's Cakewalk," Debussy reveals his fondness for carnival music and comedians. It's a little uncomfortable to listen to today, knowing the racist associations of the word "golliwog," an outlandish black rag doll that long appeared in children's books. Still, Debussy's affection for the musical style of the cakewalk comes through in this beguiling piece. It's a jaunty dance, though the golliwog keeps tripping himself up, vividly depicted through lumpy, clashing chords. Then, in the middle section, Debussy slyly mocks Wagner. We hear a prolonged version of the opening motif from the Prelude to *Tristan und Isolde*. But each short phrase is followed by a burst of high, needling chords, as if Debussy were saying: *Nyah-nyah-nyah, nyah-nyah-nyah.*

For me, the greatest Debussy piano pieces are the two books of Préludes: the first twelve completed in 1910, the second twelve in 1913. Some of Debussy's best-known pieces are among these volumes, including the lovely "Girl with the Flaxen Hair" and "The Sunken Cathedral." Some are puckish and funny, like the strumming "Minstrels." Others have shock value that has not lessened a century later. The powerhouse Russian pianist Sviatoslav Richter brought demonic intensity and kaleidoscopic colors to his recording of Book II. The final prelude, aptly titled "Feux d'artifice" (Fireworks), emerges in Richter's account in a blazing fire of unhinged, keyboard-spanning runs and crackling bursts of flinty chords. The mood is almost scarier during the few episodes when the music seems to hover in wait, readying itself for the next rocket blast. The prelude still sounds stunningly modern.

Though hearing either book performed complete is fascinating, Debussy did not really conceive of them as integrated collections. Pianists are free to put together their own choices. The one I always included whenever I performed a selection of Debussy preludes in recital was the seventh from

Book II, with the difficult to translate title "La Terrasse des audiences du clair de lune" (usually rendered as "The Terrace of Moonlit Audiences" or "Audiences of Moonlight"). As much as any Debussy work, this one conveys his daring approach to suspended time, with spans of nearly pulseless rhythm.

This slow, restrained piece begins with a fragmentary theme in soft chords. It sounds like some surreptitious, almost shy theme is daring to speak. Then the left hand plays a low sustained C-sharp, as the right hand traces a quizzical line that descends slowly from on high, taking winding turns along the way. In the middle register of the keyboard a motif sounds in hushed yet pinging octaves: it could be a melodic whiff of pagoda music drifting in from afar. These elements keep coming, in increasing complexity but always hushed. Yet for all the shifts and inner activity, the music somehow just seems to hang in space. When well into the prelude that low sustained C-sharp (an implied pedal tone) slips up a step to D-sharp, it's as if a tectonic musical plate has shifted. What next?

In a 1910 letter to the composer Edgard Varèse, Debussy complained about the "so-called" pianists who "deformed" his piano music. Deformed! That's a strong word. What bothered him, surely, were those pianists who took the "Impressionist" label as an invitation for playing Debussy with excessively loose rhythms and overly blurry textures. That approach is still common. We have some precious examples of Debussy the pianist that show what he intended. In 1904 he recorded a few of his songs and some brief excerpts from *Pelléas* with Mary Garden, the soprano who created the role of Mélisande.

I especially love his playing in "Green," from the song cycle *Ariettes oubliées*. If you can listen through the scratchy surface noise, you hear Debussy playing the lilting opening of the piano part with crisp, light clarity. The arpeggios that break out later have the requisite milky colorings, to be sure, but also scintillating vitality. Garden's singing, with her focused sound, wistful delicacy, and directness, show why Debussy wanted her as his Mélisande.

In 1909 Debussy experienced rectal bleeding. A diagnosis revealed rectal cancer. His health deteriorated steadily. In 1915 Debussy underwent surgery, a colostomy. The results were frustrating, giving him only temporary relief.

During the final phase of his career, in an intriguing departure, Debussy looked back, in a manner, and composed in a Neoclassical vein. He planned to write a set of six sonatas, but only completed three: one for cello and piano; one for the unusual combination of flute, viola, and harp; and, his final work, written in 1917, the austerely beautiful Sonata for violin and piano, with its fanciful middle movement, and an elfin finale.

Debussy died from the effects of cancer at his home on March 25, 1918, at fifty-five. Chouchou, his daughter, survived him by less than a year, dying during a diphtheria epidemic.

In time, Maeterlinck came around in his attitude toward *Pelléas et Mélisande.* He attended a performance in 1920 and openly commented that he had been completely wrong in his objections to the opera, and that Debussy had been "entirely right."

In 1911 Maeterlinck won the Nobel Prize in Literature. The citation emphasized his dramatic works, distinguished by "a wealth of imagination" and "poetic fancy." Maeterlinck, who admitted to being musically dense, had caused Debussy endless distress during their collaboration, convinced that the composer was ruining his play. Today, even with his Nobel glory, Maeterlinck is probably best known as the librettist of *Pelléas et Mélisande.*

CHAPTER THIRTEEN

"THE PUBLIC WILL JUDGE"

GIACOMO PUCCINI (1858–1924)

Intellectual condescension toward Giacomo Puccini, which still persists, started during his lifetime, when his operas played the world's houses and made him wealthy. How wealthy? When Puccini died at sixty-five, in 1924, he left behind an estate estimated in today's dollars at nearly $200 million, making him arguably the most financially successful opera composer in history.

That very popularity has long rendered Puccini suspect in high-minded circles. For one, his operas are deemed shamelessly sentimental. Consider the stories. A consumptive seamstress and a struggling poet in the Latin Quarter of Paris around 1830, living in near-poverty amid bohemian friends, meet and fall in love at first sight. They break up, make up, and break up again, until she returns to die in his arms.

Then there is the tale of a plucky young woman who owns a saloon in a small California town during the Gold Rush, a place she makes a home away from home for the rugged miners who have left families behind to seek their fortune. Though yearning for love, she keeps herself at a motherly distance, reading from the Bible to the illiterate men and offering them an example of decency—until she falls for a bandit, rescues him from an imperious sheriff, and rides off with her redeemed lover as they sing "Addio, California."

Another staple of international houses tells the story of a steamy love affair in Rome in 1800 between a renowned opera diva and a handsome painter who, betraying his aristocratic lineage, embraces antiroyalist causes. The city's villainous police chief, a lecherous baron who lusts for the diva, sadistically tortures her lover practically in her presence to elicit information about an escaped political prisoner the artist has protected.

The distinguished musicologist Joseph Kerman, in his noted 1956 book *Opera as Drama*, famously dismissed this last work, *Tosca*, as a "shabby little shocker." For Kerman and many other Puccini debunkers, including towering (possibly envious) composers like Mahler and Stravinsky, the problem is not just the sappy stories, but, as they deem it, the schlocky music. Puccini whips up intensity with cinematically graphic symphonic effects and manipulates your emotions with opulent vocal lines, often doubled for extra punch in the orchestra.

Do not believe it.

For me, Puccini is not only an indispensable, but one of the most dramatically astute and musically expert composers to write for the stage. Opinion within the academy has for some time been catching up with the opera-going public. Serious Puccini scholarship has thrived. In my experience, some of the most coolheaded admirers of Puccini have been composers who marvel not just at his melding of music and drama but at his compositional skill, harmonic daring, and colorful orchestration.

In Puccini's day Mahler may have dismissed him. But of all people, Anton Webern—a Mahler devotee and proud student of Schoenberg, a composer who embraced twelve-tone technique and wrote works of radical concision—was a Puccini fan. After hearing a Vienna performance of Puccini's Gold Rush opera *La fanciulla del West* in 1919, Webern described the work in a letter to Schoenberg as "a score with an *original* sound throughout, splendid, every bar a surprise." Webern found "no trace of *Kitsch*" in the opera. "I must say I enjoyed it very much. . . . Am I wrong?"

He was right. But it's revealing that Webern felt the need to run his opinion past his teacher.

Even Schoenberg, though he had scant affinity for Puccini's emotive Italianate style, expressed admiration for his craftsmanship and curiosity. In a 1930 essay, he wrote of how touched he was that in 1924, though Puccini was grappling with the disease that would claim him that year, he made an arduous trip to attend a performance in Florence of Schoenberg's path-breaking *Pierrot lunaire,* an unabashedly atonal song cycle for voice and chamber ensemble. The piece was received on this occasion with overt hostility, Schoenberg recalled, not by the "art lovers," but by the "expert judges," as he put it. "I was indeed honored that Puccini, not an expert judge but a practical expert, already ill, made a six-hour journey to get to know my work, and afterwards said some very friendly things to me; that was good, strange though my music may have remained to him."

Actually, Puccini was deeply interested in the musical experiments going on during this period in Vienna, Paris, and elsewhere. Even in his early works the influences of Debussy and Richard Strauss come through: you hear Puccini deftly folding hints of their styles into his own distinctive voice. The more radical modernist developments intrigued Puccini as well: he had to make sure he wasn't missing out on something, so he could go back to doing what he did best.

And what did his best entail?

Puccini has long been hailed as a supreme melodist. Yet in his day detractors complained that his music was overly symphonic, the product of a composer who lacked understanding that opera always had been, and should remain, a voice-driven art form. Today those scores seem ingenious amalgams of orchestral and vocal richness. Still, the general perception that Puccini filled his operas with soaring, endless melodies seems a simplification. His melodic writing can often be complex and elusive.

Imagine this. It's 1896 and you're at the Turin premiere of *La Bohème.* You've not heard a note of it before. You love it. But what tune do you leave the house whistling after one hearing? Maybe Musetta's Waltz, which is pretty catchy. Otherwise I'm not sure there's anything.

Think of Rodolfo's Act I aria "Che gelida manina," in which he tells Mimì, who had knocked on his garret door just moments before, all about his life. The aria is like a monologue in which melodic phrases segue into stretches of arioso writing that straddle aria and recitative. Rodolfo's lyrical effusions are disrupted by sudden dramatic bursts as he lets down his guard. The music is too episodic and impetuous to be described as simply melodious.

Harmonically, Puccini's music never really loosened its tethering to tonal harmony, though he explored whole-tone scales (à la Debussy) and even bitonality (in which strands of music in clashing keys overlap). Puccini often juxtaposed chords that had far-flung harmonic relationships and enriched his language with thick, dissonance-saturated sonorities to engender ambiguity and intensity.

The most impressive element of Puccini's craft, though, may be his sophisticated use of motifs. Wagner tended to use his leitmotifs, as they've been called, more loosely: a musical motif associated with a character, an incident, or a thematic element of the drama will routinely be transformed and deployed for more generalized purposes.

Puccini, in contrast, used motifs and melodic phrases mostly as identification tags for characters or locales: a bohemian garret, a favorite haunt, a statue of the Madonna in a church. Think of the opening of *Tosca,* which begins with a series of three fearsome, brassy chords in the orchestra: the motif of Scarpia, the fiendish police chief of Rome. The specific chords (B-flat, A-flat, and E major) are essentially unrelated harmonically, suggesting that Scarpia exercises his power in fits and starts. Also, the chords spread apart menacingly, with the top line creeping upward and the bass line plunging downward. Puccini manipulates this motif constantly throughout the opera, deploying versions of it as an ominous undercurrent, a suspenseful premonition, even, at one point, a deceptively playful dance that percolates in the orchestra while Scarpia hatches his schemes.

Over many years, starting in high school, as I got to know Puccini's operas and played through the scores on the piano, I would discern subtle uses of some motif that I'd never noticed before. These discoveries were like epiphanies that finally explained why I had always been so affected by a particular moment, without knowing why.

Regarding structure, Puccini kept pushing himself to take more chances and create almost through-composed scores. *La fanciulla del West* (1910) represented a significant advance: the score is a near-seamless unfolding of lyrical flights, choral stirrings, melodies that suggest an aria is coming only to slip into elusive arioso, and gripping dramatic episodes that are driven by the shrewd deployment of motifs and themes. *Fanciulla* has only one stand-alone aria: for Dick Johnson, the bandit, during the final act, when he is about to be hanged by an avenging posse of miners (or so we think).

Finally, what about this idea that Puccini's stories are sentimental? Well, not if you explore them a little deeper, which Puccini does in our behalf through his music.

Take *La Bohème.* Our hero, Rodolfo, the wannabe poet, survives by writing articles that bore him for little journals. He shares a cramped garret with three buddies: an aimless painter and the household's most gregarious guy; an all-purpose musician who manages to find little gigs now and then; and a would-be philosopher, adrift in the real world, who mostly struts around cracking bad puns and uttering ponderosities. The guys share food and money when they have any and hang out at a cafe they can't afford. Their poverty is self-imposed, the result of their antiestablishment attitudes. Not one of them ever mentions a family member.

But why does Rodolfo, who is so swept away by Mimì, flee lasting attachment to her? Puccini and his librettists take us step by step to the answer, which is the core message of *Bohème,* a tough life lesson that all the bohemians learn by the end. It's fine to be artsy, penniless, and carefree when you're young and healthy. But terminal illness is an adult problem. Though he can't admit this to her, or even to himself, Rodolfo soon realizes that Mimì is not just frail and prone to coughing fits but seriously ill. What can he do for her? How can he help her? He loves her but can't face her illness; he can't "hack it," as we might say today.

Mimì's death is a brutal wake-up call. Rodolfo and his friends finally understand that they must take stock and grapple with real-life responsibilities. Generations of young people—from idealistic college roommates, to striving artists sharing apartments in big cities, to thirtysomethings trying to start businesses and raise children while feeling wistful for carefree earlier days—have seen themselves in Puccini's characters, which may be one reason *Bohème* remains the most popular opera ever.

With *Madama Butterfly* (1904) Puccini turned a David Belasco play—an unabashed melodrama—into an unflinching examination of racism, including disturbing elements of a racial inferiority complex within Cio-Cio-San, the opera's tragic heroine. As we learn, ever since the young Cio-Cio-San's prosperous father was given a "gift" by the Mikado (a knife with which to commit hara-kiri), Cio-Cio-San has supported herself by being a geisha. Then B. F. Pinkerton, a dashing, confident United States Navy lieutenant, smitten with his "Butterfly" (the meaning of "chocho" in Japanese), impulsively decides to marry her. Of course, as the caddish Pinkerton admits to the American consul in Nagasaki, he considers this marriage a sham. He's just playing house temporarily with a lovely fifteen-year-old Japanese bride. Naturally, someday he will take a proper American wife.

The consul warns Pinkerton that Cio-Cio-San considers this marriage a godsend, an honor. She is the happiest woman in Japan, Cio-Cio-San tells her assembled friends and family, some of whom snipe about her decision and predict disaster, others of whom seem envious. Her husband is about to make her an American wife, she boasts. She has even renounced her religion, which causes shocked relatives to reject her cold. That she is captivated by Pinkerton's American ways, including his whiteness, however disturbing to observe, comes across as tragically true. Cio-Cio-San has never met a Japanese man like Pinkerton, she says, who laughs so heartily and loves so openly, who says whatever comes to mind. We Japanese, she tells him, are people accustomed to little things, humble and quiet. Just love me a little, she pleads.

To prevent Pinkerton from being the most detestable character imaginable, Puccini provides the newlywed couple with a transporting love duet. At least on this night, Pinkerton does not just lust after Cio-Cio-San; he seems to adore her. The most unbearably beautiful moment comes when Pinkerton gently asks his bride why she has never come right out and said she loves him. "Don't you know the words?" he asks. Butterfly answers that she's afraid to say them, for fear of dying of happiness at hearing them.

This turns out to be an eerie premonition. Pinkerton departs on his ship and stays away for three years. When he returns with a pretty American wife at his side, he is so wracked with guilt he cannot face Cio-Cio-San. The struggling Madama Butterfly has been caring as best she can for their little boy. To make amends, Pinkerton wants to bring the boy home to be raised as an American. Who could not see this as the best course?

Butterfly agrees to this proposal, but, as she tells the American consul, on one condition: Pinkerton must come in person to claim the child. When he nears the house, Butterfly stabs herself with her father's knife. In this horrific moment Puccini exposes the anger that underlies her suicide. Butterfly is saying to Pinkerton, in effect: You take the boy, I'll take my life— but you will never forget the sight of my death!

Sentimental? Not to me.

In getting his operas right—that is, making the words and music mesh to his rigorous dramatic demands—Puccini famously mistreated his librettists. He insisted upon endless changes and then changed his own mind about the alterations, dismissing writers as incompetents one moment, flattering them into loyalty the next. Some of this was prodded by his genuine insight into what makes a good story, what makes poeticized Italian words flow without becoming self-consciously literary. But his abusive behavior may also have been a coping mechanism for his chronic indecision. Puccini was a lifelong procrastinator who went on trips supposedly to clear his head and then composed in frenzied all-night sessions tanked up on coffee and cigarettes.

Critics who valued opera's long history of putting myths, legends, and historical events on stage carped about Puccini's "little" subjects, tales of seamstresses and geisha girls and such. But early on Puccini gravitated toward the emerging school of verismo ("realism" or "truthfulness"), a movement that had originated in Italian literature and embraced naturalistic, everyday subjects. Puccini's *Bohème* (1896) and *Tosca* (1900) were embraced as watershed operas by verismo agitators. Yet Puccini felt neither bound to nor defined by this movement. And he never made excuses for being attracted to humble characters whom he could ennoble through his music.

Puccini grew to hate cities and everything associated with them, except for automobiles, a passion. Writing to a friend in his hometown of Lucca in 1898, Puccini said that he was sick of Paris. "I am panting for the fragrant woods, for the free movement of my belly in wide trousers and no waist-coat; I pant after the wind that blows free and fragrant from the sea."

From 1891 onward he spent most of his time in Torre del Lago, a small lake town about fifteen miles from Lucca. There he could drive the country roads and go hunting, a favorite pastime. Puccini often quipped that he was a tireless hunter of fowl, librettos, and women. To the despair of his wife, he was indeed a voracious womanizer. Even in middle age, though a little portly, Puccini had a stylish look—with dark, curly hair, a mustache, and penetrating eyes—and exuded charisma.

His life story would make a great opera, if only Puccini were around to compose it.

Giacomo Puccini was practically compelled by family heritage to become a composer. Four prior generations of Puccini men had been musicians based in Lucca, a trade center of some twenty thousand residents during Giacomo's youth. The family had a lock on the post of organist and choir director at the Cathedral of San Martino, an appointment that fell in due course to Michele Puccini, Giacomo's father, a skilled musician who also taught composition in the local music institute. Born in 1813 (the same year as Verdi and Wagner), Michele completed his training in Naples, where one of his teachers was Donizetti.

Michele took up his duties at the cathedral in Lucca in the late 1840s, when he married Albina Magi, the daughter of a prominent local family. A woman of great personal dignity, Albina was nineteen when she wed Michele, then thirty-seven. They lived with his matronly widowed mother in the Puccini home, a storehouse of family lore. In quick order the couple had five daughters (one of whom died within a year), until, finally, on December 22, 1858, Giacomo, the long-awaited son, was born. Two more daughters followed. Then tragedy struck.

In early 1864 Michele, just fifty-one, died suddenly, leaving seven children and another on the way (a son, born three months later and named for his father). At the funeral an eminent elder of Lucca essentially announced that Giacomo, then five, would in time take his father's place at the cathedral.

The most respected senior member of Albina's extended family, Dr. Nicolao Cerù, helped provide for the young widow, and she received a modest pension from the town. Still, finances were a continual worry. Two daughters were dispatched to a convent school; another daughter married a physician, a great relief to Albina.

At the school affiliated with the cathedral, Giacomo studied music and sang in the choir. Records reveal that he was a poor student prone to pranks. Upon Giacomo's graduation, Albina, who was counting on her older son to succeed, agitated to get him admitted to the music institute in Lucca. This proved easier after her brother, Fortunato Magi, joined the school's composition faculty. The hot-tempered Magi became his inattentive nephew's exasperated teacher, though Giacomo's instruction was eventually taken over by Carlo Angeloni, a kindly composer who had studied with Puccini's father and loved opera.

In 1876, with a group of musical friends, Giacomo, then eighteen, traveled the eleven miles to Pisa for a performance of Verdi's *Aida*. Culturally, Lucca had a rich heritage of church music, but a mediocre local orchestra that performed infrequently. There were theaters where musical programs and spoken dramas were performed. Puccini had been introduced to the opera literature through his studies. But this *Aida* in Pisa may well have been the first opera he saw "decently mounted and performed," the Puccini biographer Julian Budden suggests. The experience confirmed the young composer's career path.

The next step was obvious: to enroll in the prestigious conservatory in Milan. The resourceful Albina again went to work, securing a modest study grant from the queen. Dr. Cerù also came through with some support.

In October 1880 Puccini took the two-hundred-mile trip by train to Milan, then a city of three hundred thousand. Various acquaintances from Lucca, including a cousin, housed him. In time he took the entrance exams for the conservatory and received high grades. So he was admitted, despite being, at twenty-two, several years older than most incoming students.

He wound up living in a series of meager apartments with a changing roster of roommates. When he found a place with a working wood stove it was a big step up.

In a letter to his mother he vividly described his daily routine. He rose at 8:30 in time for lessons at school. If he had none he practiced piano. After a mid-morning meal he headed out, returning in the early afternoon to prepare for courses in analysis and composition. At 5:00 he went for a frugal dinner ("but really frugal!"), usually three bowls of minestrone soup, cheese with fava beans, and a half liter of wine. In the evening, after a cigar and a stroll, he returned home and applied himself to studying counterpoint. He earnestly asked his mother to send him some proper Tuscan olive oil, impossible to find in Milan. "You can't imagine how much I want to see you again," he concluded, adding that "if I have made you angry so often, it is not because I don't love you, but because I am an animal and a rascal."

Though in letters home he emphasized his industriousness, Puccini was routinely reprimanded by teachers for skipping classes. Still, in July 1883 Puccini's *Capriccio sinfonico,* which he had written for the school year's concluding concert, was conducted by the renowned Franco Faccio, who praised the piece. Following this ceremony Puccini left the conservatory, after three years of study, determined to make it in the professional world.

That summer the prominent composer Amilcare Ponchielli, a professor at the conservatory who had mentored Puccini, invited him to spend a few days at his country place near Lake Como. This beautiful region was home to an artistic enclave frequented by intellectuals who espoused the Scapigliatura Milanese movement, a phrase that translates as the Disheveled Ones from Milan. Starting in the 1860s, forward-looking novelists, artists, composers, and journalists found common cause in this movement. Determined to modernize Italian culture, they looked to Germany and France for inspiration and debunked the so-called old guard. In opera, this meant Verdi. Though deeply curious about French and German music, including Wagner, Puccini had developed an informed respect for the great Verdi. Besides, despite his insecurities, the young Puccini was too full of his own ideas about music and opera to fall under the sway of any aesthetic. By the mid-1880s the movement was becoming passé.

Then, in 1883, the publishing firm of Sonzogno, hoping to find the next great native talent, announced in its monthly journal a competition open to young musicians of Italian nationality for a one-act opera based on an idyllic, serious, or comic subject. The prize would be two thousand lire plus a Milan performance of the piece at the journal's expense. The panel of judges included two notables who had demonstrated belief in Puccini's potential: Ponchielli and the conductor Faccio. Indeed, Ponchielli brought Puccini together with a librettist: Ferdinando Fontana, nine years Puccini's senior, an artist who identified strongly with the Scapigliatura movement. The two met at Ponchielli's country house, hit it off, and got to work.

For a subject they freely adapted the French writer Alphonse Karr's short story "Les Willis," a supernatural tale set in the Black Forest involving the ghosts of jilted maidens, called Willis.

Full of hope, Puccini and Fontana entered the competition, one of twenty-nine contestants. *Le Villi* (as the opera was called) was not even among the five honorable mentions. Puccini was crushed and, worse still, broke. However, the well-connected Fontana turned to influential colleagues and, together with Puccini, presented the opera in private sessions.

Their efforts generated support for a subscription performance at a theater in Milan as part of a triple bill in May 1884. *Le Villi* was an improbable success. At the end, Puccini was called to the stage eighteen times; four performances were added to the run; the reviews were strong. Puccini's imagination was "singularly inclined to melody," one critic wrote, praising his freshness and craftsmanship. In words echoed by others, this reviewer concluded that with Puccini, "we may have the composer for whom Italy has been waiting for a long time."

One crucial member of the audience agreed: Giulio Ricordi, the head of the renowned publishing house. Ricordi would become the most steadfast and consequential supporter of Puccini's burgeoning career.

In his 2005 book on Puccini, Budden explains how a handful of important publishing houses dominated Italian opera. These rival firms promoted their composers tenaciously: securing productions, quashing competition, issuing piano-vocal scores for public consumption, and more.

Ricordi placed his bet on Puccini and acquired the rights to *Le Villi*.

First, though, he persuaded Puccini and Fontana to turn this one-act piece into a full-evening opera, which they did. He provided Puccini a monthly stipend of two hundred lire, enough to settle his student debts and keep him afloat. The expanded opera was introduced in late 1884 at the Teatro Regio, in Turin, a prestigious staging arranged by Ricordi. The reception was excellent, with enthusiastic ovations and good reviews. Early the next year it played La Scala, another major step.

The music of *Le Villi* shows the influence of Ponchielli and Jules Massenet, whose *Manon* had premiered in Paris earlier that year. There are also hints of Wagnerian orchestral weightiness. Yet Puccini's emerging voice comes through affectingly. The dramaturgy of the work, however, is vague and ineffective.

The overall success of *Le Villi* emboldened Ricordi to commission Puccini and Fontana to write another work. It would be four years before that opera, *Edgar,* finally had its premiere, at La Scala, in April 1889. Progress was slowed down by crises in Puccini's life, including a scandalous affair.

Just as Puccini was gaining attention for *Le Villi* he suffered the devastating loss of his mother. Weakened by a long illness, Albina died in July 1884 at fifty-four. Puccini spent idle days in Lucca consumed by the dark moods and insecurities that would plague him throughout his life. There he fell in love with an attractive, dark-blond married woman, Elvira Bonturi Gemignani, whose husband, Narciso, a grocer and traveling salesman, had been Puccini's school chum. The couple had two small children, Fosca and Renato. Narciso, who played in the local amateur orchestra, was impressed by Puccini's burgeoning career. *Le Villi* had made the hometown boy a celebrity. Narciso asked Puccini to give Elvira piano lessons. By that fall teacher and student were lovers, though they managed to keep this a secret for nearly a year.

That Narciso took long trips for work made it easier for the lovers. His absences also allowed Narciso to enjoy liaisons on the road. By mid-1885 Lucca was percolating with gossip about Puccini and Elvira. Puccini kept moving in and out of town. By the winter of 1886 Elvira was pregnant with

Puccini's child. Narciso seems to have remained ignorant of the affair until one night when he returned home after a business trip and learned from a sobbing maid that Elvira had abandoned him and the children and run off with Puccini, a scene that the scholar Mary Jane Phillips-Matz relates vividly in her Puccini biography.

Narciso's own infidelities were, of course, irrelevant. Italian law stood firmly with the wronged husband. Narciso agreed to a formal separation. Fosca went to live with her mother; the boy stayed with his father. Puccini's sisters reacted with abject dismay, especially Iginia, who had become a nun and prayed ceaselessly for her sinful brother's salvation.

On December 22, 1886, Elvira gave birth to Antonio, Puccini's only child. You have to feel for Antonio, who had a hectic childhood. His parents moved often and spent long periods apart, during which Elvira would take refuge with sympathetic relatives. Puccini's work on *Edgar* surely suffered from the turmoil of his personal life, though the project was probably ill-conceived to begin with.

The story is drawn from a French play in verse by Alfred de Musset about an antisocial Tyrolean peasant who burns his house down and undertakes a journey of self-discovery. Fontana's adapted libretto compresses the timeline and relocates the story to Flanders in 1302, the year the Flemish defeated the French in battle, providing a ready backdrop for the hero's exploits. Puccini and Fontana tried to fashion Musset's poetic play into an action drama, a near-epic four-act opera. The premiere at La Scala in 1889 was coolly received and had an abbreviated run. Sympathetic critics today find things to savor in the stirring, harmonically plush music. But *Edgar* is a bloated work. Puccini trimmed and revised it several times, finally settling on a three-act version in 1905 that still seemed a "blunder," as Puccini later admitted.

Ricordi's shareholders wanted him to drop Puccini from its roster and cease his monthly stipend. But, Budden reports, Ricordi threatened to resign rather than abandon his protégé. It worked. Ricordi held fast and urged Puccini to try again. The composer was done, though, with Fontana, whose penchant for philosophical drama was ill-suited to Puccini's meaty style.

Ricordi had second thoughts, though, when Puccini told him his new idea: an opera based on the Abbé Prévost's 1731 French novel *Manon Lescaut,* in its day a controversial work, initially banned in France for its scandalous story. But Massenet's *Manon* had been an international success, and Ricordi feared that Puccini would be viewed as an upstart for attempting another version.

Puccini would not budge. At Ricordi's urging, Puccini met with librettists to discuss the project. Though never satisfied with any writer's work, Puccini was frustratingly unclear about his objections. He went through five librettists, all of whom were demoralized by the experience. Rather than mediate among the squabbling writers, the publisher issued the libretto without a credited author.

The scenario and text were mainly the work of Domenico Oliva, a young poet, and Luigi Illica, just one year younger than Puccini and already receiving attention as a playwright and librettist. There were strong disagreements among the creators until Giuseppe Giacosa, a playwright and poet, intervened and saved the day, fashioning the final versified version of the libretto. Erudite, dignified, and eleven years Puccini's senior, Giacosa found the composer intemperate and stubborn. In time, though, Giacosa and Illica became Puccini's go-to librettists, jointly producing, and gladly sharing credit for, *La Bohème, Tosca,* and *Madama Butterfly.* (Giacosa died in 1906.)

The Turin premiere of *Manon Lescaut,* on February 1, 1893, was Puccini's triumphant breakthrough. Within a year, after playing houses throughout Italy, the opera had productions in European capitals, in cities as far-flung as St. Petersburg and Rio, bringing Puccini renown and riches. Now, other than for business trips to Milan and extended stays to oversee productions of his operas wherever, Puccini could base himself in bucolic Torre del Lago. Elvira, who liked cities and socializing, regularly complained about country living but had little say.

There are miscalculations in *Manon Lescaut,* including some abrupt shifts within the score and holes in the storytelling. But you sense an emerging composer utterly confidant of his musical and dramatic vision.

With the story shifted to the second half of the eighteenth century, *Manon Lescaut* opens in a public square in Amiens, in northern France, bustling with soldiers and townsfolk. We meet the young Chevalier des Grieux, who, his name notwithstanding, is a poor student come to meet friends at a cafe. Puccini conveys Des Grieux's character in a beguiling tenor aria, "Tra voi, belle, brune e bionde," in which the coy young man, addressing the crowd, asks if there is among them a beauty, dark or fair, for him to romance. The buoyant melodic lines and jaunty gait of the music subtly convey Des Grieux's smooth-talking ways.

He notices a lovely, retiring adolescent, Manon, the little sister of Lescaut, a restless, chronically debt-ridden sergeant in the royal guard. Manon is bound for a convent school. But she entrances Des Grieux, who makes his feelings known in an impassioned aria. Suddenly, this cocky charmer seems undone. The aria leads to a deftly conceived love duet, beginning with conversational, halting phrases that evolve into fervent, rapturous outbursts.

The story immediately takes a cynical turn. Manon has been observed by an older man, Geronte, a treasury official, who convinces Lescaut that he would like to elope with his sister. Lescaut, thinking he might get something out of the arrangement, agrees to help. Des Grieux senses what's up and alerts Manon, who impulsively runs off with him in the very coach Geronte had ordered for his elopement with her. Lescaut, laughing about this folly, assures Geronte that Manon is too fond of luxury to remain with a poor student. He's right.

Massenet's *Manon* shows us why. That opera includes an entire act depicting the lovers contending with deprivation in Paris, a life Manon finds miserable. Puccini's opera has been criticized for skipping this crucial episode. Instead, like some fast-paced 1940s Bette Davis melodrama, the scene shifts to Manon living as Geronte's mistress in an elegant Paris salon, with jewels and gowns galore and a retinue of servants. Puccini trusted that his audiences could imagine how Manon's sojourn with a poor student would have turned out.

The determined Des Grieux shows up at Geronte's house and pleads with Manon to escape with him. She gives in, but obstinately stops to gather up jewelry, which gives Geronte time to arrive with guards and have her arrested.

The bleak turning point of the opera comes in the next act, at a square near the harbor of Le Havre. A group of haggard prostitutes, some humiliated, others defiant, have been held in prison awaiting deportation to America. That time has come. The shattered Manon is among them. Des Grieux turns up and tries to bribe a guard into letting Manon go; the scheme fails. As the prisoners board the ship, Puccini's heaving music, touched with bitterly lyrical strands, conveys the desperation of these powerless women. Des Grieux, his enduring love compounded by guilt, rashly decides to join Manon in exile.

In the short last act we see the lovers isolated and dying of thirst on what the libretto describes as a vast desert near the outskirts of New Orleans. Puccini and his librettists apparently mistook flood-prone southern Louisiana for arid west Texas. As Des Grieux goes in search of water, Manon, her humiliation turned to fear of dying in isolation, sings "Solo, perduta, abbandonata" ("Alone, lost, forsaken"). In the most wrenching moments of this great aria, Manon's vocal lines sweep up from dark, chesty low tones to pleading peaks, and then wend their way down despairingly as the orchestra heaves forward, prodded by a numbing repeated two-note riff.

I agree with one contemporaneous critic who praised the "remarkable clarity" of Puccini's inspiration, as opposed to those "who mistake obscurity for profundity." Puccini's temperament is robust and passionate, the critic explained; this is "healthy music."

Healthy. That seems right. Puccini looks straight into our feelings, weaknesses, and contradictions. *Manon Lescaut* also assails frivolousness, greed, and injustice. But Puccini seems more concerned with the emotional impact of these human traits and civic conditions.

As it happened, on February 9, 1893, just eight days after *Manon Lescaut* premiered in Turin, *Falstaff*, Verdi's last opera, opened at La Scala in Milan. It's as if opera in Italy had staged a symbolic passing of the torch.

As a fellow critic who understands that we're all prone to misjudgments, I shall refrain from identifying the reviewer who predicted that *La Bohème* will "leave no great trace upon the history of our lyric theater." Actually, even the more favorable reviews of the opera at its 1896 premiere in Turin expressed reservations, a reaction hard to fathom today. Almost everyone involved in creating *La Bohème* had been optimistic. Though Puccini had concerns that the cast was a little green, he was ecstatic over the work of the exacting young conductor, Arturo Toscanini.

The opera had gone through a rocky genesis of nearly three years. Puccini had considered several subjects before settling on Henri Murger's *Scènes de la vie de bohème*, a romanticized semi-autobiographical tale of impoverished bohemian friends and local characters living in the Latin Quarter of Paris during the 1830s. Murger's work had first appeared as a loosely related series of stories in a literary magazine, then as a play, and finally as a popular novel.

Giacosa and Illica, now Puccini's preferred librettists, signed on to the project and set to work shaping Murger's teeming tale into a compact libretto. Conflating various plot lines and combining aspects of different characters, they devised a story centered on six people. The love-at-first-sight relationship between Rodolfo and Mimì was contrasted with the on-again, off-again romance of the short-fused painter Marcello and the tempestuous cafe singer Musetta.

Just as the opera was coming together, Puccini met up with Leoncavallo (the composer of *Pagliacci*), a rival with whom he'd been on friendly terms, only to discover that they were both writing operas based on Murger's novel. Infuriated, Leoncavallo demanded that his publisher take action: written contracts proved that plans for his *Bohème* predated Puccini's. Leoncavallo staked his claim in a newspaper story. In a signed public statement, Puccini responded with cool detachment, writing, "Let him compose, and I will compose, and the public will judge for themselves." Leoncavallo's *Bohème* enjoyed a good reception at its 1897 premiere, then steadily sank into near-oblivion, unable to compete with Puccini's opera, which in short order became an international sensation.

Read today, the mixed reviews of the Turin premiere of Puccini's opera reveal much about the initial perceptions of the composer's work. His music was generally praised as an advance over *Manon Lescaut*, nobler and less prone to emotive overstatement. But some critics felt that Puccini repeated himself too much, that his idiom was a "trifle restricted," as Budden recounts.

La Bohème represented a big leap over *Manon Lescaut* in another way, specifically, Puccini's reliance on short motifs and themes, usually identified with characters, that keep coming back, sometimes boldly restated, but often subtly altered, slyly disguised, and lurking around in the orchestra. Maybe that's what initially struck certain listeners and critics as restricted or repetitive. Though this innovative aspect of his style took getting used to, Puccini's intricate command of the technique was crucial to his achievements in opera. *La Bohème* is full of marvelous examples, starting from its opening measures.

The scene takes place in the bohemians' garret. Rodolfo, who should be writing, is staring out the window; Marcello is painting at his easel. It's Christmas Eve, the place is freezing, and the two roommates are starving.

The orchestra begins with an irreverent, animated mini-theme associated with Marcello built from two complementary parts: a jumpy figure that slinks downward on three half steps and a rising riff that sounds like a jittery fanfare. Though Marcello never quite sings his whole theme straight out, motifs from it course through the entire opera, representing not just his character but the bohemian lifestyle.

Marcello asks Rodolfo what he's staring at. Brightly singing his own theme, Rodolfo answers that he's looking at smoke rising from chimneys all over Paris, while their own sluggard of an iron stove is doing nothing, living like some grand lord. Rodolfo's theme is bouncy and singsong. Yet there's something forced about the bravado in this first rendition of Rodolfo's tune. Later in the act, in the midst of Rodolfo's ardent aria sung to Mimì, Puccini transforms his tune into a tender, arching melody lifted by the rich orchestra. Though he has no worldly riches, Rodolfo says, in dreams and fantasies he's a millionaire. Now rid of its earlier bluster, his identifying theme sounds ardent and honest; this passage reveals the true poet within the character.

Colline, the philosopher, arrives; then Schaunard, the musician, who comes, amazingly, with some food, wine, and cash, the result of a bizarre musical task he performed for a wealthy eccentric. Eventually everyone decides to head to the Cafe Momus for a Christmas Eve meal, except for Rodolfo, who stays behind to finish an article.

But he can't concentrate. He hears a knock on the door. A woman's voice from the stairwell says, "Excuse me," then "Please, my candle has gone out." Rodolfo opens the door. He and this lovely woman he's never met begin by exchanging conversational phrases, mostly in near-monotone lines. But in the background the orchestra tells us—the audience—who she is.

In warm strings and swelling sonorities we hear for the first time the opening phrase of Mimì's demure, wistful theme, a melody that, a little later in the scene, will begin her revealing aria "Mi chiamano Mimì." ("They call me Mimì, but my name is Lucia.")

Here's a clear example of Puccini's craft. Why does this lovely melody in Mimì's aria move us so deeply? Because, whether or not we noticed it consciously, we heard the phrase earlier in the orchestra: when this winsome intruder meekly asked Rodolfo to light her candle. That theme returns again and again, sometimes in full-out romantic mode, but more often tweaked to fit dramatic twists in the story, however playful, poignant, or, by the end, tragic.

As the fourth and final act starts, both couples—Mimì and Rodolfo, Marcello and Musetta—are on the outs. At the garret the four friends, poorer than ever, horse around like frat boys, until Musetta bursts into the room with the dying Mimì. Rodolfo and Mimì have a panicked, achingly emotional reconciliation, during which Puccini weaves gossamer strands from the motifs of their love.

The most remarkable, and elusive, appearance of a motif comes at the very end of the opera. Mimì has fallen asleep; the shaken Rodolfo is wracked with dread and guilt. Fearing the worst, the garret mates and Musetta have left to give the lovers some time alone. Mimì then sings a sad melody we haven't heard, asking Rodolfo if everyone has gone now. She explains that she was only pretending to be asleep, so that their friends might take a hint.

After the friends have returned, bearing medicine, food, and a muff for the frail Mimì's cold hands, at the precise moment when Rodolfo realizes that Mimì has died, he cries out her name in anguish while the orchestra blares in the background, reprising Mimì's tender theme when she told Rodolfo that she was just pretending to be asleep. But now, hearing that theme played by searing strings driven by relentless, brassy fortissimo chords, we realize that Mimì is no longer pretending.

The opera ends with the orchestra, grimly subdued, playing a series of solemn chords, a mini-phrase that melodically sinks down three steps of a C-sharp minor scale, then rises again and trails off. (The bass line moves in contrary motion, rising and falling.) Have we heard these chords before?

Yes, in the most unlikely place. Earlier in the scene, Colline, wanting to do something to help Mimì, decides to pawn his only valued possession: his overcoat. He sings a short, lumbering, but dignified aria of farewell to his coat, which has served him so ably. It ends with that series of three descending then rising chords in the orchestra.

But this seems a strange motif to reference in the opera's tragic final moments. What does Colline's coat have to do with Mimì's death?

Well, the original manifestation of that motif, in a major key, came much earlier, with the rousing theme associated with the Cafe Momus. Trumpets blare the theme like a joyous fanfare at the opening of Act II, the scene in a bustling square next to the cafe.

That spirited theme, tamed, turned grave, and reduced to bare essentials as a motif, is what we hear at the end of Colline's aria, and then, with bitter finality, when the curtain goes down. To me it's clear what Puccini intends. The placement of that motif at these three crucial moments conveys the moral of the opera better than any words could: those carefree days of dropping out on the Left Bank, of good times and easy romance, of meals they can't afford at a local cafe, of a worn but dignified overcoat, are gone for good. Now these bohemians, like all of us, must grow up.

Though Puccini continued to torment his co-librettists, they forged on to create *Tosca*, adapted from a French melodrama by Victorien Sardou. The opera opened in Rome in 1900, a hugely anticipated premiere attended by the queen and the prime minister of Italy. Once again, most critics hedged their initial assessments. Before long, though, *Tosca* was another international sensation.

For all the theatrical intensity of this dramatically inexorable opera, which tells of the renowned diva Tosca; her lover Mario, a painter; and the sadistic police chief Scarpia, who lusts for Tosca and despises Mario, Puccini's score unfolds as a sophisticated matrix of motifs and themes that comes close to being a through-composed score.

Tosca will always hold a special place for me: it was the first opera I ever saw. I was thirteen, had just started junior high school, and was taken to the Metropolitan Opera by my former fifth-grade teacher, a bachelor who loved music, admired my piano playing, and couldn't believe I'd never been to an opera. The radiant American soprano Dorothy Kirsten sang Tosca, the great Brooklyn-born tenor Richard Tucker was Mario, and the formidable American bass-baritone George London was the malevolent Scarpia. With my very first exposure to opera I learned that this art form often asks you to adjust expectations of dramatic realism: in this case, the villain was tall and handsome; the hero was a little dumpy. I wasn't clear about the story, which confused me. I sort of liked Scarpia. George London exuded charisma.

I hardly remember a detail about the staging. But I sure remember the sound of the orchestra and the wondrous voices. I was engrossed with every moment of the music. More than five decades later, I still am.

In late February 1903, Puccini and Elvira drove from Torre del Lago to Lucca to see friends and tend to business. Some months earlier Puccini had been in a car accident, sliding into a ditch and escaping with only bruises. After dinner at a restaurant in Lucca, despite foggy conditions, Puccini ignored the warnings of friends and set off for home, with his chauffeur at the wheel. Elvira and Antonio were passengers. A few miles out of town the car overturned on a country road and fell down a gully near a bridge. Phillips-Matz describes the incident in grim detail.

The chauffeur's leg was broken; Elvira and Antonio were shaken up but not seriously injured. Puccini, initially unconscious, was trapped under the overturned car, though nestled in a small hollow. Some nearby residents came to the rescue. Brought to a home down the road, Puccini learned that he had severely injured his right leg. He was taken to Torre del Lago, where physicians began a torturous process of treatments. Puccini needed a full leg cast, then progressed from a wheelchair to crutches to a cane, which he would require for the rest of his life. He lost weight; his leg muscles shriveled; he learned he had diabetes and calmed himself by chain-smoking.

It's possible, as Phillips-Matz suggests, that while in Lucca, Puccini and Elvira might have attempted to see Gemignani, still legally her husband, who was gravely ill. Whatever the case, Gemignani died the day after the accident. Elvira and Puccini were now free to marry, after seventeen years together.

But Puccini had been involved, seriously and openly, with a woman in her twenties who expected Puccini to marry her and threatened legal recourse. Puccini's fretful sisters hectored him to give up his current flame and marry Elvira, who during one argument over this affair attacked him with her fists and fingernails. Though it took months of negotiations and a monetary settlement for Puccini's lover, on January 3, 1904, in a small civil ceremony at their house, he and Elvira were married.

Six weeks later *Madama Butterfly* had its premiere, at La Scala, in Milan, to a quite negative reception. Puccini revised the work extensively, softening the portrayal of Pinkerton as a self-indulgent creep, and dividing the long second act in half to create the three-act *Madama Butterfly* that has maintained a central place in the repertory ever since.

Being married didn't stop Puccini from cultivating what he dubbed his "little gardens." His infidelities finally pushed Elvira to a breaking point. Doria Manfredi, a pretty young woman from the Torre del Lago region, entered the Puccini household as a maid. The volatile Elvira, convinced that Doria was Puccini's latest lover, hounded her relentlessly, cursing the young woman in public and fomenting a scandal, despite Puccini's protestations of innocence. In January 1909, the beaten-down, unstable Doria died from an overdose of pills. Elvira was convicted of slander, though a compensatory payment to the Manfredi family saved her from imprisonment. An autopsy report declared that Doria died a virgin.

Puccini continued to create ambitious works. To understand Puccini's dominance of the field during these years, consider this: in 1912 alone, Covent Garden, in London, presented runs of *Manon Lescaut, Tosca, Madama Butterfly,* and *La fanciulla del West* (which had been premiered at the Metropolitan Opera in 1910, with Emmy Destinn as Minnie, Enrico Caruso as Jack Rance, and Toscanini conducting). Here was one London company presenting four recent works by a single living composer in a single year. It's impossible to imagine Covent Garden, or any company, doing something comparable today. In fact, it's common these days for a season at the Met to include two, three, or even four Puccini operas. Puccini still rules.

Given his ambitious efforts to make Italian opera dramatically and musically contemporary, Puccini's choice of a Carlo Gozzi dramatic fairy tale as a subject for what turned out to be his last work, *Turandot,* might seem a retrenchment. The opera received its premiere at La Scala in 1926, conducted by Toscanini, fifteen months after Puccini died, not having completed the crucial last scene of the third and final act.

The story, set in ancient Peking, tells of an icy young princess, Turandot, who nurses a vehement hatred of all men. We find out why in Act II, during Turandot's tell-all aria "In questa reggia." Every day Turandot broods over the story of an ancestress, a princess, who long ago was ravished and murdered by an invading barbarian soldier. Turandot has sworn to honor the memory of this innocent woman by taking revenge on any man foolish enough to court her. All suitors who seek to marry Turandot must answer three riddles she poses or pay with their lives. No suitor has survived the test.

Calaf, a prince in exile, son of the disposed King of Tartary, arrives at the palace and, to his amazement, discovers his lost father, now blind, tended to by a loyal slave, Liù, who still has unrequited love for Calaf. But then Turandot appears, and with one look at the radiant, fearsome princess, Calaf is hooked. Keeping his identity secret, he accepts Turandot's challenge. To her shock, shame, and horror, Calaf answers her riddles.

The libretto by Giuseppe Adami and Renato Simoni would seem ready-made for an old-fashioned grand opera. Indeed, *Turandot* has several massed scenes with chorus, including when the people of Peking sing praises to their old, frail emperor and, later, break into heady joy when Calaf proves victorious.

Turandot's aria "In questa reggia" is a showpiece to end all showpieces. During a climactic scene, the soprano singing Turandot must send a grand melodic line (which Puccini adapted from a book of Chinese folk songs) soaring over a stage full of choristers and slicing through the full orchestra. And Puccini never wrote a more inspired aria than Calaf's "Nessun dorma," which Luciano Pavarotti made as famous as a pop song.

Yet below its grand-opera trappings, Puccini's score includes some of his most advanced and complex music. Whole passages bristle with dissonance-tinged sonorities and modernist chords that evade tonal grounding. Puccini incorporates elements of bitonality and daring uses of whole-tone and pentatonic scales to evoke the colors of Asian music as he understood it.

Alas, Puccini left us five-sixths of a masterpiece. He completed the score up to the point where Liù takes her own life rather than reveal Calaf's identity to Turandot's avenging guards. Liù's death scene is hauntingly beautiful and nobly tragic.

But the next scene, the final one, calls for Turandot to undergo, in effect, a spiritual transfiguration. The icy princess who loathes all men must melt in the face of Calaf's fearless love. As he tried to complete the score, Puccini was already weakened by illness, including, it turned out, throat cancer.

Still, I'm convinced that this final scene had stumped him. As a passionate Italian, Puccini could understand emotional contradictions: that you could both love and hate someone. But he couldn't understand emotional transfiguration: the notion that feelings could suddenly emerge from an unfeeling woman. And why does Calaf, who has every reason to condemn Turandot after watching Liù's sacrificial suicide, still desire her? Is this just a typical ritual of male conquest? Turandot's unmotivated change of heart would have to be conveyed by music alone. For nearly two years Puccini could not write this final scene.

In October 1924 he traveled to Brussels with his son to consult a renowned specialist. "Here I am! Poor me!" he wrote to Adami. Describing the treatment he was about to undergo, Puccini added: "They say that I shall have six weeks of it. You can imagine how pleased I am! And *Turandot?*"

But soon after the surgery his health began to fail. Two days later, Puccini died, a few weeks shy of sixty-six.

His colleagues, though devastated, had to decide what to do about *Turandot.* At Toscanini's suggestion the publisher recruited the Neapolitan composer Franco Alfano to complete the work. Puccini had left some thirteen pages of minimal sketches. Alfano recycled and tweaked some melodies and passages from earlier in the score. The crucial duet of transformation was essentially written by Alfano, a serviceable but undistinguished effort. After some trimming, Alfano's version was published and has remained the standard ending.

In 2001 the Italian composer Luciano Berio wrote a new ending for *Turandot,* which was performed in a production at the Salzburg Festival in 2002 that I attended. And it's fascinating.

Berio was an ingenious modernist with a feeling for Italianate lyricism and a flair for drama. Though he took Puccini's sketches into account, the music he wrote sounds like Berio. This is not faux Puccini with contemporary touches.

In his version, which lasts some twenty-three minutes (about eight minutes longer than Alfano's), Berio prods and adapts Puccini's harmonic style and, in a respectful way, brings Puccini into the twenty-first century. There are passages of old-time operatic magic: offstage choruses sing celestial *ah*'s when Calaf refers to the fragrances of flowers. But the orchestra swirls with contrapuntal intricacies and quizzical harmonic writing. Berio veils the scene with emotional and musical ambiguity. You sense Turandot feeling rattled and unsure, wondering what she might be feeling. Berio's ending leaves things open-ended. Even the chorus of commoners who watch Turandot and Calaf come together seem unsure what to make of it.

Turandot diehards cling to Alfano's old-fashioned ending. I much prefer Berio's work. In a way, he pays Puccini the compliment of treating him like a fellow twentieth-century composer. He shows us where Puccini might have been going had he lived to complete this work and write additional operas.

I can't write about Puccini without relating how *La Bohème* prompted the most meaningful interview of my career, in January 1996. I'd heard that Jonathan Larson, a musical theater composer, then thirty-five, had written a rock musical version of *La Bohème*, a work that zapped the story from the Left Bank of Paris in the 1830s to the East Village of the 1990s. Larson's characters were modern-day equivalents to Puccini's bohemians: aspiring artists coping with drugs, poverty, sexual confusion, and AIDS. The piece, called *Rent*, was about to open a multi-week run at the New York Theatre Workshop, a small but prestigious venue.

It happened to be the hundredth anniversary of *La Bohème* that year. I was intrigued that the opera still spoke to a new generation of musical theater artists.

I went to a dress rehearsal, which was troubled by technical glitches. Still, I was impressed by the originality of Larson's book, lyrics, and music. The score had propulsive rock-infused and pop-style numbers, as well as lyrical songs and intricate ensembles that nodded to the heritage of American musical theater. That Larson revered Sondheim came through in the way he wedded vibrant music to inventive, snappy, and affecting lyrics.

And there on stage were the descendants of Puccini's characters. Roger (Rodolfo) is a charismatic punk-rock guitarist and recovering drug addict, struggling to heal himself and write a breakout song. Mimi is a sultry dancer at an S&M disco, an active user, a troubled but vulnerable woman willing to risk romance who breaks down Roger's resistance. (Both are HIV-positive.) Larson gives them a grunge love duet. Marcello becomes Mark, a filmmaker who hides in his work, a decent guy whose free-spirited girlfriend, Maureen (Musetta), has left him for a woman. Colline is Tom Collins, a bookish gay man and community activist who is living with AIDS. Tom is mugged one night and rescued by Angel Schunard, an irrepressible cross-dressing Hispanic, also living with AIDS. Tom and Angel quickly form the most loving, devoted relationship within this circle of friends.

After the rehearsal I sat with Larson for an interview. The only private place in the theater was its cramped box office. Bushy-haired, soft-spoken, and looking understandably tired, Larson told me about the struggles of his career and the friends of his who inspired *Rent*, especially those living with HIV/AIDS. He was clear about the musical's message. It's not how long you live but how you live, what you do with your life, that really matters, Larson said.

In writing *Rent* he had analyzed the *Bohème* libretto closely, "beat by beat," he said, to create his personal, updated version of the opera. *Rent* represented a long-sought breakthrough, he said proudly. Because of this production he had been able to quit his job as a waiter after ten years. "I'm happy to say that other commissions are coming up," he told me, "and I think I may have a life as a composer."

We parted late that night, shaking hands on the street. Then he returned to his walk-up apartment where, while heating some water for tea, he collapsed and died from what was later diagnosed as an aortic dissection. *Rent* opened to near-universal acclaim. The production moved to Broadway and, in time, around the world. Larson won two posthumous Tony Awards and the Pulitzer Prize for Drama.

In speaking with Larson's friends for a Sunday piece I later wrote, I learned how confident he had managed to remain, even during periods of bitter frustration. He used to tell all his friends to just wait, that someday he would have a Broadway hit, win a Tony Award, and be interviewed for the *New York Times*.

I'm so grateful that by showing up to speak with him, and telling him how much I admired *Rent*, Jonathan Larson lived to see one of those predictions come true.

And love of Puccini brought us together.

CHAPTER FOURTEEN

NEW LANGUAGES
FOR A NEW CENTURY

ARNOLD SCHOENBERG (1874–1951)

IGOR STRAVINSKY (1882–1971)

BÉLA BARTÓK (1881–1945)

Arnold Schoenberg never intended to be a radical.

In a jocular anecdote from a 1930 essay, Schoenberg recalled that while serving in the military during the First World War he was confronted one day by a superior officer who said: "So, you are this notorious Schoenberg, then." Schoenberg replied: "Beg to report, sir, yes. Nobody wanted to be, someone had to be, so I let it be me."

He was only half joking. Though Schoenberg devised the twelve-tone technique, a method of composition that completely upended the language of diatonic tonality that had prevailed in Western music for centuries, he acted as if he had no other choice. Even as his compositions were castigated by critics of his day as radical outrages, Schoenberg did not think of himself as some wild-eyed revolutionary.

But he certainly viewed music, like all the arts, as fundamentally evolutionary. And from his perspective, music, at least serious music of the Austro-German Classical heritage, had reached a crisis point by the early twentieth century. The traditional tonal language, in all its manifestations, no longer served the emerging creative imperatives of a new era, he felt. Music's natural evolution had stalled. Something had to be done.

Born in 1874 into a lower-middle-class Jewish family (his father kept a shoe shop) in a district of Vienna that had once been a Jewish ghetto, Schoenberg embraced the honored Germanic tradition and its revered masters. Drawn early to music, he started violin lessons at eight, made musical friends, and taught himself the cello and other instruments. He learned compositional forms by subscribing to an encyclopedia's instructional series. Yet this essentially self-taught composer would eventually write two sophisticated books on harmony that are still in use today.

In 1889 his father died, and at around sixteen Arnold had to leave school and take a job at a bank. But he played the cello in an amateur orchestra led by the composer Alexander Zemlinsky, who recognized Schoenberg's talents. Though only three years older, Zemlinsky became Schoenberg's valued, if informal, composition teacher (and, in 1901, his brother-in-law, when Schoenberg married Zemlinksy's sister, Mathilde).

Schoenberg credited Zemlinsky with helping him bridge the late nineteenth-century stylistic divide between, on the one side, the followers of Brahms, deemed the inheritor of the great tradition, and, on the other, devotees of Wagner, who espoused the music of the future. Schoenberg had been a Brahmsian. But Zemlinsky wrote works that reconciled Brahms's ingenious formal thinking with Wagner's visionary harmonic innovations.

In 1898 Schoenberg converted to Christianity, a common choice for Jews with cultural ambitions during a period of rising anti-Semitism. The next year, he composed a breakthrough piece, *Verklärte Nacht* (Transfigured Night), a string sextet in one episodic but continuous movement.

This thirty-minute work was inspired by a Richard Dehmel poem of the same name describing a slow walk by two lovers through a dark forest on a moonlit night. The woman haltingly tells the man a dark secret: she is carrying the child of another. But, as the title suggests, the man is transfigured by her confession. Through their love this infant will be born as his own child, he says.

In 1917 Schoenberg rescored the sextet for full string orchestra. But I love the clean lines and intimacy of the original.

Schoenberg's harmonic language here is beholden to Wagner, rich with chromatic ambiguities and, in the most tempestuous episodes, evasive of tonality. But the piece's structure nods to Brahms's use of small linking motifs. The way Schoenberg writes for the six strings, with shimmering sonorities and restless, tugging undertows, uncannily suggests emotional and spiritual transfiguration. He expresses the healing of the lovers in an extended final passage in plush D major, rich with subdued tremolos, wide-spaced pizzicato chords, and an angelic sustained high D that eases into a gently descending phrase.

At its 1902 premiere, many critics and listeners considered Schoenberg's musical language amorphous and exasperating. The language *is* amorphous, but in a sensual and engrossing way.

Here, in his first important work, Schoenberg was already grappling with the crisis of music as he perceived it. The tonal language (the system of diatonic major and minor keys) had long depended upon relatively clear harmonic grounding points (those tried-and-true tonic and dominant chords). Composers like Wagner and the elder Brahms, along with contemporaries like Zemlinsky and Richard Strauss, took exploration of wayward chromatic harmonic to extremes. But they could push only so far without forgoing the tethers that gave the language coherence.

Throughout his life, Schoenberg struggled to balance conflicting creative urges. On the one hand he venerated tradition and classical forms and wanted to compose sonatas and symphonies. On the other, in keeping with an era of radical cultural and scientific discoveries, Schoenberg felt compelled to direct his art toward change and renewal. He continued writing some instrumental pieces that had key signatures and were beholden to traditional forms, like his Quartet No. 1 in D Minor, completed in 1905.

Yet, feeling restless, he increasingly turned to vocal works, including many in a darkly dramatic vein. After all, in a sung piece, listeners had a text to follow, which lent the score dramatic impetus and structure; and the more disturbing the text, the more the music could viscerally reflect these emotions through tonal ambiguity, intense dissonance, and rhapsodic structure.

During these years, Schoenberg was also very involved in painting, and not just as an amateur. He was instinctively drawn to painters of the Expressionist movement, like Munch, Kandinsky, and Kirchner, who rejected objective reality, believing that individuals create their own realities from their own perceptions. For these painters, the personal became the real. But this approach necessitated rejecting all conventional notions of beauty, design, order, symmetry.

Schoenberg's paintings, especially his many self-portraits, resemble Munch's in style. The canvases are filled with splotches of garish colors and surreal depictions of Schoenberg's own bald pate, sunken cheeks, and penetrating eyes. In some he looks like a severe Old Testament prophet come to issue us a last-chance warning before the apocalypse.

In 1910 a solo exhibit of Schoenberg's paintings brought him a complimentary letter from Kandinsky, who also admired Schoenberg's music and theories. A lasting friendship developed, even as the composer increasingly focused on music.

Schoenberg came to believe that tonality was almost the equivalent in music to the representational reality that the Expressionist painters considered spent. He started describing tonality in the same way he dismissed stuffy Viennese society—as archaic and conformist, even diseased, and beholden to decadent cultural habits. But Vienna was changing. By 1900, after waves of immigration, only one in four residents had been born there.

In music, those old "cultural habits" involved lingering fixations on keys, tonal centers, and symmetrical phrasing. Schoenberg began imagining a musical language unbounded by the traditional expectations that harmonies would hew to consonant points of grounding. His goal, as he eventually put it, was the "emancipation of the dissonance." Why should a dissonance have to be an interval or a chord of harshness and tension, demanding resolution? Why couldn't a dissonance be valued for all its stinging beauty?

Schoenberg took a leap into the beyond. In 1908 he began composing

Das Buch der hängenden Gärten (The Book of the Hanging Gardens), a cycle of fifteen songs set to German Symbolist poems by Stefan George that loosely describe a failed love affair between two adolescents, set in a verdant, disintegrating garden. Though most of these dark songs slip around in some vestige of functioning tonality, a few are considered to be Schoenberg's first atonal works, though Schoenberg, as I noted earlier, hated hearing his music described as "atonal," a term that, to him, defines a musical language by what it's not.

That same year he composed his Second String Quartet, a piece that at its Vienna premiere in 1908 caused "riots which surpassed every previous and subsequent happening of this kind," Schoenberg later recalled. The agitated first movement is supposedly written in F-sharp minor, though knowing this doesn't help listeners much, since the hypercharged music is all over the place harmonically. In the third and fourth movements, which introduce a solo soprano singing settings of two George poems ("Litany" and "Rapture"), Schoenberg dispenses with key signatures altogether.

In the first line of "Rapture" the soprano sings, "I feel air from another planet." So did Schoenberg in this piece. Somehow, in daring to break away from expectations of tonality, he wrote music of rapture, sadness, and pinpoint colorings. At least that's the way it sounds today. After its premiere, one Berlin critic complained of having "suffered physical pain," as if having been "cruelly abused."

In 1949, looking back on this brave period in his work, Schoenberg tried to convey his mind-set at the time as he grappled with the dilemma of tonality. "The overwhelming multitude of dissonances cannot be counterbalanced any longer by occasional returns to such tonal triads as represent a key," Schoenberg wrote. It seemed "inadequate," he added, "to force a movement into the Procrustean bed of a tonality."

In other words, someone, on behalf of all living composers during the early years of a momentous new century, had to stand up, point to tonality, and declare that the emperor had no clothes. Such was Schoenberg's lot.

The Second Quartet is dedicated to Schoenberg's wife, Mathilde, a poignant yet bitterly ironic tribute: at the time she was having an affair with the Expressionist painter Richard Gerstl.

Schoenberg had befriended this intrepid young Viennese artist. Schoenberg and his wife now had two small children. When the affair was exposed in the summer of 1908, Mathilde went to live for a while with Gerstl. Devastated, Schoenberg contemplated suicide. Mathilde was persuaded to return home for the sake of her family. That November it was Gerstl, just twenty-five, who killed himself.

The crisis provoked a feverish year of creativity for Schoenberg. In early 1909 he composed his remarkable Three Piano Pieces, Op. 11. There are no key signatures; the harmonic language almost defiantly abandons any vestiges of tonality. The first piece shifts from passages that seem drenched in late-Romantic longing to hurtling moments that stretch thematic lines across several octaves. The slow second piece heaves and groans with Expressionist ruminations, prodded by a recurring two-note tread in the low register. The fitful third piece begins with leaping, crazed chords thick with dissonances in both hands. After this shocker of a start, the rest of the piece tries to figure out what on earth just happened, trundling forward in a succession of disgruntled, curt phrases.

The work that pulled together the strands of Schoenberg's intense domestic life and arduous creative pursuits was *Erwartung* (Expectation), a twenty-seven-minute monodrama in one act, a Freudian music drama. Schoenberg wrote the rough score in a feverish seventeen days during the late summer of 1909, taking some three weeks more to finish the full orchestra score.

The libretto is by the writer and physician Marie Pappenheim, a friend of Schoenberg's who was knowledgeable about Freud's theories of hysteria and repression. The story begins with a woman poised at the edge of a dark forest on a moonlit night. At first she describes her fears, expressing her thoughts in short, broken phrases and many open-ended questions. She is searching for "him," her lover. She enters the woods and then thinks she sees a body. But it's the stump of a tree. Her words turn into a delusional conversation with "him." She plunges deeper into the woods. Distraught and confused, now bloodied, her dress torn, she heads toward a bench, but her foot strikes something. It's a man's bloody body—her lover. She goes off into the shadowy distance. What happens to her? It's unclear.

The score is still remarked upon because it seems to lack any repetitions. It's like stream-of-consciousness musical Expressionism. (*Erwartung* was not performed until 1924, in Prague.)

In 1910 Schoenberg applied for, and won, a position as a lecturer in theory and composition at the music and performing arts academy in Vienna. The musicologist O. W. Neighbour reports that, amid anti-Semitic attacks, the question of Schoenberg's further advancement at the academy was actually raised in parliament. At the end of the academic year, feeling thwarted, Schoenberg moved his family to Berlin to try his luck in that cosmopolitan city. He wound up doing arrangements, teaching privately, and giving poorly attended lectures.

In 1912 Schoenberg produced another work that, in time, would alter the contours of twentieth-century music: *Pierrot lunaire* (Moonstruck Pierrot or Pierrot in the Moonlight), which originated from a commission by the vocalist and cabaret actress Albertine Zehme. It's a monodrama in the form of a song cycle, settings of twenty-one French poems (or "three times seven" poems, as Schoenberg, who had a lifelong fascination with numerology, specifies in the title) by the Belgian writer Albert Giraud, translated into German.

The texts relate exploits of the timeless Pierrot clown character in a moon-drunk state, singing of love, sex, violence, and heresy. In the third part, returned to his home in Bergamo, Pierrot seems haunted by the surreal and crazed things that have happened to him.

Schoenberg wrote the solo part, tailored to Zehme's talents, in a vocal style called *Sprechstimme* (speech-song), sort of half spoken, half sung. The instrumentation is unusual: flute (doubling on piccolo), violin (doubling on viola), clarinet (doubling on bass clarinet), cello, and piano. This scoring caught on among composers in later generations, who wrote works for what became known as the "Pierrot ensemble."

During the most terrifying songs, there are bouts of savagery, screeching sounds, grating sonorities, and frantically racing lines. In the more ruminative ones, however, diaphanous textures, teasing riffs, and rippling instrumental streams almost, but not quite, disguise Pierrot's seemingly demented state.

After some forty rehearsals, Schoenberg led the Berlin premiere in an intimate performance space in 1912, with Zehme dressed in a Columbine costume and the instrumentalists playing behind a veil. There was whistling from the audience and the expected scathing reviews. But the piece won supporters. The musicians took it on tour through Germany and Austria, an almost-success and, at the least, a curiosity.

One might assume that Schoenberg, a convert from Judaism, an ostracized figure within the Austro-German musical establishment, would have resisted the calls to German nationalism that fueled the First World War. Not so, as comes through in a disturbing letter he wrote on August 28, 1914, to Alma Mahler, the widow of Gustav Mahler, who had died in 1911. Mahler had been a singular ally and mentor to Schoenberg, even when the younger man's music baffled him.

In this letter, Schoenberg welcomes the war and hails a "glorious victory of the Germans against France, England and Belgium." He expresses certainty that "our Austria is approaching a new, more beautiful future." Now even Japan and America have "shown their true face as our enemy" and "my eyes are open," he writes. He dismisses "foreign music" as "stale, empty, disgusting, cloying, false, and awkward." But now comes the reckoning, Schoenberg asserts: "Now we shall send these mediocre purveyors of kitsch back into slavery, and they shall learn to honor the German spirit and to worship the German God."

In fact, the war to end all wars would open Schoenberg's eyes. His best pupils, Anton Webern and Alban Berg, were called to military service. In May 1915, then forty, Schoenberg was called for medical examination by the military in Vienna and rejected. He moved his family back to that city. That winter he volunteered for one year of service. When his asthma became an issue he applied for release, which came late the next year.

The cataclysmic experience of the war pushed Schoenberg to dig deeper into his ideas about the next stage in music's evolution. It took several years, until the mid-1920s. But the result would shake up music ever after in ways that even Schoenberg, who could be arrogant to the point of obnoxiousness, never imagined.

It's common to think of major and minor scales as a series of pitches rising from the tonic note up to the repeat of the tonic an octave higher. We all know do, re, mi, and many of us have practiced ascending and descending scales on various instruments.

But at its core a scale is less a series than a hierarchy of pitches, all related by various intervals (drawn from the overtone series) to a central, stabilizing tonic tone. Play them in succession and you get the familiar scale. But in a way, a starlike pattern, with pitches shooting out from the central note, might be a more apt representation.

During the late nineteenth century, composers increasingly explored chromatic areas of harmony, using the notes in between the seven tones of the scale (and chords based on those in-between notes), thereby lessening the grounding impact of the tonic pitch through whole passages of a piece. It was Schoenberg's perception—an astute and defensible one—that the more progressive composers of his day, himself included, had pushed chromatic harmony to such an extent that they were undermining the whole hierarchical point of the scale—that, in effect, they were using all twelve chromatic pitches equally.

So, he argued, let's just admit it!

His response, following his experiments with atonality, was to throw out the notion of organizing pitches through a hierarchy. If we're all writing for the twelve tones more or less equally, he reasoned, why not come up with an approach that embraced and facilitated, even assured, equality?

Using the piano, mostly, to work out his ideas, he composed two pathbreaking works, more or less simultaneously: Five Piano Pieces, Op. 23, and Suite for Piano, Op. 25.

The first of Schoenberg's Five Piano Pieces begins like a somber rumination, unfolding in three slow yet shifting contrapuntal lines. Here Schoenberg utilizes three three-note groups of pitches; these are not quite motifs in the manner of Brahms, but more like collections of pitches organized into pitch cells from which Schoenberg spins out the music. The dark, impetuous second piece uses a cell of nine pitches, employed horizontally in short, furious spurts, and vertically through leaping chords. In the third piece—a work of intensely complicated counterpoint broken up by anxious passages that sound almost improvisatory—he uses a cell of five pitches.

In the fifth piece, an impish waltz, Schoenberg takes his experiment to its logical final step: using a cell of all twelve pitches, what he would call a tone row. Schoenberg came up with a basic ground rule to maintain a sense of equality between the twelve tones of a row. The notes of the row (the series) had to be played, that is, gone through, in order. A note within a row could not be repeated until its turn came up again. Of course, just as with scales, pitches from a row could be played successively (as melody) or simultaneously (as harmony).

But as he developed his system, Schoenberg devised all sorts of ways around the basic rule to create all manner of permutations, which lent striking variety to the new technique. The tone row could be broken in half into two so-called hexachords; it could be transposed so that it started on another pitch (while maintaining the same interval relationships); it could be gone through upside down (inverted) or backward (in retrograde). And crucially, a row could be used simultaneously with a tweaked version of itself—say, the row in retrograde, or inversion, or transposed. So in twelve-tone music various strands of the basic series routinely overlap.

The obvious objection to this technique concerns the very idea of putting pitches in an order. Isn't that inherently unmusical and rigid?

Not exactly. Masterpieces of tonal music are full of stretches that, at least loosely, deploy pitches in patterns that are pretty close to preordained orders. Think of virtuosic passage-work in, say, a Mozart or Beethoven piano concerto, when the piano races up and down the keyboard in scale patterns, or goes through a progression of standard chords played in arpeggios, or takes some lyrical phrase and repeats it almost exactly in rising (or falling) sequences.

Still, the concept of putting pitches in order is the definitional component of the twelve-tone method. Admittedly, Schoenberg's breakthrough may seem an intellectual conceit.

Yet for me, the resulting music is inventive and exhilarating. That waltz from Op. 23, the first official twelve-tone piece, is a good example—a slightly fractured and skittish yet charming dance in homage to the *oom-pah-pah* Viennese waltz. The familiar harmonic dichotomy between consonance and dissonance essentially disappears as dissonances are "emancipated."

With this discovery Schoenberg could now indulge his penchant for tradition and write works that, in form and character, looked back to Baroque and Classical models. His first large-scale twelve-tone piano work was the Suite for Piano, Op. 25, a six-movement piece in which Schoenberg tips his hat to Bach's keyboard suites. The musical language is rigorously twelve-tone; the piano writing is angular and spiky. Yet in the manner of Bach, the suite begins with an industrious prelude, includes a graceful minuet, and ends with a slightly demonic gigue.

When I taught music in college I won over a lot of twelve-tone skeptics with a simple demonstration. I would play a Bach gavotte (a similar type of dance) on the piano, and then play the musette from this Schoenberg suite. In every respect, except for the way the pitches were picked, the Schoenberg musette was just like Bach's piece: the same short-short-long dance rhythm; the same bagpipelike drone characteristic of this seventeenth-century dance; the same skipping, playful character. When students stopped fretting about tone rows and just listened, they would hear the elements of Bach's gavotte in Schoenberg's stunning transformation.

The twelve-tone method may sound brainy and mathematical. But for Schoenberg it was liberating. With equivalence of pitch rendered almost automatic, he could achieve subtlety, complexity, delicacy, tension, darkness, tenderness—whatever quality he was after—through rhythmic gesture, contrapuntal intricacy, accent, and dynamic contrasts. Walking with a colleague on a summer day in 1921, Schoenberg boasted that he had "discovered something which will assure the supremacy of German music for the next hundred years."

That's where he went wrong. Schoenberg viewed the arts as continually evolving. He excitedly thought that he had taken music to the next stage in its evolution.

But an art form may progress and change, even radically, without "evolving." To claim that the twelve-tone method was the next stage in music's evolution and that it would recharge the art form (and keep Germanic composers on top) buys into the notion that music inherently evolves.

What Schoenberg discovered, what he pioneered, was radical, to be sure, but it was a fascinating new language, a "new metaphorical speech through one huge, convulsive transformation," as Leonard Bernstein put it in his Norton Lectures at Harvard in 1973. Looked at in a larger context, this development was more like an exhilarating offshoot in music history, not its next stage. Visual artists today overwhelmingly see Abstract Expressionism similarly. This was also a challenging and dazzling development that changed everything in its wake. But it was not the next stage in art history; it was not the only valid approach to contemporary painting (though many imposing artists and polemical critics touted it as such at the time).

There is also the question of whether in doing away with some semblance of tonality, twelve-tone music was violating the acoustical properties of sound. Leonard Bernstein pressed this view in that Norton lecture series, titled *The Unanswered Question*. Though he ranged over many topics, Bernstein mainly set out to argue, to prove, even, that all music in all cultures throughout time hewed, however loosely, to some kind of tonality; that notwithstanding the many varieties of scales, modes, and practices, there was a worldwide, inborn musical grammar; and that the human ear, by virtue of the inherent acoustical properties of the overtone series, craved some hewing to fundamental tones.

Now, Bernstein was a hero of my youth, and the televised lectures were riveting. But during one of them, while comparing Schoenberg's twelve-tone method to an artificial language, he played that impish waltz from the Five Pieces, Op. 23, and asked, "How many music lovers do you know who can say, today, in this fiftieth year of Op. 23, that they *love* to hear it, that they listen with love to it, as they might listen to Mahler or Stravinsky?"

Actually, I can. I had first studied Op. 23 at Yale and had played three of its pieces at my senior-year recital. At the time the music challenged me technically and intellectually. But once I knew them, I never dropped a note. Maybe listening to this music—and certainly playing it—makes demands on your intellect. But it also invites you to let go.

That's what Schoenberg's later works, and the best twelve-tone music by other composers, can offer, a chance to take a leap, to enjoy denying your ear tonal grounding, to bask for a while in a realm beyond tonality and, without mentally straining, try to hear the alternative coherence and logic of this new language. If after a while you have savored your journey through tone rows and want to return to tonality, fine. Being a music lover should never involve an either-or choice.

In the years following his discovery, Schoenberg's twelve-tone works continued to stir up extreme reactions, mostly hostile. Recalling this period, Schoenberg later wrote that he "stood alone against a world of enemies." With one exception, he added: "That small group of faithful friends, my pupils, among them my dear Anton von Webern, the spiritual leader of the group, a very Hotspur in his principles, a real fighter, a friend whose faithfulness can never be surpassed, a real genius as a composer."

Webern (1883–1945) absorbed Schoenberg's method in its entirety and produced austerely captivating works in which complex content is conveyed in a highly concentrated style: most of his pieces are extremely short, with whole gestures reduced to essentials, like musical haiku. By the mid-twentieth century Webern would be seen as the avatar of serialism, an extension of the twelve-tone system that involved orderings not just of pitch but of rhythm, duration, and other elements.

Schoenberg's other steadfast student was Alban Berg (1885–1935), whose death at fifty shattered Schoenberg: he could barely speak for days.

Berg was also excited by twelve-tone technique. But Berg's late-Romantic lyrical yearnings and powerful feeling for Expressionist turmoil combined to make his music viscerally dramatic. If I ever did a Top Ten Operas project, I'd keep one spot for Berg's *Wozzeck*, a work whose composition predates Berg's exploration of twelve-tone technique. First performed in 1925, *Wozzeck* is the raw, anguished tale of a delusional soldier with a common-law wife and small son, who is stationed in a small Austrian garrison town. He supplements his meager pay by performing menial tasks for superior officers and a quack doctor. This taut, relentless music drama (three acts lasting less than ninety minutes) shows Berg ingeniously blending atonal angst with dwindling echoes of late-Romantic chromaticism. I'd be tempted to claim another spot on that list for Berg's *Lulu,* essentially a twelve-tone score, left incomplete at his death, a shattering masterpiece.

In embracing twelve-tone music Berg was never rigid about the rules. He didn't see why, if so inclined, he should not drop some tonal sonority into a piece. Interestingly, in later years Schoenberg would follow suit and, taking a break, return to tonality (or mix it with twelve-tone elements) in certain pieces.

However, Schoenberg mostly persevered with his discovery, writing, among many other works, his colossal Variations for Orchestra, Op. 31, in 1926. And for two years, ending in 1932, he worked on a formidable opera, *Moses und Aron,* adapting his own libretto. He could never find the time to compose the third and final act.

Schoenberg's wife, Mathilde, had died in 1923. The following year he married Gertrud Kolisch, the sister of a student, the violinist Rudolf Kolisch, a founding member of the Kolisch Quartet, an ensemble that would tenaciously champion Schoenberg's works.

Schoenberg was vacationing with his family in France in 1933 when Hitler came to power in Germany. Schoenberg responded by returning to Judaism. In coming years his music would be consigned by the Third Reich to the waste heap of "degenerate" art. Hitler and his henchmen reviled modernist art for its supposed abstruseness and decadence, seeing telltale traces of Bolshevik sympathies and perverse Jewish spirit.

Schoenberg immigrated to America, first teaching at a conservatory in Boston and then settling in Los Angeles, where he taught at the University of Southern California and UCLA. With an appointment to UCLA in 1935 as a visiting professor and promotion the following year to professor, he was able to purchase a commodious Spanish colonial house in Brentwood.

George Gershwin had a house nearby, and they became friends and tennis partners.

In 1944, upon turning seventy, Schoenberg was compelled to retire from UCLA, with a pension of only thirty-eight dollars a month. He now had three children ages thirteen and under from his second marriage to provide for. In 1945 he applied to the Guggenheim Foundation for a fellowship. Private lessons, he explained in his letter, were now his only means of support. He hoped to use a fellowship to compose the final act of *Moses und Aron,* as well as an oratorio, and to write a harmony textbook.

Schoenberg's application was denied. He died in 1951 at seventy-five, having spent a day sick in bed, anxious with premonitions.

He never finished *Moses und Aron.*

IGOR STRAVINSKY

During the first couple of minutes, the audience attending the May 29, 1913, world premiere of *Le Sacre du printemps* (The Rite of Spring), at Paris's new, nineteen-hundred-seat Théâtre des Champs-Élyseés, refrained from reacting.

This hotly anticipated ballet—an evocation of pagan Russian rituals in adoration of the earth and glorification of the spring, culminating with a sacrificial dance—was the latest volley from the audaciously contemporary Ballets Russes, the itinerant company based in Paris that the Russian impresario Sergei Diaghilev had started in 1909. *The Rite of Spring* was choreographed by Vaslav Nijinsky, the company's twenty-five-year-old star dancer; the sets and costumes were by Nicholas Roerich. Igor Stravinsky, then thirty-one, had written the music.

Before the curtain went up, the orchestra, swollen to ninety-nine players to accommodate Stravinsky's score, began the Introduction, which evokes the ballet's primitive setting and ritualistic aura. However wary and restless, the audience listened quietly as Pierre Monteux conducted the music, which started so strangely.

A solo bassoon, playing in an unusually high register (was it some kind of oboe? or saxophone?), spun out a bare melody in which an insinuating sustained pitch kept breaking into eerie squiggles. As the melody continued, atop a two-note intrusion from lower horns, some clarinets slinked down in stark parallel fourths. Other instruments joined the fray, squirreling around, needling the music with sputtering repeated tones and rude trills, finally cutting loose into jumpy riffs that sounded crazed. And where were the strings? They mostly seemed sidelined, except for flecks of pizzicato, a strange soft trill. During one sudden episode, the weird sounds of sustained string harmonics somehow broke through a mass of madhouse brass and woodwinds.

Before long, some members of the audience had enough. They laughed and scoffed; a few whistled and catcalled. Then the curtain went up to reveal the first scene, showing a tribe of maidens, as Stravinsky's music for the Dance of the Adolescents began.

The orchestra erupted with brisk, pile-driving repetitions of a barbarously dissonant chord (*ugh-ugh-ugh-ugh*), played in low, weighty strings, while a battery of horns slammed down only on certain beats, at random, it seemed. For many in the audience this was the limit, as the music historian Thomas Forrest Kelly reports in an engrossing account of this notorious premiere. People were incensed not just by the "laborious and puerile barbarity" of the music (as one critic would put it) but by the attempt to conjure "prehistoric" movements in the choreography, with dancers decked in "bathrobes, animals skins or purple tunics," stamping the "same gesture a hundred times." Half the audience, it seemed, started jeering loudly. Shouts rang out from the orchestra seats to the balconies.

Yet as the ballet continued, others in the theater got swept up with frenetic enthusiasm, a "sort of ejaculatory delirium," as the critic Pierre Lalo put it in *Le Temps*. Neighbors began to "hit each other over the heads with fists, canes or whatever came to hand," Monteux later recalled. Disgusted at the uproar, Stravinsky stormed out, slamming a door behind him, and retreated backstage. For the duration of the thirty-eight-minute performance, which never broke down, Stravinsky stood beside the distraught Nijinsky, who kept shouting inaudible cues to the dancers. "I had to hold

Nijinsky by his clothes, for he was furious, and ready to dash onto the stage at any moment and create a scandal," Stravinsky later recalled.

At the time Paris was a teeming city of three million that boasted not just established opera and ballet companies but the popular Moulin Rouge and Folies Bergère. The savvy Diaghilev stoked what became a craze for Russian music and art in Paris. His company was founded for foreigners and never performed in Russia. As the influential musicologist Richard Taruskin has pointed out, Stravinsky's three career-defining ballets—*The Firebird* (1910), *Petrushka* (1911), and *The Rite of Spring* (1913)—were "composed for cosmopolitan, which is to say Parisian, consumption and were calculated to appeal to an audience that prized Russianness as sexy, violent exoticism."

Born in 1882 in St. Petersburg, where his father was a principal bass singer at the Maryinsky Theater, Stravinsky was scrounging for work when Diaghilev and his Russian agents discovered him in the city in 1909. He had married a cousin, Katya, in 1906 and already had two children to support. (There would eventually be four.) Commissioning this untried composer to write a major work for his new Paris company took a leap of faith on Diaghilev's part.

The Firebird, based on Russian fairy tales and choreographed by Fokine, proved an enormous success at its 1910 premiere. The story and music are steeped in Russian folklore, including tunes Stravinsky borrowed from a handy catalogue of one hundred Russian folk songs that his beloved teacher Nicolai Rimsky-Korsakov had compiled. Stravinsky's score has diaphanous sonorities right out of Debussy. The gyrations of the Firebird are evoked through music steeped in the flickering orchestral effects and murky chromatic harmonies of Scriabin. If at times the musical language has an exotic cast, that quality owes to Rimsky-Korsakov's use of unusual scales, including what came to be labeled the octatonic scale (with eight notes, alternating whole and half steps).

The next year, *Petrushka,* also choreographed by Fokine, gave Stravinsky a second consecutive hit. He composed the piece while flush with childhood memories of carnival festivities in St. Petersburg. The story tells of an ill-fated love triangle between three puppets—the clown Petrushka, the petite Ballerina, and the jealous Moor—who are uncannily brought to life by a magician (called here a Charlatan), or so it appears to a crowd at the fair. The music is run through with angular, catchy folk tunes. The score's most famous excerpt, a breathless Russian dance, is loosely borrowed from a Rimsky work.

Still, the score had radical elements that seem not to have troubled Paris audiences very much, probably because the cinematic colors and kinetic energy of the music were so engaging. Yet there are stretches of metrically fractured rhythmic writing, which disrupt expectations of symmetry, and in-your-face bitonality. The jittery, swirling music of the opening scene—which seems to skip atop but never settle into a steady meter—vividly conjures the frenetic bustle of a street fair.

But *The Rite of Spring* was another matter. For Stravinsky, this score was a fearless salvo. Even some of the enthusiastic reviews can be construed as damning with praise. The French composer Florent Schmitt, extolling Stravinsky's "genius," described the music's evocations of "the prehistoric epoch of a stammering and savage humanity . . . its frenetic agitation . . . the senseless whirl of its hallucinating rhythms . . . its aggregations of harmonies beyond any convention or analysis."

The critic Adolphe Boschet, feigning open-mindedness, said that Stravinsky's "apparent desire" was to create something primitive, to "make his music like noise." To that end, Stravinsky "set to work to destroy any impression of tonality." Boschet was quite wrong.

Whole sections of the *Rite* are written, at least loosely, in keys or modes, including the "primitive," pummeling Dance of the Adolescents. (That fiercely dissonant repeated chord is made up of two standard diatonic chords blended into a bitonal cluster.)

Yes, the music crackles with cluster chords, snarling brass, and hell-bent dissonances. But the most radical elements of the *Rite* were rhythmic. Boschet would have had a stronger case if he had denounced Stravinsky for trying to destroy meter, that is, symmetrical units of pulse. The final Sacrificial Dance, in which a girl enters into a frenzied state and must dance herself to death, hurtles forward in aggressive spurts and mini-phrases that seem unhinged from downbeats. During extended stretches the time signatures change almost measure to measure, with complex shifts like 2/8, 3/16, 3/16, 5/16. It's hard to imagine how Monteux (who in later interviews claimed that he "detested" the piece) managed to keep the orchestra in sync. Over time, the rhythmic writing of twentieth-century music caught up with Stravinsky, you could say, and musicians learned how to execute these shifting meters. Today, any good conservatory orchestra can play the *Rite* comfortably, though in my experience, young newcomers hearing it for the first time, even fans of hard rock and rap, still find the *Rite* a shocker.

Looking back to radical shake-ups of the 1910s and 1920s and thereafter, Leonard Bernstein saw twentieth-century music as split, much like a "river divides into two forks" into "hostile camps," as he said in his Norton Lectures, with "tonal composers," led by Stravinsky on one side, and "non-tonal composers," led by Schoenberg, on the other. Though he was not alone in this view, I think he oversimplified the extent of the divide. Still, Bernstein got it right in characterizing Stravinsky and those he influenced as "seeking to extend musical ambiguities as far as possible by constant new kinds of transformations, but always somehow remaining within the confines of the tonal system." That qualification "somehow remaining" seems crucial.

Stravinsky continued employing the general language of the *Rite* even in works of a very different character, like *Le Rossignol* (The Nightingale), a fairy-tale opera from 1914 that, like the best fairy tales, is often grim and dissonant. When World War I broke out, Stravinsky took his wife and children to neutral Switzerland, where they remained until 1920. While there, fretting about his homeland, he immersed himself in Russian wedding folk lyrics, as he later wrote in his autobiography (an admittedly unreliable, partially ghostwritten book, first published in 1936).

What fascinated him "was not so much the stories," which were "often crude," as the "sequence of the words and syllables, and the cadences they create, which produces an effect on one's sensibilities very closely akin to that of music." The resulting piece, long in gestation, would be *Les Noces* (The Wedding), a ballet and concert work scored for four vocal soloists, mixed chorus, and two batteries of percussion instruments, including four pianos. *Les Noces* is like some alternative, frantically joyous *Rite of Spring*, a raucous, mechanistic, dizzying din of a piece, with catchy tunes and driving riffs.

The Russian Revolution finally made it impossible for Stravinsky to visit his homeland. (He would not see Russia again until 1962.) During the war years, he fashioned a new aesthetic.

On commission from Diaghilev, Stravinsky wrote a very different kind of ballet score, *Pulcinella,* based on a tale from eighteenth-century Italian commedia dell'arte. For the music he refashioned some works by the eighteenth-century composer Pergolesi (or so he thought—some of the borrowed pieces turned out to be by other Italian composers of the period) into a tart, animated, and slightly elusive score. With choreography by Léonide Massine and sets and costumes by Picasso, *Pulcinella* proved a major success at its 1920 Paris premiere.

That same year, working in another vein entirely, Stravinsky composed the Symphonies of Wind Instruments, scored originally for an ensemble of twenty-four wind and brass instruments. In using the plural "symphonies" in the title, Stravinsky was referencing the broader connotation of the Greek word for "sounding together." He dedicated this piece, with its uncanny blend of austere solemnity and captivating colors, to his good friend Debussy, who had died in 1918.

Though written in just one nine-minute movement, the Symphonies of Wind Instruments seems to compress extended episodes into passages of stunning concision made up of clipped, fragmentary phrases, using metrical dislocations as radical as anything in the *Rite* and harmonies voiced with such unusual spacing of pitches as to make essentially tonal chords seem strangely new. Taruskin has persuasively described the piece as a distilled, instrumental stylization of a Russian Orthodox funeral service.

With these seemingly opposite 1920 scores Stravinsky segued into his Neoclassical period. This shift may have been in part a reaction to the global chaos of war or an expression of Stravinsky's well-honed anti-Romantic sensibility. In the most often-quoted comment from his 1936 autobiography, Stravinsky declared that "music is, by its very nature, essentially powerless to express anything at all, whether a feeling, an attitude of mind, a psychological mood, a phenomenon of nature, etc. *Expression* has never been an inherent property of music."

Now, most of us find it impossible to hear *Les Noces,* let alone *The Rite of Spring,* without experiencing the music as expressing something. The comment smacks of aesthetic posturing. Yet it also rings true. Stravinsky goes on to argue that music is "the sole domain in which man realizes the present." And, you can certainly hear *Les Noces* as an attempt to do this very thing: to use music to animate old Russian words in the present moment; and, even more, to establish a coordination between "*man* and *time*," as Stravinsky wrote.

During the 1920s Stravinsky dug even deeper into his anti-Romantic orientation. To Stravinsky, a piece like Schoenberg's *Pierrot lunaire,* for all the radicalism of its mostly atonal language, still carried elements of Germanic, late-Romantic, self-expressive emotionalism. He began, at least in his own mind, to distance himself from his Russian background and to embrace more objective, modernist thinking about music. So music was powerless to express feelings? Then Stravinsky would write music that was, in a sense, about itself. Almost every one of the Neoclassical works he would compose over the next three decades referenced some other, earlier style of music. So these pieces are, in effect, music about other music.

For some, Stravinsky's Neoclassical aesthetic represented a conservative retreat. Indeed, he started writing works whose very titles seemed like throwbacks: Octet for wind instruments, Violin Concerto in D.

Yet even while paying homage to older musical styles, these distilled, formalist scores present another aspect of Stravinsky's modernism. His subtly intricate and beautiful Serenade in A for piano (in four movements: Hymne, Romanza, Rondoletto, and Cadenza Finala) is not really in A major or A minor. You could describe the overall harmonic language as hovering *around* the tone of A, using A as a force of tonal grounding, but nothing more. Even today musicians and scholars analyze Stravinsky's remarkable Neoclassical works, including the Serenade, trying to decipher these chords. How did he come up with these striking notes and rhythms? It still seems miraculous.

A milestone of Stravinsky's Neoclassical period, and one of my favorite pieces of all time, is the Symphony of Psalms, from 1930. Serge Kousse-vitzky, the Russian-born conductor of the Boston Symphony Orchestra, secured the commission for this work to help celebrate the ensemble's fiftieth anniversary. The piece is scored for four-part chorus and an unusual orchestra of winds, brass, timpani, bass drum, harp, two prominent pianos, and only low strings (cellos and basses, but no violins or violas). The symphony's three movements—lasting just twenty-three minutes—set verses from three Psalms of David (Nos. 38, 39, and 150). Stravinsky revealingly wrote to a friend at the time that the psalms are poems of exultation, but also of anger and judgment, even curses. The work is not, he emphasized "a symphony in which I have included psalms to be sung." On the contrary, "It is the singing of psalms that I am symphonizing."

Here is Stravinsky composing music to help him understand, in a sense, earlier music. As I listen, I can almost imagine him asking himself: What is it about the heritage of sacred music that I love? What baffles me? What speaks to me as a contemporary composer?

The opening movement, a setting of "Hear my prayer, O Lord, and give ear unto my cry," begins with a curt, emphatic E minor chord. But the way the notes are doubled and voiced—with wide spaces throughout the instruments—makes the harmony seem elemental and startling, at once ancient and modern. Oboes and a bassoon enter playing restless figurations that evade the implied key, then stop short, as another emphatic, strange E minor chord is struck.

In time, just the altos in the chorus sing a chantlike setting of the opening line of the psalm, "Exaudi orationem meam," that hovers on just two notes (E and F, a half step apart) as the orchestra industriously bustles along playing severe eighth-note riffs that trace chords in arpeggio figures. Then the full chorus breaks out, still dominated by that two-note melodic refrain but backing it with spare-textured, almost elemental-sounding harmonies.

The slow second movement ("I waited patiently for the Lord"), like an homage to a Baroque sacred work, begins with a somber double fugue starting with woodwinds, one instrument at a time, until the chorus enters and takes the music to mysteriously spiritual realms. The final movement ("Alleluia, Praise the Lord") begins counterintuitively. Wistful woodwinds and brass seem to rise hesitantly and halt. Then the chorus sings the most sadly beautiful harmonization of the word "Alleluia" in three chords, the first sung twice, with cellos and basses gently supporting the second and third chords.

In time, the music erupts with bursts of repeated notes and skittish flourishes to evoke the psalm's call to praise the Lord ("Laudate Dominum") with the trumpet, psaltery, harp, and timbrel (an instrument resembling the modern tambourine), and with dance. But the movement ends in an august hymnal episode in which the chorus keeps intoning a simple melodic turn over an orchestral backdrop of pungent, hushed harmonies and a treading bass line. There is one last statement of that aching "Alleluia" before the chantlike "Laudate" melody ends with a final "Dominum" sung on a spacious chord: a C major harmony, but missing the crucial fifth of the triad. There seems to be a hole in the middle of this familiar chord, which gives the sonority a timeless, mystical cast.

After the war Stravinsky moved his family to Paris, but in coming years they spent time in Nice as well. He took a house in Southwest France, in part for his wife's health: Catherine (Katya) had contracted tuberculosis. He also took a mistress, Vera Sudeikina, whom he met in Paris in 1921, the wife of a stage designer who had worked with Diaghilev. They were brazenly open about the relationship; Vera left her husband in 1922. Katya had to endure the humiliation.

Stravinsky made a good living from his compositions, and also from performing his works as a conductor and pianist. Many of his colleagues, not just the Jewish ones, were more outspoken against the Nazis than Stravinsky. Still, by nature he abhorred disorder and disdained the Germans for the savagery and dislocation they inflicted on Europe.

In 1938, while working on his Symphony in C, his elder daughter, who had contracted her mother's tuberculosis, died at twenty-nine. Four months later Katya succumbed; Stravinsky, also ill, was hospitalized for months.

He spent most of the academic year of 1939–1940 in Cambridge, Massachusetts, as the Norton lecturer at Harvard. He and Vera married during these months in a nearby Massachusetts town. Having decided to move to

America, he bought a house in West Hollywood, which meant that for some eleven years he and his supposed rival Schoenberg resided in the same city, though they did not mingle.

The St. Petersburg–born choreographer George Balanchine, nearly twenty-two years Stravinsky's junior, steadily became his closest colleague. Their partnership remains one of the greatest artistic collaborations of the twentieth century. Like Stravinsky, Balanchine was a formalist who brought an abstract, modern sensibility to classical ballet. For Balanchine the subject of dance was dance. He preferred creating ballets unencumbered with stories. Even in devising choreography for Stravinsky's *Apollo* and *Orpheus,* two astonishing scores based on mythological tales, Balanchine made dance itself the focus.

He asked Stravinsky to write a series of pieces for his company, the New York City Ballet. But Balanchine also saw the dance potential in many Stravinsky works that had never been intended as ballet scores. It was not just the complex rhythmic character of the music that attracted Balanchine, but the way the pieces seemed to unfold in blocks: episodes with teeming vitality would simply stop, and something else would happen. For Balanchine these Stravinsky works screamed for dance.

For nearly three years, Stravinsky was consumed with writing an opera, *The Rake's Progress,* which finally had its highly anticipated premiere in Venice, in 1951. Among the attendees were the intellectual elite of contemporary music, composers who had thoroughly embraced twelve-tone techniques and serialism, and were intensely curious to see what the eminent Stravinsky was up to.

Many of them found the resulting work a curious Mozartian takeoff, with a stylized Neoclassical score and a wry, elegantly poetic libretto by W. H. Auden and Chester Kallman. Inspired by a series of Hogarth engravings, the opera tells of the indolent young Tom Rakewell, who inherits a fortune and, rather than turning responsible and marrying his wholesome fiancée, Anne Trulove, is led astray by the Devil in the person of Nick Shadow, who lures Tom into a life of debauchery in London. At the end the Devil is foiled, but not completely: he turns Tom mad. In the last scene, the devoted Anne sings the delusional Tom to sleep in the Bedlam insane asylum.

The music may have struck avant-garde composers as a negligible pastiche of eighteenth-century Italian opera, complete with recitatives accompanied by harpsichord. Yet every measure of this ingenious score represents Stravinsky, the formalist-modernist, tweaking that style, transfiguring it into his own piercing and audacious music. Today *Rake* is rightly included among the handful of twentieth-century opera masterpieces.

Still, the negative reactions and intellectual condescension rattled Stravinsky, who had added a crucial colleague to his inner circle a few years earlier: the aspiring American conductor Robert Craft. Born in 1923, Craft, then twenty-four, wrote to Stravinsky in 1947, eager to conduct the composer's Symphonies of Wind Instruments but unable to locate a score. They met the next year. In short order Craft, who was forty-one years younger, became Stravinsky's secretary, assistant, and surrogate son. With the blessing of Vera, Craft moved into the Stravinsky home.

During the years when Columbia Records engaged Stravinsky to conduct his complete works for a series of historic albums, Craft often rehearsed the orchestras and ensembles in preparation. He also collaborated with Stravinsky on a series of published conversations and chronicles. Some people saw Craft as Stravinsky's invaluable amanuensis, his Boswell. Others considered him a Svengali-like manipulator who authored some of the texts that bore Stravinsky's name.

One thing that Craft fully owned up to was his role in steering Stravinsky to embrace the twelve-tone imperative. "I say in all candor that I provided the path and that I do not believe Stravinsky would ever have taken the direction that he did without me," Craft wrote in 1993. But why this path?

It was Schoenberg who had attracted the attention of a new generation of composers and performers, Craft among them. The twelve-tone method had become too significant to ignore. Stravinsky came to believe that he risked being seen as dated if he did not explore the new language and master the method.

If, indeed, Craft led Stravinsky into taking this step, that says more about Stravinsky than it does about Craft. Stravinsky was a living legend. He made his own decisions; he could have ignored Craft's arguments. Besides, exploring serialism on his own terms gave Stravinsky a jolt of vitality. He wrote a series of, to me and to many, remarkable twelve-tone pieces. One of them is Movements for Piano and Orchestra, composed in 1959, a compact, nine-minute work in five sections, with fleeting interludes between the movements for orchestra alone. Rather than submitting his creativity to a method, Stravinsky devised ways to absorb the twelve-tone technique into his distinctive voice. In place of pulsing rhythmic writing, the piece progresses in short, skittish fragments and statements. Somehow, the austere harmonic allure and precise delineation of textures make the music seem not that far removed in character from Stravinsky's Neoclassical works.

In *Requiem Canticles* (1966), scored for alto and bass soloists, chorus, and orchestra, Stravinsky collapses the imposing legacy of the Latin requiem mass into a fifteen-minute, nine-part, twelve-tone masterpiece. Every aspect of his music seemed uncannily, starkly compressed into small gestures. Yet the music eerily combines Debussy-inspired lushness, ancient solemnity, and pinpoint rhythmic incisiveness, similar to the gestural rhythmic writing of pieces like Movements. *Requiem Canticles* was performed at Stravinsky's funeral in Venice; Vera Stravinsky said that her husband sensed he was writing the piece for himself.

Not surprisingly, Balanchine seized on these twelve-tone scores to turn them into ballets. By the time Stravinsky adopted twelve-tone technique, this music had been around for decades. So in a similar way to his earlier Neoclassical pieces, the subject of Stravinsky's twelve-tone works is twelve-tone music. Here is Stravinsky looking back, offering his thoughts on this technique and language, while transforming it into something new.

On April 6, 1971, a pleasant spring day in New Haven, I arrived at Stoeckel Hall, the main building of the Yale School of Music, a little late for a piano lesson. But I stopped cold at the dark wood front door.

Someone had tacked up a small white note card on which these simple words were written: "Igor Stravinsky died today."

It felt like the floor upon which twentieth-century music stood had suddenly dropped away. I remember thinking about the incredible longevity of Stravinsky's career. He came from the Russia of Rimsky-Korsakov to shake up Paris. In 1912 he and Debussy gathered a group of friends together and played through Part I of *The Rite of Spring* in a preliminary version for piano four-hands. Imagine attending that soirée.

And yet, that very semester, the spring of 1971, in an analysis class I was taking, we had studied the score to *Requiem Canticles,* trying to fathom Stravinsky's adaptation of twelve-tone technique in this five-year-old piece. He was still at the center of twentieth-century music.

The closest I came to meeting him was during the intermission of a New York Philharmonic concert in the early summer of 1966. Leonard Bernstein had organized a Stravinsky festival. The opening program ended with Bernstein conducting a stunning account of *The Rite of Spring.* At the end, Bernstein pointed to Stravinsky in the first tier. The composer stood and waved to Bernstein, the players, and the audience. During intermission he stayed in his seat and I tried to greet him, but an usher kept me away. He did wave, though. At least I think he did.

The final concert in that series ended with Stravinsky conducting the orchestra and chorus in his Symphony of Psalms. He walked out, a frail, stooped old man with a cane, and sat on a stool to conduct. Still, his gestures were brusque, emphatic, and effective.

Imagine being in the hall when Beethoven conducted one of his symphonies. Being there for Stravinsky's performance of his Symphony of Psalms felt like that to me.

BÉLA BARTÓK

During the summer months of 1904 the twenty-three-year-old Béla Bartók stayed at a resort in northern Hungary, where he retreated to practice the piano and work on his compositions. Having finished his training at the

Budapest Academy, he was earning increasing attention as a pianist. The previous year he had played Beethoven's *Emperor* Concerto to acclaim in Vienna and enjoyed a notable debut in Berlin. Still, he was feeling aimless in his career and unsure of himself as a composer.

One day at the resort, he overheard a woman singing in an adjacent room. She was, Bartók later learned, Lidi Dósa, a young woman from Transylvania employed as a maid, who was singing folk songs from her homeland to a child in her care. Fascinated, Bartók approached and asked her to sing it again so he could jot it down.

This chance encounter changed the course of twentieth-century music.

The melodies Dósa sang—and, over subsequent days, Bartók kept asking her to sing more of them—were nothing like the tuneful, easygoing folk songs and dances that Bartók's mother, a schoolteacher who played the piano, had taught him when he was a shy, sickly child growing up in southern Hungary, in the province of Torontál. Dosa's songs, so strange, earthy, and elusive, were certainly different from the popularized Hungarian "gypsy" music Bartók later endured in Budapest cafes—the kinds of tunes that Liszt used in his dazzling Hungarian Rhapsodies.

Bartók had to learn more. In December of that year, in a letter to his sister, he wrote of a new plan: "to collect the finest Hungarian folk songs and to raise them, adding the best possible piano accompaniments, to the level of art-song." From this initial description, Bartók sounds somewhat patronizing about the indigenous music of his homeland. By implication, these melodies and dances needed proper accompaniments to improve them. Bartók soon learned better.

He set about turning himself into what today we call an ethnomusicologist. In 1905 in Budapest, Bartók met the composer Zoltán Kodály, then at work on a dissertation about the poetic and musical phrase structures of Hungarian folk song. In 1906 Bartók and Kodály made a public appeal to the Hungarian people to support a venture to produce a collection of native folk songs, gathered with "scholarly exactitude." They were determined to rescue this heritage from the diluting influx of what they deemed "light music" and "imitative folksongs." As the musicologist Malcolm Gillies has explained, Bartók and Kodály came to idealize "rural peasants" as "the conveyors of the pure musical instincts of the nation."

Over the next few years, sometimes joined by Kodály, Bartók took extended field trips into the Hungarian countryside, collecting tunes, thousands of them, including Slovak, Romanian, Serbian, and Bulgarian melodies and dances. There is a charming 1907 photograph of Bartók in the village of Darázs (now in Croatia) mingling with Slovak peasants in their native dress, showing one woman his small Edison gramophone. Bartók made a series of early recordings for his research, while writing down everything he heard. As he studied the tunes he notated, he increasingly discovered that the music was based on early modes, like the Dorian and Aeolian, and unusual scales, including the pentatonic scale, common to Asian music. He was affected by the expressive powers of this music, which was devoid of sentimentality. And the metrical dislocations of the dance rhythms astonished him.

The most essential task, Bartók felt, involved collecting and publishing the tunes and dances in relatively faithful arrangements, to preserve the heritage, to make the music widely available. He also slightly adapted the melodies and arranged them in sets of songs and dances with more inventive accompaniments. The best-known example is his 1915 Romanian Folk Dances, a suite of six dances for piano, based on Romanian tunes from Transylvania, which Bartók probably heard played on country fiddle or shepherd's flute, or sung. Like countless piano students today, I learned Bartók's Romanian Folk Dances and especially loved the slow, sad one, "Pe loc," with its elegiac melody, odd accents, and clipped grace notes (tinged, as I learned years later, with Aeolian modal and Arabic elements) that waft above a steady two-pulse pattern of minor chords. The rousing, wild-eyed final "Măruntel" dance was a blast to play. I had a big success with Bartók's Romanian dances at a student recital when I was fifteen.

From the start, Bartók purposefully incorporated folk materials into his emerging musical voice, which proved decisive to his development as a modernist master. That understanding really hit me during the summer of 1995, when I attended "Bartók and His World," a two-weekend, fourteen-event festival at Bard College, directed by Leon Botstein. During panels and lectures linked to chamber programs and orchestra concerts, many perspectives on Bartók were offered. But, as I would report in the *New York Times*, one theme kept emerging: that during this fraught period in music history, when some composers were determined to lift themselves above their origins and fashion an international style of cutting-edge modernism, and others seemed hopelessly bound to their provincial backgrounds, Bartók offered an empowering alternative approach. Through his comprehensive explorations of Eastern European folk music, Bartók discovered a wellspring of unvarnished idioms that he assimilated into a musical style that was of a place and yet audaciously modern.

The festival began with a performance by five musicians and two dancers from the Muzsikás Folk Ensemble from Hungary (which still thrives). Like Bartók and Kodály, these musicians had traveled through Eastern Europe learning folk songs from peasants. How close the music they presented at the festival was to what Bartók heard firsthand was hard to say. One scholar on a panel referred to the players as "so-called folk musicians."

Still, I found their performance revelatory. There were plaintive songs with pungent modal melodies; driving dances that thwarted one's expectations of regular meter; some fancy fiddle playing over droning accompaniments supplied by the kontra, a three-stringed viola with a flattened bridge that makes it easier to play thick block chords.

With this raucously captivating music still in mind, I listened keenly for elements of folk music in Bartók's works during subsequent concerts. I was surprised by my reactions. The familiar Romanian Folk Dances, performed vigorously in an arrangement for violin and piano, had never sounded so tame to me. Yet Bartók's astonishing four-movement, twenty-five-minute Sonata for Solo Violin, a late work completed in 1944, and no foray into nationalism, seemed run through with folkloric elements and character. Commissioned by Yehudi Menuhin, the piece was Bartók's contemporary response to the solo violin sonatas of Bach, complete with a fugue movement. Still the music teems with angular, twisting lines, sudden shifts of meter, raw modal harmonies, and raspy chords.

By blending components of folk music into his musical language Bartók found an alternative way to be avant-garde. In a revealing comment, Bartók once explained to Menuhin that he "wanted to show Schoenberg that one can use all twelve tones and still remain tonal." He meant tonal not just in terms of major and minor keys but in a larger, organic sense. For all the thick textures and dissonances in, say, Bartók's formidable Piano Sonata (1926), with its granitic slow movement packed with cluster chords, and for all the jaggedness of the contrapuntal writing in the composer's visionary string quartets, the overall musical language comes across as harmonically grounded in some essential way. Maybe "earthbound" is the better word.

Without his immersion in folk music, Bartók might have developed in an entirely different manner. During his student days he was swept away by Richard Strauss. He described hearing the first Budapest performance of Strauss's epic tone poem *Also sprach Zarathustra* in 1902 as a "lightning stroke" that roused him from "stagnation." He was so enthusiastic about Strauss's *Ein Heldenleben* that he wrote and performed an elaborate piano transcription of the piece. The glittery scoring, plush chromatic harmonic idiom, and episodic structure of that Strauss work permeated Bartók's youthful symphonic poem *Kossuth*, a piece forgotten today.

Bartók may have set about to rescue Hungarian folk music from obscurity, before it was subsumed into popular culture and lost. Yet you could also say that Hungarian folk music rescued Bartók from becoming a Richard Strauss wannabe.

Bartók did not discover Debussy until 1907, when Kodály came back from Paris with scores to peruse. The influence of Debussy, along with effectively embedded elements of Hungarian folk music, runs through Bartók's one-act opera *Bluebeard's Castle*, a disturbing psychological thriller composed in 1911. The libretto is by Béla Bálazs, a writer who, like Bartók, was interested in creating something both idiomatically Hungarian and bracingly modern.

Bartók submitted the score to two opera competitions in Budapest. Deeming it unperformable (due to its musical difficulties) and unworkable (the opera has only two roles and demands a huge orchestra), the jurors rejected it. Bartók revised the score, and *Bluebeard's Castle* made it to the stage of the Budapest Opera in 1918.

Loosely based on a fairy tale by Charles Perrault, set in legendary times, the story begins with the sullen Duke Bluebeard leading his new young wife, Judith, into his bleak Gothic castle. Judith has heard rumors that the fearsome Bluebeard murdered his previous wives. But she seems drawn by his brooding nature and neediness, convinced that her love can bring life to his dark soul.

The main hall of Bluebeard's castle has seven locked doors. Judith insists on knowing what's behind them. Despite warnings from her husband, she is given the keys. Each door reveals fantastical and horrific sights: a torture chamber; an armory of weapons; a horde of bloodied jewels; a sea of tears. The links to Debussy are metaphoric, thematic, and musical. As in *Pelléas et Mélisande,* the story is drenched in ambiguity and implication. Bartók's vocal lines conform closely, almost slavishly, to the contours and sounds of the Hungarian words. Bluebeard's lines have a distinct musical character, steeped in ancient modes, while Judith's radiate chromatic richness. There's very little you could call melodic.

When the door to the bloodied horde of jewels is thrust open, the orchestra erupts in a riot of harps and celesta. Another door reveals a vista of Bluebeard's domain reinforced by the swelling sounds of an organ and brass choir, though the sonorities have dissonant edges and, buried within, clusters so dense they almost swallow you.

Sure enough, the final door reveals three silent, vacant-eyed women: Bluebeard's previous wives, who are, he explains, the loves of his dawns, his noons, and his evenings. Judith, the most beautiful of all, will become the love of his nights.

In what might seem a strange tribute, Bartók dedicated *Bluebeard's Castle* to Márta Ziegler, whom he had married in 1909, when he was twenty-eight and she sixteen. A son, also named Béla, was born the next year. Bartók's chronically poor health, exacerbated by the turmoil in Hungary during the First World War, contributed to the couple's marital problems. Bartók had been called up by the military but was deemed unfit. Romania had entered the war on the Allied side. The threat of military incursions into Budapest stoked tensions within Bartók's small family and curtailed his trips to uncover folk music. He and Márta divorced in 1923, two months before Bartók, then forty-two, married Ditta Pásztory, a piano student of his. She was nineteen, and would become the mother of Bartók's other son, Peter.

Bartók's study of folk music went hand in hand with a deep interest in music education that emanated from a genuine sense of social consciousness. He composed four volumes of short pieces for young piano students, 85 in all, based on folk tunes and dances, a collection published as *For Children,* and still in use. He wrote *Ten Easy Pieces* and other suitable works. Bartók believed that there was no reason for elementary piano students to practice only bland white-key pieces. His works for children—even the easy ones of the five-finger variety—revel in the unusual sounds and modes of indigenous folk music and contain inventive moments in every measure. His most systematic contribution to music education was *Mikrokosmos,* a six-volume series of 153 progressively challenging piano pieces. The first volume, beginning with unison melodies, introduces students to repetitions, syncopations, canons, the Dorian mode, and much more. With each book the musical substance of the pieces becomes more sophisticated along with the technical challenges. Some of the titles are playful, like "Dragon's Dance" and "Village Joke." But most simply identify the challenge at hand, like "Thirds against a Single Voice" and "Broken Chords." The final volume ends with the exciting, technically demanding "Six Dances in Bulgarian Rhythm," and any young pianist who can play these dances is well advanced. Even today, in every home where children study piano, Bartók is part of the family conversation. What could be a greater legacy?

In 1971 I enrolled in an advanced analysis seminar at the Yale School of Music taught by a visiting professor from the Juilliard School, the composer and jazz musician Hall Overton, one of the most impressive musicians I ever encountered. Tall and stocky with thick white hair, Overton, a chain-smoker, was just fifty-one but looked older. He started playing jazz piano during combat service in World War II and later collaborated with Stan Getz, Duke Jordan, and, most awesome to me (a budding jazz fan), the astonishing Thelonious Monk, who chose Overton to score his piano works for orchestra.

Though Overton (who sadly died the next year) did not know Bartók personally, he was close to musicians who had been the composer's colleagues. Overton argued that Bartók essentially had a public and a private style. A composer who put so much energy into pedagogical pieces and devoted himself to collecting folk music had no reservations, Overton suggested, about aiming particular concert works toward a wide audience. In other scores, as Overton saw it, Bartók pushed himself to extremes of experimentation and complexity, understanding that these pieces might be of interest primarily to musicians.

In the seminar we closely analyzed one Bartók piece from each style. Bartók's visionary Music for Strings, Percussion, and Celesta (1936) was the composer's greatest work, Overton suggested, in his public style. The String Quartet No. 3 (1927) was an ingenious, uncompromising piece in Bartók's private style, as Overton saw it.

The originality of the Music for Strings, Percussion, and Celesta begins with its scoring, which includes diverse tam-tams, drums, and xylophone, but no woodwinds or brass. The first movement begins as a bleak fugue for subdued strings, with a theme in four short phrases that moves mostly by half steps and minor thirds within a narrow span of chromatic pitches. Though restrained and steady in tempo, the fugue keeps shifting through time signatures and never feels settled. The musical language is harmonically elusive.

Overton insisted that we all learn how to sing the fugue theme solo, on any *ah* or *dah* syllable we preferred and exactly on pitch, which is not easy. The fugue inexorably builds in intensity and complexity during a fiendish, dissonance-saturated, screeching climax. Then the fugue theme inverts and, having wound its way up to this point, now winds its way down, settling into a hushed, spent conclusion, during which a celesta plays delicate, eerie arpeggios, that segues right into the next movement: a whirling, metrically wild, and percussively pummeling dance. The third movement is an engrossing experiment in Bartók's "night music" style, full of mysterious sonorities, static-seeming passages of ominous, whispered instrumental colors, and stretches of diffuse, thick harmonic writing. The finale bursts forth like a breathless, giddy folk dance.

Overton's take convinced me that Bartók was thinking of mainstream audiences when he wrote this piece. But the composer's six string quartets, written over a span of thirty years between 1909 and 1939, Overton asserted, were mostly intended for insiders.

To Bartók's mind, in his string quartets he was daring to pick up the mantle of Beethoven, especially the audacious late quartets, works that confounded most listeners in Beethoven's day. Bartók won champions for his string quartets, notably the intrepid Kolisch Quartet, which premiered the last two and played all six. These scores are the most compelling examples of Bartók transforming earthy, modal, rhythmically fractured elements of folk music into a blazingly modernist language. His explorations of pioneering string techniques and sounds in these scores have been emulated by every subsequent composer. During that seminar I became obsessed with the Third Quartet, a brooding, turbulent, and tightly structured piece written in one continuous, mood-shifting span, but divided into four parts.

Bartók probably assumed that these quartets would remain beyond general public comprehension for some time. It took a century, even longer, for Beethoven's late quartets to enter the repertory. Bartók would have been amazed at how popular his quartets have become. Adventurous ensembles have given marathon concerts playing all six works, packing concert halls and college auditoriums with eager listeners, young people who respond to the unabashed extremes of the music and don't realize that they are supposed to find these quartets forbidding.

Bartók's life ended sadly. Though a Hungarian patriot, he was a fierce anti-fascist pained by his country's siding with Germany. Yet, with a family to support, he had to be cautious about speaking out too forcefully. After the Nazis came to power in Germany he refused to perform there.

In 1940, with the war worsening, Bartók reluctantly immigrated with Ditta to America, where neither his works nor his renown as a pianist were very well known. They settled in New York City and were joined there in 1942 by Peter, who enlisted in the navy and served during the war. (Béla Jr. remained in Hungary, eventually working for the Hungarian railway company.)

Bartók found some prominent supporters, especially the Hungarian conductor Fritz Reiner. The Columbia University music department appointed Bartók to an associate position with no teaching responsibilities. Instead he worked on a project to transcribe a collection of recordings of Yugoslav folk songs that had been given to the library. Yet he had chronic financial difficulties.

During these years Bartók showed symptoms of leukemia. As his health worsened he received a gratifying major commission from Serge Koussevitzky to write a piece for the Boston Symphony Orchestra. That work, the Concerto for Orchestra, is the final completed example of Bartók at the height of his public style. It received splendid reviews at its 1944 premiere. Bartók lived to see that this piece, at least, would become popular.

The next year he died in a New York hospital at sixty-four. His estate was valued at less than $10,000.

❦ EPILOGUE ❦

In the fall of 1969, the start of my senior year at Yale, I was having lunch one day at a pizza place next to the main music building with a few graduate students and younger faculty members from the School of Music. Most were composers, as I remember. Opera came up. I mentioned how sorry I was to have missed hearing the great tenor Jon Vickers sing the title role of Britten's *Peter Grimes* the previous spring at the Metropolitan Opera.

My comment was mostly met with you've-got-to-be-kidding condescension. The implication was that Benjamin Britten, a composer I revered, was some fusty British conservative whose operas were mawkishly melodramatic.

Such was the general climate that prevailed in academic musical circles at the time. The field incongruously dubbed "contemporary classical music" was essentially split into hostile camps.

On one side were the serialist composers, who claimed the intellectual high ground and held forth from prestigious university posts. Their ranks included the slightly less rigorous rearguard composers who used various adaptations of the twelve-tone method. Schoenberg and his allies in the Second Viennese School, especially Webern, were the acknowledged forefathers of this new language. But starting in the 1950s, serialists like Pierre Boulez had taken composition to levels of complexity and systematization that even Schoenberg never imagined.

On the other side were those composers clinging, however loosely, to tonality. These holdouts were regarded by the self-appointed modernists as, at best, so yesterday and, at worst, a drag on the evolution of music.

To a young musician like me—and I was hardly alone—the schism seemed pointless and confusing. It made the field of contemporary classical music look weirdly disconnected from contemporary culture. Like most sixties youths, my tastes were broad. In my dorm room, along with the recordings of Glenn Gould playing Bach and Rudolf Serkin playing Beethoven, I had albums by Dionne Warwick, Otis Redding, and The Band that I played all the time. I turned several friends on to Miles Davis's *Kind of Blue*. I had trouble winning my roommate over to *Simply Streisand*. The awesome *Abbey Road* had just come out.

At the time I was a member of an undergraduate composer-performer collective that we called Interface, an offshoot of a seminar for music majors. Earlier that semester we had presented a program with several knotty, complex new scores on it. On another night we performed Terry Riley's *In C*, a pioneering work of Minimalism, then only five years old. That Riley concert drew a big crowd to a dining hall of one of Yale's residential colleges, where we played the piece on a large assortment of instruments, including three upright pianos. Curiously, the composers who saw Britten as negligible found *In C* quite fresh and striking.

So from what I could make out, serialism and other complex styles set the intellectual standard for contemporary classical music, while Minimalism and other postmodern ventures emerging just then were accepted as inventive, plucky experiments. It was just those composers hewing in any way to tonal procedures who represented the hopelessly dated middle ground.

The good news is that this absurd battle ended decades ago. Today young composers at colleges and conservatories write any kind of music they want to, drawing upon all manner of techniques, models, and styles. The climate for new music could not be more inviting and open.

Still, the stylistic wars between modernists and traditionalists over many decades stifled creativity and alienated general audiences from contemporary music. Today, among all the performing arts classical music remains the most conservative. In comparison with dance and theater companies,

America's major orchestras and opera houses devote much more of their calendars, and their resources, to the standard repertory. More recently, institutions have been paying more attention to contemporary music, partly, I believe, because their leaders need to draw in new generations of patrons to survive, and young people are by nature curious about what's new—in every realm of life. Still, to maintain goodwill between audiences and living composers into the future, it's important to understand a little about this dismaying, and damaging, period in contemporary music.

As I've argued many times, during the years when composers were employing the most complex methods and procedures, the problem was less about the music they wrote, some of which was fascinating, than the dogma associated with it. As a student I discovered Boulez's *Le Marteau sans maître,* a 1955 vocal work for alto voice and six instruments that sets surrealist poems by René Char. Written with pervasive serialist procedures, the piece sounds astoundingly complex. Yet the music is alive with ravishing sounds, inventive instrumental effects, and intensely animated vocal writing. Though Boulez's jumpy rhythmic idiom negates any hint of a steady pulse, the music courses with breathless energy. When I first listened to a recording of *Marteau,* I found it simultaneously baffling and exhilarating.

Yet back then Boulez was a polemical advocate of serialism. In 1952 he had written: "Every musician who has not felt—we do not say understood, but indeed felt—the necessity of the serial language is USELESS."

What was there to say? I was amazed by Boulez's *Marteau.* But I also loved Britten's *Illuminations,* a 1940 song cycle for soprano (or tenor) and string orchestra, which sets French texts by Rimbaud.

During the late 1970s a roster of composers based in universities were still touting the supremacy of twelve-tone methods. In *Simple Composition,* a 1979 textbook, Charles Wuorinen, a composer and Columbia professor, made this unequivocal pronouncement: "While the tonal system, in an atrophied or vestigial form, is still used today in popular and commercial music, and even occasionally in the works of backward-looking serious composers, it is no longer employed by serious composers of the mainstream," he wrote. "It has been replaced or succeeded by the 12-tone system." Note that serialist composers now constituted the "mainstream."

It must be said that Wuorinen and colleagues in his corner of contemporary music tell a very different story about what happened back then, namely, that it was the serialists who were besieged and powerless, while the Samuel Barbers and John Coriglianos of the day got the big commissions from the Metropolitan Opera and major orchestras. In 1997, for a *New York Times* article by the critic K. Robert Schwarz, Wuorinen debunked as a "big fake" the notion that serialist composers were "a bunch of beady-eyed theoreticians" who were "forcing innocent students to do terrible, nameless things" and write twelve-tone music.

Even if no actual strong-arming was taking place in the field of contemporary classical music, the intimidation factor was quite real. It was easy for composers to fear being marginalized if they did not get with the twelve-tone program.

How did it happen in the first place? It's a complex saga involving a perfect storm of factors, as I see it.

At the dawn of the twentieth century, when the traditional tonal language, having been pushed to extremes, seemed spent (the "crisis of tonality," as Schoenberg put it), contemporary music entered a period of unfettered experimentation. Parallel to this, new developments in recording and radio made music more accessible than ever. So music lovers with a traditionalist orientation could take a pass on the challenging new music of the day and sit at home enjoying their old favorites.

Also, and perhaps related, the economic boon from recordings fostered the emergence of star performers as the heavyweights in classical music. In earlier eras, performers were also composers, like Mozart, Beethoven, Liszt, and Brahms. Though that tradition continued into the twentieth century with figures like Prokofiev and Bartók, for the most part the disciplines of performing and composing became separate specialties. Increasingly, powerful maestros, master pianists maintaining the great repertory, and superstar virtuosos ruled the field, and few of them made their marks by championing living composers—including those many vibrant "middle ground" composers who might have held real appeal for audiences.

As audiences became more entrenched in the standard repertory, composers, feeling squeezed out, retreated into universities. This was both good and bad: good, in that composers had stable livelihoods; bad, in that they got cut off from the public. Much like scholars who wrote articles for journals aimed only at other scholars, composers started writing pieces to impress other composers. Going to a new-music concert during the 1960s often felt like the musical equivalent of attending an academic conference or a workshop demonstrating the latest scientific discoveries.

By the 1970s, the terrain was ripe for a postmodernist backlash. Philip Glass, Steve Reich, and their Minimalist colleagues leapt into the breach, shaking up the field and enticing a new generation into concert halls. Suddenly irreverent experimentation took off, including empowering attempts to find commonalities between diverse contemporary styles.

From his base in Boston, Gunther Schuller fostered what he called the Third Stream, music that drew from both contemporary classical and jazz traditions. In New York the feisty Bang on a Can organization, founded in 1987, championed new voices that synthesized complex contemporary idioms with all kinds of pop, rock, and ethnic music. Composers interested in electronic resources drew inspiration from both the rocker Frank Zappa and the serialist Milton Babbitt, who had helped develop the important Columbia-Princeton Electronic Music Center (now the Computer Music Center at Columbia University) in the 1950s.

Complex methodologies for composition remained. But dogma was no more. Even Boulez mellowed, a process that began in 1971 when, in a stunning development, he became Bernstein's successor as music director of the New York Philharmonic. (His tenure lasted six years.) He used the post, in part, to champion the most challenging new music, while also fostering a general climate of tolerance and discovery at Lincoln Center. As his performing career flourished, Boulez conducted Neoclassical works by Stravinsky that he had earlier deplored and became an acclaimed interpreter of Wagner and Mahler.

Wuorinen has stuck to his principles. But with the new openness in classical music, he no longer comes across as a scold to tonality holdouts. He just writes his pieces his own way. I've met students at Juilliard who relish the challenges of learning and playing Wuorinen's audaciously intricate scores.

The cessation of hostilities allowed different strands of contemporary music to be experienced on their own terms. In 2008, on the day the fearlessly complex composer Elliott Carter turned one hundred, James Levine led the Boston Symphony Orchestra in the New York premiere of Carter's *Interventions* for piano and orchestra at Carnegie Hall with the pianist Daniel Barenboim as soloist. At the end, when the composer, walking unsteadily with a cane, climbed the few stairs to the stage, the audience responded with a prolonged ovation.

Yet that same year Philip Glass, in every way Carter's opposite, received a hero's welcome at the Metropolitan Opera during the ovations on the opening night of a new production of *Satyagraha,* his 1979 opera based on the life of Gandhi. In 1976, when he still sometimes drove a taxi to support himself, Glass had to rent out the Met in order to present his landmark opera *Einstein on the Beach.*

There is a new sense within the field that contemporary music will prosper just fine on its own if we simply give living composers a chance. That so many composers today, unbeholden to any school or aesthetic, draw so deliberately from sundry styles testifies to what feels like an empowering new freedom.

The British composer George Benjamin, for one, has had a much-deserved international success with his 2012 opera *Written on Skin,* with a libretto by Martin Crimp—a gothic tale introduced by a chorus of angels, who recount a story from eight hundred years earlier, a tragic love triangle that we see take place. Though Benjamin's music has mysterious and radiant qualities, the score unabashedly employs complex techniques and styles. *Written on Skin* is a triumph of modernism.

On the other hand, I think of *Fellow Travelers,* a notably successful 2016 opera by a younger team, the composer Gregory Spears and the librettist Greg Pierce, based on Thomas Mallon's 2007 novel. It centers on a troubled gay love affair between two government employees in 1950s Washington, D.C., who get caught up in the "lavender scare" purges and persecutions of the McCarthy era. In his boldly personal score Spears blithely combines two seemingly disparate styles: the melismatic singing of medieval troubadours and American Minimalism. Good for him, I say.

And finally, classical music is addressing centuries-long barriers by giving opportunities to women and minority composers. That the major institutions had much ground to make up was made painfully clear in 2016 when the Metropolitan Opera presented the New York premiere of the Finnish composer Kaija Saariaho's mystical, haunting opera *L'Amour de loin* (2000), a tale of an idealized love from afar between a medieval French troubadour and a princess in Tripoli. Incredibly, this was the first opera by a woman composer at the Met in nearly a century. The conductor, Susanna Mälkki, making her Met debut, became only the fourth woman to lead an opera in the company's history.

Sticking with opera, in 2017 I attended the Opera Philadelphia premiere of *We Shall Not Be Moved,* a collaboration among three African American artists: the composer Daniel Bernard Roumain, the librettist Marc Bamuthi Joseph, and the director (and famed dancer-choreographer) Bill T. Jones. This raw, compelling work looks at the deadly 1985 incident when Philadelphia police, after armed standoffs, dropped bombs on a row house where members of Move, a group of black separatists, had been living, killing eleven people. The fires spread to sixty-five nearby buildings. The opera reflects on that harrowing incident by telling a story of North Philadelphia teenagers in 2017, runaways who take refuge in that abandoned house. Roumain's music skillfully folds gospel, funk, jazz, and sinewy contemporary classical idioms into an urgent and personal score. There are bold stretches of spoken words in the fast-paced, poetic libretto.

Here were three creators claiming the opera genre on their own terms for today's times.

This book has been an attempt to explore the unfathomable achievements of indispensable—and indisputably great—composers. Yet, as I said at the start, the best thing about contemporary music, like contemporary work in all the arts, is that in the moment, questions of greatness are swept aside. Where Spears, Roumain, Saariaho, Benjamin, and dozens of other living composers whose work has affected me will place in the pantheon seems irrelevant right now. We are too close to say, and too immersed in the exciting newness of the music to care.

RECOMMENDED RECORDINGS

BOXED SETS

For many years there have been ominous predictions about the coming demise of the CD, especially within classical music. Yet CDs just keep coming, both new releases and reissues of historic recordings. Of special interest to those hoping to boost their collections quickly are multi-disc boxed sets, often available at bargain prices. These items fall in and out of availability, though with some online searching (or streaming) they are not hard to find. Here are four recommendations.

RUDOLF SERKIN PLAYS BEETHOVEN (SONY CLASSICAL, 11 DISCS)

If you can find this set, grab it. Here are a master pianist's Beethoven recordings from over many years collected into one handy box, containing the five piano concertos, seventeen of the thirty-two piano sonatas (including the last five, with an exhilarating account of the mighty *Hammerklavier*), and other works.

ARTHUR RUBINSTEIN PLAYS CHOPIN (RCA, 10 DISCS)

What to say? An incomparable Chopin pianist in repertory he was born to play. Here are the concertos, mazurkas, ballades, nocturnes, and more.

BERNSTEIN HAYDN (SONY CLASSICAL, 12 DISCS)

"Bernstein Haydn" is how this box is billed, and pairing these two names says it all. Early music specialists have brought new expertise and style to Haydn, but few conductors got Haydn's inventiveness and style the way Bernstein did. This collection includes his recordings with the New York Philharmonic of Haydn's six *Paris* Symphonies, twelve *London* Symphonies, the oratorio *The Creation*, and four masses, including one recorded with the London Symphony Chorus and Orchestra.

MOZART: THE COMPLETE PIANO CONCERTOS
(SONY CLASSICAL, 12 DISCS)

This acclaimed set offers Murray Perahia as pianist soloist and conductor, with the English Chamber Orchestra, in winning accounts of the twenty-seven Mozart piano concertos. The music making combines elegance, brio, and imagination.

INSTRUMENTAL AND CHORAL WORKS

Though this list is frustratingly selective, here are various recommendations of some favorite individual albums and smaller sets, followed by some essential operas.

BACH: MASS IN B MINOR (HARMONIA MUNDI, 2 DISCS)

A fresh period-instrument take on a seminal masterpiece. The probing conductor Philippe Herreweghe draws a lucid, stirring performance from the Collegium Vocale. And the recorded sound is splendid.

BACH: *ST. MATTHEW PASSION* (ARCHIV PRODUKTION, 3 DISCS)

An engrossing and dramatically urgent account from the towering Bach conductor John Eliot Gardiner, leading the Monteverdi Choir, the English Baroque Soloists, and a fine roster of singers.

BARTÓK: SIX STRING QUARTETS
(DEUTSCHE GRAMMOPHON, 2 DISCS)

Bartók's string quartets still come across as shockers—arresting, teeming, and inspired shockers. Take the plunge. You can't go wrong with these 1988 recordings from the early years of the Emerson String Quartet.

BRAHMS: PIANO CONCERTO NO. 2 IN B-FLAT
(RCA RED SEAL/BMG, 1 DISC)

Here is the first recording Sviatoslav Richter made in the United States at the time of his 1960 American debut with the Chicago Symphony Orchestra, Erich Leinsdorf conducting. A colossal recording of a colossal concerto.

MONTEVERDI: VESPERS OF 1610 (CORO, 2 DISCS)

A luminous, splendid account of a choral masterpiece performed by The Sixteen, an exceptional period instrument vocal and instrumental ensemble, conducted with verve and insight by Harry Christophers.

SCHOENBERG: *PIERROT LUNAIRE* AND OTHER WORKS
(DEUTSCHE GRAMMOPHONE, 1 DISC)
There are many fine, compelling recordings of this pathbreaking 1912 song cycle for a narrator (delivering texts in quasi-spoken *Sprechstimme* style) and six-piece instrumental ensemble. This riveting account, with Pierre Boulez leading Christine Schäfer and members of the Ensemble InterContemporain, is especially exciting.

SCHUBERT: *WINTERREISE* (DECCA, 1 DISC)
In 1963, the tenor Peter Pears and the composer (and fine pianist) Benjamin Britten, partners in life and in art, made this sublime recording of Schubert's profound song cycle.

SCHUMANN: PIANO CONCERTO IN A MINOR; GRIEG: PIANO CONCERTO IN A MINOR (EMI CLASSICS, 1 DISC)
These popular concertos have often been paired on recordings. These accounts by the splendid pianist Leif Ove Andsnes and the conductor Mariss Jansons, leading the Berlin Philharmonic, are especially fine.

STRAVINSKY: *LE SACRE DU PRINTEMPS* (THE RITE OF SPRING) (SONY CLASSICAL, 1 DISC)
Leonard Bernstein was my early guide to this piece when I heard him lead the New York Philharmonic in a stunning performance with Stravinsky in the audience. His first recording is still my favorite.

OPERAS

BERG: *WOZZECK* AND *LULU* (DEUTSCHE GRAMMOPHON, 3 DISCS)
Alban Berg's two great operas are pioneering twentieth-century scores, and the masterful Austrian conductor Karl Böhm conveys that in these recordings. But, leading the orchestra of the Deutsche Oper Berlin, Böhm also brings out the vestiges of late Romantic richness and intensity in the music. You hear where Berg was coming from, not just where he was heading to. The 1965 recording of *Wozzeck* offers the great Dietrich Fischer-Dieskau in an anguished account of the title role. The 1968 *Lulu* recording, made live in concert, features Evelyn Lear at her riveting best as Lulu. (This is the incomplete two-act version that Berg left at his death.)

BRITTEN: *PETER GRIMES* (PHILLIPS, 2 DISCS)
Britten wrote the title role of this shattering 1945 work for his partner, Peter Pears, and the historic 1958 recording that features Britten conducting Pears (Decca, 3 discs) is wrenching. But the astonishing tenor Jon Vickers claimed this role as his own and revealed the dark, thwarted sides of Grimes, a dreamy fisherman feared and ostracized by his village neighbors. Vickers's 1978 recording on Phillips, with Colin Davis conducting, is overwhelming.

DEBUSSY: *PELLÉAS ET MÉLISANDE* (SONY, 3 DISCS)
While Pierre Boulez, conducting the orchestra of chorus of the Royal Opera, Covent Garden, brings out the sensual allure and mystery of this symbolist story of ill-fated love, he conducts the score like the pathbreaking work of early twentieth-century modernism it is. The elegant tenor George Shirley and the exquisite soprano Elisabeth Söderström are exceptional as the title characters.

HANDEL: *ORLANDO* (ARCHIV PRODUKTION, 2 DISCS)
Bejun Mehta, the exciting countertenor in the title role of the tormented, love-struck knight Orlando, heads an exceptional cast in the conductor René Jacobs's distinguished 2014 recording with the B'Rock Orchestra of an opera that reveals Handel as a genius of musical drama.

MOZART: *LE NOZZE DI FIGARO* (THE MARRIAGE OF FIGARO)
(DEUTSCHE GRAMMOPHON, 3 DISCS)
There are so many classic recordings of this essential opera, but try the Claudio Abbado's 1994 account with the Vienna Philharmonic and a winning cast.

MOZART: *DIE ZAUBERFLÖTE* (THE MAGIC FLUTE) (EMI CLASSICS, 2 DISCS)
The 1964 recording led by Otto Klemperer with the Philharmonic Orchestra and Chorus will always be my favorite *Magic Flute*. Though Klemperer captures the music's whimsical elements, he also probes deeply and treats the opera as a sublime tale of confused people on a spiritual journey. The matchless cast includes Nicolai Gedda, Lucia Popp, and Walter Berry. (The libretto's spoken dialogue is omitted.)

PUCCINI: *TOSCA* (EMI, 2 DISCS)
With Maria Callas as a blazing, impassioned, and vulnerable Tosca, the ardent tenor Giuseppe di Stefano as Mario, the formidable baritone Titto Gobbi as the villainous Scarpia, and the thrilling conductor Victor de Sabata leading the forces of La Scala in Milan, this 1953 Tosca may be the greatest overall recording of any opera ever made.

VERDI: *AIDA* **(DECCA, 3 DISCS)**
For me, and for many others, Leontyne Price owned the title role. Of her two studio recordings I especially love the first one, from 1962, with the great Jon Vickers as Radames and Georg Solti conducting the orchestra and chorus of the Rome Opera.

VERDI: *FALSTAFF* **(DECCA, 2 DISCS)**
There are several recordings of Verdi's miraculous final opera that I cherish, but if I had to pick one I'd go with Georg Solti's 1963 version starring Geraint Evans, a lively Falstaff, with an ideal cast, especially Alfredo Kraus and the young Mirella Freni as the smitten lovers Fenton and Nannetta.

VERDI: *OTELLO* **(DECCA, 2 DISCS)**
I'll never forget hearing the legendary Renata Tebaldi as Desdemona at the Metropolitan Opera when I was fifteen. Her sumptuous voice comes through beautifully on this classic recording of *Otello,* with the powerhouse tenor Mario del Monaco in the title role and Herbert von Karajan conducting the Vienna Philharmonic.

WAGNER: THE COMPLETE *RING* **(DECCA, 14 DISCS)**
Debates over various *Ring* cycle recordings can turn Wagner fans combative. For me, this first complete *Ring* recorded in a studio, a seven-year project that began in 1958, remains the best overall choice. It's not perfect. But Solti drew glowing, exciting playing from the great Vienna Philharmonic and had a superb cast, with Birgit Nilsson, Wolfgang Windgassen, Hans Hotter, and other great singers.

For a video of a production, though, there is only one choice: the landmark centennial *Ring* staging for the Bayreuth Festival directed by Patrice Chéreau, with Pierre Boulez conducting (Deutsche Grammophon, 8 DVDs). Chéreau interprets Wagner's epic as a story of Industrial Age corruption, pointless greed, and tragically decaying family dynamics.

❦ ACKNOWLEDGMENTS ❦

In many ways this personal look at indispensable composers is the result of six decades immersed in music. So it feels right to acknowledge the teachers who inspired me early on, especially my piano teachers: Gladys Gehrig during my childhood, Donald Currier at Yale University, and Leonard Shure for my doctoral studies at Boston University.

Still, as I explained in the introduction, the specific impetus for the book was my Top Ten Composers project at the *New York Times* in 2011, a two-week series of articles, videos, blog posts, and online interactions with readers in which I attempted to come up with a list, in order, of the all-time top ten composers. This venture was an intellectual game, played seriously.

But many readers, though they enjoyed the game, expressed some frustration with the series. They felt I had much more to say about the composers I grappled with. So I decided to essentially drop the game, open up the examination, and really grapple with the greatness of the composers who have, in a sense, guided me through life as much as my teachers. Though I wanted my essays to be informative, I was determined to make them personal as well. I was not sure how to proceed. For that I will always be grateful to those who embraced the idea and helped me figure out how.

Starting with my agent, Andrew Wylie, who immediately grasped what I wanted to try. Scott Moyers, publisher of Penguin Press, proved eager to take on the project, and from our first meeting at his office his confidence was empowering. Most of all, I want to thank Virginia Smith Younce, my editor, who guided me with such insight, sensitivity, and encouragement. She understood the balance I was striving for: to tell the stories of these composers and their careers in the context of their times, while also bringing in my personal experiences: not just teachers I have had and performances I have heard, but performances I've given from my childhood to recent years. And I thank Ginny especially for being so patient with me, even as my determination to come up with something to say made me dig deeper and, inevitably, take much more time. Ginny is a passionate music lover but not a musician, which made her an ideal editor: she was my target reader.

Her stalwart assistant, Caroline Sydney, provided invaluable help during the later stages of my writing and the editing process. And Bruce Giffords, senior production editor at Penguin Group, tirelessly steered the edited manuscript into final form and publication. Everyone I dealt with at Penguin, including several editors and designers whom I have never met, offered crucial support.

The idea of writing this book may have stemmed from the Top Ten Composers series, but it's truly the result of my work for more than thirty years as a music critic, first as a freelancer at the *Boston Globe,* then, for two decades now, at the *New York Times.* I must thank Richard Dyer, who was the influential music critic at the *Globe* when, in early 1986, he tried me out as a critic and started using me immediately. He believed in my talent and knew I had knowledge, but also sat me down and taught me how to write a lively, to-the-point review, how to do an interview, a feature, a news story. And I was honored that during those early years of my writing career the composer Virgil Thomson, who was one of the best critics ever, became my critic-mentor, offering me practically a one-on-one tutorial.

At the *Times,* I thank Joseph Lelyveld, who as executive editor hired me in 1997, and the culture editors I worked for, among them John Darnton, my first; Jonathan Landman, who encouraged me to do the Top Ten series; Danielle Mattoon, who provided steady support; and now Gilbert Cruz, who was excited about the book as soon as he heard of it. The classical music editors at the *Times* I have worked with— first James Oestreich, then Myra Forsberg, and now Zachary Woolfe—also encouraged me in this endeavor, even when it distracted me from my beat now and then. And I thank the video editors and reporters who have worked with me over the years on my informal music videos, filmed at my apartment, where I sit at the piano and talk about, explain, and play music. Gabe Johnson (now at the *Wall Street Journal*) was especially eager to work with me on these videos and helped me become more informal and relaxed.

୶ NOTES ୶

INTRODUCTION: THE GREATNESS COMPLEX

4 **it traps "a tenaciously living art":** Alex Ross, *Listen to This* (New York: Farrar, Straus & Giroux, 2010), 3.

5 **"great, melancholy, natural scenery":** Edvard Grieg, *Letters to Colleagues and Friends,* ed. Finn Benestad, trans. William H. Halverson (Columbus, Ohio: Peer Gynt Press, 2000), 417.

5 **"taste of cod":** Quoted in Michael White, "The Greatest Pianist of His Generation," *Independent,* June 8, 1996, http://www.independent.co.uk/life-style/the-greatest-pianist-of-his-genera tion-1336170.html.

7 **"almost said a hoax":** Quoted in Nicolas Slonimsky, *Lexicon of Musical Invective* (New York: W. W. Norton, 2000), 44.

11 **"I thought the serial-dominated":** Quoted in Harold C. Schonberg, "A Critic Reflects on 44 Years in the Business," *New York Times,* July 6, 1980.

CHAPTER 1: CREATOR OF MODERN MUSIC

19 **towering Italian master:** Leo Schrade, *Monteverdi: Creator of Modern Music* (New York: W. W. Norton, 1950).

21 **hometown and family background:** Tim Carter, "Monteverdi," *New Grove Dictionary of Music and Musicians,* ed. Stanley Sadie (London: Macmillan, 2001), 17:29.

22 **Parma and Mantua:** Denis Arnold, *Monteverdi* (London: J. M. Dent, 1963), 1.

22 **new realms of sophistication:** Carter, "Monteverdi," 17:29.

23 **women and gambling:** Arnold, *Monteverdi,* 8.

24 **maestro della musica:** Carter, "Monteverdi," 17:30.

24 **the dissonant irregularities:** Arnold, *Monteverdi,* 12.

24 **an easy target:** Carter, "Monteverdi," 17:30.

24 **"service of text expression":** Carter, "Monteverdi," 17:30.

28 **though not quite:** Arnold, *Monteverdi,* 17.

31 **parent to three children:** Carter, "Monteverdi," 17:31.

32 **seemed to help:** *The Letters of Claudio Monteverdi,* trans. Denis Stevens (Cambridge: Cambridge University Press, 1980), 58.

33 **renowned musical heritage:** Carter, "Monteverdi," 17:31–32.

33 **fifty ducats:** Arnold, *Monteverdi,* 26.

33 **took all his money:** *Letters,* 91.

34 **religion and sensuality:** Ellen Rosand, "L'Incoronazione di Poppea," *New Grove Dictionary of Opera,* ed. Stanley Sadie (London: Macmillan, 1992), 2:795.

37 **composed this music:** James R. Oestreich, "A Conductor Celebrates Monteverdi's 450th," *New York Times,* October 14, 2017.

CHAPTER 2: MUSIC FOR USE, DEVOTION, AND PERSONAL PROFIT

39 **"to its founder":** Quoted in C. Stanford Terry, "Bach," in *From Bach to Stravinsky: The History of Music by Its Foremost Critics,* ed. David Ewen (New York: W. W. Norton, 1933), 56.

39 **"a daily confession":** Quoted in Robert Schumann, *On Music and Musicians,* ed. Konrad Wolff, trans. Paul Rosenfeld (New York: W. W. Norton, 1969), 93 (originally published 1946).

39 a **"benevolent god":** Quoted in Edward Lockspeiser, *Debussy* (New York: McGraw-Hill, 1972), 239.

39 **"man *of* God":** Leonard Bernstein, "The Music of Johann Sebastian Bach," in *The Joy of Music* (New York: Simon & Schuster, 1959), 265.

40 simply as **"Genesis 1,1":** *H. L. Mencken on Music,* ed. Louis Cheslock (New York: Schirmer Books, 1975), 185. Originally from *Smart Set,* May 1912, 158.

40 **"invisible to us":** John Eliot Gardiner, *Bach: Music in the Castle of Heaven* (New York: Alfred A. Knopf, 2013), xxv.

41 **"not at all opposed":** Jeremy Denk, "Bach's Music, Back Then and Right Now," *New Republic,* November 15, 2012.

41 **"succeed equally well":** Quoted in Gardiner, *Bach,* xxvi.

41 **"'envy and persecution'":** Quoted in Gardiner, *Bach,* xxvii.

42 **basic music theory:** Christoph Wolff, "Johann Sebastian Bach," *New Grove Dictionary of Music and Musicians,* ed. Stanley Sadie (London: Macmillan, 2001), 2:310.

42 a **"profound"** composer: Wolff, "Bach," 2:310.

43 **guardian of two boys:** Gardiner, *Bach,* 78–79.

43 **"triumph over death":** James R. Gaines, *Evening in the Palace of Reason: Bach Meets Frederick the Great in the Age of Enlightenment* (New York: Harper, 2005), 45.

45 **an elaborate piece:** Hans T. David & Arthur Mendel, eds., *The Bach Reader: A Life of Johann Sebastian Bach in Letters and Documents,* rev. ed. (New York: W. W. Norton), 277.

46 **of whom six survived:** Wolff, "Bach," 2:317.

46 **Christoph Graupner:** David & Mendel, *Bach Reader,* 22.

47 **Mass in B Minor:** Wolff, "Bach," 2:319.

53 **"use and profit":** David & Mendel, *Bach Reader,* 85.

59 **"refresh their spirits":** David & Mendel, *Bach Reader,* 171.

60 **"most overrated keyboard disc":** Quoted in liner notes by Tim Page, *Glenn Gould, A State of Wonder: The Complete Goldberg Variations* (1955 & 1981), Sony Music Classical, 2002.

61 **tempted by opera:** Anthony Tommasini, "Swept Up in Bach's All-Consuming Passion," *New York Times,* October 9, 2014.

63 **"really too expensive":** Quoted in David & Mendel, *Bach Reader,* 183.

CHAPTER 3: "VAST EFFECTS WITH SIMPLE MEANS"

66 **by significant artists:** Handel & Hendrix in London, http://handelhendrix.org.

67 **loose in practice:** Ellen T. Harris, *George Frideric Handel: A Life with Friends* (New York: W. W. Norton, 2014), 203.

68 **friend Anne Donnellan:** Harris, *Handel,* 7.

68 **in Great Britain ever since:** Harris, *Handel,* 1–2.

68 **identity of Great Britain:** Harris, *Handel,* 2.

69 **and died wealthy:** Harris, *Handel,* 55.

69 **"exempt from pedantry":** Harris, *Handel,* 12.

70 **"with simple means":** Quoted in *Beethoven: The Man and the Artist, as Revealed in His Own Words,* ed. Friedrich Kerst, trans. Henry Edward Krehbiel (New York: B. W. Huebsch, 1905), 54.

71 **his provincial hometown:** Harris, *Handel,* 17.

71 **we have to go on:** Anthony Hicks, "George Frideric Handel," *New Grove Dictionary of Music and Musicians,* ed. Stanley Sadie (London: Macmillan, 2001) 10:748.

71 **in civil law:** Hicks, "Handel," 748.

72 **took the boy along:** Harris, *Handel,* 18.

72 **voices and instruments:** Harris, *Handel,* 19.

72 **public opera house:** Hicks, "Handel," 10:748.

73 **was now no composer:** Harris, *Handel,* 23–24.

73 **just one intermission:** Anthony Tommasini, "Duets, Ensembles, Dance Music and Arias, All in the Lobby," *New York Times,* May 31, 2012.

74 **embryonic opera scenes:** Winton Dean, *Handel and the Opera Seria* (Berkeley: University of California Press, 1969), 25.

75 **after every aria:** Harris, *Handel*, 28.

75 **naturalized British subject:** Harris, *Handel*, 31–32.

75 **"courts of Italy":** Quoted in Dean, *Handel*, 5.

76 **scenes and decorations:** Edward J. Dent, *Handel* (Port Washington: Kennikat Press, 1972; first published in London, 1934), 45–46.

77 **"near as possible antidramatic":** Quoted in Dean, *Handel*, 19.

78 **"of his age":** Dean, *Handel*, 2.

79 **a terrible rush job:** Dent, *Handel*, 40.

80 **to musical matters:** Anthony Tommasini, "Jerusalem under Siege, a Sorceress Intervenes," *New York Times*, March 2, 2012.

81 **feel more intimate:** Anthony Tommasini, "Handel Discovers Big Home at the Met," *New York Times*, December 4, 2004.

82 **suffering grows worse:** English translation of libretto by Kenneth Chalmers, 1987, in George Friderik Handel, *Rodelinda*, Il Complesso Barocco, orchestra. Conductor, Alan Curtis. Archiv Produktion, 2005, audio CD.

83 **in Handel's works:** Dean, *Handel*, 32.

84 **"the solar system":** Quoted in Andrew Porter, "Love's Mazes," *New Yorker*, February 22, 1982.

85 **"struck me as near-miraculous":** Porter, "Love's Mazes."

86 **"stroke of the palsy":** Quoted in Edward Blakeman, *The Faber Pocket Guide to Handel* (London: Faber & Faber, 2009), 87.

86 **"forgotten than recorded":** Quoted in Blakeman, *Handel*, 88.

86 **"can well be imagined":** Quoted in Blakeman, *Handel*, 88.

86 **was an "irrational entertainment":** Quoted in Hicks, "Handel," 10:753.

87 **urged them on:** Julianne Baird, "Mr. Handel and His Singers," http://juliannebaird.camden .rutgers.edu/HprogramNotes.htm.

88 **Great Music Hall:** Hicks, "Handel," 10:758.

90 **anguish and pensive self-reflection:** Anthony Tommasini, "Once a Flop, a Handel Departure Is Celebrated," *New York Times*, October 9, 2014.

90 **"hearing him perform":** Quoted in Blakeman, *Handel*, 103.

CHAPTER 4: THE "VIENNA FOUR"

92 **for his compositions:** James Webster, "(Franz) Joseph Haydn," *New Grove Dictionary of Music and Musicians*, ed. Stanley Sadie (London: Macmillan, 2001), 11:171.

93 **"in our own":** Harvey Sachs, *The Ninth: Beethoven and the World in 1824* (New York: Random House, 2010), 28.

CHAPTER 5: "I HAD TO BE ORIGINAL"

97 **becoming a priest:** A. C. Dies, in *Haydn: Two Contemporary Portraits*, trans. Vernon Gotwals (Madison: University of Wisconsin Press, 1968), 80–81.

97 **convivial family evenings:** G. A. Griesinger, in *Haydn: Two Contemporary Portraits*, trans. Vernon Gotwals (Madison: University of Wisconsin Press, 1968), 9.

98 **"thrashings than food":** Quoted in Griesinger, *Haydn*, 9.

98 **this prestigious institution:** James Webster, "(Franz) Joseph Haydn," *New Grove Dictionary of Music and Musicians*, ed. Stanley Sadie (London: Macmillan, 2001), 11:172.

98 **was still intact:** Griesinger, *Haydn*, 11.

98 **on his own:** Griesinger, *Haydn*, 10.

99 **"great and unknown world":** Dies, *Haydn*, 89.

99 **fluent in Italian:** Griesinger, *Haydn*, 12.

99 **giving private lessons:** Webster, "Haydn," 11:174.

100 **"suited him thoroughly":** Quoted in Griesinger, *Haydn*, 15.

100 **"or an artist":** Griesinger, *Haydn*, 15–16.

101 **de facto music director:** Webster, "Haydn," 11:176.

101 **and "fashion follower":** Quoted in H. C. Robbins Landon, *Oxford Composer Companions: Haydn* (New York: Oxford University Press, 2002), 436.

102 **historical curiosity today:** Webster, "Haydn," 11:177.

102 **in London and Paris:** Webster, "Haydn," 11:181.

102 **separate fee for each:** Webster, "Haydn," 11:181.

103 **"had to be original":** Quoted in Griesinger, *Haydn,* 17.

104 **go to the country:** Webster, "Haydn," 11:179.

104 **brought in from Vienna:** Webster, "Haydn," 11:180.

105 **"or anyone to follow":** Bernard Holland, "Quartets as Mirrors of Haydn," *New York Times,* January 22, 2002, http://www.nytimes.com/2002/01/22/arts/music-review-quartets-as-mirrors -of-haydn.html.

110 **period of his life:** Webster, "Haydn," 11:184.

111 **"sighed for release":** Quoted in Webster, "Haydn," 11:191.

111 **"should not outdo me":** Quoted in Griesinger, *Haydn,* 33.

112 **world did not end:** Anthony Tommasini, "No Requiem for Earth, Only Celebration," *New York Times,* December 25, 2012.

CHAPTER 6: "RIGHT HERE IN MY NOODLE"

114 **was about ten:** Cliff Risen & Stanley Sadie, "Wolfgang Amadeus Mozart," *New Grove Dictionary of Music and Musicians,* ed. Stanley Sadie (London: Macmillan), 17:276.

114 **rebellious streak:** Maynard Solomon, *Mozart: A Life* (New York: Harper, 1995), 28.

114 **potential way out:** Risen & Sadie, "Leopold Mozart," 17:270.

115 **homes of noblemen:** Risen & Sadie, "Mozart," 17:276–77.

115 **salary at court:** Jane Glover, *Mozart's Women: His Family, His Friends, His Music* (New York: Harper, 2005), 18.

115 **Nannerl, almost twelve:** Glover, *Mozart's Women,* 19.

115 **for eight days:** Solomon, *Mozart,* 53–54.

116 **"beyond all conception":** *Letters of Wolfgang Amadeus Mozart,* ed. Hans Mersmann, trans. M. M. Bozman (New York: Dover, 1972), 3 (originally published 1928).

116 **rings, and necklaces:** Glover, *Mozart's Women,* 27.

117 **died in infancy:** Glover, *Mozart's Women,* 95–97.

117 **before hearing a note:** Risen & Sadie, "Mozart," 17:279–80.

118 **"all mannerist traces":** Charles Rosen, *The Classical Style: Haydn, Mozart, Beethoven,* rev. ed. (New York: W. W. Norton, 1997), 59.

120 **all of the above:** Glover, *Mozart's Women,* 58–59.

120 **"pursuit of pleasure":** Quoted in Solomon, *Mozart,* 166.

121 **all of whom became singers:** Glover, *Mozart's Women,* 72.

121 **"against the world":** Solomon, *Mozart,* 213.

121 **"amazement and horror!":** *Letters,* 69.

121 **"even for an hour!":** *Letters,* 72.

122 **begun in 1725:** *Letters,* 105–8.

123 **wrote to Leopold:** *Mozart's Letters, Mozart's Life,* ed. & trans. Robert Spaethling (New York: W. W. Norton, 2000), 255.

123 **and stood firm:** Risen & Sadie, "Mozart," 17:284.

123 **"to avenge myself":** *Mozart's Letters,* 269.

124 **"so far as have mine":** *Letters,* 202.

125 **"dropping from your boat":** Peter Shaffer, *Amadeus* (New York: Harper, 1981), 16.

126 **"had me trembling":** Shaffer, *Amadeus,* 18.

127 **"rest's just scribbling":** Shaffer, *Amadeus,* 58.

129 **"without knowing why":** *Mozart's Letters,* 336.

131 **a letter to Nannerl:** Risen & Sadie, "Mozart," 17:287–88.

131 **of sincere friendship:** *Mozart's Letters,* 375.

136 **among his listeners:** Wye Jamison Allanbrook, *Rhythmic Gesture in Mozart: Le Nozze di Figaro and Don Giovanni* (Chicago: University of Chicago Press, 1983), 2–3.

139 **"is scarcely started":** *A Virgil Thomson Reader,* ed. John Rockwell (Boston: Houghton Mifflin, 1981), 206–7.

144 **and do the math:** Anthony Tommasini, "If Mozart Had Had Better Health Care," *New York Times,* September 17, 2006.

CHAPTER 7: THE GIFT OF INEVITABILITY

·149 **"listening to Beethoven":** Leonard Bernstein, *The Joy of Music* (New York: Simon & Schuster, 1959), 29.
150 **Ludwig's later life:** Joseph Kerman & Alan Tyson with Scott G. Burnham, "Ludwig van Beethoven," *New Grove Dictionary of Music and Musicians,* ed. Stanley Sadie (London: Macmillan, 2001), 3:73.
150 **plenty to eat:** Jan Swafford, *Beethoven: Anguish and Triumph* (New York: Houghton Mifflin, 2014), 23.
150 **stories, sometimes torturous:** Swafford, *Beethoven,* 32.
150 **is not clear:** Kerman & Tyson, "Beethoven," 3:73.
151 **"to violent passions":** Quoted in *Beethoven: Impressions by His Contemporaries* (New York: Dover, 1967, 15 (originally published 1926).
152 **"my youthful works":** *Beethoven's Letters,* ed. A. Eaglefield Hull, trans. J. S. Shedlock (New York: Dover, 1972), 1 (originally published 1926).
152 **to the boy:** Kerman & Tyson, "Beethoven," 3:74.
153 **a mentor in, Mozart:** Swafford, *Beethoven,* 90–91.
153 **"my best friend":** *Beethoven's Letters,* 2.
153 **and the theater:** Kerman & Tyson, "Beethoven," 3:74.
154 **a work of his:** Kerman & Tyson, "Beethoven," 3:75.
154 **"rules of grammar":** *Beethoven: Impressions,* 15.
154 **with Haydn's sanction:** *Beethoven: Impressions,* 15–16.
155 **"extrinsic, nonmusical metaphors":** Leonard Bernstein, *The Unanswered Question: Six Talks at Harvard* (Cambridge, Mass.: Harvard University Press, 1976), 157.
156 **"tune in F major":** Bernstein, *Unanswered Question,* 159.
156 **"the *only* material":** Bernstein, *Unanswered Question,* 157.
158 **"of a rivulet":** Harold C. Schonberg, *The Great Pianists* (New York: Simon & Schuster, 1963), 72.
159 **"of barbarous chords":** Quoted in Nicolas Slonimsky, *Lexicon of Musical Invective* (New York: W. W. Norton, 2000), 42.
160 **"to the music":** *Beethoven: Impressions,* 58.
160 **"crockery at them":** *H. L. Mencken on Music,* ed. Louis Cheslock (New York: Schirmer Books, 1975), 40.
160 **"and they pay":** *Beethoven's Letters,* 19.
160 **"they say to this?":** *Beethoven's Letters,* 20.
160 **"can ever be healed":** *Beethoven's Letters,* 17.
163 **"for I am deaf":** *Beethoven's Letters,* 38.
163 **"came before him":** Alex Ross, "Deus Ex Musica," *New Yorker,* October 20, 2014, 44.
163 **"a sonic revelation":** Ross, "Deus," 44.
164 **"of terror, of pain":** Ross, "Deus," 44.
165 **"confused and unintelligible":** Quoted in Slonimsky, *Lexicon,* 46.
165 **"a move to Paris":** Ross, "Deus," 46.
165 **"himself and the world":** Swafford, *Beethoven,* 363.
166 **"great and so forth":** Quoted in Leo Carey, "The Beethoven Mystery Case," *New York Review of Books,* October 23, 2014, 34.
167 **"third element, or synthesis":** *A Virgil Thomson Reader,* ed. John Rockwell (Boston: Houghton Mifflin, 1981), 267–68.
168 **solo piano improvisations:** Kerman & Tyson, "Beethoven," 3:84.
170 **married his companion:** Maynard Solomon, *Beethoven,* 2nd rev. ed. (New York: Schirmer Books, 1998; originally published 1977), 282.
170 **joint custody of Karl:** Kerman & Tyson, "Beethoven," 3:89.
170 **won sole guardianship:** Kerman & Tyson, "Beethoven," 3:89.
171 **bullets only grazed him:** Kerman & Tyson, "Beethoven," 3:94.
171 **"over his hands":** *Beethoven: Impressions,* 167.
172 **"to teach *Minerva*":** *Beethoven's Letters,* 342.

CHAPTER 8: "WHEN I WISHED TO SING OF LOVE IT TURNED TO SORROW"

175 **he grew impatient:** Robert Winter, "Franz (Peter) Schubert," *New Grove Dictionary of Music and Musicians,* ed. Stanley Sadie (London: Macmillan, 2001), 22:657.

176 **Schubert playing viola:** Winter, "Schubert," 22:657.

176 **a lifelong friend:** Winter, "Schubert," 22:656.

177 **"his song-writing destiny":** Graham Johnson, *Franz Schubert: The Complete Songs* (New Haven: Yale University Press, 2014), 1:794.

177 **"My peace is gone":** Quoted in Johnson, *Schubert,* 1:793.

177 **"drained of expression":** Quoted in Johnson, *Schubert,* 1:796.

178 **"experienced such feelings":** Tom Huizenga, "After 200 Years, a Schubert Song Still Resonates," *Deceptive Cadence,* October 19, 2014, https://www.npr.org/sections/deceptivecadence/2014/10/19/352513546/after-200-years-a-schubert-song-still-resonates.

179 **"how often do I!":** *Franz Schubert's Letters and Other Writings,* ed. Otto Erich Deutsch, trans. Venetia Savile (New York: Vienna House, 1974), 51 (originally published 1928).

179 **"one is kept busy!":** *Schubert's Letters,* 54.

180 **with solid finances:** Winter, "Schubert," 22:666.

181 **"eagerly burning sensuality":** Quoted in Maynard Solomon, "Franz Schubert and the Peacocks of Benvenuto Cellini," *19th-Century Music,* vol. 12, no. 3 (Spring 1989), 193.

181 **"sociability and melancholy":** Quoted in Solomon, "Schubert," 193.

181 **"cesspool of slime":** Quoted in Solomon, "Schubert," 194.

181 **"or wanton sensuality":** *Schubert's Letters,* 32.

182 **"they ought to be":** *Schubert's Letters,* 31–32.

182 **underage boys, in Vienna:** Solomon, "Schubert," 201.

183 **sign of Schubert's homosexuality:** Anthony Tommasini, "'Outing' Some 'In' Composers," *New York Times,* August 6, 1995.

186 **"from his sight":** *Schubert's Letters,* 59.

186 **"for me into love":** *Schubert's Letters,* 60.

187 **school for good:** *Schubert's Letters,* 59n.

187 **in Schubert's life:** Solomon, "Schubert," 197.

187 **"Schubert's honest susceptibility":** Winter, "Schubert," 22:659.

187 **"you once were":** *Schubert's Letters,* 75.

188 **lodgings with Schober:** Solomon, "Schubert," 197.

188 **"history of Western music":** Winter, "Schubert," 22:658.

188 **"for the applause":** *Schubert's Letters,* 26.

189 **"to us again, transformed":** Ian Bostridge, "The Magic in Schubert's Songs," *New York Review of Books,* April 2, 2015, 60.

189 **I thank you:** Quoted in Johnson, *Schubert,* 1:175.

190 **dead in his arms:** Johnson, *Schubert,* 1:518.

190 **met in 1817:** Winter, "Schubert," 22:661.

191 **"out of it":** *Schubert's Letters,* 74.

191 **"in Upper Austria":** Solomon, "Schubert," 200.

191 **and his circle:** Solomon, "Schubert," 203.

193 **tried out as well:** Winter, "Schubert," 22:664.

194 **in severe punishments:** Ian Bostridge, *Schubert's Winter Journey: Anatomy of an Obsession* (New York: Alfred A. Knopf, 2015), 221.

194 **"a severe reprimand":** Bostridge, *Schubert's Winter Journey,* 224.

194 **"badly with me too":** *Schubert's Letters,* 121.

195 **"makes me pretty furious":** *Schubert's Letters,* 42.

196 **carried this infection:** Winter, "Schubert," 22:665.

197 **impact of his illness:** *Schubert's Letters,* 78.

198 **"then, my path":** Quoted in Johnson, *Schubert,* 2:812.

200 **for their daughter:** Bostridge, *Schubert's Winter Journey,* 9.

200 **"Let stray dogs howl":** Quoted in Johnson, *Schubert,* 3:630.

202 **"like them too":** Quoted in Winter, "Schubert," 22:673.

202 **"armchair and bed":** *Schubert's Letters,* 143.

CHAPTER 9: AN UNFORGETTABLE DAY IN 1836

206 "the artists here": Frédéric Chopin, *Chopin's Letters*, ed. Henryk Opieński, trans. E. L. Voynich (New York: Dover, 1988), 54 (originally published 1931).

206 "the orchestra's *tutti*": *Chopin's Letters*, 53–54.

207 "very much to myself": *Chopin's Letters*, 192.

208 device for practicing: John Daverio, "Robert Schumann," *New Grove Dictionary of Music and Musicians*, ed. Stanley Sadie (London: Macmillan, 2001), 22:763.

209 crack down on Poland: Kornel Michałowski & Jim Samson, "Fryderyk Chopin," *New Grove Dictionary of Music and Musicians*, ed. Stanley Sadie (London: Macmillan, 2001), 5:708.

209 demonstrations in Paris: Tad Szulc, *Chopin in Paris: The Life and Times of the Romantic Composer* (New York: Scribner, 1998), 20.

209 "premonitions and recollections": Daverio, "Schumann," 22:764.

210 great Polish opera: Arthur Hedley, "Chopin: The Man," in *The Chopin Companion: Profiles of the Man and the Musician*, 2nd ed., ed. Alan Walker (New York: W. W. Norton, 1973), 13–14.

211 in Schumann's words: Daverio, "Schumann," 22:767.

212 in an adjacent building: Michałowski & Samson, "Chopin," 5:706–7.

212 among the elite: Michałowski & Samson, "Chopin," 5:707.

212 self-taught as a pianist: Michałowski & Samson, "Chopin," 5:707.

212 "exceptional talent, musical genius": Quoted in Michałowski & Samson, "Chopin," 5:707.

213 "gentlemen, a genius": Robert Schumann, *On Music and Musicians*, ed. Konrad Wolff, trans. Paul Rosenfeld (New York: W. W. Norton, 1969), 126 (originally published 1946).

214 a lyrical line: Joao Paulo Casarotti, "Chopin the Teacher," http://www.forte-piano-pianissimo .com/Chopin-the-Teacher.html.

214 "our bel canto": Quoted in Owen Jander, "Bel Canto," *New Grove Dictionary of Opera*, ed. Stanley Sadie (London: Macmillan, 1992), 1:381.

216 "its throat cut": Quoted in John Warrick & Sandro Corti, "Gilbert(-Louis) Deprez," *New Grove Dictionary of Opera*, ed. Stanley Sadie (London: Macmillan, 1992), 1:1281.

218 "praises of the journalists": *Chopin's Letters*, 76.

218 culture in music: Michałowski & Samson, "Chopin," 5:708.

220 of the Russians: Michałowski & Samson, "Chopin," 5:708.

220 "bear this feeling": *Chopin's Letters*, 149–50.

221 "so many virtuosi": *Chopin's Letters*, 154.

221 "Kalkbrenner is his equal": *Chopin's Letters*, 154.

222 in his day: George Steiner, "Liszt Superstar," *New Yorker*, June 3, 1983, 126.

223 "We are such snobs": Quoted in Anthony Tommasini, "Horowitz at 85: Still Playing Free," *New York Times*, September 25, 1988, http://www.nytimes.com/1988/09/25/arts/horowitz-at-85-still -playing-free.html.

224 as a pianist: *Chopin's Letters*, 160–61.

224 "faces oppress me": Quoted in Franz Liszt, *Life of Chopin*, trans. Martha Walker Cook (New York: Dover, 2005), 46 (originally published 1863).

225 show "feverish vehemence": Frederick Niecks, *Frederick Chopin as a Man and Musician* (Neptune City, N.J.: Paganiniana Publications, 1983), 2:183 (originally published 1888).

227 "is not music": Schumann, *On Music*, 142.

227 horrific, final outburst: Michałowski & Samson, "Chopin," 5:720.

229 "really a woman?": Michałowski & Samson, "Chopin," 5:709.

230 accommodations proved difficult: Michałowski & Samson, "Chopin," 5:709.

230 company in Paris: Szulc, *Chopin in Paris*, 213.

230 "judging things human": George Sand, *Lucrezia Floriani*, trans. Julius Eker (Chicago: Academy Chicago Publishers, 1985), 10 (originally published 1847).

230 "remote to him": Sand, *Lucrezia*, 11.

232 "fever of indecision": *Chopin's Letters*, 391.

232 reunion in Carlsbad: Michałowski & Samson, "Chopin," 5:712.

232 a second mother: Peter Ostwald with Lise Deschamps Ostwald, *Schumann: The Inner Voices of a Musical Genius*, rev. ed. (Boston: Northeastern University Press, 2010), 15.

232 the boy's improvisations: Ostwald, *Schumann*, 19.

232 **music studies continued:** Daverio, "Schumann," 22:760.

233 **with mental instability:** Ostwald, *Schumann,* 21.

233 **for music and literature:** Daverio, "Schumann," 22:761.

233 **"my inner being":** Daverio, "Schumann," 22:761.

233 **major touring pianist:** Anna Beer, *Sounds and Sweet Airs: The Forgotten Women of Classical Music* (London: Oneworld Publications, 2016), 205.

234 **bungled a performance:** Beer, *Sounds,* 207.

234 **foster in Clara:** Beer, *Sounds,* 208.

234 **about the same:** Daverio, "Schumann," 22:762.

234 **joined the festivities:** Beer, *Sounds,* 209.

235 **as a pianist:** Daverio, "Schumann," 22:763.

235 **final mental breakdown:** Daverio, "Schumann," 22:765.

235 **major affective disorder:** Ostwald, *Schumann,* 303.

235 **contracted syphilis:** John Daverio, *Robert Schumann: Herald of a "New Poetic Age"* (New York: Oxford University Press, 1997), 484.

236 **owner and editor:** Daverio, "Schumann," 22:766.

236 **"honor once again":** Schumann, *On Music,* 25.

236 **"in humorous fashion":** Schumann, *On Music,* 26.

236 **bring social disadvantages:** Daverio, "Schumann," 22:767.

237 **"lament for Clara":** Daverio, "Schumann," 22:768.

238 **"you will smile fondly":** Quoted in Ostwald, *Schumann,* 140–41.

241 **considered themselves pledged:** Ostwald, *Schumann,* 129.

241 **named for her:** Beer, *Sounds,* 215.

241 **"things more easily":** Beer, *Sounds,* 220.

241 **"my music and I":** Beer, *Sounds,* 220.

242 **endeavor than performing:** Beer, *Sounds,* 224.

242 **"work of a woman":** Beer, *Sounds,* 227.

243 **write dramatic works:** Daverio, "Schumann," 22:777.

243 **"wears me out":** Quoted in Ostwald, *Schumann,* 140.

244 **"have stood watch":** Schumann, *On Music,* 253.

244 **the icy waters:** Ostwald, *Schumann,* 1.

245 **he seemed calm:** Ostwald, *Schumann,* 6–7.

245 **suburb of Bonn:** Ostwald, *Schumann,* 9.

245 **might shock her:** Daverio, *Robert Schumann,* 487.

245 **in her diary:** Quoted in Daverio, *Robert Schumann,* 488.

CHAPTER 10: THE ITALIAN REFORMER AND THE GERMAN FUTURIST

248 **"yet understand everything":** Quoted in Richard Taruskin, *The Oxford History of Western Music* (New York: Oxford University Press, 2005), 3:563.

249 **this paid position:** Roger Parker, "Verdi," *New Grove Dictionary of Music and Musicians,* ed. Stanley Sadie (London: Macmillan, 2001), 26:435.

250 **"culture and commerce":** Mary Jane Phillips-Matz, *Verdi: A Biography* (New York: Oxford University Press, 1993), 24.

250 **have been lost:** Phillips-Matz, *Verdi,* 30.

250 **in Verdi's promise:** Phillips-Matz, *Verdi,* 37.

250 **at the conservatory:** Parker, "Verdi," 26:435.

250 **piano technique unconventional:** Parker, "Verdi," 26:435.

250 **"like a father":** *Letters of Giuseppe Verdi,* ed. & trans. Charles Osborne (New York: Holt, 1972), 140.

251 **Milanese musical circles:** Parker, "Verdi," 26:435.

251 **to civil records:** Phillips-Matz, *Verdi,* 101.

251 **from music completely:** Parker, "Verdi," 26:436.

252 ***Nabucco* for Merelli:** Charles Osborne, *The Complete Operas of Verdi* (New York: Da Capo, 1969), 48.

252 **"opera was written":** Quoted in Osborne, *Operas of Verdi,* 48.

253 **begun a relationship:** Parker, "Verdi," 26:437.

253 **"I boast of it":** *Letters of Verdi,* 83–84.

253 **family in attendance:** Parker, "Verdi," 26:447.
254 **"right and proper":** Quoted in Parker, "Verdi," 26:439.
255 **"creations of man":** Quoted in Julian Budden, *The Operas of Verdi* (New York: Oxford University Press, 1973), 270.
256 **he insisted, even "diabolic":** *Letters of Verdi*, 59.
257 **attended few sessions:** Parker, "Verdi," 26:447.
257 **1832 Paris premiere:** Osborne, *Operas of Verdi*, 228.
258 **as *La maledizione*:** Osborne, *Operas of Verdi*, 227.
259 **"give it character":** *Letters of Verdi*, 76–77.
264 **her white lover:** Anthony Tommasini, "From Diva to Unlikely Movie Star, at 90," *New York Times*, December 24, 2017.
264 **"was my costume":** Anthony Tommasini, "Aida Takes Her Story to Harlem," *New York Times*, May 30, 2000.
267 **as crowds cheered:** Osborne, *Operas of Verdi*, 416.
268 **"How? . . . Who knows":** Quoted in Osborne, *Operas of Verdi*, 434.
268 **"put on at Sant'Agata":** *Letters of Verdi*, 246.
270 **in Bayreuth, Germany:** Frederic Spotts, *Bayreuth: A History of the Wagner Festival* (New Haven: Yale University Press, 1994), 172.
270 **"cultural values alone":** Quoted in Spotts, *Bayreuth*, 164.
271 **"to cultural sterility":** Barry Millington, "Richard Wagner," *New Grove Dictionary of Music and Musicians*, ed. Stanley Sadie (London: Macmillan, 2001), 26:935.
272 **in opera, to attend:** Spotts, *Bayreuth*, 165.
272 **from the festival:** Spotts, *Bayreuth*, 170.
272 **Winifred's four children:** Spotts, *Bayreuth*, 143.
273 **of their parents:** Millington, "Wagner," 26:931.
273 **He never did:** Millington, "Wagner," 26:931.
273 **(The Wedding), never completed:** Millington, "Wagner," 26:931–32.
274 **married in November:** Millington, "Wagner," 26:932.
274 **"arms once more":** *Selected Letters of Richard Wagner*, ed. & trans. Stewart Spencer & Barry Millington (New York: W. W. Norton, 1988), 38.
279 **finally to Switzerland:** Millington, "Wagner," 26:935.
292 **"only ultimate redemption":** *Letters of Wagner*, 323.
292 **"full-blooded musical conception":** *Letters of Wagner*, 324.
296 **biographer Oliver Hilmes:** Oliver Hilmes, *Cosima Wagner: The Lady of Bayreuth*, trans. Stewart Spencer (New Haven: Yale University Press, 2010), 44.
296 **"Wagner's overpowering genius":** Hilmes, *Cosima Wagner*, 57.
296 **"tears and sobs":** Hilmes, *Cosima Wagner*, 63.
296 **Isolde, by Wagner:** Millington, "Wagner," 26:936–37.
297 **"faithful and true":** *Letters of Wagner*, 600.
297 **"would never end":** *Letters of Wagner*, 600.
297 **some financial support:** Millington, "Wagner," 26:937–38.
298 **progressed to delirium:** *New Grove Dictionary of Opera*, ed. Stanley Sadie (London: Macmillan, 1992), 4:234.
298 **"body on a reel":** Quoted in Nicolas Slonimsky, *Lexicon of Musical Invective* (New York: W. W. Norton, 2000), 232.
299 **"and ecstatic experiences":** *A Virgil Thomson Reader*, ed. John Rockwell (Boston: Houghton Mifflin, 1981), 262.
301 **north side of town for free:** Spotts, *Bayreuth*, 40–41.
301 **raked, fan-shaped level:** Spotts, *Bayreuth*, 3.
305 **joined him there:** Millington, "Wagner," 26:940.

CHAPTER 11: THE SYNTHESIZER

307 **friends, mostly musicians:** Artur Schnabel, *My Life and Music* (New York: St. Martin's Press, 1963), 15.
308 **"to a child?":** Schnabel, *My Life*, 16.
308 **"did at the piano":** Schnabel, *My Life*, 16.

308 **high speaking voice:** George S. Bozarth & Walter Frisch, "Johannes Brahms," *New Grove Dictionary of Music and Musicians*, ed. Stanley Sadie (New York: Macmillan, 2001), 4:181.

309 **"more completely overwhelmed":** Quoted in Jan Swafford, *Johannes Brahms: A Biography* (New York: Vintage Books, 1999), 64.

309 **intriguingly, a "demon":** Peter Ostwald with Lise Deschamps Ostwald, *Schumann: The Inner Voices of a Musical Genius*, rev. ed. (Boston: Northeastern University Press, 2010), 262.

309 **"world of spirits":** Quoted in Robert Schumann, *On Music and Musicians*, ed. Konrad Wolff, trans. Paul Rosenfeld (New York: W. W. Norton, 1969), 253–54 (originally published 1946).

310 **1933 radio talk:** Bozarth & Frisch, "Brahms," 4:190.

310 **for "enriched harmony":** Arnold Schoenberg, *Structural Functions of Harmony*, rev. ed., ed. Leonard Stein (New York: W. W. Norton, 1969), 84.

311 **polemicist promptly retired:** Bozarth & Frisch, "Brahms," 4:183.

311 **as a synthesizer:** Bozarth & Frisch, "Brahms," 4:180.

312 **and philharmonic society:** Bozarth & Frisch, "Brahms," 4:180.

313 **after a week:** Karl Geiringer, *Brahms: His Life and Work*, rev. ed. (New York: Da Capo Press, 1981), 5 (originally published 1948).

313 **brother's burgeoning success:** Bozarth & Frisch, "Brahms," 4:180.

313 **Friedrich Wilhelm Cossel:** Geiringer, *Brahms*, 16.

313 **on these reports:** Bozarth & Frisch, "Brahms," 4:180.

314 **"beer into him," and worse:** Swafford, *Brahms*, 29.

314 **"childhood like mine":** Quoted in Swafford, *Brahms*, 547.

314 **music and dance:** Geiringer, *Brahms*, 26.

314 **impossible to imagine:** Swafford, *Brahms*, 67–68.

315 **"mastery of form":** Quoted in Ostwald, *Schumann*, 263.

316 **"the greatest ease":** Quoted in Ostwald, *Schumann*, 263.

316 **"bubbling over with mirth":** Quoted in Geiringer, *Brahms*, 37.

316 **"charming and comfortable":** Quoted in Geiringer, *Brahms*, 45.

316 **before the end:** Bozarth & Frisch, "Brahms," 4:182.

317 **"tired of adoring you":** *Johannes Brahms: Life and Letters*, ed. Styra Avins, trans. Josef Eisinger & Styra Avins (Oxford: Oxford University Press, 1997), 134.

317 **their separate ways:** Bozarth & Frisch, "Brahms," 4:182.

318 **"enough for me":** Quoted in Michael Steinberg, *The Concerto: A Listener's Guide* (New York: Oxford University Press, 1988), 108.

318 **"of the movement":** Quoted in Steinberg, *The Concerto*, 109.

320 **"portrait" of Clara:** Bozarth & Frisch, "Brahms," 4:183.

321 **"most unpleasant sounds":** Quoted in Swafford, *Brahms*, 190.

321 **"forbade such demonstrations":** *Brahms: Life and Letters*, 189.

321 **"raises one's courage":** *Brahms: Life and Letters*, 189.

321 **they were engaged:** Geiringer, *Brahms*, 57.

322 **"I love you":** Geiringer, *Brahms*, 60.

326 **and public buzz:** Bozarth & Frisch, "Brahms," 4:183.

326 **conquering the city:** Geiringer, *Brahms*, 73–74.

326 **also a friend:** Geiringer, *Brahms*, 74.

326 **"to his art":** Geiringer, *Brahms*, 77.

326 **providing financial support:** Geiringer, *Brahms*, 87.

326 **including his own:** Geiringer, *Brahms*, 79–80.

327 **the German Requiem:** Bozarth & Frisch, "Brahms," 4:184.

327 **Bible for his text:** Bozarth & Frisch, "Brahms," 4:196–97.

327 **call it a "Human" requiem:** Quoted in Swafford, *Brahms*, 317.

327 **a large orchestra:** Swafford, *Brahms*, 328.

327 **"awe and grace":** Swafford, *Brahms*, 330.

329 **of course, himself:** Geiringer, *Brahms*, 111.

330 **not yet been written:** Geiringer, *Brahms*, 128.

330 **"a black border":** Quoted in Swafford, *Brahms*, 436.

330 **"on a Prater merry-go-round":** Swafford, *Brahms*, 441.

330 **"unsurpassable pianistic perversions":** Quoted in Steinberg, *The Concerto*, 116.

330 **"wisp of a scherzo":** Steinberg, *The Concerto*, 115.

331 **over three months:** Bozarth & Frisch, "Brahms," 4:185.

332 **Liszt and Wagner:** Bozarth & Frisch, "Brahms," 4:189.

332 **a Russian-born violinist:** Michael Musgrave, *A Brahms Reader* (New Haven: Yale University Press, 2000), 113.

332 **"as a genius":** Quoted in Nicolas Slonimsky, *Lexicon of Musical Invective* (New York: W. W. Norton, 2000), 73.

333 **"care for his music":** Quoted in Bradley Bambarger, "When Tchaikovsky Met Brahms . . . ," June 22, 2015, http://tch15.medici.tv/en/news/when-tchaikovsky-met-brahms.

334 **"as easy as it looked":** *H. L. Mencken on Music*, ed. Louis Cheslock (New York: Schirmer Books, 1975), 79.

335 **sweet and clear:** Swafford, *Brahms*, 572–73.

336 **"the two sonatas":** Berthold Litzman, ed., *Letters of Clara Schumann and Johannes Brahms, 1853–1896* (Westport, Conn.: Hyperion Press, 1976; first published in London, 1927), 262.

336 **father in 1872:** Bozarth & Frisch, "Brahms," 4:188.

336 **in the harbor:** Geiringer, *Brahms*, 196.

337 **"healing it is now":** Anthony Tommasini, "Brahms and Masur Touch the Heart of the Matter," *New York Times*, September 22, 2001.

CHAPTER 12: THE REFINED RADICAL

339 **"nature of tone":** Arnold Schoenberg, "Problems of Harmony," in *Style and Idea: Selected Writings of Arnold Schoenberg*, ed. Leonard Stein, trans. Leo Black (Berkeley: University of California Press, 1984), 283.

339 **Ellington ruefully noted:** Bill Crow, "Jazz Anecdotes: Second Time Around," *Jazz Revisited Radioshow*, http://www.bixeibenhamburg.com/some-stories-about-the-word-jazz.html.

340 **"in a word, musical impressionism":** François Lesure, "Claude Debussy," *New Grove Dictionary of Music and Musicians*, ed. Stanley Sadie (London: Macmillan, 2001), 7:102.

340 **"the whole of art":** *Debussy Letters*, ed. François Lesure & Roger Nichols, trans. Roger Nichols, rev. ed. (Cambridge, Mass.: Harvard University Press, 1987), 188.

341 **seemed to vibrate:** Margaret Samu, "Impressionism: Art and Modernity," Metropolitan Museum of Art Heilbrunn Timeline of Art History, https://www.metmuseum.org/toah/hd/imml/hd_imml.htm.

341 **"than that seascape":** Michael Prodger, "The Man Who Made Monet: How Impressionism Was Saved from Obscurity," *Guardian*, February 21, 2015, https://www.theguardian.com/artanddesign/2015/feb/21/the-man-who-made-monet-how-impressionism-was-saved-from-obscurity.

341 **"fakir casting spells":** *Debussy Letters*, 178.

343 **"screen of bristling irony":** Edward Lockspeiser, *Debussy* (New York: McGraw-Hill, 1972), 22 (originally published 1936).

343 **these Tuesday gatherings:** Lesure, "Debussy," 7:97.

344 **"by sound alone":** Quoted in Brad Bucknell, *Literary Modernism and Musical Aesthetics: Pater, Pound, Joyce and Stein* (Cambridge: Cambridge University Press, 2001), 11.

344 **by Debussy's *Faun*:** Pierre Boulez, *Notes of an Apprenticeship*, trans. Herbert Weinstock (New York: Alfred A. Knopf, 1968), 345.

344 **"than any color":** *Debussy Letters*, 218.

344 **"of not being one":** Stéphane Mallarmé, "The Afternoon of a Faun," trans. Alex Cohen, in *Debussy*, 293.

348 **on his marriage:** Lockspeiser, *Debussy*, 3–4.

348 **liked collecting butterflies:** Lockspeiser, *Debussy*, 6.

348 **home of Manuel's sister:** Lesure, "Debussy," 7:96.

348 **"(as you pleased)":** *Debussy Letters*, 189.

348 **his civil rights:** Lesure, "Debussy," 7:96.

348 **a successful virtuoso:** Lockspeiser, *Debussy*, 7.

349 **worldly, cultured life:** Lesure, "Debussy," 7:97.

350 **a work of genius:** Lookspeiser, *Debussy*, 22.

350 **"work to come":** Bernard Holland, "Prodigal Son and a Brat, a Whimsical Pairing," *New York Times*, December 10, 2004.

350 **"so lonely I've cried":** *Debussy Letters*, 5.

350 **"your family circle":** *Debussy Letters*, 5.

350 **spring of 1887:** Lesure, "Debussy," 7:97.

350 **"rules of courtesy":** Lockspeiser, *Debussy,* 26.

351 **"rampage of chromaticism":** Leonard Bernstein, *The Unanswered Question: Six Talks at Harvard* (Cambridge, Mass.: Harvard University Press, 1976), 238.

351 **"a lot of countries":** *Debussy Letters,* 232.

351 **"for a sunrise":** Jack Sullivan, program notes, Strauss, *Don Juan,* Mariinsky Orchestra concert, Carnegie Hall, November 15, 2017.

352 **"to stupid children":** *Debussy Letters,* 76.

354 **"human feelings," he explained:** *Debussy Letters,* 8.

354 **"no time or place":** Lockspeiser, *Debussy,* 46.

355 **"thanks to this opera":** *Debussy Letters,* 34.

355 **the couple met:** Lockspeiser, *Debussy,* 75.

355 **"middle-class drawing rooms":** François Lesure, Introduction to *Debussy Letters,* xvi.

355 **in November 1893:** Lesure, "Debussy," 7:97.

355 **the composer Ernest Chausson:** *Debussy Letters,* 60.

356 **Maeterlinck shyer still:** *Debussy Letters,* 61.

357 **"a puff of smoke!":** *Debussy Letters,* 62.

357 **and start over:** *Debussy Letters,* 54.

359 **"is made of":** *Debussy Letters,* 62.

361 **"well-balanced listener giddy":** *Debussy Letters,* 73.

361 **"gives me nightmares":** *Debussy Letters,* 73.

362 **at the piano:** *Debussy Letters,* 66.

362 **"a death wish":** *Debussy Letters,* 106.

362 **from conventional forms:** Lesure, "Debussy," 7:98.

362 **account rings true:** Lockspeiser, *Debussy,* 79–81.

363 **"and decided failure":** Quoted in Lockspeiser, *Debussy,* 81.

363 **"and without life":** Quoted in Nicolas Slonimsky, *Lexicon of Musical Invective* (New York: W. W. Norton, 2000), 90.

363 **"become a cathedral":** Mary Garden & Louis Biancolli, *Mary's Garden Story* (New York: Simon & Schuster, 1951), 71.

364 **lack of refinement:** Lockspeiser, *Debussy,* 88.

364 **friends abandoned him:** Lockspeiser, *Debussy,* 87.

364 **"ever loved anybody really":** Garden & Biancolli, *Mary Garden's Story,* 80.

364 **his creative imagination:** James M. Keller, "La Mer: Trois Esquisses symphoniques," January 11, 2018, https://nyphil.org/~/media/pdfs/program-notes/1718/Debussy-La-Mer.pdf.

367 **his piano music:** *Debussy Letters,* 222.

368 **only temporary relief:** Lesure, "Debussy," 7:100.

368 **"entirely right":** Quoted in Richard Langham Smith, "Maurice Maeterlinck," *New Grove Dictionary of Opera,* ed. Stanley Sadie (London: Macmillan, 1992), 3:146.

CHAPTER 13: "THE PUBLIC WILL JUDGE"

370 **"shabby little shocker":** Joseph Kerman, *Opera as Drama* (Berkeley: University of California Press, 2005), 205 (originally published 1956).

370 **"Am I wrong?":** Quoted in Julian Budden, *Puccini: His Life and Works* (New York: Oxford University Press, 2002), 331.

371 **"remained to him":** Arnold Schoenberg, "My Public," in *Style and Idea: Selected Writings of Arnold Schoenberg,* ed. Leonard Stein, trans. Leo Black (Berkeley: University of California Press, 1984), 97.

376 **"from the sea":** *Letters of Giacomo Puccini,* rev ed., ed. Giuseppe Adami & Mosco Carner, trans. Ena Makin (London: George G. Harrap, 1974), 117 (first published 1931).

376 **during Giacomo's youth:** Mary Jane Phillips-Matz, *Puccini: A Biography* (Boston: Northeastern University Press, 2002), 5.

376 **teachers was Donizetti:** Phillips-Matz, *Puccini,* 10.

376 **more daughters followed:** Phillips-Matz, *Puccini,* 11–12.

377 **at the cathedral:** Phillips-Matz, *Puccini,* 13.

377 **relief to Albina:** Phillips-Matz, *Puccini,* 14.

377 **composition faculty:** Budden, *Puccini,* 5.

377 **Julian Budden suggests:** Budden, *Puccini,* 4.

377 **with some support:** Budden, *Puccini,* 16.

377 **most incoming students:** Phillips-Matz, *Puccini*, 21.

378 **"and a rascal":** Quoted in Phillips-Matz, *Puccini*, 27.

378 **praised the piece:** Gabriella Biagi Ravenni & Michele Girandi, "Giacomo Puccini," *New Grove Dictionary of Music and Musicians,* ed. Stanley Sadie (London: Macmillan, 2001), 20:567.

378 **so-called old guard:** Phillips-Matz, *Puccini*, 32.

379 **the conductor Faccio:** Budden, *Puccini*, 39–40.

379 **got to work:** Budden, *Puccini,* 41.

379 **five honorable mentions:** Budden, *Puccini*, 43.

379 **"for a long time":** Quoted in Budden, *Puccini*, 44.

379 **consumption, and more:** Budden, *Puccini*, 37–38.

380 **another major step:** Budden, *Puccini*, 48.

380 **for nearly a year:** Phillips-Matz, *Puccini*, 48–50.

381 **her Puccini biography:** Phillips-Matz, *Puccini*, 57–58.

381 **Puccini later admitted:** Budden, *Puccini*, 86.

381 **abandon his protégé:** Budden, *Puccini*, 87.

382 **attempting another version:** Budden, *Puccini*, 89.

382 **intemperate and stubborn:** Phillips-Matz, *Puccini*, 76–77.

382 **renown and riches:** Budden, *Puccini*, 106.

384 **this is "healthy music":** Budden, *Puccini*, 106.

384 **"our lyric theater":** *Puccini Letters*, 90.

385 **conductor, Arturo Toscanini:** Budden, *Puccini*, 154.

385 **cafe singer Musetta:** Budden, *Puccini*, 135.

385 **"judge for themselves":** Quoted in Budden, *Puccini*, 138.

386 **a "trifle restricted":** Budden, *Puccini*, 155.

389 **in grim detail:** Phillips-Matz, *Puccini*, 136–38.

390 **fists and fingernails:** Phillips-Matz, *Puccini*, 132.

390 **he and Elvira were married:** Phillips-Matz, *Puccini*, 142.

390 **protestations of innocence:** Phillips-Matz, *Puccini*, 190.

390 **died a virgin:** Phillips-Matz, *Puccini*, 194.

393 **"I am! And *Turandot?*":** *Puccini Letters*, 325.

394 **write additional operas:** Anthony Tommasini, "Updating *Turandot,* Berio Style," *New York Times,* August 22, 2002.

395 **"as a composer":** Anthony Tommasini, "A Composer's Death Echoes in His Musical," *New York Times,* February 11, 1996.

395 **for the *New York Times*:** Anthony Tommasini, "The Seven-Year Odyssey That Led to *Rent,*" *New York Times,* March 17, 1996.

CHAPTER 14: NEW LANGUAGES FOR A NEW CENTURY

397 **"let it be me":** Arnold Schoenberg, "New Music: My Music," in *Style and Idea: Selected Writings of Arnold Schoenberg,* ed. Leonard Stein, trans. Leo Black (Berkeley: University of California Press, 1984), 104.

398 **a Jewish ghetto:** Macolm MacDonald, *Schoenberg* (New York: Oxford University Press, 2008), 27.

398 **and other instruments:** O. W. Neighbour, "Arnold Schoenberg," *New Grove Dictionary of Music and Musicians,* ed. Stanley Sadie (London: Macmillan, 2001), 22:578.

398 **encyclopedia's instructional series:** Alex Ross, *The Rest Is Noise: Listening to the Twentieth Century* (New York: Farrar, Straus & Giroux, 2007), 45.

398 **at a bank:** MacDonald, *Schoenberg,* 31.

398 **recognized Schoenberg's talents:** Neighbour, "Schoenberg," 22:578.

398 **credited Zemlinsky:** Schoenberg, "My Evolution," in *Style and Idea,* 80.

398 **of rising anti-Semitism:** MacDonald, *Schoenberg,* 39.

400 **focused on music:** Neighbour, "Schoenberg," 22:579.

400 **decadent cultural habits:** Ross, *The Rest,* 59–60.

400 **had been born there:** Leon Botstein, "Schoenberg, Munch and Expressionism," December 3, 2017, http://theorchestranow.org/portfolio-item/schoenberg-munch/.

400 **"of the dissonance":** Schoenberg, "Opinion or Insight?" in *Style and Idea,* 260.

401 **"happening of this kind":** Schoenberg, "Prefaces to the Records of the Four String Quartets," 1937, Joseph Auner, *A Schoenberg Reader* (New Haven: Yale University Press, 2003), 57.

401 **been "cruelly abused":** Quoted in Nicolas Slonimsky, *Lexicon of Musical Invective* (New York: W. W. Norton, 2000), 149.

401 **"bed of a tonality":** Schoenberg, "My Evolution," in *Style and Idea*, 86.

402 **who killed himself:** Neighbour, "Schoenberg," 22:579.

402 **full orchestra score:** MacDonald, *Schoenberg*, 12.

402 **hysteria and repression:** MacDonald, *Schoenberg*, 11.

403 **raised in parliament:** Neighbour, "Schoenberg," 22:579.

403 **translated into German:** MacDonald, *Schoenberg*, 17–18.

404 **at the least, a curiosity:** Neighbour, "Schoenberg," 22:579.

404 **"the German God":** Quoted in Joseph Auner, *A Schoenberg Reader: Documents of a Life* (New Haven & London, Yale University Press, 2003), 125–26.

404 **late the next year:** Neighbour, "Schoenberg," 22:580.

407 **"next hundred years":** Quoted in MacDonald, *Schoenberg*, 54.

408 **"convulsive transformation":** Leonard Bernstein, *The Unanswered Question: Six Talks at Harvard* (Cambridge, Mass.: Harvard University Press, 1976), 270.

408 **"Mahler or Stravinsky":** Bernstein, *Unanswered Question*, 297.

409 **"as a composer":** Schoenberg, "How One Becomes Lonely," in *Style and Idea*, 41.

410 **champion Schoenberg's works:** Neighbour, "Schoenberg," 22:580–81.

410 **returning to Judaism:** Neighbour, "Schoenberg," 22:581.

411 **and tennis partners:** MacDonald, *Schoenberg*, 79.

411 **a harmony textbook:** *Arnold Schoenberg: Letters*, ed. Edwin Stein, trans. Eithne Wilkins & Ernst Kaiser (New York: St. Martin's Press, 1965), 231–33.

411 **started so strangely:** Thomas Forrest Kelly, *First Nights: Five Musical Premieres* (New Haven: Yale University Press, 2000), 280.

412 **"laborious and puerile barbarity":** Kelly, *First Nights*, 204.

412 **"a hundred times":** Quoted in Kelly, *First Nights*, 305.

412 **in *Le Temps*:** Kelly, *First Nights*, 295.

412 **Monteux later recalled:** Kelly, *First Nights*, 292.

413 **Stravinsky later recalled:** Igor Stravinsky, *An Autobiography* (New York: W. W. Norton, 1962), 47 (originally published 1936).

413 **"sexy, violent exoticism":** Richard Taruskin, "Just How Russian Was Stravinsky?," *New York Times*, April 16, 2010.

413 **children to support:** Stephen Walsh, "Igor Stravinsky," *New Grove Dictionary of Music and Musicians*, ed. Stanley Sadie (London: Macmillan, 2001), 24:532.

414 **"convention or analysis":** Quoted in Kelly, *First Nights*, 313.

414 **"impression of tonality":** Quoted in Kelly, *First Nights*, 306.

415 **"detested" the piece:** Quoted in Kelly, *First Nights*, 274.

415 **"of the tonal system":** Bernstein, *Unanswered Question*, 270.

415 **remained until 1920:** Walsh, "Stravinsky," 24:536–37.

415 **"to that of music":** Stravinsky, *Autobiography*, 53.

416 **1920 Paris premiere:** Walsh, "Stravinsky," 24:539.

416 **Russian Orthodox funeral service:** Walsh, "Stravinsky," 24:539.

417 **"property of music":** Stravinsky, *Autobiography*, 53.

417 **"realizes the present":** Stravinsky, *Autobiography*, 54.

418 **"I am symphonizing":** Quoted in Vera Stravinsky & Robert Craft, *Stravinsky in Pictures and Documents* (New York: Simon & Schuster, 1978), 297.

419 **endure the humiliation:** Walsh, "Stravinsky," 24:539.

419 **inflicted on Europe:** Walsh, "Stravinsky," 24:546.

419 **hospitalized for months:** Walsh, "Stravinsky," 24:548.

421 **"he did without me":** Robert Craft, *Stravinsky: Glimpses of a Life* (New York: St. Martin's Press, 1993), 16–17.

424 **could jot it down:** Malcolm Gillies, *Bartók Remembered* (New York: W. W. Norton, 1991), 50–52.

424 **"the level of art-song":** Quoted in Malcolm Gillies, "Béla Bartók," *New Grove Dictionary of Music and Musicians*, ed. Stanley Sadie (London: Macmillan, 2001), 2:789.

425 **"instincts of the nation":** Gillies, "Bartók," 2:790.

426 **yet audaciously modern:** Anthony Tommasini, "Casting an Ear on Béla Bartók," *New York Times*, August 22, 1995.

427 **"still remain tonal":** Quoted in David Cooper, *Béla Bartók* (New Haven: Yale University Press, 2015), 304.

427 **roused him from "stagnation":** Gillies, "Bartók," 2:788.

427 **jurors rejected it:** Gillies, "Bartók," 2:794.

428 **the next year:** Gillies, *Bartók Remembered,* xx–xxi.

429 **to uncover folk music:** Gillies, *Bartók Remembered,* xxi.

432 **Hungarian railway company:** Cooper, *Bartók,* 376.

432 **to the library:** Cooper, *Bartók,* 329–30.

432 **less than $10,000:** Edith Evans Asbury, "22-Year Battle by Son of Bartók over Estate Is Nearing Decision," *New York Times,* March 23, 1981.

EPILOGUE

435 **"language is USELESS":** Quoted in K. Robert Schwarz, "In Contemporary Music, a House Still Divided," *New York Times,* August 3, 1997.

435 **"the 12-tone system":** Quoted in Schwarz, "House Divided."

436 **write twelve-tone music:** Schwarz, "House Divided."

ILLUSTRATION CREDITS

Insert page 1: Title page of *Fiori poetici,* by Giovanni Battista Marinoni, 1644, engraving, Beinecke Rare Book & Manuscript Library.

Page 2, top: Johann Sebastian Bach, by Elias Gottlob Haussmann, 1748, painting, Bach-Museum Leipzig.

Page 2, bottom: George Frideric Handel, by E. H. Schroeder, date unknown.

Page 3, top: Joseph Haydn, by Thomas Hardy, 1791, oil on canvas, Royal College of Music.

Page 3, bottom: The Mozarts, by Johann Nepomuk della Croce, c. 1780, oil on canvas, Mozarteum Foundation.

Page 4, top: Ludwig van Beethoven, by Carl Jaeger (reproduction), original painted c. 1870, photograph of reproduction, Library of Congress.

Page 4, bottom: Unattributed portrait of Franz Schubert.

Page 5, top right: Frédéric Chopin, by Louis-Auguste Bisson, 1849, photograph, Musée de la Musique.

Page 5, bottom left: Robert Schumann, by Adolph von Menzel, before 1856, drawing.

Page 5, bottom right: Clara Schumann, by Elliott & Fry, 1887, photograph.

Page 6, top: Richard Wagner, by unknown artist, 1861, photograph.

Page 6, bottom: Giuseppe Verdi, by Giovanni Boldini, 1886, painting, Galleria Nazionale d'Arte Moderna e Contemporanea.

Page 7, top: Johannes Brahms, by unknown artist, c. 1866, photograph.

Page 7, bottom left: Giacomo Puccini, by Mario Nunes Vais, c. 1900, photograph, Archivi Alinari, Florence.

Page 7, bottom right: Claude Debussy, by Otto Wegener, c. 1900, photograph, Bibliothèque Nationale de France.

Page 8, top left: Arnold Schoenberg, by Florence Meyer Homolka, 1948, photograph, Arnold Schönberg Center.

Page 8, top right: Igor Stravinsky and Claude Debussy, by Erik Satie, 1910, photograph, Paul Sacher Foundation.

Page 8, bottom: Béla Bartók, by unknown artist, 1908, photograph.

P.O. 0005471791 202